WITHDRAWN

BASIC READINGS IN
ANGLO-SAXON ENGLAND
VOL. 1

BEOWULF

GARLAND REFERENCE LIBRARY
OF THE HUMANITIES
VOL. 1431

Basic Readings in Anglo-Saxon England

CARL T. BERKHOUT, PAUL E. SZARMACH, AND JOSEPH B. TRAHERN, JR.
General Editors

OLD ENGLISH SHORTER POEMS
Basic Readings
edited by Katherine O'Brien O'Keeffe

BEOWULF
Basic Readings
edited by Peter S. Baker

ANGLO-SAXON MANUSCRIPTS
Basic Readings
edited by Mary P. Richards

BEOWULF

Basic Readings

edited by

Peter S. Baker

GARLAND PUBLISHING, Inc.
New York & London / 1995

Library of Congress Cataloging-in-Publication Data

Beowulf : basic readings / edited by Peter S. Baker.
    p.   cm. — (Basic readings in Anglo-Saxon
England ; v. 1) (Garland reference library of the humanities ; vol. 1431)
    Includes index.
    ISBN 0–8153–0098–0 (alk. paper). — ISBN 0–8153–
0491–9 (pbk. : alk. paper)
    1. Beowulf.   2. Epic poetry, English (Old)—History
and criticism.   3. Civilization, Anglo-Saxon, in literature.   I. Baker, Peter S. (Peter Stuart), 1952–   . II.
Beowulf.   III. Series.   IV. Series: Garland reference
library of the humanities ; vol. 1431.
PR1585.B27   1995
829'.3—dc20   94–28245
                                                   CIP

Cover design by Patti Hefner.

Printed on acid-free, 250-year-life paper
Manufactured in the United States of America

Contents

Preface of the General Editors

BASIC Readings in Anglo-Saxon England (BRASE) is a series of volumes that collect classic, exemplary, or ground-breaking essays in the fields of Anglo-Saxon studies generally written in the 1960s or later, or commissioned by a volume editor to fulfill the purpose of the given volume. The General Editors impose no prior restraint of "correctness" of ideology, method, or critical position. Each volume editor has editorial autonomy to select essays that sketch the achievement in a given area of study or point to the potential for future study. The liveliness and diversity of the interdisciplinary field, manifest in the annual bibliography of the *Old English Newsletter* and in the review of that bibliography in the *Year's Work in Old English Studies,* can lead only to editorial choices that reflect intellectual openness. BRASE volumes must be true to their premises, complete within their articulated limits, and accessible to a multiple readership. Each collection may serve as a "first book" on the delimited subject, where students and teachers alike may find a convenient starting point. The *terminus a quo,* approximately the 1960s, may be associated with the general rise of Anglo-Saxon Studies and a renewed, interdisciplinary professionalism therein; other collections, particularly in literature, represent the earlier period. Changes in publication patterns and in serial-acquisitions policies, moreover, suggest that convenient collections can still assist the growth and development of Anglo-Saxon studies.

In this first volume of the series, Peter S. Baker selects essays illustrating the evolution of *Beowulf* studies from the mid-1960s, when the New Criticism dominated the field, to the present, in which that formalist mode is being supplanted by the array of methodologies that go under the labels "post-structuralist" and "post-modern." This critical sea-change has been accompanied by a slow but sweeping shift in orientation: Earlier scholarship was informed by philological techniques developed in the early nineteenth century, which focused attention on reconstructed archetypes—textual, linguistic, historical, and mythological—presumed to be more "correct" than those that actually survive. Later scholarship, on the other hand, in a movement recently codified as "The New Philology," tends to look instead at immediately accessible contexts—the surviving manuscript, the attested language, Anglo-Saxon history, and the scholarly culture in which the poem is read now. Both the older position and the restlessness of thoughtful scholars working with that position are well represented here by such classic essays as E.G. Stanley's "Beowulf," Larry D. Benson's "The Pagan Coloring of *Beowulf*," Fred C. Robinson's "Elements of the Marvellous in the Characterization of Beowulf," and others. Recent trends are well illustrated in such essays as Kevin S. Kiernan's "The Legacy of Wiglaf," Gillian R. Overing's "The Women of *Beowulf*," and two studies written especially for this volume, Mary Blockley and Thomas Cable's "Kuhn's Laws, Old English Poetry, and the New Philology" and Roy Michael Liuzza's "On the Dating of *Beowulf*." Anglo-Saxonists will therefore recognize that this collection marks a notable departure from previous collections of this kind and helps lay the foundation for future study of the world masterpiece of Old English literature.

The General Editors would like to thank Professor Baker for preparing this inaugural volume in the series. Other BRASE volumes available in 1994 are *Old English Shorter Poems,* edited by Katherine O'Brien O'Keeffe, and *Anglo-Saxon Manuscripts,* edited by Mary P. Richards. Further volumes are in preparation or in planning.

Carl T. Berkhout
Paul E. Szarmach
Joseph B. Trahern, Jr.

Acknowledgments

IN preparing this volume I have incurred many obligations which it is a pleasure to acknowledge. For permission to reprint the articles here I wish to thank the Brown University Press, the *Bulletin of the John Rylands University Library of Manchester,* the Cambridge University Press, the *Kentucky Review,* the Medieval Academy of America, the Modern Language Association of America, the Southern Illinois University Press, the University of Toronto Press, and the Wilfrid Laurier University Press. The article by E.G. Stanley was published by Thomas Nelson and Sons and is reprinted with Professor Stanley's kind permission. Three of the authors represented here—Fred C. Robinson, Kevin S. Kiernan, and Gillian R. Overing—revised their studies for this volume, and I am indebted to them for their trouble and care.

The articles by Mary Blockley and Thomas Cable and by Roy Michael Liuzza appear here for the first time. I thank these scholars for their cooperation and good cheer in permitting me to include their work in this volume. For expert advice on the design of this book I wish to thank my sister, Christine Bouchelle, and for help with individual points I thank Garrett W. Brown, Monique Willemien Dull, and Eric Miller.

While planning the project I benefited greatly from conversations with Carl Berkhout, Fred Robinson and Paul Szarmach. Carl Berkhout read almost the whole of this book and made many valuable suggestions. Paul Szarmach read the introduction and—what was more valuable—kept me going with his friendly entreaties that the book might one day be done.

Finally, I am grateful to the students who have studied Old English and *Beowulf* with me over the last fourteen years at Emory University and the University of Virginia. Their interests have guided me in assembling this collection, which is for them and for *Beowulf*ians everywhere.

Introduction

READERS of this anthology of *Beowulf* scholarship will find that it differs from its predecessors in two major respects. First, it excludes several articles that have long been part of the standard reading list for a *Beowulf* course. Some of these, such as J.R.R. Tolkien's "*Beowulf*: The Monsters and the Critics,"[1] continue to be influential and are still worth the student's attention. But by the middle of the 1960s, when the coverage in this anthology begins, several of the critical approaches that had long dominated scholarship on *Beowulf* had begun to play themselves out, and certain positions that had been a matter of consensus were beginning to be questioned, if not yet abandoned. Here I am concerned less with older orthodoxies than with the movement away from them and the development and testing of new ways to think about the poem. Second, this anthology takes as its range of interest *Beowulf* scholarship generally, and does not focus exclusively on "criticism" or "interpretation." The broad scope of the collection reflects my conviction that the student of *Beowulf* ought to encounter not only literary criticism but also studies of paleography, metrics, textual criticism, analogues, and history. Criticism dominates this collection, of course, as it does the bibliography of *Beowulf* scholarship each year; further, all of the articles here have implications for literary critics. But I hope to demonstrate to students that there are many things one can do with *Beowulf*, and that these things are not merely ancillary to criticism, but have a life and legitimacy of their own.

It is not always a good idea to begin reading an anthology with the first item, but that is the place to start with this one. E.G. Stanley's "Beowulf" appeared in 1966 in a volume called *Continuations and Beginnings,* whose title aptly characterizes its mission—to assess the state of Old English studies and lead the discussion in new directions. Stanley contributes a detailed study of the poem's complex and subtle style, which employs an "additive and annexive method of progression" in both its small and its large structures. Implicit in this view of *Beowulf* as sophisticated and highly wrought is a rejection of the Romantic longing for a genuinely primitive poem that had led many to see its style as simple and artless. Related to that longing for the primitive was the "oral-formulaic" view of *Beowulf* as the extemporaneous composition of an illiterate minstrel; Stanley argues strongly that the poem's sophistication makes extemporaneous composition unlikely.[2]

Stanley has always been known for his care in distinguishing what can be known from what can only be guessed at. Several of these essays aim to distinguish "what can be known" by studying the literary, historical, and intellectual background of the poem. The title of Larry D. Benson's "The Pagan Coloring of *Beowulf*" situates it in the long-running debate about the poem's religious outlook. It is an echo of the title of F.A. Blackburn's famous essay "The Christian Coloring of *Beowulf*" (1897),[3] which, accepting the prevailing view that the poem was "essentially" pagan, attempted to show that its Christian passages could be accounted for by interpolation and revision. By 1967, when Benson's essay was published, the critical position had been almost precisely reversed: the selection of essays in Lewis E. Nicholson's *Anthology of Beowulf Criticism* (1963) illustrates very well the triumph of the notion that *Beowulf* is "essentially" Christian. Benson points out, however, that the sympathetic depiction of pagan Danes and Geats in *Beowulf* must still be accounted for; he argues that, "beginning in the last years of the seventh century and extending throughout the eighth, the dominant attitude of Christian Anglo-Saxons toward the Germanic pagans was one of interest, sympathy, and occasionally even admiration" (36) and reconsiders the "pagan coloring" of the poem against the background of Latin accounts of the English missions to the continent. Benson ends his essay with an allusion to the viking age, a period later than the one he discusses, but which recent scholarship has suggested cannot be ruled out as a possible home for *Beowulf*. Interestingly, Benson's arguments may apply as well to the vikings as they do to the continental Germans, for there is a growing body of evidence suggesting that friendly relations were possible between the vikings and the Anglo-Saxons, who were indeed capable of looking at their adversaries with "interest, sympathy, and occasionally even admiration."

Some of this evidence was presented in a volume of essays, *The Dating of Beowulf* (1981), edited by Colin Chase.[4] In his own essay for the collection, "Saints' Lives, Royal Lives, and the Date of *Beowulf*," Chase argued that the hagiographical literature of the viking age seemed more informed by the heroic sensibility than did that of the age of Bede. In his "*Beowulf*, Bede, and St. Oswine: The Hero's Pride in Old English Hagiography" (1985), printed here, Chase develops this argument with particular reference to two accounts of the death of St. Oswine, one from Bede's *Historia Ecclesiastica* (735) and the other from an anonymous eleventh-century retelling of Bede's story. In both accounts, Oswine, seeing that he cannot prevail militarily against his enemy Oswy, dismisses his army and goes into hiding, but the later writer adds that Oswine's soldiers beg him to allow them to fight, fearing that they will "become a byword for cowardice in the songs of the people, as deserters of our lord" (187). The soldiers' desire to fight is undoubtedly heroic, and the hagiographer appears to be in sympathy with it; Oswine too, though he will not allow his men to die for his sake, is aware that his saintly resolve conflicts with an ethos that is not without value. Chase's article not only demonstrates that the heroic ideal was alive and well in late Anglo-Saxon England but also sheds light on the long-running debate concerning the propriety of Beowulf's decision to fight the dragon.[5]

If Benson and Chase read *Beowulf* against the background of the Anglo-Saxons' understanding of their own present and past, Marijane Osborn reads it against a background of theology and cosmic history. In "The Great Feud: Scriptural History and Strife in *Beowulf*" (1978), she argues that the poet distinguishes "between two levels of knowledge, that bound by the secular world of the poem and that perceived from our initiated Christian perspective" (112). The poet's Christian audience, she argues, understood such narrative elements as Scyld's funeral and the creation song sung in Heorot before Grendel's first attack in a way that the pagan inhabitants of the poem's world could not; she notes further that the poem's few explicit scriptural references are directed to the Anglo-Saxon audience, not to the poem's characters. This article, like Benson's, represents a modern trend toward viewing the poem as the work of a Christian looking sympathetically, albeit with regret, at the pagan past.

Beowulf scholarship has always looked to Old Icelandic literature for analogues. Such scholarship has traditionally identified analogues with a view to determining the historical reality underlying the events as narrated or, in the case of the "marvellous elements," to reconstructing the "original" folk-tale from which *Beowulf* and analogue are ultimately derived.[6] The method applied to such analogues is affiliated with the reconstruction of archetypes in textual criticism and of proto-languages in historical linguistics. In "The Germanic Context of the Unferþ Episode," Carol J. Clover takes a different approach: leaving aside questions of "origins" and "originals," she offers a "morphology" of the *flyting*, a narrative set-piece common to *Beowulf* and several Norse sources. Borrowing more linguistic terms, one might say that if the study of analogues has traditionally been "diachronic," Clover's essay is "synchronic."[7]

It has long been debated whether the relationship between *Beowulf* and its Norse analogues is genetic—stories having descended from an original told by both cultures during the heroic age—or is the product of cultural commerce at a later period. Roberta Frank takes on this problem in "Skaldic Verse and the Date of *Beowulf*" (1981), which considers "whether Old Norse skaldic verse can persuade us that the Old English poet's interest in and knowledge of things Scandinavian was the result of the Danish settlements in England and not part of a distant folk memory imported by the Anglo-Saxons from their continental homeland" (156). Frank identifies a striking number of parallels between the large corpus of surviving skaldic verse and *Beowulf,* and finds Norse influence on the Old English poem by far the most likely explanation. Further, she argues, her evidence points to the period between 890 and 950 as the most likely date of composition for *Beowulf.*

Beowulf has often been mined for historical information. Rather more rarely have historians applied their expertise to the elucidation of the poem's literary qualities, though classic studies by such scholars as Dorothy Whitelock and Patrick Wormald show very well the benefits to be gained from this approach.[8] In "*Beowulf* and the Margins of Literacy," historian Eric John argues "that we must move out of the traditional centres of our disciplines to what seem to be the margins: if we do this we shall find . . . that these margins overlap" (52). To the historian, *Beowulf* is marginal, but such institutions as the state, landholding, and the feud are not. John chooses to read the poem against the background of these institutions rather than that of Christian exegesis or other Old English poetry; the resulting interpretations of some of the poem's features seek to look beyond the ideologies offered by the text itself to the real-world conditions that generated them.

Because the unique manuscript of *Beowulf* is damaged and is, like virtually every other medieval manuscript, corrupt in some degree, textual criticism has always occupied a prominent place in the bibliography of *Beowulf* studies. Articles with titles like "Six Notes on *Beowulf*" promise little by way of entertainment for the non-specialist, and yet the critical implications of editors' emendations and restorations, and even of their punctuation, can be immense. In his several studies of the texts of *Beowulf* and other Old English poems, Fred C. Robinson has generally foregrounded such critical implications, producing work that offers both technical sophistication and penetrating, often startling, critical insight. In one of his most influential studies, "Elements of the Marvellous in the Characterization of Beowulf: A Reconsideration of the Textual Evidence" (1974), Robinson examines three passages—the descent into

Grendel's mere, the return from Frisia, and the swimming feat with Breca. In each passage, Robinson finds, the text does not support the interpretation that has traditionally been given it, that the hero's strength is superhuman; the hero is indeed very strong, but finally he is nothing more than a man. "The reason for the supernaturalizing interpretations," he suggests, "is that in reading the poem scholars may have been excessively influenced by its folktale analogues and so have sometimes read back into the sophisticated text of the poet a wild extravagance which he had carefully purged from the material he adopted" (81).

So far in my discussion of the essays in this book, several trends have become evident. Recent scholarship has tended to see *Beowulf* as less romantic and more sophisticated than earlier scholarship did; it has de-emphasized folklore, mythology, and legendary history as preferred contexts for reading *Beowulf* in favor of the social and political life of Anglo-Saxon England itself; it has moved away from a genetic or philological model for understanding the poem's relationship to comparable literatures and toward a model based on cultural commerce and literary influence. I have surely oversimplified these trends: interest in the political background of *Beowulf,* for example, goes at least as far back as 1892, when John Earle argued that it was composed at the court of King Offa of Mercia,[9] and some contemporary critics continue to interest themselves in the prehistoric antecedents of the poem. Like all intellectual trends, the one I am describing has been messy and uneven, manifesting itself less as new consensus than as a shift in the field where argumentation takes place.

For a variety of reasons—including, perhaps, the wish to place the poem as near as possible to its legendary origins and England's own pagan past, and to have in it a product of the golden age of Anglo-Saxon letters—eighth-century Northumbria provided the most congenial home for the *Beowulf* read by scholars of the late nineteenth century and the first half of the twentieth.[10] The *Beowulf* read by later scholars, on the other hand, might well seem more at home in a time and place rich with Danish political and cultural contacts—for example, the late ninth-century Danelaw, as suggested by Levin L. Schücking as early as 1917.[11] Pressure for a later date was steady from 1951, when Dorothy Whitelock argued for late eighth-century Mercia, until 1980, when two events fundamentally altered the nature of the debate: First, the publication of Ashley Crandell Amos's *Linguistic Means of Determining the Dates of Old English Literary Texts* cast doubt on many of the "scientific" tests that had been used to support an eighth-century *Beowulf.* Second, several of the papers read at a conference in Toronto in April of that year presented powerful arguments in favor of late rather than early dates.[12]

One of those papers, Roberta Frank's "Skaldic Verse and the Date of *Beowulf*," is printed here and has already been discussed. Another, Kevin S. Kiernan's "The Eleventh-Century Origin of *Beowulf* and the *Beowulf* Manuscript," was followed in the next year by the publication of his *Beowulf and the Beowulf Manuscript*, which presented his arguments in greater detail. Kiernan's "The Legacy of Wiglaf: Saving a Wounded *Beowulf*" (1986), printed here, summarizes the complex linguistic and paleographical arguments of his book. Kiernan places *Beowulf* even later than most "late-daters" have done. He dates the manuscript itself to the very end of the period that paleographers assign it to—the reign of Cnut—and detects in it signs that the poem was under revision at the time it was copied; thus the poem as we have it, he says, is contemporary with the manuscript in which it is preserved. Reaction to Kiernan's theory in the early 1980s was lively and intense, and it continues to be at the center of contemporary debate concerning the origin and provenance of the poem. Most agree on at least this much: Kiernan is essential reading for all who study *Beowulf* seriously.

Arguments about the date of *Beowulf* normally present themselves as rational assessments of historical, metrical, stylistic, or paleographical evidence. But how rational are such arguments in fact, and are they motivated by the spirit of dispassionate inquiry or by our desire to read one kind of poem rather than another? In "On the Dating of *Beowulf*," published here for the first time, Roy Michael Liuzza takes on these difficult questions, suggesting that "the assumptions made in dating the poem . . . tell us a great deal about our sometimes unspoken and unformulated critical attitudes towards Old English literary texts; each effort to date the poem contains an implicit *ars poetica*" (283). Liuzza examines these assumptions under two headings, "the internal evidence of meter and language" and "the external evidence of historical context" (284). In both areas he sees the major arguments as circular and often undermined by the instability of the evidence on which they are based. Thus the establishment of the poem's date—which we would like to be a matter of fact—"is itself an act of interpretation, in some respects one of the hermeneutic activities most productive of knowledge of the poem and its meanings" (295).

A valuable aspect of Liuzza's study is its demonstration of the relationship between fact and interpretation, and in particular the inevitable involvement of interpretation in the development of "facts" from undigested "observations." In 1933 Hans Kuhn made some observations about the position in clauses of Germanic poetry of a category of words he called "particles," and from these observations he developed two "laws" governing the placement of these words. "Kuhn's Laws" have been accepted as fact by many scholars of metrics and syntax. But our use of the word "law" suggests that what Kuhn discovered was a prescriptive rule that constrained the practice of poets in various ways, when in fact other interpretations are possible. In "Kuhn's Laws, Old English Poetry, and the New Philology," published here for the first time, Mary Blockley and Thomas Cable argue that while Kuhn seemed to have discovered "surprising facts in need of an explanation," he had in fact observed "the rather ordinary and expected results of other principles of meter, syntactic placement, and phrasal stress" (263). Blockley and Cable demonstrate the inadequacy of Kuhn's Laws as descriptions of Old English poetic syntax and sketch the outlines of a metrical and syntactic theory that will account for the evidence more adequately.

In the last part of their essay, Blockley and Cable place their theory in the context of the study of English metrics, and also in the context of the New Philology, the recent movement that aims to reformulate medievalists' traditional approaches to the text in light of postmodern developments in literary theory and related disciplines.[13] Indeed, the New Philology may well provide a context for reading this collection as a whole. Compare, for example, the conceptions of "the *Beowulf* poet" in Benson's "The Pagan Coloring of *Beowulf*" and Kiernan's "The Legacy of Wiglaf." As I have said, Benson's essay was preceded by a movement in the critical community away from seeing *Beowulf* as "essentially" pagan; that movement was almost inevitably accompanied by a rejection of the older view of the text as composite, consisting of a pagan core and later Christian interpolations. Benson instead sees *Beowulf* as the unitary product of one poet's labor. For Kiernan, on the other hand, "the *Beowulf* poet" is the person responsible for collecting existing Beowulf stories, ordering them, writing narrative links, and assembling the whole into the poem as it now survives. This "poet" is almost unrecognizable as such to the reader who brings to the poem modern ideas of "authorship," but is quite at home in the culture of variance posited by the New Philology, in which each scribe displaces the poet responsible for the exemplar he is copying and revising, and becomes in effect the author of his unique copy. Or compare the idea of the "voice" in Stanley B. Greenfield's "The Authenticating Voice in *Beowulf*" (1976). Greenfield was a formalist in the tradition of the New Criticism, and indeed this essay shows his preference for finding material for his arguments within the boundaries of the text under discussion. Nor does his method evince any discomfort with the Old Philology; rather he quietly makes use of the body of knowledge developed by a century and a half of philological study. And yet one can detect in Greenfield's notion of the "authenticating voice"—the voice that not only reports events but also "validates the way or ways in which it understands and wishes its audience to understand them" (99)—some discomfort with the interdependent concepts of authorial integrity and textual stability that the Old Philology assumed: for he pointedly declines to answer the obvious question, "whose voice?" Instead he speaks in negatives: the voice is not a *persona,* not the "poet." The one thing that the voice does not authenticate is the text of *Beowulf* itself.

If Greenfield hears in *Beowulf* an "authenticating voice" that tends to stabilize meaning in the text (if not the text itself), Gillian R. Overing, in "The Women of *Beowulf*: A Context for Interpretation," hears instead "a polyphony of voices" (220). The dominant discourse in this most masculine of poems is "about death: how to die, how to seek out death . . . how to choose it, privilege it, embrace it" (220). It is also about the desire for resolution, and in the masculine world of the poem, that resolution is always death. Yet "there are other elements in the poem that speak for desire as life, elements of marginal desire that disrupt the dominant discourse, that escape appropriation and operate against resolution in a simple, binary sense" (221). To seek out the poem's "other voices," Overing examines three of the women of *Beowulf*—Hildeburh, Wealhtheow, and Modthryth—using a variety of critical methodologies. She sees each of these women as a "hysteric," whose desires challenge the masculine desire for death, and indeed for resolution itself, and destabilize the symbolic order of the poem. Overing is not concerned only with the desires of the poem's characters but also with the readers' desires, which lead them to privilege some of the poem's elements over others. In one sense, Overing's project is to see what happens when one approaches the poem with a set of desires different from those that have dominated criticism of *Beowulf* in the past. That the result has been to destabilize critical discourse, much as the "hysterics" she discusses destabilize *Beowulf* itself, is shown by the controversy her work has provoked.[14]

Desire has been a prominent topic in recent discussions of Old English literature;[15] certainly I have had something to say about it in discussing the scholarship in this volume and its intellectual background. Overing's assertion of the desire that motivates her particular approach to *Beowulf* is refreshing; such assertions are rare, though they would often be appropriate. The reader of this introduction may well be left

with the impression that recent *Beowulf* scholarship has cleared away
the illusions generated by the desires of the past, revealing a truer and
more authentic *Beowulf*. The first part of this proposition may well be
true; the second part asks for a little reflection. The *Beowulf* that scholars of the nineteenth and early twentieth centuries desired was not merely
wished into existence, but built with the powerful assistance of the logical and evidential machinery of the Old Philology and the New Criticism. We are building the *Beowulf* we desire with the assistance of the
New Philology and postmodern modes of literary criticism. This is not
to say that the exercise is futile: we need not inevitably end up with a
Beowulf that tells us about nothing but our own desires. Those earlier
scholars whose views we sometimes reject also bequeathed to us a vast
corpus of evidence, analysis and interpretation, which we continue to
rely upon and regard as valid. So it may be with this anthology. To some
future generation many of the positions taken in this book may seem
quaint or wrong-headed, but I believe that the essays collected here—
and many more besides—add to a base of knowledge about the poem
that is essentially stable. Whatever *Beowulf* we desire to read, we are still
capable of saying something about it that is true.

NOTES

1. *Proceedings of the British Academy* 22 (1936): 245–95. Reprinted in Lewis
E. Nicholson, *An Anthology of Beowulf Criticism* (Notre Dame, 1963), 51–103, and
in R.D. Fulk, *Interpretations of Beowulf* (Bloomington, IN, 1991), 14–44.

2. The classic statement of the "oral-formulaic" theory of the composition
of Old English verse is Francis P. Magoun, Jr., "The Oral-Formulaic Character of
Anglo-Saxon Narrative Poetry," *Speculum* 28 (1953): 446–67. Reprinted in Nicholson,
189–221, and Fulk, 45–65. Work on the oral component of Old English literature
continues, but has evolved far beyond the position taken by Magoun. See particularly John Miles Foley, *Traditional Oral Epic: The Odyssey, Beowulf, and the Serbo-
Croatian Return Song* (Berkeley, 1990), and Katherine O'Brien O'Keeffe, *Visible
Song: Transitional Literacy in Old English Verse* (Cambridge, 1990).

3. *PMLA* 12 (1897), 205–25. Reprinted in Nicholson, 1–21.

4. *The Dating of Beowulf* (Toronto, 1981). See especially R.I. Page, "The
Audience of *Beowulf* and the Vikings," 113–22, and Roberta Frank, "Skaldic Verse
and the Date of *Beowulf*," 123–39, reprinted in this volume.

5. For the critics whom Chase answers, see nn. 10 and 16 of his article.

6. For a survey of scholarship up to 1958, see the various discussions in R.W.
Chambers, *Beowulf: An Introduction to the Study of the Poem*, 3rd ed. with a supplement by C.L. Wrenn (Cambridge, 1959). For a convenient collection of analogues,
most of them translated from Old Icelandic sources, see G.N. Garmonsway *et al.*,
Beowulf and Its Analogues (London, 1968).

7. Readers interested in continental analogues of the Unferth episode should
see Kathryn Smits, "Die 'Stimmen' des schweigenden Königs: ein Erzählmotiv im

Beowulf, im *Nibelungenlied* und im *Parzifal,*" *Literaturwissenschaftliches Jahrbuch* 27 (1986): 23–45.

    8. Whitelock, *The Audience of Beowulf* (Oxford, 1951); Wormald, "Bede, *Beowulf* and the Conversion of the Anglo-Saxon Aristocracy," in *Bede and Anglo-Saxon England,* ed. R.T. Farrell, British Archaeological Reports 46 (Oxford, 1978), 32–95.

    9. Reference in Whitelock, *Audience,* 64.

    10. For a convenient survey of scholarship on dating, see Colin Chase, "Opinions on the Date of Beowulf, 1815–1980," in *The Dating of Beowulf,* 3–8.

    11. "Wann entstand der *Beowulf* ? Glossen, Zweifel, und Fragen," *Beiträge zur Geschichte der deutschen Sprache und Literatur* 42 (1917): 347–410. Summarized in Chase, "Opinions," 5–6.

    12. Most of the papers were published, in revised form, in Chase's *The Dating of Beowulf.* See especially the essays by Kevin S. Kiernan, Walter Goffart, Alexander Callander Murray, R.I. Page, Roberta Frank (reprinted here), and Colin Chase. Essays by Peter Clemoes and John C. Pope argued for the traditional early date, while some others came to no conclusions.

    13. The standard reference-point for the "New Philology" is the January 1990 issue of *Speculum,* which collects six essays on the topic by noted medievalists. See especially Stephen G. Nichols's manifesto, "Introduction: Philology in a Manuscript Culture," *Speculum* 65 (1990): 1–10.

    14. For references to some reviews of her *Language, Sign, and Gender in Beowulf* and her response, see her "Recent Writings on Old English: A Response," *Æstel* 1 (1993): 135–49.

    15. See especially Allen J. Frantzen, *Desire for Origins: New Language, Old English, and Teaching the Tradition* (New Brunswick, 1990). Of particular interest to students of *Beowulf* is chapter 6, "Writing the Unreadable *Beowulf.*"

Beowulf

Beowulf[1]

by E.G. STANLEY

This essay first appeared in Continuations and Beginnings: Studies in Old English Literature, *ed. Eric Gerald Stanley (London: Nelson, 1966), 104–40.*

WE have no traditional approach to *Beowulf.* We are entirely ignorant of the author's intentions except for what we may claim to be able to infer from the poem itself. Even the subject and the form of the poem are in doubt; words like epic and elegy are applied to it, epic because it is heroic, early and fairly long, and elegy because it commemorates and mourns men who were honoured in their generations and were the glory of their times. Some have seen the poem in its entirety as an *exemplum* in illustration of Hrothgar's great "sermon" (1700–84); others have held that the poem celebrates a dynasty of kings, gloriously founded by Beowulf son of Ecgtheow, a Wægmunding like his successor Wiglaf, whose nobility of purpose was, as the poet tells us (2600f.), such that nothing could make him turn aside the claims of kinship.

We are ignorant of the reception the poem had among the Anglo-Saxons, how widely it was known or how highly it was regarded. Those modern readers who see in Beowulf the personification of the Anglo-Saxon heroic ideal must be surprised that, as far as our evidence goes, only a couple of Anglo-Saxons bore his name. There is some evidence that *Beowulf* may to some extent have served one other Old English poet, the poet of *Andreas,* as a model.

If we wish, we can compare *Beowulf* with other Old English poems. We may find that *Beowulf* is not only longer but also better than the others. That is not necessarily high praise; we may try to turn this relative praise into something more nearly absolute by protesting that the poem is the product of a great age, the age of Bede, an age which knew artistic achievements of the kind buried at Sutton Hoo, an age in which art and learning were united to produce great gospel books like the Lindisfarne Gospels, now in the British Museum, and the Codex Amiatinus, now at Florence. Even so, we cannot tell how good *Beowulf* was compared with the best works of that age. Is it not possible that at a time when the country was full of poems, no longer extant, of the stature of *Paradise Lost*, *Beowulf* (which happens to survive) had the standing roughly of Davenant's *Gondibert* or Cowley's *Davideis*? Or are we to believe that some special dispensation preserves the best of every age? That, surely, is a romantic superstition: from the thirteenth century to the sixteenth, and after, Old English was not sufficiently understood for an Old English text to be preserved deliberately because of its literary merit.[2] And more particularly, the fire which on 23 October 1731 raged in the Cotton Library at Ashburnham House in Westminster is not likely to have held back from doing worse harm to MS Vitellius A xv, the *Beowulf* Manuscript, than to scorch its edges, merely because the first taste the fire got of the poem convinced it of the excellence of *Beowulf* as a work of literature.

The evidence of the Anglo-Saxons' own interest in the poem lies chiefly in the manuscript itself. It is of the late tenth or early eleventh century, a long time after the composition of the poem, which is usually thought to have taken place no later than the eighth century. Several copyings (probably made in different parts of England where different dialects of Old English were spoken) lie between the only extant manuscript and the author's original. Of course, we cannot be sure what in each case made them copy the poem; as far as the extant manuscript is concerned, however, it seems that a finer sense of its value as poetry was less to the fore than its associations with monsters. The manuscript contains also some prose texts. One of them is a life of the dog-headed St Christopher, in the course of which we learn that the saint was twelve fathoms tall—twelve cubits, or roughly eighteen feet, in the Latin source—and he is treated and behaves accordingly. Another text in the manuscript is about *The Wonders of the East*; the monsters there are so numerous and so varied that strangely tall men are among the lesser marvels, for

> Đar beoð dracan cende, þa beoð on lenge hundteontiges fotmæla lange 7 fiftiges. Hy beoð greate swa stænene sweras micle. For þara dracena micelnesse ne mæg nan man na yþelice on þæt land gefaran.

> There are dragons born which are a hundred and fifty feet long. They are as big as great stone pillars. On account of the size of those dragons no man can easily travel into that land.[3]

A third text in the manuscript, *Letter of Alexander the Great to Aristotle*, has its monsters too; though it is disappointing to find that where the Old English text has a great battle between men and water monsters, *nicras*, the Latin source reads something like *hippopotami* for the Old English *nicras*.

Now a dragon and water monsters belong to the Beowulf story, and in England Beowulf's king, Hygelac of the Geats, was renowned because he was exceptionally tall. In a book, probably roughly contemporary with *Beowulf*, called *Liber Monstrorum* or *De Monstris et de Belluis* ("Book of Monsters" or "Of Monsters and Wild Beasts") the following passage occurs:

> And there are monsters of wonderful size; such as King Higlacus who ruled the Getæ and was killed by the Franks, whom from his twelfth year no horse could carry. His bones are preserved on an island in the Rhine, where it flows forth into the ocean, and are shown to those who come from afar as a miracle.[4]

It has been shown that the *Liber Monstrorum* is English in origin. It preserves a reasonably good form of Hygelac's name and a form of the name of his people, the Geats, not remembered otherwise (as far as our evidence goes) on the Continent at that time. It is not an unreasonable speculation to think it possible that the centre which produced the *Liber Monstrorum* would have been interested in the subject-matter of *Beowulf*; the direction of that interest runs parallel with that shown by those who put together (long after the composition of the poem[5]) the material in our *Beowulf* Manuscript. A dragon, monsters, strangely tall men, these excited the Anglo-Saxons and seem to have done so over a long period. Nothing more literary than that is needed to explain the preservation of the poem.

All this need not redound to the glory of *Beowulf* as a literary masterpiece. It might seem rather to confirm the most cynical opinions about the intolerably naive views of the Anglo-Saxons, who delighted in those parts of the poem of which many modern apologists are most ashamed, and that includes the dragon.

Dragons are a common occurrence in the Bible; and in the Vulgate the word *draco* comes not only on the numerous occasions when the Authorised Version has *dragon,* but also often when the Authorised Version has *serpent.* It is not difficult to find in the Bible confirmation for the view that the dragon (or the serpent) is in league with the devil. Revelation 20:2 makes the dragon one with the devil: "And he laid hold on the dragon, that old serpent, which is the Devil, and Satan, and bound him a thousand years." The dragon in *Beowulf,* however, does not seem at all like that; it is very much more like the dragon of another book of the Bible, that of the story of Bel and the Dragon in the Book of Daniel.[6] Daniel among the Babylonians has destroyed their brass and clay idol, Bel. Verses 23–27 tell the next event, an historical event:

> And in that same place there was a great dragon, which they of Babylon worshipped. And the king said unto Daniel, Wilt thou also say that this is of brass? lo, he liveth, he eateth and drinketh; thou canst not say that he is no living god: therefore worship him. Then

said Daniel unto the king, I will worship the Lord my God for he is
the living God. But give me leave, O king, and I shall slay this dragon
without sword or staff. The king said, I give thee leave. Then Daniel
took pitch, and fat, and hair, and did seethe them together, and made
lumps thereof: this he put in the dragon's mouth, and so the dragon
burst in sunder: And Daniel said, Lo, these are the gods ye worship.

The dragon in *Beowulf* is more like that: lo, he liveth, he eateth and
drinketh, and can be destroyed, by Daniel's trick or by the courage of
men like Beowulf and Wiglaf—suitably protected by a flame-proof
shield. And when dragons perish they may burst in sunder like that of
Babylon or melt in their own heat like that slain by Sigemund (*Beowulf*
897). The dragon slain by Beowulf (as much as that slain by Daniel) is an
evil adversary; but the words used by the poet to describe it, *niðdraca*
(2273), *se laða* (2305), *manscaða* (2514), *inwitgæst* (2670), and the like,
seem less definitely links with hell than the words used by the poet of the
fiendish brood of Grendel and his mother. The killing of the dragon is
described as a terrible exploit from which men who at other times bear
themselves valiantly may shrink: their fear is of a real being, a mon-
strously powerful creature—mercifully rare on this earth.[7]

It seems inconceivable that the poet of *Beowulf* should have intended to sublimate his evil dragon into draconity, making what has
reality in the Bible into something abstract or symbolic, something
acceptable to a twentieth-century audience willing to swallow monsters
only as myths or symbols. Moreover, however we ourselves may wish to
read *Beowulf*, of one thing we can be pretty sure on the evidence of the
manuscript: the Anglo-Saxons read the poem as an account of Beowulf
the monster-slayer, and preserved it with other accounts of monsters.

Nevertheless, it would be a highly imperceptive reading of *Beowulf*
which finds in it nothing except monster-slaying. We may not go all the
way with Klaeber when he says, "The poet would not have selected so
singular a fable if it had not been exceptionally well-suited to Christian-
isation";[8] yet that judgment points in the right direction. Most of us
now think tales of monsters a low order of literature, unless redeemed in
the handling. The poet of *Beowulf* handles his story with literary
artistry; he has made the story rich with spirituality. That has led some
modern critics to look away from the reality of the monsters, to make
them *be* wholly the powers of darkness towards which they *tend* (and
from which Grendel's race is derived).

It is worth considering at the very outset one clear example of the
poet's great skill in handling the customary material of Old English
verse. Jacob Grimm, writing of Old English poetry with particular
reference to *Elene,* said:

The way in which battles and war, the favourite occupation of our antiquity, are described deserves our attention before all else. There is something glorious in every battle-scene. Wolf, eagle and raven with joyous cry go forward in the van of the army, scenting their prey.[9]

In Old English poetry the wolf, the eagle and the raven occur as satellites of battle some sixteen times in all. Wherever they come they convey the expectation of slaughter. The lean wolf leaves the forest for that, and the wings of eagle and raven, dark and glistening with dew, seem to reflect impending carnage. The *Beowulf* poet uses the same imagery at the end of the speech which near the end of the poem foretells the destruction of the Geatish nation now that Beowulf is dead:

> Forðon sceall gar wesan
> monig morgenceald   mundum bewunden,
> hæfen on handa,   nalles hearpan sweg
> wigend weccean,   ac se wonna hrefn
> fus ofer fægum   fela reordian,
> earne secgan,   hu him æt æte speow,
> þenden he wið wulf   wæl reafode.   (3021–27)

Therefore many a morning-cold spear must be gripped, raised by the hand; not the sound of the harp shall awaken the warriors, but the black raven, eager in pursuit of doomed men, shall speak of many things, tell the eagle how he prospered at the feast when in competition with the wolf he despoiled the slain.[10]

In no other poem is an attempt made to establish a relationship between the beasts of battle: they are attendants of carnage operating singly though pursuing the same end. In *Beowulf* they are more than that: there is on the one hand the grim conversation between the birds, and on the other the cadaverous eating match. The purposeful combination of the beasts of battle expresses effectively the certainty that the Geats shall be extirpated:[11] the three will have much to tell of things to their liking.

Other poets may refer to the beasts of battle to convey lustily the impending downfall of an enemy; the poet of *Beowulf* invokes them when friends must fall. If, as may well be, the beasts of battle first had a place in poems exulting in the overthrow of an enemy, like that of the Danes in *The Battle of Brunanburh* (60–65) and of the Assyrians in *Judith* (204–12, 294–96), the formulas turn sour in the hands of the poet of *Beowulf,* who uses them to call up all that is most abhorrent to warriors. There is deliberate artistry in that.

It would be pleasant to think that the poet's art did not remain unrecognised in Anglo-Saxon times. There is, outside the context of the *Beowulf* Manuscript itself, only one point which might provide evidence of how the Anglo-Saxons themselves regarded the poem: there seems to be some connection between *Beowulf* and one other of the longer Old English poems, *Andreas*. Klaeber surveys the material in the introduction (cx ff.) of his edition of *Beowulf* and so does Mr K.R. Brooks, the most recent editor of *Andreas,* in the introduction to his edition. Parallels have been adduced between *Beowulf* and Old English poems other than *Andreas,* but they seem less striking than those with *Andreas,* nothing that cannot be readily explained as arising from the fact that *Beowulf* and *Andreas* share their poetic traditions with other Old English poems.[12] Often traditional phrases were available to an Old English poet for subjects occurring frequently in traditional poetry. Some of the details which *Andreas* shares with *Beowulf* can be ascribed to that cause. For example, Heorot, the Danish hall in *Beowulf* (82), like the Temple of Jerusalem (*Andreas* 668), is described as *heah ond horngeap.* There are *stræte stanfage* in *Andreas* (1236) and *stræt wæs stanfag* in *Beowulf* (320). Such parallels do not provide evidence of indebtedness; after all, if "lofty and wide-gabled" represents an ideal in a hall and if roads paved with stones in the Roman manner are an impressive sight it is not very surprising that two suitable and alliterating epithets should be used of a hall in a number of Old English poems and that *stræt* should come in collocation with *stanfah* in more places than one.

Nevertheless, when due allowance has been made for what may be derived independently from the common poetic heritage of the nation, there remain one or two parallels that do seem to be the result of one poet imitating the other. It should be possible to deduce from this special relationship between *Beowulf* and *Andreas* something that might help us to evaluate how *Beowulf* was regarded by at least one other Anglo-Saxon.

Perhaps the clearest of the parallels connecting *Beowulf* and *Andreas* are the words *ealuscerwen* (*Beowulf* 769) and *meoduscerwen* (*Andreas* 1526) and the opening lines of the two poems. The *Beowulf* poet's use of the word *ealuscerwen* almost certainly implies the image of Death's bitter cup.[13] In his use of the word the image lies all in the word *ealuscerwen* itself. Literally *ealu* means "ale" and *meodu* means "mead," and *scerwen* probably means "dispensing" or possibly "privation" (though the meaning "privation" would not fit the context of *meoduscerwen* in *Andreas* at all well). The words do not occur except here. In the *Beowulf* context *ealuscerwen* refers to disaster: ale is a bitter drink. When the poet of *Andreas* uses the word *meoduscerwen* he labours away at the image. He applies it to a sea-flood overwhelming a multitude. The bitterness implicit in the *Beowulf* image is made explicit in *Andreas* as a *biter beorþegu* 'bitter beer-drinking' (1533), and he further exploits the metaphor by a reference to a *sorgbyrþen* 'brewing of sorrow' (1532). Unfortunately for the image, when the *Andreas* poet was introducing the idea expressed by the *Beowulf* poet as *ealuscerwen,* he happened to be writing a second half-line, following a first half-line which used *m*-alliteration, *myclade mereflod* 'the sea-flood increased'; and so forgetting that mead (unlike the ale of *ealuscerwen*) is a sweet honey-drink quite unconnected with brewings of sorrow and bitter *beer*-drinking, he wrote *meoduscerwen.* If his use of that word is indebted to *Beowulf* it is clear that he bungled what he borrowed. A skilful versifier would have found no difficulty in producing a first half-line with vocalic alliteration to allow the use of the *Beowulf* word *ealuscerwen* in the second half-line: that word is presumed in the clumsy exploitation of the image in *Andreas.*

A comparison of the opening lines of *Beowulf* with those of *Andreas* reveals further similarities which it would be difficult to explain simply by reference to their common poetic inheritance:

> Hwæt, we Gardena   in geardagum,
> þeodcyninga þrym gefrunon,
> hu ða æþelingas   ellen fremedon!
>   (*Beowulf* 1–3)

[Lo, we have heard of the Spear-Danes, of the nation's kings, in days of yore, how those princes did deeds of valour!—P.S.B.]

> Hwæt, we gefrunan   on fyrndagum
> twelfe under tunglum   tireadige hæleð,
> þeodnes þegnas.   No hira þrym alæg . . .
>   (*Andreas* 1–3)[14]

The opening word *hwæt* is common as the opening word of many Old English poems, and that both *Beowulf* and *Andreas* begin with the same word is of no special significance. The formula *we* (. . .) *gefrunon* is also a common one in Old English verse, but the two poets handle it quite differently. In the *Beowulf* opening the two verbs *gefrunon* and *fremedon* play no part in the alliteration of the lines in which they come. The complex alliterative scheme rests on nouns: *Gar* alliterates with *gear, dena* with *dagum,* both second elements of compounds; *þeod* alliterates with *þrym,* and the initial vowels of *æþelingas* and *ellen* alliterate. The sense requires Spear-Danes and days of yore, the glory of a nation's kings, princes and deeds of valour to be stressed. The metre requires those syllables to be stressed which are emphasised also by the sense, and the alliteration reinforces the stress. By its positioning, the subject *we* at the beginning of the clause and the verb *gefrunon* at the end, the phrase *we . . . gefrunon* frames the glory of the Spear-Danes' royal dynasty in days of yore, and leads on to the next clause. It is quite different in *Andreas*. His word-order is pedestrian; his statement merely asserts, first, the apostles' existence, secondly, their glory. Without in any way complicating the alliteration the poet tells us that he has heard tell of twelve glorious heroes under the stars in distant days, the Lord's retainers; the word *þrym* comes in the next sentence: their glory did not fail. The ingredients of the two openings are similar, but they have been used with differing degrees of skill. The devices available to Anglo-Saxon poets are used together in *Beowulf* to produce that harmony of sense and metre which it is possible for Old English poets to achieve if they know how to exploit the relative freedom of word-order permitted in verse. There is nothing wrong with *Andreas*—unless it is wrong for the opening of a poem to lack every distinction.

It is not always profitable to look for modern analogies and to transfer subjective judgments of poems of one age to poems of another. It is not possible to say how high in absolute terms *Beowulf* is to be rated, where it might be allowed to stand in relation to *Paradise Lost,* for example. Even so, it is perhaps possible to discern that the poet of *Beowulf* achieved something that was achieved also in the opening of *Paradise Lost*; and that the difference between the opening of *Beowulf* and that of *Andreas* (whatever its degree) is something of the *kind* of difference between the opening which begins "Of Man's first Disobedience" and:

> I sing the *Man* who *Judah's Sceptre* bore
> In that right Hand which held the *Crook* before;
> Who from best *Poet,* best of *Kings* did grow;
> The two chief *Gifts Heav'n* could on *Man* bestow.

That is the opening of Cowley's *Davideis*. It was published earlier than *Paradise Lost,* so that there can be no question of Cowley's being indebted to Milton—and there is of course not much similarity. There is similarity between the opening of *Beowulf* and that of *Andreas,* and to assume indebtedness is a likelier explanation than any other that might explain the similarity.

The dating of Old English poems is tricky. *Andreas* is generally held to be later than *Beowulf.* The possibility that *Andreas* is imitated in *Beowulf* is unlikely; the fact that *ealuscerwen* fits its context in *Beowulf* well whereas *meoduscerwen* fits its context in *Andreas* badly may be regarded as sufficient evidence that (if there is indebtedness at all) the borrowing is from *Beowulf* into *Andreas.* It seems inconceivable also that the successfully ornate opening of *Beowulf* should owe anything to the indifferent opening of *Andreas.* There are, of course, instances of a better poet borrowing from a worse. Thus, Lord Lyttleton's line

Poured forth his unpremeditated strain

(from James Thomson's *Castle of Indolence,* Canto I, stanza lxviii) does seem to have contributed something to the opening stanza of Shelley's *To a Skylark,* written in 1820, nearly three-quarters of a century later:

That from heaven or near it
Pourest thy full heart
In profuse strains of unpremeditated art.

But the line from *The Castle of Indolence* is sufficiently competent for it to have jingled in Shelley's mind even if the possibility of conscious borrowing were to be ruled out by those who know about Shelley. It is difficult to believe that the mind of the *Beowulf* poet was chiming with memories of *Andreas.*

It seems likely, therefore, that one Old English poet, the poet of *Andreas,* drew on *Beowulf.* Can we base anything on such borrowing in our attempt to establish whether or not *Beowulf* was highly regarded by the Anglo-Saxons? A first reaction, to base nothing on what a poetical dunderhead like the poet of *Andreas* may happen to choose as his models, should probably be rejected as too hasty. An inferior versifier's critical acumen may well be better than his practice, not merely on account of the general principle that one need not be a hen to know if an egg is rotten, but rather on account of the particular principle that many who do not themselves excel in an art nevertheless make sensitive critics of other practitioners, their failure having given them better insight into what success is possible. There is something in the view that imitation implies admiration; the imitation of *Beowulf* in *Andreas* is testimony to the regard in which one Anglo-Saxon, whose own efforts made him a competent judge of what we now call Old English literature, seems to have held the poem. We have a right to show greater faith in him, for all his faults as a poet, than in the monster-mongers who preserved the poem. It is poor evidence of the original reception of the poem: we have no better evidence.

If we have little to go on in assessing the original reception of the poem, we have still our own judgment to tell us that in *Beowulf* certain details of poetic expression are put to better use than in other poems of the Old English period. In this kind of comparative analysis we cannot be sure that the details we single out for praise would, in fact, have been among things considered important by the Anglo-Saxons themselves.

The superior use made by the poet of *Beowulf* of the beasts of battle has been cited already as an example of the poet's special skill. The poet uses the traditional material of Old English verse with an aptness which makes it often seem the fresh product of his mind. His skill shows itself in his exploitation of the resources of the Old English poetic vocabulary, in his manipulation of complicated sentences, and in his use of the alliterative metre to convey his meaning effectively. These particulars are in the first place aspects of the poet's art of expression and therefore only less immediately aspects of what is being expressed. We have no means of knowing how these things were valued by the Anglo-Saxons themselves, and we may find that if we value these accomplishments of poetic expression highly and turn to them as criteria for judging the merits of Old English verse we may come to think less well of such pieces as *The Battle of Maldon, The Dream of the Rood,* and *The Later Genesis,* however good these may be at communicating pathos and passion.

Comparison must occupy an important place in any analysis of the poetic art of *Beowulf.* But there is a limit to what can be subjected to comparison. This is especially true of Old English poetic vocabulary, the greatest glories of which may well be the coinages: they were created to fill a special need and cannot for that reason be compared. In the *Beowulf* passage which ends in the figure of the beasts of battle, for example, the word *morgenceald* 'morning-cold' (3022[15]) demonstrates what can be done with words in Old English verse. The adjective applies to the hand-gripped spear, and satisfactorily communicates the clammy fear of the Geatish warriors as they wake to their last battle. The substantival and adjectival compounds used by the *Beowulf* poet have often been singled out for their excellence.[16] G. Storms's careful discussion of a small group of adjectives, including words like "lordless," "joyless," "soulless," well illustrates the poet's skill with words. Thirty years before Storms's analysis of words ending in -*leas* Hoops discussed compounds beginning with *ær-*. He suggested convincingly that in words like *ærgod* (the first element of which means "previously" and the second means "good") the prefix *ær-* means "old and venerable," so that the compound *ærgod,* for example, means "excellent as things were formerly"; it does not mean "formerly good, but not so good now." Weohstan, Wiglaf's father—a most important personage if the poem should in any way be thought of as celebrating a dynasty—is described (line 2622) as *ærfæder.* The meaning of the word is "father, old and venerable"—not "a good old man but a little senile" like Goodman Verges in Dogberry's eyes. The poet describes ancient treasure as *ærgestreon, ærgeweorc, ærwela*; and we know from descriptions of ancient treasure in *Beowulf* that it was admired for excellence, presumably because some of the skill that made the treasure in former times was not to be found among the poet's contemporaries. From the poet's use of the prefix *ær-* we can see his attitude to *le temps perdu* some part of which may be recalled as the hand touches the hilt of an ancient sword great in associations and glorious in workmanship (cf. 1677–98).

These are detailed points, and *Beowulf* is rich in such points. Compounds are a common occurrence in the poem. On average there is a compound every other line of the poem. This very high frequency is, of course, of some interest in itself. It would be of greater interest if we could tell which of them the poet coined. Klaeber, in the excellent glossary to his edition of the poem, indicates by means of a double dagger those words which do not occur outside the poem. It is likely enough that the poet made up many of these compounds, but we can never be sure that any particular compound which we think bears the stamp of his individuality, *morgenceald* for example, might not have been more widespread. Too much has been lost. In a few cases we know that a word only found in *Beowulf* must have had wider currency in English at one time. Thus the adjective *niðhedig* 'hostile thinking' (3165) only comes in *Beowulf*; but the cognate *niðhugdig* occurs in Old Saxon (*Heliand* 1056). Similarly the word *nydgestealla* 'companion in need' (882) occurs in *Beowulf* alone of extant Old English texts; but Old High German forms of the word (e.g. *notgistallo,* Otfrid's *Evangelienbuch* 4.16.4) are not uncommon. It is best, therefore, not to praise the *Beowulf* poet's originality in coining words. We must content ourselves with praising that he used words aptly.

The way in which the poet manipulates complicated sentences distinguishes his work among Old English poets (though other Old English poems also contain long sentences). If we take the *Beowulf* Manuscript as our starting-point, the organisation of ideas can be discerned to some extent from the rudimentary punctuation and sporadic capitalisation, rudimentary and sporadic, that is, when compared with modern editions. Except for that, no help is given to the reader, who has to rely on his familiarity with the alliterative metre to guide him to correct metrical phrasing, and in Old English verse metrical phrases correspond to meaningful phrases. Since the poem is written continuously like prose (that is, not in lines of verse) it is obvious that the Anglo-Saxon readers of the manuscript must have been helped by the metre to a meaningful reading of the poem.

In selecting the passage which covers lines 864 to 886 for the following discussion the hope is that, though perhaps no individual passage can be called typical of *Beowulf,* nothing atypical will have been chosen. In Klaeber's edition the lines are printed as follows (ignoring the macrons and other diacritics he uses):

Hwilum heaþorofe   hleapan leton,
on geflit faran   fealwe mearas,   865
ðær him foldwegas   fægere þuhton,
cystum cuðe.   Hwilum cyninges þegn,
guma gilphlæden,   gidda gemyndig,
se ðe ealfela   ealdgesegena
worn gemunde,   word oþer fand   870
soðe gebunden;   secg eft ongan
sið Beowulfes   snyttrum styrian,
ond on sped wrecan   spel gerade,
wordum wrixlan;   welhwylc gecwæð,
þæt he fram Sigemunde[s]   secgan hyrde   875
ellendædum,   uncuþes fela,
Wælsinges gewin,   wide siðas,
þara þe gumena bearn   gearwe ne wiston,
fæhðe ond fyrena,   buton Fitela mid hine,
þonne he swulces   hwæt secgan wolde,   880
eam his nefan,   swa hie a wæron
æt niða gehwam   nydgesteallan;
hæfdon ealfela   eotena cynnes
sweordum gesæged.   Sigemunde gesprong
æfter deaðdæge   dom unlytel,   885
syþðan wiges heard . . .

At times men famed in battle made their bay horses gallop, run races
where paths seemed suitable, known for their excellence. At times the
king's retainer, a man filled with high rhetoric, with the memory of
songs, who remembered a multitudinous wealth of ancient traditions,
came upon other words (?) bound in truth (?). The man did then tell
with art the exploit of Beowulf, set forth with happy skill a well-told
tale, weaving words; he said all that he heard tell of Sigemund's deeds
of valour, much of things unknown, the Wælsing's strife, distant
exploits, of such things, hostility and crimes, as the sons of men knew
little of, had Fitela not been with him whenever he wished to tell
something of such a matter, uncle to nephew, friends in need as they
were at all times in every enmity. They had laid low a numerous race
of giants with their swords. No little glory came to Sigemund after his
hour of death when bold in battle. . . .

In the manuscript the following punctuation is used. *Hwilum* (864) is
preceded by a punctuation mark and the word begins with a capital.
There is a mark of punctuation after *wiston* (878), but the mark is less
prominent than that preceding *Hwilum* (864) and *fæhðe* (879) has no
initial capital. There is again a prominent mark of punctuation after
gesteallan (882) and the next word, *Hæfdon* (883), begins with a capital.

The next mark of punctuation, again prominent, comes after *unlytel* (885), and the next word, *Sypðan* (886), begins with a capital.

A comparison of the manuscript punctuation with Klaeber's shows that, though there is some correspondence, the manuscript punctuation is insufficient to enable a modern reader to grasp the meaning at the kind of speed needed for reading the poem to an audience. Yet there is nothing unusual about the punctuation of this passage or of the rest of the poem. It is not known if the punctuation of the manuscript goes back to the poet; there is no need to claim authorial authority for the punctuation for the present purpose, which is to consider how an Anglo-Saxon reader of the manuscript would have understood the text before him in spite of the sparseness of marks of punctuation, and how the author's characteristic style might be particularly well suited for the kind of reading which an Anglo-Saxon reader used to alliterative verse might have achieved.

An Anglo-Saxon reader of the poem had to rely on the metrical phrasing for a meaningful delivery. We may assume him to have been familiar with alliterative verse, and for that reason he can have had no difficulty in splitting up the text into the units we call half-lines and lines. The poet's syntax depends on the metre for its clarity, so that his art of discourse is poetic not only in his exploitation of the vocabulary available to him, but poetic also in the more prosaic virtue of clarity. This is not lowering the dignity of the word *poetic*: what is involved is the characteristic sentence paragraph of the *Beowulf* poet; that is, the poet depends on the metre for his ability to formulate his ideas at length and for his complexity of utterance.[17] It may well be that those Old English prose writers, Ælfric and Wulfstan among them, who at times wrote metrical prose, did so partly because they gained in clarity of expression, but mainly because metrical phrasing would more easily enable their readers to achieve meaningful delivery; however, the use to which metre is put in Old English prose has only an indirect bearing on the present discussion.

In all Old English verse, words which have the function of joining phrases or clauses or sentences (that is, metrically unstressed connectives) precede the first stressed syllable of the half-line in which they come. This is simply the result of the fact that the beginning of phrases, clauses and sentences must coincide with the beginning of metrical phrases: a break within a half-line is not tolerated. As in any other passage of Old English verse, the connectives, e.g. *hwilum* (867), *buton* (879), *þonne* (880), come in the initial dip of the half-line. *Hwilum* at line 864 is (or, at least, could be) stressed; that is borne out by the alliteration of the line, *h*-alliteration, in which *Hwilum* shares. The word does so also at line 2107, and at line 2020 it takes part in cross-alliteration. It follows that *hwilum,* though not always stressed, is stressable; and stressable particles when they are in fact not stressed must come in the first dip (i.e. unstressed position) of the clause.[18] When, as at line 867 for example, the stressable particle (here *hwilum*) is a connective it must come in the dip which precedes the first stress of the clause.

Though there are exceptions,[19] the vast majority of clusters of three or more unstressed syllables come in the position between the last stress of a half-line and the first stress of the following half-line. Not more than one unstressed syllable may end a half-line (except insofar as an additional unstressed syllable may be required for resolution of the last stressed syllable of the half-line). It follows that an Old English reader who comes upon a cluster of syllables consisting of words (or parts of words) which are unstressable and particles which are occasionally stressed will recognise that he is very probably at the beginning of a clause, even though he is reading a manuscript which, by modern standards, is insufficiently punctuated and not split up into lines and half-lines of verse.

Unstressed syllables in clusters may be regarded as signals to tell the reader how the construction of the sentence continues. The dip at the beginning of a half-line is a signalising position, especially clear when it is used in excess of the minimum requirements of the metre.[20] All this applies to all Old English verse. There is every reason for thinking that the poets knew what syntactical advantages were to be derived from the regularity of metre.

The method of composition in *Beowulf* is usually additive and annexive. That is not to say that the poet simply tacks phrase to phrase without premeditation. Though sentences in which the subordinate clauses precede their main clause are not very common in the poem there are enough of them (examples occur at lines 1368–72 and 1822–30) to show that the poet's complexity of utterance is premeditated. Other examples of complex sentence structure include the embedding of one clause within another, as occurs, for instance, at lines 867–71, where (however we may relate *word oþer fand* / *soðe gebunden* to what precedes it) the relative clause *se ðe ealfela ealdgesegena* / *worn gemunde* comes between *cyninges þegn,* the subject, and its verb. Other examples are to be found at lines 731b, 1613b, 1831b, and 2855b. Nevertheless the commonest shape of long sentences in the poem begins with the main clause, and clauses and phrases are added and annexed one after the other.

Correlatives enable Old English poets to construct their very long sentences. Modern editors not infrequently punctuate passages containing a pair of correlatives as two separate sentences, each beginning with a correlative. An example is provided by Klaeber's punctuation of lines 864ff., where he has two sentences each beginning with *Hwilum*. Modern writers on the whole prefer a set of logically connected short sentences to a single long sentence containing them all, and Klaeber's punctuation accords well with their practice. His punctuation is unexceptionable, as long as we remember that the reference of the correlative at each of its two occurrences is not identical: at its first occurrence the reference of *hwilum* is forward, at its second occurrence it refers back. The meaning of *hwilum* at its first occurrence is "at certain times (which are to be given)," at its second occurrence "at other times (than those already named)." When the word first occurs the reader or listener cannot know if there is going to be another occurrence of the word; for *hwilum* does exist in constructions other than correlative constructions (just as "at certain times" does). An Anglo-Saxon reader or listener would know the way in which the word *hwilum* could be used. The first occurrence would alert him for any second occurrence. At both occurrences here the word comes at the beginning of the clause, in the dip at line 867 and in what could be the dip (if we knew more about the rules of double-alliteration involving particles) at line 864. The initial dip of a clause is a signalising position. At line 916, fifty-odd lines away from the first occurrence of *hwilum* the word comes again, also in the signalising position:

> Hwilum flitende   fealwe stræte
> mearum mæton.

[At times, contending, they measured with their horses the pale yellow road.—P.S.B.]

There is good reason for thinking that *hwilum* here (though Klaeber makes it begin a new paragraph) refers back to the two earlier occurrences of the word. They introduce related ideas (though the use of *hwilum* at line 916 is not strictly correlative)—and we cannot call the whole passage from lines 864 to 917 one single sentence, because the passage consists of an organism greater than is covered by our concept of a sentence, a concept for practical purposes defined by practical rules of permissible punctuation. By utilising the initial dips of clauses, occupying them with connectives—*hwilum,* for example—the poet is able to embark on a complex idea, extending it over one sentence or two or more, without losing lucidity, even if (as in the case of Anglo-Saxon manuscripts) the punctuation is only rudimentary.

The device of variation acts in the same direction, though not at such length. Variation, as usually defined, is prosodically of stressed units only: it does not include personal pronouns, for example. In the passage under discussion the subject *cyninges þegn* (867) is varied by *guma gilphlæden* (868), which adds to the description of the king's retainer, and is varied further by *secg* (871), which continues the idea, lucidly enabling the reader to follow the sense of the passage without the help of punctuation; and *secg* is taken up by the pronoun *he* (875), though that is not strictly "variation."

There is more to the sentence than that. The word *gemyndig* (868) is echoed paronomastically by *gemunde* (870); the adjective *gilphlæden* is varied and made explicit by *gidda gemyndig* (868), and the word *gidda* dependent on *gemyndig* is varied by *ealfela ealdgesegena / worn* (869f.) dependent on *gemunde*. Whatever it may mean, the phrase *word oþer fand* (870) is answered across Klaeber's semi-colon by *wordum* (874); *wordum,* a dative plural used adverbially, goes with the infinitive *wrixlan,* and is parallel to *snyttrum* (872) which goes with the infinitive *styrian.* It would not be difficult to go on: there is more to the passage; and almost every passage in the poem can be analysed in this way. Of course, it is not likely that the original audience would have apprehended these interweavings at a first hearing. Their effect is twofold: these interweavings enable the poet to proceed in an additive and annexive progress, which is far from simple and can nevertheless be understood; and they give to his verse a peculiar density of texture, only rarely found in Old English verse outside *Beowulf.*

It is pleasing to trace in the totality of the poem the patterns which we discern in a small part of it. Conversely, it is pleasing to find in a short passage of the poem the patterns which seem to underlie the structure of the poem as a whole. Professor J.R.R. Tolkien has said that "*Beowulf* is indeed the most successful Old English poem because in it the elements, language, metre, theme, structure, are all most nearly in harmony."[21] But the overall pattern which he selects in illustration of this statement is balance: that is, the static principle which to his mind governs the total structure of the poem as much as it governs the individual lines with their "opposition between two halves of roughly equivalent phonetic weight, and significant content, which are more often rhythmically contrasted than similar."[22] There are many ways of regarding the poem. If there is a balance either in the smaller units or in the total structure of the poem it is perceived only on looking back. As the poem advances, as it is read or heard, it is surely a continuum: the listening ear strains for what is to come. The adding of bit to bit in that continuum and the diversity of the means by which the continuity is attained provide evidence of the poet's art.

The passage under discussion is a good example of the poet's skill in sentence structure. It is also an excellent example of how he uses an additive and annexive method of progression for a much larger unit. The general statement of what the king's retainer does (867–77), with its specific statement (868–71) about the traditional nature of what he sings, is followed by a statement (871–74) that Beowulf is the subject still in the account of Sigemund the dragon-slayer and his fame; and that Beowulf is still the subject of the song even when it proceeds to speak of Heremod, the Saul-like king of the Danes, is made clear when at line 913 the singer reverts to Beowulf.[23] The modern reader (waylaid and beset by linguistic difficulties and background notes of exceptional length) thinks the transitions sudden. The forward-listening members of the original audience, told at the beginning of the song that it is of Beowulf, make the connection and apprehend the unity. It is of great importance for an understanding of how the poem compares with other Old English poems to realise that it is unusual in Old English verse other than *Beowulf* to attempt such long organisms. In *Beowulf* the attempt is successful because the poet exploits all the devices of Old English versification (including the syntax peculiar to Old English verse) to prepare the listener for long units and to give them clarity.

Twice in the course of *Beowulf* the poet gives expression to a poetic ideal, once in the passage some aspects of which have been discussed already, lines 867–74, and once at lines 2105–14. The former is a difficult passage: we are not sure what is meant by the two half-lines *word oper fand / soðe gebunden*; but its beginning is clear. The other passage, lines 2105–14 is easier:

> Þær wæs gidd ond gleo; gomela Scilding,   2105
> felafricgende feorran rehte;
> hwilum hildedeor hearpan wynne,
> gomenwudu grette, hwilum gyd awræc
> soð ond sarlic, hwilum syllic spell
> rehte æfter rihte rumheort cyning;   2110
> hwilum eft ongan eldo gebunden,
> gomel guðwiga gioguðe cwiðan,
> hildestrengo; hreðer inne weoll,
> þonne he wintrum frod worn gemunde.

There was singing and revelry: the aged Scylding, a man of wide learning, told of far-off things; at times the man brave in battle touched his joyful, pleasure-giving harp of wood; at times he set forth a song true and sad; at times the magnanimous king told a wondrous story according to what is right; at other times the aged warrior, in the grip of years, did lament his youth, his strength in battle; his heart

within him was moved whenever he, old in years, recalled a multitude
of memories.

A comparison of these two passages shows that they have much in
common. The singer tells a wondrous tale, *syllic spell,* true and sad, *soð
and sarlic.* And in both passages the emphasis is on the memory. In the
first passage the phrase *soðe gebunden* may refer to the technicality of
alliteration, "truly linked"; on the other hand, *soð ond sarlic* of the
second passage may lead us to prefer the translation "bound in truth" for
soðe gebunden. The phrase *æfter rihte* in the second passage should
probably be regarded as a vague statement, meaning "according to what
is right," rather than a specific reference to accurate alliteration. The best
explanation of the words *wordum wrixlan* does seem to be[24] to regard it
as a reference to the "weaving of words" in the rhetorical devices of
variation, specifically, and paronomasia, more generally.

There is good reason for taking the two passages together, for they
both refer to the same occasion. The first is the poet's account of the
festivities at Heorot after Beowulf's defeat of Grendel, the second is
Beowulf's own account to Hygelac, his king, of what is presumably a
later stage of the same festivities. It is an ideal picture of a society deeply
rooted in its traditions, recalling past events to provide fit comparison
for present deeds of glory.

The crux *word oðer fand* (870) has sometimes been interpreted in
contradistinction to *ealdgesegen* (869); that is, "he composed new words"
in contradistinction to "he remembered a great multitude of *old* traditions." That view is not accepted by Professor Else von Schaubert in her
edition of the poem, and the reasons of syntax which led her to reject it
(and which led Klaeber to follow her in the second supplement (466f.)
of his edition) seem convincing. In any case, there is nothing that might
lead one to the view that old traditions in new words represents an ideal
among the Anglo-Saxons; and, even if it were possible to parallel in Old
English the meaning "new" for *oþer,* that alone would make one doubt
the interpretation. This is the value of Professor F.P. Magoun's application to Old English poetry of the theories relating to preliterate poetic
composition, and this, as Professor C.L. Wrenn has shown,[25] is one
important aspect of the miracle of Cædmon: that Old English had only
one form of poetic utterance; it was aristocratic and traditional whatever
the subject and whatever the mood. According to Bede, Cædmon was
the first in England to take Christian themes as subjects for that traditional poetry. Since traditional diction is as much a part of the definition
of Old English verse as the use of regular rhythms and the use of regular
alliteration, Christ, Lucifer, the saints and the Patriarchs appear as

Germanic liege-lords with their retainers. That is the reason for the Germanisation of the Orient, as Heusler called it. The audience expected what they were used to, and the poet supplied it: there was no other way of telling in verse of the deeds of men.

So far we have considered the means of poetic expression and the use made of them by the poet of *Beowulf*. The passage selected for closer analysis contains a statement of the poet's ideal in poetry, the singing of a song about deeds performed that day. The singer in Heorot is the poet's fiction, part of his picture of the society of the past. Before we consider that picture as a whole we must take issue with the application to *Beowulf* of theories which may help to explain some of the characteristics of oral poetry such as is found in the Balkans. That poetry makes use of a stock of formulas traditionally associated with it. Old English verse, like the verse of related Germanic tribes, for example the Old Saxons, is formulaic. Formulas found again and again in different Old English poems, a seemingly unique phrase found in the same or a very similar form in some other poem, all confirm that Old English poets draw not merely on an ancient hoard of poetic words, but also on an ancient hoard of whole poetic phrases when they wish to give expression to something already expressed in a set formula. No doubt, very often the availability of a formula will influence poets to make use of it.

As we have seen, in descriptions of battles poets introduce in traditional terms something on the beasts of battle. The traditional formulaic element is available for a very wide range of ideas, at times for an absence of ideas, as when they introduce some tag like *heard under helme* 'strong under his helmet' to describe—very vaguely—some hero, or *under heofones hwealf* 'under the arch of heaven' to localise—very vaguely— some action. The origin of the use of such phrases may well lie in the characteristics of oral poetry, the product of an extemporising singer. This has been the opinion of scholars for a long time. It is sufficient to quote A.F.C. Vilmar's view of a hundred and twenty years ago:

> These formulas, which rest as much on ancient tradition as they characterise oral tradition, create the refreshing impression that what we are concerned with here is nothing invented, nothing artificial or fictive, no mere book-learning, but rather a living tale which wholly fills the teller and stands at all times at his command.[26]

Vilmar distinguishes the traditional origin of the formulas of Germanic verse, and their connection with oral poetry, from the *impression* given by their use. That is an important distinction to be borne in mind when we come to *Beowulf*; that poem survives in written form only: whether we think it the work of an extemporising poet or of a man who composes pen in hand depends on our response to the *impression* made on us by the poem.

Professor F.P. Magoun's discussion[27] of oral-formulaic versification has deepened our understanding of the kind of poetry that underlies the Old English poetry surviving in such manuscripts as have been preserved. To understand the use of tags and set phrases, whole half-lines of verse used repeatedly, it is useful to know about some kinds of preliterate composition. But we should not necessarily assume that what applies to the poetry of a genuinely preliterate society has an immediate and direct bearing on the elaborately literate poetry of the Anglo-Saxons. When we come to *Beowulf,* I agree with Professor Kemp Malone: "The *Beowulf* poet was no minstrel, strumming a harp and composing verse as he strummed."[28] Though the devices of sense and sound, variation and paronomasia, could in themselves be explained as the vehicles of an associative imagination working *extempore,* when they come, as in *Beowulf,* in combination with the careful exploitation of every aspect of what was available to an Old English poet, it seems more likely that this highly wrought poem is the product of a lettered poet, or at least of a slow, non-extemporising poet.

In his analysis of Old English verse Professor Magoun has made crucial use of the example of Cædmon.[29] It may be worth considering Cædmon again to see if we are really presented by Bede with "the case history of an Anglo-Saxon oral singer" in the sense in which Magoun and his school interpret that phrase. We have the authority of Bede for the fact that Cædmon was illiterate. Except for the nine lines of his *Hymn* none of his poems survives. Even so, we know from Bede's account that he recited his orally composed verses to his teachers who acted as scribes. We are told also that they were long poems. However, nothing in Bede's account suggests that Cædmon composed *extempore* before an audience; nothing suggests even that he composed harp in hand; nothing suggests that he composed long poems other than bit by bit. Bede's famous phrase that Cædmon composing was like a clean beast ruminating, *quasi mundum animal ruminando,* calls to mind slow and deliberate, many-stomached digestion, remouthing again and again the same material. This does not support Magoun: not even the case of Cædmon, the illiterate neat-herd. We have no account of how the *Beowulf* poet went about his work. Nevertheless, the product of his art, with its sophisticated interweaving of devices, and the mechanics of elaborate, long, sentence-like structures composed with metrical precision, all aptly matching a subtle and complex set of ideas, makes one doubt that *Beowulf* should have been the work of an oral singer.

Magoun makes a distinction between good and bad oral verse, by saying that "a good singer is one able to make better use of the common fund of formulas than the indifferent or poor singer."[30] This is obvious enough: the putting together is part of the art. Aptness and organisation make suitable criteria for judging a poem. More recently a disciple of Magoun's, writing "On the Possibility of Criticizing Old English Poetry," has told us,

> Our praise is misplaced when we would offer it to the poet for the *wording* of a verse or line, as much misplaced as if we should praise Yeats for *inventing the words* of his poems.[31]

This seems misguided. The *wording* is not the same as the *words*. There is a degree of contrivance and invention in putting together words and phrases from the hoard of oral formulas. There is invention in the use of compounds, and we can judge that invention by the criteria of aptness and organisation. We are not in a position to know which individual phrase or compound is new, but we are in a position to detect good use made of traditional language. In *Beowulf* good use is made of it; in *Andreas* less so. Regardless of whether the technique of composition is fully *extempore*, or slow composition refined by revision, or even written composition painfully corrected, putting together words from the customary poetic vocabulary of the nation, making use of customary compounds and phrases can lead to good poetry or bad.

As we have seen, the *Beowulf* poet himself twice gives expression to a poetic ideal: the creative activity of the singers thought by him worth the attention of heroes in Heorot consists in the memory of ancient strife recalled in language that lies beyond the tickle of novelty. These idealised singers belong to the glorious past, to which oral poetry also belonged.

The poet does not advert to this ideal *simpliciter,* but uses the scop's song to bring out also certain ulteriors, perhaps the crimes of Sigemund (879), perhaps the hopes men had of Heremod (909–13). The *Beowulf* poet is sophisticated: his art cannot be identified with the scop's. The scop sings *extempore* a song in praise of Beowulf. So the poet imagines him as he peoples the heroic past; but that in no way implies that he, like his creature, Hrothgar's singer, also sings *extempore*.[32]

When we consider the *Beowulf* poet's treatment of Hrothgar's scop we should perhaps distinguish two phases in the use of formulaic poetry: the oral and the written. The oral stage, that of the scop in Heorot, is well described by Magoun. It is fully *extempore*; the minstrel as he stands before his audience composes with the use of ready-made formulas. Sometimes he introduces old tags, virtually meaningless; much of the time he describes traditional happenings, battles or feasting for example, in traditional words and phrases. Sometimes a minstrel working in the oral-formulaic tradition coined a phrase, for every phrase must have been new before it grew old, and one man can coin a multitude of phrases for use by himself at first and later for use by others in admiring imitation. Nevertheless, tradition is tenacious and change slow in that kind of literature; and in any case we have no means of knowing what is new.

Much has been said of the singers, and less of the audience. For a hearer (as for a reader) there are many ways of feeling pleasure in poetry; but, at one level of appreciation at least, a great part of the pleasure seems to lie in pleasurable recognition of the expected and pleasurable surprise at the unexpected. An audience used to formulaic verse is presumably conditioned to feeling pleasure in recognition of the familiar.[33] It is characteristic of the secondary stage in the use of formulaic poetry that it still draws on the formulas descended from the primary, the extemporising stage of poetic composition, partly because there is no other conception of poetry and partly because the audience demands the traditional. The Christian poetry of the Anglo-Saxons may well have been written to supply a audience's craving for what they had always had.

Gregory the Great wrote for the guidance of St Augustine that well-constructed pagan temples in England should not be destroyed but dedicated to the glory of Christ, so that the nation, seeing their temples preserved, might gather with a new spirit more familiarly in the places to which they were accustomed. In the extant Anglo-Saxon verse we see the customary poetic formulas of the nation deliberately, artificially even, put to a new use. Tags like *heard under helme* 'strong under his helmet', *ecg wæs iren* 'its blade was of iron', *maðma mænigeo* 'a multitude of treasures', serve as reminders of an old order, and as such have new meaning. In origin they may have been the *hums* and *haws* of hesitating poetic extemporisation: in their new context they have become living tokens of a heroic past which the Christian present still wears among its ornaments.

A long time ago Adolf Ebert wrote of the Anglo-Saxons:

> The quick acceptance and ready assimilation of the civilisation of Latin Christianity, assimilation moreover which soon turned into prolific learned activity in Latin, was not merely a consequence of the great talent of this Germanic nation: it presupposes a higher degree of indigenous refinement. This refinement, of course, was not of a scholarly nature; but rather a refinement of disposition, a refinement of the affections, and a refinement of the imagination.[34]

It would perhaps be too fanciful to say that Gregory sensed this refinement when he saw the English slave-boys for sale in Rome, and took to punning on angels and Angles. We know, however, that he thought their outward appearance so full of grace that he lamented the darkness of their souls; and he must have thought them capable of responding to missionary efforts. The conversion of the English became the object of his special zeal; he laboured to fill the minds and altars of the nation with a different spirit; he condemned in them only that they were pagan. It is not likely that when the English neophytes looked back they would condemn and despise the past which had nurtured them and given them a mind to apprehend the new faith. Their past did not lack nobility, and when they came to sing of God and his saints they turned to the past to furnish them with the means of expression. In the vernacular they had no other means.

It goes deeper than that. When the Anglo-Saxons turned to their language to express their thoughts they would have found, if they had been capable of such Humboldtian reasoning, that it had been at work already, and had shaped not merely their thoughts but also the mode of perception that underlay them. There is a statement of Wilhelm von Humboldt's which seems highly pertinent to the study of Old English literature:

> Since languages, or at least their constituent parts . . ., are transmitted by one age to the next, and since we can speak of incipient languages only by going right outside the range of our experience, it follows that the relationship in which the past stands to the present reaches down into the uttermost depths of all that shapes the present.[35]

We delude ourselves if we believe that we can catch a nation in its infancy and hear its first babblings. When in the fifth century the Anglo-Saxon tribes left their Continental homes they brought with them a group of closely related, ancient dialects including the tribes' poetic word-hoard, their oral-formulaic stockpile. Centuries earlier, Tacitus, writing of the Germanic tribes in general, refers to song as the vehicle of their tribal memory, that is, of their history. We have evidence that some memory of the origin of the nation in northern lands was preserved, and survived to be recorded in definite form by Bede and in the genealogies of the English royal dynasties.

Beowulf, both as a young man and as king, is represented as embodying the traditional ideals of the nation. The language in which this ideal is expounded is the traditional diction in the traditional metre of the English. Of course, the poem owes a great deal to Christianity, but it does not owe everything to Christianity; the language in which the ideal is expressed and the mode of perception by means of which the Anglo-Saxons were able to grasp the ideals of the new faith, relating them to their indigenous ideals, go back to the pagan past.

In the passage we have been considering (lines 864–915) the ideal seems absolute. Beowulf has triumphed against an evil being, has deserved the gratitude of a good and wise king, and his merit calls forth a song of praise from a panegyrist filled with the memory of ancient traditions. The poet presents the scop to us as singing the hero's praise in the traditional manner in the traditional poetic medium. *Secg eft ongan /* *sið Beowulfes snyttrum styrian* (871–72), we are told; surely, we may expect something about Beowulf himself. Instead we get the ideal which is embodied in Beowulf expressed in terms of Sigemund and Heremod. The relevance of Sigemund, the dragon-slayer, is not made explicit, it is too obvious to need explanation; but how love fell to Beowulf whereas iniquity took possession of Heremod is clearly stated. It would be going too far to claim that a traditionalist, such as the *Beowulf* poet imagines Hrothgar's minstrel to be, could only have praised Beowulf by borrowing some of the actual words which belong to the praise of men like Sigemund or to the dispraise of men like Heremod. All that we have the right to claim is that the merit of Beowulf, however it might have been expressed, could only have been perceived in terms which had their application to earlier heroes. There is a special directness in the *Beowulf* poet's adduction of Sigemund and Heremod. The poet's associative habit of mind working in the same direction as his annexive syntax, which is in part based on the devices of the alliterative metre, leads him to take for granted the transitions. Without expressing the transitions he puts down directly the whole of the circumstances of a comparable or contrasting personage or situation. Other poets might have stripped the parallel of some of the words in which it is expressed and taken them over for their own use. The poet of *Beowulf* takes over the parallel whole, perhaps because he is conscious that he perceives the hero of his poem at this point as being all that, in descriptions known to him, made Sigemund glorious and all that Heremod was not.

A number of the passages in the poem referred to by critics of *Beowulf* as "digressions and episodes" owe their place to the poet's habit of mind. Far from being intrusions or excrescences they are the result of his directness of expression. The sorrow to be experienced by Wealhtheow, Hrothgar's queen, who presumably lives to see the treacherous enmity of Hrothulf to her poor sons, is expressed, not by telling us proleptically how *she* suffered, but how her parallel, Hildeburh suffered when her son and brother and later her lord were slain (1063–1191). The poet makes it appear by his use of Hildeburh's manifold sorrows that she is the *locus classicus* of a queen's suffering in intestine strife. There is, of course, a strong element of foreboding in all this: as Hildeburh mourned, so shall Wealhtheow. The poet shapes his account of the wars between Finn (Hildeburh's husband) on the one hand and Hnæf (Hildeburh's brother) and Hengest (who succeeds Hnæf) on the other to bring out to the full the misery of Hildeburh.

At the first appearance of Hygd, Hygelac's young and gracious queen, she is described chiefly by the device which the poet had used when he drew on the evil Heremod to expound the virtues of Beowulf. The mind of Modthryth, the untamed shrew, was disgraced by every opposite of Hygd's many graces (1925–62, especially 1929–43). Here, as in the case of Heremod, the transition is abrupt, the connection is not made explicit, so that some of the best critics of the poem suspect (unnecessarily, it seems to me) a gap.[36] Once again, the abruptness is the result of the directness with which the poet habitually lays the past under contribution to set forth the present: his mode of perception of the present is as much part of his heritage as the language in which he expresses it. It has been suggested[37] that the reference in this passage to Offa, the legendary king of Angle, may be in the nature of a compliment to Offa of Mercia, his historical descendant. Offa of Angle is praised in a very similar way in the Old English poem *Widsith*. If, as seems very likely, this is the correct analysis of why Offa of Angle is twice praised in Old English verse, it follows that two Old English poets at least, and Offa of Mercia too if he understood their praise, were accustomed to direct reference to the glorious past for an exposition of the present; those not very close kinsmen of the then reigning king of Mercia who gave the new-born Offa his name must have looked back similarly (as royal families do in name-giving). In *Beowulf,* however, this is not just an occasional device for a graceful compliment: the poem is about the past and is furnished with instances drawn from the past.

It is not to be inferred from all this that the *Beowulf* poet, going to his nation's word-hoard, has come away with something equivalent to the Elgin Marbles, where his fellow poets were content to pick up bits and pieces the size of acanthus leaves or vine-leaf scrolls. Whatever the poet of *Beowulf* takes over, little units and large ones, he moulds and modulates to suit his specific purpose. In the same way as he makes apt use of the smaller units and organises them well, so he does not leave the larger units strewn about unhewn and unaltered in his work like a scatter of erratic boulders.

We know, merely through the poet's choice of subject, that he resembles the ideal minstrel whom he presents to us on two occasions in this, that he too delights in the exercise of a well-stored memory deeply imbued with traditions, enshrined also in some of the genealogies of the Anglo-Saxons by which their kings appear as descendants of Scyld. The genealogies contain some of the Danish names in the poem: Beow,[38] Scyld, Sceaf, and Heremod. It seems likely that before these names, all appearing as ancestors of Woden, were incorporated in the genealogies, Woden must have been euhemerised (as he is explicitly in the *Chronicle* of Æthelweard, almost certainly a member of the West Saxon royal house living in the tenth century). This act of euhemerisation is clear evidence that members of the royal families took these genealogies seriously, even in Christian times. The extension of the genealogies beyond Woden, though presumably quite unhistorical, shows that they wished to associate these figures, of whom they knew (*Beowulf* is witness to that), with their own royal dynasties. *Beowulf* could well have been written late enough for at least some of the Danes mentioned in the poem to have been regarded by the poet and his audience as ancestors of Anglo-Saxon kings in England.[39]

It is likely that the rulers who knew of their ancient descent were stirred by the memory of glorious deeds of those men from whom they were descended. The use to which the *Anglo-Saxon Chronicle* puts Offa's genealogy in the annal for the year of his accession (in 757) seems to indicate a deliberate exploitation of the list of kings going back to Woden as contributing to the glorification of Offa. If, as is natural, Anglo-Saxon rulers delighted in the ancient nobility of their dynasty their retainers must have been aware of these traditions also. The beginning of the poem with its piece of Danish history is relevant to England, to English kings and therefore to their retainers, as much as the Trojan origins of the British dynasty relevantly introduce poems, like *Sir Gawain and the Green Knight,* on British themes.

There is evidence that there was in Anglo-Saxon England a considerable knowledge of the legends of the Germanic heroic age. Interest in these legends is not likely to have been swiftly reduced when Christianity came, and the poet of *Beowulf* was able to rely on his audience's familiarity with the ancient traditions to such an extent that he introduced allusive references and not fully coherent accounts of feuds, apparently without needing to fear that he would not be understood. The Finn Episode (1063–1159) could not be understood by an audience not already familiar with the facts; perhaps the original audience was familiar with these events because (if the Hengest of the Episode was identified with the Hengest of the Anglo-Saxon Settlement) the feud was held to belong to proto-Kentish history.[40] The wars between the Geats and the Swedes are not told by the poet in chronological sequence, but allusively and selectively. In lines 2177–89 praise of Beowulf and a reference to his ignominious youth encloses an allusion to Heremod, who had been trusted in his youth: change came to both of them. The allusion is missed by anyone who fails to seize on Heremod as one pattern of evil in a king.

As the poet's ideal minstrel relates Beowulf's merit, gained from present exploits in Denmark, to the merit of past figures, Sigemund and Heremod, so the poet analyses a Christian ideal, appropriate to the English audience for whom he is writing, in terms of an ideal figure of the past: Beowulf. The language which he uses, the traditional poetic vocabulary of the Anglo-Saxons, with many formulas expected by the audience to whom no other language seemed fit for poetry, has led the poet to seek his material outside Christian story in the Germanic traditions to which his language had had its first, its most direct application. His habit of mind which finds expression in an annexive syntax, such as goes well with the alliterative metre, is associative. He does not always make explicit how his associations are linked to his main theme, no more than the minstrel does in Heorot who fails to make explicit why in singing the praise of Beowulf he should recall what he heard tell of Sigemund's exploits and the tyranny of Heremod.

The excellence of the poem is in large measure due to the concord between the poet's mode of thinking and his mode of expression. An associative imagination works well in annexive syntax: each is the cause of the other's excellence. At the same time, he is good with the smaller units, the words and formulas which all Anglo-Saxon poets had to handle. Perhaps there is a deeper reason why *Beowulf* is satisfactory. The Christian poet chose to write of the Germanic past. His ideal king is Beowulf the monster-slayer, whom he compared, not with Daniel, but with Sigemund, and contrasted, not with Saul, but with Heremod.

His success lies in that choice. The elements of Old English poetic diction, the words and the traditional phrases feel at home in the world which they first celebrated in song.[41] Old English poetic diction is retrospective: it looks back to the civilisation that gave it shape and which in turn it helped to shape. Heusler[42] said rightly of the Germanisation in Old English verse of Genesis and of Exodus, of the legends of St Andrew and of St Helena's Invention of the Cross, of Christ even (of whom *The Dream of the Rood* (39–41) reports "that the young hero armed himself, strong and fierce of mind he mounted the high gallows, brave in the sight of many"), that all this Germanisation was not taken seriously. But the language of his poetry is something a poet must feel serious about. The Germanisation of biblical narrative is a good device only where its spirit can be accepted as part of a fuller transformation. In the account of the Crucifixion in *The Dream of the Rood* the ideal raised by the Germanising language clashes with the idea of the Crucifixion.

There are good things in Old English verse, in the Elegies especially, but also in some of the saints' lives, the second part of *Guthlac,* for example; but it is difficult to see how the inapposite application of the Germanic battle-style to Christian themes could ever have called forth critical praise. The beginning of *Andreas* reads in rough translation:

> Lo, we heard tell of twelve in far-off days under the stars, glorious heroes, the Lord's retainers. Their glory did not fail in warfare, whenever banners clashed . . . They were men famous on earth, eager leaders of nations, men active in the army, warriors renowned whenever in the field of assault buckler and hand defended the helmet on the plain of destiny.

Here is a poet who can do the big bow-wow like any man going. But he was writing of those twelve whom Christ ordained with the words, "Behold, I send you forth as sheep in the midst of wolves" (Matthew 10:16).

The *Beowulf* poet avoided that mistake.

So far we have been less concerned with what the *Beowulf* poet says than with how he says it. The poem is obviously about the past. In Professor Tolkien's words:

> When new *Beowulf* was already antiquarian, in a good sense, and it now produces a singular effect. For it is now to us itself ancient, and yet its maker was telling of things already old and weighted with regret, and he expended his art in making keen that touch upon the heart which sorrows have that are both poignant and remote.[43]

The sadness of the poem lies in that. But there is glory in it too, such as is proper to a noble society presented as an ideal. Beowulf himself is of heroic stature. His strength and valour, made manifest in every exploit, his wisdom, his regard for the etiquette of an aristocratic society, his long victorious reign, the assurance of his speeches and the nobility of his intentions, all these are the proper ingredients of heroism; and that the heroic ideal embodied in Beowulf goes deeper still follows from his loyalty to Hygelac, his king, and to Heardred, Hygelac's son (2373–79), from his mildness, praised by his survivors (3180–82), and from the speech, modestly expressed, in which, surveying a world of deceit and murderous perfidy, he finds himself at the end of his days unperjured and guiltless of the blood of kinsmen (2736–43). He is the ideal ruler of a society held together by bonds of love and service. Though less fashionable now as a theme for literature, strength is emphasised in the poem and is gloried in. Beowulf brought strength to Hrothgar, the aged king of the Danes, bowed down with care for his people; and with strength he survived the proud Frisian raid in which Hygelac was slain; with strength also he kept the Swedes out of the land of the Geats.

It seems as if the poet's intended audience looked back to the nation's past (as adumbrated in the royal genealogies), and took pleasure in it. The poet gratifies his audience's idealising love of the Germanic past. The opening of the poem by means of its specific references to the ancestors of kings in England plays on an audience's memory of the past. There is in the poem a strong element of regret for a noble order which will never come back.

I have said elsewhere[44] that it seems to me that, though the poet presents the heroic ideal of his people lovingly, he presents it as ultimately unavailing and therefore not worth ambition. Perhaps there is a hint even that Beowulf, being a pagan too eager in the hour of his death for posthumous fame and the sight of gold—what else *can* pagans think about when they die?—will not, for all his virtues, be saved from everlasting damnation in hell. Once the modern reader feels that hint he ceases to read the poem simply as the Germanic heroic ideal presented elegiacally. What is implied is that the poet is aware of the fact that the pagan heroic ideal stands in conflict with the ascetic ideal of Christianity, as it was known in the English monasteries of the poet's time. By the standards of that higher ideal the heroic ideal is insufficient. The poet, however, nowhere states unambiguously (except at lines 175–88) that the pagan ideal he presents is insufficient, and some readers will be reluctant to read the poem in that way (especially if they first delete lines 175–88 as an interpolation).

We have no means of telling who the poet's first audience was: perhaps in some royal hall, where the lord and his men still delighted in the ancient nobility of the dynasty; or perhaps in some monastery to which a king retired, as we know King Sigeberht of East Anglia did when he gave up his throne in the second quarter of the seventh century, and as King Ethelred of Mercia did in 704, and Ceolwulf of Northumbria in 737, and Eadberht of Northumbria in 758. Kings like these proved by their abdication that they thought the pagan glory of pledging in the hall, of victory in the field, of treasure-giving and of loyalty to an earthly throne, a vain ideal. A poet might have written a poem like *Beowulf* for one of many courts, to teach a king wisdom, or for some monastery whose refectory contained a man descended from a line of Spear-Danes and not contemptuous of that ancestry. It is only a guess; but that is the kind of original audience that would have heard *Beowulf* with understanding.

NOTES

1. I wish to thank Professors Randolph Quirk and Geoffrey Shepherd for reading this essay in typescript, and for their help and criticism.

2. Two pieces of evidence, neither of them conclusive, that Old English verse may have ceased to be fully understood as early as the twelfth century are Simeon of Durham's misunderstanding of *Bede's Death Song* (cf. M. Förster, "Paläographisches zu *Bedas Sterbespruch* und *Cædmons Hymnus*," *Archiv für das Studium der neueren Sprachen und Literaturen* 135 (1917): 282–84) and a possible misunderstanding of *The Battle of Maldon* in the *Liber Eliensis* (cf. E.O. Blake, ed., *Liber Eliensis*, Camden Society, 3rd Series, 92 (London, 1962), 134f., footnotes). Cf. also K. Sisam, *The Structure of "Beowulf"* (Oxford, 1965), 70f.

3. Stanley Rypins, ed., *Three Old English Prose Texts in MS. Cotton Vitellius A xv*, EETS os 161 (London, 1924), 59.

4. Quoted from Dorothy Whitelock, *The Audience of "Beowulf"* (Oxford, 1951), 46. Professor Whitelock's discussion of the relationship between the *Liber Monstrorum* and *Beowulf* is of fundamental importance in this connection.

5. See the important discussion by Kenneth Sisam, "The Compilation of the Beowulf Manuscript," in *Studies in the History of Old English Literature* (Oxford, 1953), 65–96.

6. In the Authorised Version the story is relegated to the Apocrypha, for excellent textual reasons.

7. Cf. W.W. Lawrence, *"Beowulf" and Epic Tradition* (Cambridge, Mass., 1928), 207; T.M. Gang, "Approaches to *Beowulf*," *Review of English Studies* NS 3 (1952): 6ff.; K. Sisam, "Beowulf's Fight with the Dragon," *Review of English Studies* NS 9 (1958): 128–40, and also *Structure*, 25.

8. "Die christlichen Elemente im *Beowulf*," *Anglia* 36 (1912): 195.

9. *Andreas und Elene* (Cassel, 1840), xxvii. For recent discussions of the beasts of battle, considered from widely different points of view, see F.P. Magoun, Jr., "The Theme of the Beasts of Battle in Anglo-Saxon Poetry," *Neuphilologische Mitteilungen* 56 (1955): 81–90, E.G. Stanley, "Old English Poetic Diction and the Interpretation of *The Wanderer, The Seafarer* and *The Penitent's Prayer*," *Anglia* 73 (1956): 442f., A. Bonjour, "*Beowulf* and the Beasts of Battle," *PMLA* 72 (1957): 563–73 (and *Twelve "Beowulf" Papers* (Neuchatel, 1962), ch. X). For Grimm's discussion see E.G. Stanley, "The Search for Anglo-Saxon Paganism," *Notes and Queries* 209 (1964): 244.

10. R. Quirk (in *Early English and Norse Studies Presented to Hugh Smith* (London, 1963), 166) also selects this passage (3014–27) to demonstrate the excellence of *Beowulf*: "We see here the use of incongruous collocations to form a critical undercurrent of a kind which notably enriches *Beowulf* from time to time and which is prominent among the features making it a great poem."

11. For a different view, see Sisam, *Structure*, 54–59.

12. Cf. A.F.C. Vilmar, *Deutsche Altertümer im "Heliand,"* etc. (Marburg, 1845), "Epische form" (3ff. of the edition of 1862); and, more recently, F.P. Magoun, Jr., "Oral-Formulaic Character of Anglo-Saxon Narrative Poetry," *Speculum* 28 (1953): 446–67. See also H. Schabram, *"Andreas* und *Beowulf,"* *Nachrichten der Giessener Hochschulgesellschaft* 34 (1965): 201–18.

13. See G.V. Smithers, "Five Notes on Old English Texts," *English and Germanic Studies* 4 (1952): 67–75.

14. See p. 30 below for a translation.

15. See p. 7 above.

16. An excellent account of the diction of *Beowulf* is provided by A.G. Brodeur, *The Art of "Beowulf"* (Berkeley, 1959), ch. 1. See also G. Storms, "The Subjectivity of the Style of *Beowulf,"* in *Studies in Old English Literature in Honor of Arthur G. Brodeur* (Eugene, 1963), 171–86, and J. Hoops, *Beowulfstudien* (Heidelberg, 1932), 20–24. Among earlier studies, O. Krackow, *Die Nominalcomposita als Kunstmittel im altenglischen Epos* (Weimar, 1903), is still useful.

17. See A. Campbell's important "The Old English Epic Style," in *English and Medieval Studies Presented to J.R.R. Tolkien* (London, 1962), especially in this connection 19f.

18. See H. Kuhn, "Zur Wortstellung und -betonung im Altgermanischen," *Beiträge zur Geschichte der deutschen Sprache und Literatur* 57 (1933): 1–109 (summarised in English by D. Slay, *Transactions of the Philological Society* (1952): 1–14).

19. Cf. E. Sievers, *Altgermanische Metrik* (Halle, 1893), §82; an example of an exceptionally long multisyllabic medial dip (given by Sievers) is *sealde þam þe he wolde* (*Beowulf* 3055).

20. Cf. J. Ries, *Die Wortstellung im "Beowulf"* (Halle, 1907), 72–75, who rightly insists on the similarity of verse and prose in this respect. The difference lies in the greater regularity and, therefore, predictability of verse. For a discussion, not always convincing, of the style and syntax of *Beowulf,* cf. S.O. Andrew, *Syntax and Style in Old English* (Cambridge, 1940), and the same author's *Postscript on "Beowulf"* (Cambridge, 1948). The earlier book is especially good on co-ordinate clauses in *Beowulf*; ch. VIII (on asyndetic co-ordinate clauses) deals with an important aspect of the additive style of *Beowulf,* a characteristic uncommon elsewhere in Old English verse, as Andrew notes.

21. *"Beowulf": The Monsters and the Critics* (London, 1936), 31 (*Proceedings of the British Academy* 22 (1936): 273).

22. Ibid.

23. See Hoops, *Beowulfstudien,* 52–55.

24. But cf. the use of the phrase at line 366 (and elsewhere in verse), where the meaning is quite unspecifically "to converse."

25. "The Poetry of Cædmon," *Proceedings of the British Academy* 33 (1946): 277–95.

26. *Deutsche Altertümer im Heliand,* 1862 ed., 5.

27. "Oral-Formulaic Character" (see n. 12 above).

28. Review of G. Storms, *Compounded Names of Peoples in "Beowulf,"* *English Studies* 41 (1960): 204 (quoted by Bonjour, *Twelve "Beowulf" Papers,* 149). See also Brodeur, *The Art of "Beowulf,"* ch. 1.

29. F.P. Magoun, Jr., "Bede's Story of Cædman: The Case History of an Anglo-Saxon Oral Singer," *Speculum* 30 (1955): 49–63.

30. "Oral-Formulaic Character," 447.

31. R.P. Creed, *Texas Studies in Literature and Language* 3 (1961): 98.

32. For a different view, cf. R.P. *Creed,* "The Singer Looks at His Sources," *Studies in Old English Literature in Honor of Arthur G. Brodeur* (Eugene, 1963), 44–52.

33. Cf. in this connection R. Quirk's important paper "Poetic language and Old English metre" in *Early English and Norse Studies Presented to Hugh Smith* (London, 1963), 150–71.

34. *Allgemeine Geschichte der Literatur des Mittelalters im Abendlande* (Leipzig, 1880–89), 3:3.

35. *Sprachphilosophische Werke,* ed. H. Steinthal (1883), 225.

36. Among others, Sisam, *Studies,* 41 (reprinting *Review of English Studies* 22 (1946): 266); Whitelock, *Audience,* 58ff.; E. von Schaubert (in the *Kommentar* to her edition (Paderborn, 1961), 114f.) has a fuller list of critics who suspect a gap here.

37. By Whitelock, *Audience,* 58ff.

38. For the view that the name *Beowulf* at lines 18 and 53 is probably an error for *Beow* see A.J. Bliss, *The Metre of "Beowulf"* (Oxford, 1958), 58, as well as the editions.

39. For a comprehensive and fundamental account of the genealogies, see K. Sisam, "Anglo-Saxon Royal Genealogies," *Proceedings of the British Academy* 39 (1953): 287–348.

40. Cf. Sisam, *Studies,* 136.

41. F.P. Magoun, "Some Notes on Anglo-Saxon Poetry" (in *Studies in Medieval Literature in Honor of Albert Croll Baugh,* ed. MacEdward Leach (Philadelphia, 1961), 280–82) suggests that the merits, which, he claims, all readers of Old English poetry see in *The Battle of Maldon,* are grounded on the harmony of subject matter and diction in that poem.

42. *Die altgermanische Heldendichtung* (1926), 140.

43. *"Beowulf": The Monsters and the Critics,* 35f. (277f.).

44. "Hæthenra Hyht in *Beowulf,*" *Studies in Old English Literature in Honor of Arthur G. Brodeur,* ed. Stanley B. Greenfield (Eugene, 1963), 136–51.

The Pagan Coloring of *Beowulf*

by Larry D. Benson

This essay first appeared in Old English Poetry: Fifteen Essays, *ed. Robert P. Creed (Providence: Brown University Press, 1967), 193–213.*

THE old theory that *Beowulf* is an essentially pagan work only slightly colored with the Christianity of a later scribe has now been dead for many years, and critics today generally agree that the poem is the unified work of a Christian author.[1] Indeed, most of the elements in *Beowulf* that once supplied arguments for its essential paganism—the function of Wyrd, the emphasis on the comitatus, the duty of revenge—are now recognized not as pagan but as secular values that were easily incorporated into the framework of Anglo-Saxon Christianity.[2] Likewise, though the stories of Beowulf and the monsters probably originated in pagan times, it is now generally acknowledged that they have been assimilated into a Christian world view with the monsters allied with the devil and Beowulf (or so Friedrich Klaeber and others have held) fitted to the pattern of Christ himself.[3] Yet the ghost of the old pagan-versus-Christian dispute still lingers, for along with the Christian and Christianized secular elements the poem does contain some indisputably pagan features that have remained intractable to modern criticism. Moreover, the knockings of that spirit have become steadily more insistent, for the more deeply Christian the meanings of *Beowulf* are discovered to be, the more difficult become the still-unanswered questions raised by H.M. Chadwick in 1912: "If the poem preserves its original form and is the work of a Christian, it is difficult to see why the poet should go out of his way in v. 175 ff. to represent the Danes as offering heathen sacrifices. . . . Again why should he lay Beowulf himself to rest with heathen obsequies, described in all possible detail . . . ?"[4] Why, one must ask, should the poet's whole representation of the Danes and Geats include all the other details that Chadwick notes—the funeral ship (27 ff.), the observation of omens (204), and the use of cremation (1108 ff., 2124 ff., 3137 ff.)?[5]

The intrusion of these pagan elements into an otherwise completely Christian work presents more difficult problems than the simple matter of factual inconsistency. Certainly the poet is inconsistent in first showing us the Danes listening to the Christian account of the Creation and then, a few lines later, telling us that they knew nothing of God and sacrificed to idols. That is only the sort of historical inaccuracy that one expects in medieval poetry; Chaucer and Shakespeare confused pagan and Christian elements in much the same way.[6] Poets (especially medieval poets) are responsible for total aesthetic effect rather than documentary accuracy. The difficulty in *Beowulf* is that the pagan elements seem to confound the aesthetic effect, to destroy the consistency of tone. Instead of casually mixing pagan and Christian, as so many medieval poets do, the *Beowulf* poet goes out of his way to draw our attention to the Danes' heathen sacrifices. Furthermore, the paganism that he describes is not simply literary or historical; it was a still strong and threatening force in his own day. For him to present his characters as heathens is, so we assume, to show them in the worst of possible lights. Alcuin, in his famous letter to the monks at Lindisfarne, defines for us the Christian Englishman's attitude toward the pagans: *Quid Hinieldus cum Christo? Angusta est domus: utrosque tenere non poterit. Non vult rex cęlestis cum paganis et perditis nominetenus regibus communionem habere* 'what has Ingeld to do with Christ? Narrow is the house; it cannot hold both. The King of Heaven wants no fellowship at all with pagan and damned kings.'[7] Given this attitude toward the heathens, our poet's insistence that his characters are both emphatically pagan and exceptionally good seems self-contradictory, and that apparent contradiction has seemed to many critics a touch of feebleness at the very heart of the poem, so feeble that even his warmest admirers have been forced either to fall back on the old theory of scribal tampering or to conclude that the poet simply blundered.[8]

The blunder may be our own, for the apparent contradiction arises, not from the poem itself, but from our assumptions about the meaning of paganism to the poet and his audience. These assumptions have been based on our knowledge of one letter by Alcuin, written in a spirit of reforming zeal at the end of the eighth century, and scattered comments by Bede, who is not quite so inflexible in his attitude toward pagans as his doctrinal pronouncements make him seem.[9] The extreme distaste for everything pagan that these comments exhibit is not typical of the age to which the composition of *Beowulf* is usually assigned; beginning in the last years of the seventh century and extending throughout the eighth, the dominant attitude of Christian Englishmen toward the Germanic pagans was one of interest, sympathy, and occasionally even admiration. This was the period during which the English church was engaged in an intense missionary activity on the Continent, sending missionaries in significant numbers first to the Frisians and Danes and then to the Old Saxons and the tribes in central Germany. This major undertaking, the great interest that it aroused in England, and the attitude it fostered toward pagandom has received relatively little attention from students of *Beowulf*; yet it can shed considerable light on the problems raised by the pagan elements in the poem, revealing artistry where we thought we detected blunders.

I

THE MISSIONARY activity of the English church began by accident when Wilfred, on his way to Rome to protest his deposition as Bishop of York, landed in Frisia to avoid falling into the hands of his political enemies and spent the winter of 678–79 as guest of the pagan king Aldgisl.[10] He preached the gospel to the heathens, apparently with some success, and then traveled on to Rome. He returned to England, where he occupied a number of sees during his contentious career, but evidently he always maintained an interest in the missionary work in Frisia. In 697 he consecrated a bishop, Suidbert, for the Frisian mission, and the founder of the most successful mission there was Willibrord, who had been Wilfred's student at Ripon and whom Wilfred visited when he again passed through Frisia in 703.

The next missionary effort came from English monks living in Ireland. As Bede tells it, the mission began with the plan of Egbert, who *proposuit animo pluribus prodesse; id est, initio opere apostolico, verbum Dei aliquibus earum quae nondum audierant gentibus evangelizando committere: quarum in Germania plurimas noverat esse nationes, a quibus Angli vel Saxones qui nunc Brittaniam incolunt, genus et originem duxisse noscuntur; unde hactenus a vicina gente Brettonum corrupte Garmani nuncupantur. Sunt autem Fresones, Rugini, Danai, Hunni, Antiqui Saxones, Boructuari: sunt alii perplures eisdem in partibus populi paganis adhuc ritibus servientes.* 'set his mind on doing good to many; that is, by undertaking the apostolic work, to preach to some of those peoples that had not yet heard the word of God; he knew that there were several such nations in Germany, from which the Angles or Saxons who now inhabit Britain are known to have taken their stock and origin; hence, by the neighboring race of the Britons they are to this day corruptly called "Garmani." These are the Frisians, the *Rugini,* the Danes, the Huns, the Old Saxons, the *Boructuari*; there are many other peoples in these same parts still in servitude to pagan rites.'[11] Egbert was deterred from this undertaking by a series of visions and a shipwreck. Yet he had established the plan, basing it on the idea of the kinship between the insular and Continental "Garmani" that was to remain a basic motivation of this missionary work. One of his disciples, Wictbert, took up the task next and preached for two years, though without success, to the Frisians and to their king Rathbod.[12]

The next year, 690, Willibrord, who had spent several years in Ireland as a pupil of Egbert after his studies at Ripon, set out for Frisia with a company of twelve English missionaries.[13] Shortly thereafter, two more English priests, both named Hewald (known as "White" and "Black" Hewald, from the colors of their hair), journeyed to the Continent and met martyrdom among the Old Saxons (whose alderman, though a pagan, was incensed at this murder and avenged their deaths).[14] But despite this setback the mission flourished. Suidbert, one of Willibrord's twelve helpers, was consecrated bishop by Wilfred and carried the mission to the *Boructuari,* and Willibrord received the pallium at Rome and extended his work in Frisia. He carried the gospel even to the Danes, whose king, Ongendus, received him with "every mark of honor" but was unimpressed by his preaching.[15] Nevertheless, Willibrord brought back with him from Denmark thirty Danish youths whom he instructed in the Christian faith, and on his return journey he visited and desecrated the famous pagan shrine at Heligoland. At the time Bede was writing, Willibrord still lived among his converted flock in Frisia, one of the heroes of the English church.

The next and greatest stage in the movement was the mission of Boniface.[16] With two companions he sailed with a trader from London to Frisia in 716. He spent the winter among the Frisians and, meeting with no success, returned to England. After a trip to Rome he went again to Frisia, preaching in places as yet untouched by missionaries. He succeeded Willibrord as leader of the movement and turned his attention to the Old Saxons. From Britain an "exceedingly large number of holy men came to his aid, among them readers, writers, and learned men trained in the other arts."[17] In his last years he went back to Frisia and, pushing farther into heathendom, was martyred near the border of Denmark in 754. He was succeeded by Lull, another Englishman, and the missionary effort of the English church continued unabated throughout the eighth century; the later intellectual expeditions of scholars such as Alcuin were only extensions of the movement that Wilfred and Willibrord began.

One of the most remarkable features of these missions was the close relation that they all maintained with the homeland. We have already noted Wilfred's continuing interest in Frisia and the fact that Suidbert returned to England to be consecrated a bishop at Wilfred's hands. We also know that another of Willibrord's helpers visited Lindisfarne, and in general, even though Willibrord's correspondence does not survive, there is evidence of frequent intercourse between his mission and England.[18] Likewise, it is probable that a good many other Englishmen joined him, for the missionary expeditions were fairly large, involving not one or two wandering preachers but the mission *suorum tantum stipatus clientum numero* 'accompanied by a great number of servants,' including even armed soldiers.[19] Boniface's letters do survive, as do those of his successor, Lull, and beginning with the first quarter of the eighth century, we have ample evidence for Levison's assertion that "the continental mission was regarded as a national undertaking of the whole English people."[20] It was to England that Boniface looked for advice, books, and the help of prayer, and his correspondents included clergy and laymen alike from Thanet to Lindisfarne. On one occasion he addressed a letter, which we shall shortly examine, to the entire English nation. The nation responded by turning its eyes to the pagan Continent—hoping for the conversion of the heathen, for the prayers of the missionaries, or like King Ethelbert of Kent, for a pair of falcons of the sort that Boniface had sent along with shields and spears as a gift to the king of Mercia.[21]

II

THE EXTENT and intensity of this traffic with the Continent has long been known, but this knowledge has had little effect on the study of *Beowulf.* This is largely because the English missions have been considered only in relation to the history of the plot. As early as 1816 Outzen proposed that the missions in Frisia supplied the route by which the story of Beowulf reached the poet.[22] The more recent discovery of the possible English origin of the *Liber Monstrorum* with its account of Hygelac, which probably came to England by way of Frisia, has led critics to reflect anew that a good many Englishmen of the late seventh and eighth centuries must have seen or heard of Hygelac's grave on that island in the mouth of the Frisian Rhine.[23] It does seem likely that English travelers would have brought home some tales of Hygelac and Hrothgar, of Finn, and perhaps even of Beowulf—if not the tales our poet used, at least some related tales that helped kindle new interest in the old materials. Likewise, the Frisians, that "great trading people of the North" who dealt with Christian London on the west and pagan Scandinavia on the east,[24] are the most likely means by which tales of the Swedes and stories of Sigmund would have reached England. We know that the Frisians had a recognized class of minstrels,[25] and it would be surprising if their store of songs did not include at least some of the tales used in *Beowulf.* Yet this is only conjecture, and critics have rightly set aside the impossible task of tracing the exact sources of the plot and have turned their attention elsewhere.

Unfortunately, in turning away from the Continent as a contemporary source for the poet's plot, they have also turned away from it as a source of the poet's knowledge of heathen customs, such as the burials in *Beowulf.* The study of *Beowulf* has been needlessly complicated by a search of the English past for the possible hints and memories upon which the poet could have based his accounts of pagan funerals. Even the Sutton Hoo discovery has been of little help; but on the Continent, where the English missionaries were working, pagan burials both by cremation and by interment in mounds continued throughout the eighth century, as we know from laws directed against anyone who *corpus defuncti homini secundum ritum paganorum flamma consumi fecerit et ossa eius ad cinerem redierit* 'has had the body of a deceased man consumed by flame and returned his bones to ashes according to the rite of the pagans' or who buried the dead *ad tumulus paganorum* 'at a grave-mound of the pagans.'[26] Likewise, such practices as augury and sacrificing to idols might reflect a memory of England's own past but are more likely based on some knowledge of the Germanic pagans themselves, for throughout the Continent divination and idol-worship were widely and persistently practiced.[27] That Christians of this period were interested in learning about such practices is shown by the contemporary references to pagan beliefs that have survived,[28] and certainly some information of this sort must have been a common subject of conversation whenever a cleric or trader returned to England with news of the missions. We cannot be sure that any of the poet's plot reached him by this route, but we can be positive that he had at his disposal a good deal of information about the pagans that he chose to celebrate.

More important to the student confronted with the problem of the poet's characterization of his pagans is the attitude toward the Germanic heathen which the missionaries maintained and encouraged among their supporters in England. They had none of Alcuin's disdain, and from Egbert to Lull one of the prime motives for the missions was the sympathy fostered by the kinship between the English and *noster gens,* the Germanic tribes on the Continent.[29] This sympathy appears in Bede's account of Egbert's decision to become a missionary, quoted above, and it is stated even more emphatically in the celebrated letter that Boniface wrote in 738 to the whole English nation, from the bishops to the laymen, *immo generaliter omnibus catholicis* 'indeed, to all Catholics in general': *Fraternitatis vestrae clementiam intimis obsecramus precibus . . . ut deus et dominus noster Iesus Christus, "qui vult omnes homines salvos fieri et ad agnitionem Dei venire," convertat ad catholicam fidem corda paganorum Saxonum, et resipiscant a diabuli laqueis, a quibus capti tenetur, et adgregentur filiis matris ecclesiae. Miseremini illorum, quia et ipsi solent dicere: "De uno sanguine et de uno osse sumus"* 'We implore the mercy of your brotherhood with deepest prayers [that you pray] . . . that God and Our Lord Jesus Christ, "who wants all men to be saved and to come to the knowledge of God," may turn the hearts of the pagan Saxons to the Catholic faith, and that they may repent of the devilish snares by which they are held captive, and be joined to the sons of the Mother Church. Have mercy upon them, for they themselves are accustomed to say, "We are of one blood and one bone."'[30] The tone of this letter, its certainty that the pagan Saxons are damned if they are not converted, and its intense sympathy with their plight is almost the same as that which we find in one of the most difficult passages in *Beowulf,* the poet's overt comment on the Danes' idol worship:

> Swylc wæs þēaw hyra,
> hæþenra hyht; helle gemundon
> in mōdsefan, Metod hīe ne cūþon,
> dæda Dēmend, ne wiston hīe Drihten God,
> nē hīe hūru heofena Helm herian ne cūþon,
> wuldres Waldend. Wā bið þǣm ðe sceal
> þurh slīðne nīð sāwle bescūfan
> in fȳres fæþm, frōfre ne wēnan,
> wihte gewendan! Wēl bið þǣm þe mōt
> æfter dēaðdæge Drihten sēcean
> ond tō Fæder fæþmum freoðo wilnian![31]
>
>   (178–88)

Such was their custom, the hope of the heathens; they remembered hell in their minds, they did not know the Ruler, the Judge of Deeds, nor did they know the Lord God, nor indeed did they know how to praise the Protector of Heaven, the Ruler of Glory. Woe be to him who must, in terrible affliction, thrust his soul into the embrace of fire, expect no consolation, no change at all! Well is it for him who, after the day of death, can seek the Lord and ask for peace in the embrace of the Father!

Critics have often suggested that these lines must refer to some relapse into idolatry, but the remarkable quality of this passage is its tone of compassion, and a return to idolatry is a sin for which compassion is not the appropriate emotion.[32] To describe such relapses even the gentle Bede employs the conventional image of the "dog returning to his own vomit."[33] It is to those who have not had a chance to know of God, *ne wiston hīe Drihten God,* that one can be compassionate. Their sin, as the missionaries repeatedly tell us, is "ignorance." They are "blundering in the darkness," ensnared in devilish errors through no fault of their own. The poet's insistence on the Danes' ignorance of God (*ne wiston, ne cūþon*) places them clearly with those blameless and pitiful heathens of whom Boniface speaks.

The poet's sudden shift from the past tense, which he uses to refer to the Danes, to a more generalized present provides an even more important link between his fictional pagans and those real pagans still living on the Continent in his own time. If there is a "Christian excursus" in *Beowulf*, it is not in the account of the sacrifices themselves but in the lines beginning *Wā biþ þǣm*, for the changed tense shows that the object of the poet's compassion includes not only those long-dead Danes in his poem but also those heathens who exist at the moment he is speaking and who are compelled—*sceal*—through ignorance to thrust their souls *in fyres fæþm*. Their plight is made even sadder by the parallel consideration of those—perhaps their kinsmen—whose lot is the happier because they may *Drihten secean*. Marie P. Hamilton has suggested that "by presenting Scandinavian men of good will as looking in the main to the governance of God he [the poet] might bring them within the sympathetic ken of their English cousins."[34] This is true enough, but given the English attitude toward Continental heathens, it may also be that the poet engages his audience's sympathy for his characters by emphasizing their very paganism. Certainly in this "excursive" passage he seems to step aside from the course of his narrative to draw attention to the similarity between the Danes in *Beowulf* and the real Danes whose salvation had become a matter of widespread concern.

The characters in *Beowulf* are men of good will, despite their paganism, and this has seemed to most critics the central contradiction in the poem. In the face of the attitude represented by Alcuin the only way out of this dilemma seems to be that proposed by Charles Donahue: the possibility that the poet was touched by the Pelagian heresy, which taught that pious heathens could be saved for their natural goodness and thus made it possible for a Christian to admire a native heathen hero.[35] Donahue shows that in early medieval Ireland some native heroes were regarded as having lived under the "natural law," virtuous even though heathen and eligible for salvation because they were born outside the Judaic and Christian dispensations. Yet in England and on the Continent, as Donahue also shows, a strict Augustinian orthodoxy prevailed. Bede, writing an attack on the Pelagian heresy, states flatly that even the great philosophers *nullam veram virtutem nec nullam veram sapientiam habere potuerunt. In quantum vero vel gustum aliquem sapientiae cujuslibet, vel virtutis imaginem habebant, totum hoc desuper acceperunt* 'could have no true virtue or knowledge of God. Indeed, insofar as they had any taste of knowledge or image of virtue, they received it from above.'[36] The second sentence seems to grant that the pagans may have some virtue after all, but even so Bede affirms that all those born outside the Judaeo-Christian law are damned, even those born between Adam and Moses, *quia regnavit mors ab Adam usque Moysen, etiam in eos qui non peccaverunt* 'since Death ruled from Adam until Moses, even over those who had not sinned.'[37] This was the attitude the missionaries upheld. In the famous near-baptism of Rathbod a touch of Pelagianism would have saved that "Scourge of Christians" and made the conversion of Frisia much easier, but when Rathbod, with one foot in the water, turned to ask Bishop Wulfram whether he would meet his ancestors in heaven, Wulfram said they were in hell, Rathbod withdrew his foot, and the great chance was lost.[38] Boniface was as orthodox as Wulfram and Bede, and when it came to his attention that a Celtic bishop named Clement was teaching that Christ brought all from hell, "believers and unbelievers, those who praised God and the worshippers of idols," he lost no time in bringing the matter to the attention of Rome, where the "folly" was roundly condemned in 745.[39] The fact that Boniface and Bede paid so much attention to this heresy may indicate that Pelagianism was more widespread than is usually thought. The lives of the early missionaries, who were trained in Ireland, show that relations between the English and Celtic churches were quite close despite their differences, and the works of Pelagius himself were circulating in England (some even under the name of Augustine).[40]

However, we need not hunt for heresy to explain the poet's presentation of his heroes as both virtuous and pagan, for despite the Pelagian dispute (which turns really on the functions of nature and grace) even the most orthodox eighth-century churchmen could regard the pagans as quite virtuous, following the natural law and lacking only the knowledge of God necessary for salvation. The *Translatio Sancti Alexandri* puts this most clearly in its account of the Saxons: *Legibus etiam ad vindictam malefactorum optimis utebantur. Et multa utilia atque secundum legem naturae honesta in morum probitate habere studuerunt, quae eis ad veram beatitudinem promerendum proficere potuissent, si ignorantiam creatoris sui non haberent, et a veritate culturae illius non essent alieni* 'indeed, they made use of excellent laws for the punishment of wrongdoers. And they were diligent to maintain in their conduct a very useful and, according to the law of nature, decent probity, which would have helped them to a truly deserved blessedness, if they had not been ignorant of their Creator and were not alien to true religion.'[41] The praise for Germanic institutions in this work is drawn from Tacitus, and among early Latin writers—Horace, Tacitus, Martianus Capella—there was a slender tradition of idealizing the Germanic pagans for their good morals and institutions.[42] As early as the fifth century one finds Christian writers employing this idealized view. Salvianus writes of the Goths and Vandals who were attacking the Empire: _tantum apud illos profecit studium castimonia, tantum seueritas disciplinae non solum quod ipsi casti sunt, sed, ut rem dicamus nouem, rem incredibilem, rem paene etiam inauditam, castos etiam Romanos esse fecerunt_ 'so much did the zeal for chastity prevail among them, so great was the severity of their discipline, that not only were they chaste themselves, but—to say a new thing, a thing incredible, a thing almost unheard of—they made even the Romans chaste.'[43] This view was strong enough to survive even among those who fought against the Germanic pagans, as we see in Einhard's _Vita Karoli Imperatoris: Saxones, sicut omnes fere Germaniam incolentes nationes, et natura feroces, et cultui daemonum dediti, nostraeque religioni contrarii, neque diuina neque humana iura vel polluere vel transgredi inhonestum arbitrabantur_ 'the Saxons, though, like almost all the nations inhabiting Germany, by nature fierce and given to the worship of demons and opposed to our religion, are yet said neither to violate nor indecently to transgress divine and human laws.'[44]

In addition to the weight of this minor tradition of the "honest Germanic pagan," some of the missionaries must have been led to accept the idea that virtue can exist among the pagans simply from meeting an occasional good heathen, like this Frisian nobleman of the early eighth century: _qui quamvis fidem sanctae Trinitatis nondum sciret, erat tamen adiutor pauperum, defensor oppressorum, in iuditio quoque iustus_ 'though he did not yet know the faith of the Holy Trinity, he was nevertheless a helper of paupers, a defender of the oppressed, and also just in pronouncing judgments.'[45] Such decent men, of the sort that exist in all societies, often performed acts of kindness to the missionaries, even when they refused the chance to be converted, and they must frequently have impressed the English priests with their natural goodness.[46] They thus exemplified the most important source of the idea that pagans observe the natural law, the statements in the Bible itself, which taught that the Gentiles "show the work of the law written in their hearts, their conscience also bearing witness, and their thoughts the mean while accusing or else excusing one another" (Rom. 2:15).

Boniface drew on all three sources—the literary tradition represented by Tacitus, his own knowledge, and the Bible—in what must have been the most famous use of natural law in the eighth century, his letter to King Ethelbald of Mercia. Ethelbald's loose sexual conduct had become an international scandal, and it was a matter of concern to English churchmen (and probably laymen) on both sides of the Channel. Finally (around 745–46), Boniface wrote directly to the king, rebuking him for his sin: *Quod non solum a christianis, sed etiam a paganis in opprobrium et verecundiam deputatur. Quia ipsi pagani verum Deum ignorantes naturaliter quae legis sunt et quod ab initio Deus custodiunt in hac re. . . . Cum ergo gentiles, qui Deum nesciunt et legem non habent iuxta dictum apostoli, naturaliter ea quae legis sunt faciunt et ostendunt opus legis in cordibus suis. . . .* 'which not only by Christians but even by pagans is held in shame and contempt. For these pagans, ignorant of the true God, by nature maintain in this matter those things which are lawful and what God established in the beginning. . . . When thus the gentiles, who do not know God and have no law according to the word of the apostle, do by nature what is lawful and show the work of the law written in their hearts. . . .'[47] Since Boniface himself, the persecutor of the heretical Clement, held this opinion, we need have no lingering doubts about the theological respectability of admiring the virtues of the pagans. Even Bede, despite his doctrinal rigidity, found some admirable pagans in the course of his history, and he held that at least one unbaptized pagan had been saved.[48] Certainly the author of *Beowulf,* even if he was a cleric addressing a clerical audience, would have encountered no difficulty in presenting his characters as both virtuous and pagan.

III

IN THE LIGHT of what we now know of attitudes toward the pagans in the late seventh and eighth centuries, it appears that the paganism of the poet's characters may have been a positive advantage to him rather than the insuperable difficulty that it seemed to early critics. Those critics assumed that *Beowulf* was originally and essentially pagan, and what pagan elements the poem contains were therefore most easily explained as mere undigested lumps of primitive matter. We are still accustomed to think of the pagan elements as part of the original essence of the poem, the Christian elements as additions—beautifully integrated, but additions nevertheless. Yet our reading of the poem does not accord with our theory. Christianity is part of the very fabric of *Beowulf,* the pagan elements are not. When we examine those elements that are actually pagan rather than secular, references to practices that ceased altogether or became criminal with the introduction of Christianity—augury, cremation, the worship of idols—we find that they are few in number and easily isolable. Their removal would harm but not destroy the poem (which may explain why good critics have wanted to take some of them out), for one cannot imagine *Beowulf* in anything like its present state without its Christian basis, but one can easily conceive of it without its few touches of paganism. Without them, it would simply be a more ordinary medieval poem, a narrative in which the past is seen through the eyes of the present, as Chaucer viewed Troy in *Troilus* or Shakespeare ancient Denmark in *Hamlet*. The tales that the poet used must have come to him in that more ordinary state, originally created in pagan times but insensibly altered to fit the requirements of new audiences by each succeeding generation of oral poets.[49] Probably it was the *Beowulf* poet who deepened the Christian meanings when he reshaped the inherited material; but probably it was also he who added the "pagan coloring," drawing on contemporary information about the Germanic pagans and on the prevalent attitude toward them to add both interest and a new dimension of meaning to his materials.

The most obvious advantage that the poet gained by his use of pagan materials is that of "local color." He was able to capitalize on the general interest in pagandom that the missions had aroused, and by providing vivid, even sensational, accounts of rites such as cremation of which his audience had only heard, he was able to engage their attention for his more important purposes. For those more sober members of his audience who, like the later Alcuin, could see no good in stories of pagan kings, the very reminders that the kings in *Beowulf* are pagan serve to build interest and sympathy, for the poem functions as a kind of proof of the missionaries' reports that the heathens are indeed virtuous, while the pagan elements have something of the same function as Boniface's letter to the English nation, emphasizing the perilous condition of these good heroes and thus appealing for a compassionate, serious consideration of their state. Perhaps that is why the "Christian excursus" comes so early in the poem, providing the framework within which the good Christian can ponder the deeds of the good pagans.

There must have been a good many more in the poet's audience who, like the monks at Lindisfarne, simply enjoyed a good secular tale, and for them most of all the touches of paganism are means of building interest and sympathy in the dual purpose of this poem. *Beowulf* is now recognized as a skillful blend of secular and religious values; it is simultaneously a celebration of the ideal Germanic warrior and a statement of Christian morality.[50] These values were not necessarily opposed, as poems like *The Dream of the Rood* show, but they were nevertheless quite different. Aldhelm apparently recognized this, for we are told that he would stand at crossroads, singing the old songs until he had gathered crowds for his more edifying discourses.[51] The *Beowulf* poet seems to employ his secular materials in the same way, using his tales of monster killing as an occasion for a meditation on life and on the meaning of victory and defeat. For those who were drawn to listen primarily to hear again the deeds of heroes, the insistence on the paganism of those heroes provided the larger context of that present day, helping to reinforce the point of Hrothgar's sermon that strength alone is not enough and to state the further requirement that even that "intelligent monotheist" cannot meet, that to strength and natural piety must be added the New Law of Christ. In this way the touches of paganism in *Beowulf* place the fictional ironies and tragedy of the poem within the dimension of the real irony and tragedy of Germanic history as it was viewed by an eighth-century audience newly aware of the sad condition of their Continental kinsmen to whom the gospel had not yet been preached. Thus the poet builds a link between the doomed heroes of his poem and the sad but admirable pagans of his own time, whose way of life seemed likewise fated to disappear before the apparently certain victory of the Church.

The final irony of *Beowulf* is that which Wyrd visited on the poet himself, when the pagans he celebrated swept down to destroy their Christian kinsmen in England. After the burning of Lindisfarne in 793, it would be another two centuries before English missionaries would again set out for the Continent and the attitude toward pagandom expressed in *Beowulf* would again be appropriate. We can only speculate, but it may be that we owe the survival of the poem to its touches of paganism, for the only manuscript in which it survives was written at that other moment in English history, around the year 1000, when English churchmen were again concerned with the fate of their heathen kinsmen in northern Europe.[52]

NOTES

1. William Whallon, "The Christianity of *Beowulf*," *Modern Philology* 60 (1962): 81–94, argues that the poet is a very naive Christian who knows little except for the tales of the Old Testament, but this is as close as critics today come to assuming a pagan author. For a full discussion see E.G. Stanley, "The Search for Anglo-Saxon Paganism," *Notes and Queries* N.S. 11 (1964): 205–09, 242–50, 282–87, 324–33, 455–63, and 12 (1965): 9–17, 203–07, 285–93, 322–27, especially 11:326–31.

2. On Wyrd see, for example, Alan H. Roper, "Boethius and the Three Fates of *Beowulf*," *Philological Quarterly* 41 (1962): 386–400; on revenge see Dorothy Whitelock, *The Audience of "Beowulf"* (Oxford, 1951), 13–17; the comitatus is, of course, found throughout Old English religious poetry (e.g., *Andreas*).

3. *Beowulf and the Fight at Finnsburg*, ed. Friedrich Klaeber, 3rd ed. (Boston, 1950), cxxi: "in recounting the life and portraying the character of the exemplary leader . . . he [the poet] was almost inevitably reminded of the person of the Savior."

4. *The Heroic Age* (Cambridge, 1912), 53.

5. *Ibid.,* 52–53; I have included Scyld's funeral ship, although it seems to represent the departure of a legendary hero, as Klaeber suggests, rather than a real

burial like that of Baldr.

6. Marie P. Hamilton, "The Religious Principle in *Beowulf,*" *PMLA* 61 (1946): 309–31; reprinted in *An Anthology of "Beowulf" Criticism,* ed. L.E. Nicholson (Notre Dame, 1963), 125; in *The Knight's Tale* Chaucer shows his essentially Christian characters worshipping in pagan shrines.

7. Alcuin, *Albini Epistolae,* ed. E.L. Dummler, Monumenta Germaniae Historica, Epistolae no. 4 (Berlin, 1895), letter 124, p. 183.

8. For example, J.R.R. Tolkien, "*Beowulf:* The Monster and the Critics," *Proceedings of the British Academy* 22 (1937): 245–95; reprinted in Nicholson, *Anthology,* 101–02. In his edition of *Beowulf,* note to ll. 175–88, Klaeber holds that the poet "failed to live up to his own modernized representation of [the Danes]."

9. Chadwick, *The Heroic Age,* 73; his work is still the most recent full discussion of the problem, and it has been accepted without question.

10. Eddius Stephanus, *Vita Wilfridi Episcopi,* chap. 27, in *The Historians of the Church of York and its Archbishops,* ed. James Raine, Rerum Britannicarum Medii Aevi Scriptores no. 71 (London, 1879–94), 1:38. For a full account of the missions in Frisia see Wilhelm Levison, *England and the Continent in the Eighth Century* (Oxford, 1946), 45–69. Translations of some of the relevant materials are provided in *The Anglo-Saxon Missionaries in Germany,* ed. and trans. C.H. Talbot (New York, 1954).

11. *Historia Ecclesiastica Gentis Anglorum* 5.9, in *Baedae Opera Historica,* trans. J.E. King (New York, 1930), 2:234; the translations of Bede in this essay, however, are mine.

12. *Ibid.* 5.9, 2:238–40.

13. *Ibid.* 5.10 11, 2:240–52; Alcuin, *Vita Willibrordi,* in *Passiones Vitaeque Sanctorum Aevi Merovingici,* ed. B. Krusch and W. Levison, Monumenta Germaniae Historica, Scriptores Rerum Merovingicarum no. 7 (Hanover, 1919), 81–141.

14. Bede, *Historia* 5.10, 2:244.

15. Talbot, *Anglo-Saxon Missionaries,* 9, notes that this king has been identified with Ongentheow in *Beowulf,* but I can find no basis for the identification.

16. Levison, *England and the Continent,* 70–93. Willibald, *Vita S. Bonifacii,* in *Monumenta Germaniae Historica, Scriptores,* ed. G.H. Pertz, vol. 2 (Hanover, 1829), 331–53.

17. Willibald, *Vita S. Bonifacii,* chap. 6, pp. 340–42, trans. Talbot, *Anglo-Saxon Missionaries,* 47.

18. Levison, *England and the Continent,* 61.

19. Hermann Lau, *Die angelsächsische Missionweise im Zeitalter des Bonifaz* (Kiel, 1909), 39.

20. Levison, *England and the Continent,* 92.

21. *Die Briefe des heiligen Bonifatius und Lullius,* ed. Michael Tangl, Monumenta Germaniae Historica, Epistolae Selectae no. 1 (Berlin, 1916), letter 105, pp. 229–31; trans. Ephraim Emerton in *The Letters of St. Boniface,* Records of Civilization, Sources and Studies no. 31 (New York, 1940), 177–79.

22. See Klaeber, *Beowulf,* cxvi n. 1, for a summary of early scholars' views on this question.

23. Antoine Thomas, "Un manuscrit inutilisé du *Liber Monstrorum,*" *Bulletin du Cange: Archivum Latinitatis Medii Aevi* 1 (1925): 232–45; Whitelock, *Audience,* 50; Kenneth Sisam, *Studies in the History of Old English Literature* (Oxford, 1953),

288–90.

24. Matts Dreijer, *Häuptlinge, Kaufleute, und Missionare im Norden vor Tausend Jahren,* Skrifter Utgivna av Ålands Kulturstiftelse no. 2 (Mariehamm, 1960), 71–80.

25. Cf. Bernlaf who joined St. Liudger's retinue and was "loved by his neighbors because he was of an open and free nature, and would repeat the actions of the men of old and the contests of kings, singing to his harp," *Vita Liudgeri,* in Pertz, *MGH Scriptores* 2:403; cited and trans. W.P. Ker, *The Dark Ages* (1904; repr., New York, 1958), 57.

26. On Sutton Hoo in relation to the burials in *Beowulf* see the Supplement by C.L. Wrenn, "Recent Work on *Beowulf* to 1958," especially 513, in R.W. Chambers, *"Beowulf": An Introduction,* 3rd ed. (Cambridge, 1959); for the Continental sources quoted in the text see *Capitulatio de Partibus Saxoniae* in *Texte zur germanische Bekehrungsgeschichte,* ed. Wolfgang Lange (Tübingen, 1962), 154–55, nos. 7, 22. This text dates from about 789.

27. They are frequently mentioned in the texts collected in Lange, *Texte;* e.g., *Dicta Pirmini* (written between 718 and 724), 90–91.

28. In the ninth century more extended accounts of the pagans were written, such as the *Translatio Sancti Alexandri,* in Pertz, *MGH Scriptores* 2:673–81, and the *Indiculus Superstitionem et Paganiarum,* in *Monumenta Germaniae Historica, Leges,* ed. G.H. Pertz, vol. 1 (Hanover, 1885), 19–20.

29. Lau, *Missionweise,* 3, quotes an Englishman, Wigbert, writing to Lull (Tangl, *Briefe,* letter 137, pp. 275–76).

30. Tangl, *Briefe,* letter 46, pp. 74–75.

31. The text is from Klaeber, *Beowulf.*

32. For example, Whitelock, *Audience,* 78–79.

33. *Historia* 2.5, 1:228: *Quo utroque* [Eadbald and his wife] *scelere occasionem dedit ad priorem vomitum revertendi* 'by both crimes [Eadbald and his wife] he gave occasion for returning to the previous vomit.' Cf. Caesarius of Arles, *Sermones,* in Lange, *Texte,* 61; Prov. 26:11.

34. "The Religious Principle," in Nicholson, *Anthology,* 125.

35. "Beowulf, Ireland, and the Natural Good," *Traditio* 7 (1949–51): 263–77.

36. *In Cantica Canticorum,* in *The Complete Works of the Venerable Bede,* ed. J.A. Giles (London, 1844), 9:197. The *desuper* is a reminder that even a pagan like Ongendus (see n. 46) or Beowulf can be touched by grace.

37. *Ibid.,* 199.

38. *Annales Xantenses,* in Pertz, *MGH Scriptores* 2:221.

39. Tangl, *Briefe,* letter 59, pp. 108–20.

40. Sister M. Thomas Aquinas Carroll, *The Venerable Bede: His Spiritual Teachings,* Catholic University of America Studies in Medieval History N.S. no. 9 (Washington, D.C., 1946), 95. For a further discussion of this doctrine in relation to *Beowulf* see the suggestive article by Morton Bloomfield, "Patristics and Old English Literature: Notes on Some Poems," *Comparative Literature* 14 (1962): 36–43; reprinted in *Studies in Old English Literature in Honor of Arthur G. Brodeur,* ed. Stanley B. Greenfield (Eugene, Ore., 1963), 36–43, and in Nicholson, *Anthology,* 367–72. In writing the present article, I have had the benefit of Bloomfield's suggestions and criticisms.

41. Pertz, *MGH Scriptores* 2:675.

42. Horace, *Odes* 3.24 (referring to *Getae*); Tacitus, *Germania*; Martianus Capella, *De Nuptis Philologiae et Mercurii*, ed. F. Eyssenhardt (Leipzig, 1866), 227–28, 240. Adam of Bremen takes the references in Horace and Martianus to refer to the Danes and the Geats: see *History of the Archbishops of Hamburg-Bremen*, trans. F.J. Tschan, Records of Civilization: Sources and Studies no. 53 (New York, 1959), 195, 199, 204.

43. *De gubernatione Dei*, in Lange, *Texte*, 16. Bede takes a somewhat similar view when he (following Gildas) speaks of the Saxon invaders as agents of God's just vengeance for the crimes of the Celtic Christians: *Historia* 1.14 15, 1:64–74.

44. Pertz, *MGH Scriptores* 2:446; the same passage appears in the *Translatio Sancti Alexandri* in the same volume, 675.

45. *Vita S. Liudgeri*, in Pertz, *MGH Scriptores* 2:405.

46. See, for example, the alderman who avenged the two Hewalds (see n. 14), the Danish king Ongendus who, though a pagan, "nevertheless, through divine intervention, received the herald of truth with every mark of honour" (Talbot, *Anglo-Saxon Missionaries*, 9), the pagans who spare the lives of St. Lebuini (Pertz, *MGH Scriptores* 2:363) and of St. Willehad (Pertz, *MGH Scriptores* 2:381), those pagans *naturaliter prudentia* 'naturally wise' reported in the *Historia Translationem Sanctae Puissinae* (Pertz, *MGH Scriptores* 2:681), and the pagan Frisians who honorably received Wilfred: *Cujus loci incolae, nondum imbuti fide Christi, solo humanitatis affectu eos obvii benigne suscepere, et relevantes lassitudinem ipsorum quaeque necessitas exigebat gratis obtulere* 'the inhabitants of this place, not yet filled with the faith of Christ, moved by human kindness alone, received them kindly along the way and, relieving their weariness, brought them freely whatever necessity required,' *Breviloquium Vitae S. Wilfridi*, in Raine, *Historians* 1:231 (cf. *Vita Wilfridi*, chap. 26–27, pp. 37–58 in the same volume).

47. Tangl, *Briefe*, letter 73, pp. 146–55. In parts of the letter not quoted Boniface draws on Tacitus for his account of the pagans' attitude toward adultery, and he draws on his own experience by extending that account to cover also the Wends; in the passage quoted Boniface cites the Bible.

48. *Historia* 1.7: a pagan who refuses to execute St. Alban is himself executed, *de quo nimirum constat, quia etsi fonte baptismatis non est ablutus sui tamen est sanguinis lavacro mundatus* 'of whom it is clearly apparent that though he was not bathed in the baptismal font yet he was cleansed by the washing of his own blood' (1:43). Likewise, Edwin before his baptism is described as a man of 'extraordinary sagacity' (2:9).

49. Cf. Albert B. Lord, *The Singer of Tales* (Cambridge, Mass., 1960), 100: "I believe that once we know the facts of oral composition we must cease trying to find an original of any traditional song. From one point of view each performance is an original."

50. Arthur G. Brodeur, *The Art of "Beowulf"* (Berkeley, 1959), demonstrates that Beowulf and Hrothgar are "exemplars of an ideal and a course of conduct in harmony with both the best traditions of antiquity and the highest ideal of Christian Englishmen" (185).

51. However, William of Malmesbury is our only authority for the story.

52. Cf. Adam of Bremen, *History of the Archbishops*, 80–93; Dreijer, *Häuptlinge*, 199–207.

Beowulf and the Margins of Literacy[1]

by ERIC JOHN

This essay first appeared in the Bulletin of the John Rylands University Library of Manchester, *56 (1973–74): 388–422.*

A S a historian I take up the theme of *Beowulf* and its world with hesitation. The study of the poem must lie mainly with the literary scholars, because they alone have the time and expertise to master the complex problems it raises and the vast international literature devoted to it. It is noticeable, however, that in spite of generations of energy and ingenuity in pursuit of the real *Beowulf*, he and it are not in sight: not, that is, the subject of a scholarly consensus. There is no agreement as to the date of the poem; there is even less agreement as to its author's intentions, let alone his identity or the places in which he might be found. In the last few years two scholars have written two different books on *Beowulf,* each of obvious distinction: Dr. Sisam and Dr. Goldsmith.[2] So different, so absolutely contradictory, are their conclusions, it is difficult to believe they are writing about the same poem. Something must be seriously amiss when generations of scholarship can give us no basic facts that are undisputed outside the particular tradition or connection which discovered, I had almost said invented, them.

It seems to me that historians are after all the one relevant group of scholars who have had little to say about *Beowulf.* Of all the *Beowulf* scholars only one of the great names was equally famous as historian, Hector Munro Chadwick. A good many of his points seem to me not to have been taken by his fellow-students of literature simply because they were not altogether understood. Chadwick wrote out of a very informed and refined sense of the social context of Anglo-Saxon literature. He knew, I think, that some things that seem plausible if the text is studied in isolation must nonetheless be rejected because there was no place for them in *that* world.[3] Now the study of Chadwick has, I believe, revived somewhat amongst historians in recent years, to their considerable profit. Anglo-Saxon historians have at last learnt from him that they must not ignore the literature, even the imaginative literature, if they would understand the world. The trouble has been that the world of *Beowulf* was a single world: but its art is studied by the men of manuscripts if it is two-dimensional, by archaeologists if it is three; its literature is the province of philology, its laws, government, and institutions, of history. But whatever the date of *Beowulf,* its audience knew the *fyrd,* the *here,* the *sceattas,* the wergelds, the bots, the wites, as part of the stuff of everyday experience. The result has been that what must be taken as a whole in order to be intelligible is cut into lumps which are minutely investigated in isolation. What is needed is some recognition that we must move out of the traditional centres of our disciplines to what seem to be the margins: if we do this we shall find, as I think Chadwick found before us, that these margins overlap, and that together we shall be much better placed to distinguish sense from nonsense than we have so far been able to do separately.

Let us begin with the date of the poem. By and large Anglo-American scholarship has come to an agreement that it is not earlier than about 700 and not much later than about 800. The agreement is impressive though it conceals two differing schools who would choose, the one Bede's Northumbria, and the other Offa's Mercia. The choice of names for the epochs is not without significance. But on what is it based? Not, so far as I can see, on hard philological facts, since the manuscript tradition belongs to the tenth century and a different cultural milieu.[4] In fact, when literary scholars discuss these matters they appeal very largely to social and historical criteria and these do not seem to bear quite all the weight sometimes assumed. Recently the late Professor Robert Reynolds has revived in the English-speaking world the hypothesis, never abandoned in the German-speaking world, that *Beowulf* is post-Viking. He has drawn attention to a charter of Æthelstan (CS 677)[5] which has often been noted as containing a reference to a place-name *Grendlesmere.* Professor Reynolds had pointed out that there are a number of other echoes of the poem in the charter. In particular, the ambience of the prologue is much in tune with the proem to the charter. He concluded that the proem might have been a recent one, dating from the time of Æthelstan himself and perhaps made at his court, which it is known was the resort of recently pagan-Danish ealdormen as well as traditionally Christian ones. Its propaganda value is obvious. Since we have Æthelstan's grandfather's testimony as to the state into which religion, especially literary religion, had fallen during the wars, and very little to disprove him, the usual arguments about the relative degrees of pagan and Christian influences in *Beowulf* do not exclude Professor Reynolds's suggested dating.

It is worth citing here Professor Wrenn's point[6] about linguistic features which suggest that a text of *Beowulf* "was revised in the time of King Ælfred who did so much to preserve the older poetry." It would

obviously not be easy to separate with any certainty revisions made in
Ælfred's reign from those made in the reign of his grandson. The poet's
interest in matters of lineage, so obvious from the opening of the poem,
is relevant too. Dr. Sisam has shown us that written genealogies are not
primitive or Germanic but seem to belong to the time of the Mercian
hegemony and to be the product of its propaganda or its vanity. Interest
was beginning in the time of Bede who knew, apparently, only the East
Anglian lineage which he quotes. It is difficult to believe he would not
have quoted the Northumbrian if he had known it, and it is difficult to
believe he would not have known it if it had then existed. The Northumbrian genealogy, like the West Saxon one, is a palpable forgery[7] and
there is obvious common matter to both. Dr. Sisam argued that the
West-Saxon list was modelled on the Northumbrian: as, on his showing, the Northumbrian had even more mythical names in it than the
West-Saxon, would it not be more plausible to think that the more
florid Northumbrian version is an inflated version of its southern counterpart? We cannot deny that Anglo-Saxon genealogies were extant in
the age of Bede but the West-Saxon genealogy was hardly one of them.
But there are some interesting names in the West-Saxon Pedigree. Geat,
the eponymous ancestor of Beowulf's *folc,* is there: there is a Scyld and a
Heremod, as well as a number of names beginning with H, as is
customary amongst Beowulf's royals, but not amongst real English
royals for the most part. It is possible that Professor Whitelock is right,[8]
that the characters and incidents from the poem were common knowledge, but I doubt it. It is odd that the fabricator of a genealogy should
include Heremod, even on the brief reference to him in *Beowulf,* and
fantastic if fuller and even more villainous tales were also circulating. I
cannot help but feel that Professor Reynolds is right and something
important was happening to the poem in the early tenth century, but,
with hesitation, I cannot agree that it was written then.

The preamble to the charter in question (CS 677) has so much in
common with Aldhelm's latinity that his editor included a closely
related text in his edition of the collected works.[9] I take it that this
charter lies behind Dr. Whitelock's hint; it is no more than that, that
Aldhelm was a possible *Beowulf* poet.[10] Professor Ware has, however,
cast some doubt on the identification of the latinity of CS 677 with
Aldhelm's hysperic (or would "hysperical" be more appropriate?) style.[11]
He has pointed out that it contains indubitably later features. I do not
think it quite so obvious as he that the style is the product of Æthelstan's
day.[12] But it is unquestionable—and Dr. Ware does not question it—
that the latinity of the charter and that of Aldhelm have much in
common. This "new" latinity was a revived latinity; could not a renewed

interest in *Beowulf* be the product of the same revival? The interest of
CS 677 lies in its *Beowulf* names, personal and place-names. But is it
likely that if the poem were new at that time, grown-men or ancient
stretches of water would have been named from it? The archaeological
evidence certainly suggests a much earlier date, nearer the traditional
one.[13] Professor Girvan's well-known study *"Beowulf" and the Seventh
Century* still seems to me to make a powerful case for an early provenance, though it cannot be a conclusive one. The relationship between
authority, birth and property implied in *Beowulf* is also worth considering. In Ælfred's day to judge by "his" comments on St. Augustine's
Soliloquies,[14] bookland, a perpetual inheritance, was the normal goal,
and a goal generally achieved, of the ordinary warrior: this is not true of
Beowulf's world. Of the highest birth and close to the royal office itself,
he only obtains his inheritance after proving himself on some scale.
There are a number of other references, which will be discussed below,
which point to a very different relationship between the rank of companion and the right to heritable property. It seems to me that the type
of landholding described in *Beowulf* is much nearer to that occasionally
called *folcland*.[15] This was certainly in decay by the time of Offa. On the
other hand, there is much to relate *Beowulf* to the time of what German
scholars have called the *Heerkönigtum*.[16] Likewise, there is some resemblance between Beowulf's career and his values and those of the un-
converted Guthlac.[17] I do not think the English Scyld Scefings or even
Guthlacs survived very long into the Mercian hegemony, and I should
place their decline on the Continent in much the same period, except of
course in the peripheral areas of Carolingian power. It seems to me,
therefore, that Professor Reynolds is wrong in reviving the Schücking
hypothesis as to the post-Viking date and provenance of the poem, but
very likely right in suggesting that it had a conscious value as propaganda for the conversion of recent Vikings into new Englishmen. I
should suppose a revival of interest in the early tenth century, to which it
is even possible we owe the survival of the poem.

I have laboured the point because the date of the poem is crucial to
identifying the social context to which it belongs. Only those, and they
still exist, who see the Anglo-Saxon period as a static, comfortable world
of sturdy freemen from the invasions to the Conquest will fail to take the
importance of this question. Central to this, and to every other point in
Beowulf exegesis, is the question of the nature of the poet's relationship
to the Christian religion. I have so far avoided using any arguments from
the nature of the poem's religious values, and yet these have been the
principal arguments for most scholars who have tackled the problems of
Beowulf's date and provenance. This is because this question is the most

fundamental of all and because it is also one peculiarly difficult to get right. It is nearly half a century since Klaeber in his great edition put into currency the notion that Beowulf was a type of Christ, and a generation since Professor Tolkien's famous lecture[18] gave licence to an unbridled speculation unusual in medieval studies. Plainly in some sense *Beowulf* is a Christian poem, but the problem is in what sense?

Chadwick pointed out:[19]

> In *Beowulf* . . . there are about seventy . . . passages [of a religious (Christian) character] of which the significance is not open to question, and seven or eight others which may belong to the same category. Out of the total number thirty-three are limited to single verses or half-verses, while another sixteen affect not more than two verses in each case. The longest passage of all contains at least thirty-seven verses, the next longest fourteen. The rest vary from three to nine verses.

Too many, in other words, to be dismissed as merely superficial colouring, but only two extended passages nonetheless. He goes on:

> The theology which appears in these passages is of a singularly vague type. There are four distinct references to incidents in the early part of Genesis, viz. one to the Creation, two to the story of Cain and Abel and one to the Flood. Apart from these there appears to be no reference to any passage in the Bible except perhaps in v. 1745 ff., which are thought by some to be based on *Ephes.* vi. 16, and in v. 3069, which contains the phrase "day of judgement." We find also few references to rewards and punishments in a future life. The word *god* is of very frequent occurrence and always used in a Christian sense. . . . On the other hand there is no example of the word *gast* in a religious sense (Holy Ghost), nor of the name *Crist,* nor of any epithet denoting "Saviour" (*nergend, hælend,* etc.). Hardly less curious is the total absence of the word *engel,* for expressions such as "lord of angels" (*engla dryhten*) are among the more frequent epithets of the Deity in Anglo-Saxon religious poems. Lastly, there are no references to the saints, to the cross or to the Church, nor to any Christian rites and ceremonies.
>
> It appears then that the religious utterances of the poem are of a singularly one-sided character. Indeed, it has been observed that, with the exception perhaps of vv. 977–9, "their theology is covered by the OT. and a pious Jew would have no difficulty in assenting to them all." Certainly the facts are such as to call for some explanation, especially since the religious poems are pervaded by a wholly different tone.

In recent years, dating from Professor Tolkien's influential lecture "*Beowulf:* the Monsters and the Critics," a variety of answers has been proposed to the puzzles so succinctly set out by Chadwick, ranging from the pioneer essay of Professor Marie Hamilton, *The Religious Principle in "Beowulf,"* published in 1946, to Mrs. Goldsmith's *The Mode and Meaning of "Beowulf,"* published in 1970. There are many versions of this new learning and much is to be said in its favour. The centrality of the monsters to the discussion of *Beowulf* is not likely to be challenged again, for instance, but to the sceptical student what these versions have in common is more important than what divides them. The key assumption is made in the opening passage of Professor Hamilton's essay. "Reflective Englishmen of the seventh and eighth centuries, living under the transforming influence of classical and Christian ideas, must have satisfied a special need by revaluating their Germanic patrimony in terms of the new culture."[20] "Must have" seems unfortunate here; the question is "did they," and it will not do to beg it so early in the day. We may note in passing Professor Hamilton's wholly anachronistic use of the term Englishman for her period. I have elsewhere sought to show the confusions that flow from an over-hasty attribution of Englishry to the seventh and eighth centuries.[21] The argument continues. *Beowulf* is a pretended pagan poem, using pagan themes and a pagan *genre* with a single reference to Christ overtly, but full of covert Christian analogies drawn mainly from the fathers. The poem, read in this way, requires a very sophisticated technique of allegorizing and it demands a highly learned and specialized response in its audience. Most recently, Dr. Goldsmith has made what seems to me one of the best and most ingenious defences of this point of view. Writing after the devastating criticism of Dr. Sisam,[22] she shows great learning in marshalling a set of patristic allusions to authors who were certainly or probably known to Bede. Like most writers of this school, she assumes that eighth-century England was full of men as learned as Bede.[23] She does not ask why the pagan colouring should be, not of interest but even tolerable, to this kind of audience. To most of them the rituals described in *Beowulf* would be "devils' rites." It seems to me important to prove that some men, preferably quite a lot of men, could combine a sympathetic interest in pagan customs and feelings with a literary culture that was intended to inculcate exactly the opposite response. If on the other hand we want to argue, as some do, that the pagan atmosphere was a piece of clever missionary strategy designed to lead the newly converted from pagan to Christian things, how could we possibly impute so profound a knowledge of the Fathers to this audience that they could catch such indirect allusions at a hearing? Alcuin's famous attack on the story of Ingeld is often quoted by *Beowulf* scholars, who then proceed to ignore its implications. Alcuin would certainly not have accepted *Beowulf* as a Christian poem. What establishment theologian of the period would?

Appeal is made to Gregory the Great. It is true that Gregory makes heavy and sustained use of allegory in his spiritual writings. They do not read to me much like *Beowulf* and they are unmistakably Biblical and patristic in source and, one would have thought, obviously allegorical and analogical in development. Dr. Sisam has pointed out: "the text [of *Beowulf*] supplies no references or citations"[24] that could show the author was widely read in patristic writings; no one could make the same claim about Gregory. There is also the problem of the audience. The audience of Gregory, which no one will dispute was wider and longer lasting than that of *Beowulf,* was offered allegories so obvious that one would have said they could not be missed. But they were missed by the most learned men of the age and Gregory remarkably misunderstood.

A few years ago Dom Henry Wansbrough, in a paper that deserves more attention than it has so far received,[25] dealt with the passages in Gregory's *Dialogues* that treat of the life of St. Benedict. He pointed out what has remained hidden for nearly fifteen hundred years, that the "biography" is not and was never intended to be taken literally, but is a highly allegorized picture of the life of the ideal monk, based loosely on a real monk and real vocation. Most of the characters are not given real names but are virtues and vices like the characters in *Pilgrim's Progress.* Scholastica, for instance, is a type of contemplation. If the most *evolué* audience of the seventh and eighth centuries misunderstood Gregory so completely, where is the audience that could unravel *Beowulf* if the poem really is a sophisticated and extended allegory?

If the poem were such an allegory, it must surely have a Christ figure, and that figure could only be Beowulf himself. A number of scholars from Klaeber onwards have made this identification. It does not seem to me that this can be done without, in effect, rewriting the poem. Professor Leyerle[26] has argued, to my mind convincingly, that the poem means us to suppose that Beowulf's conduct in fighting the dragon was little short of hubris. But even if this be not accepted what are we to make of Beowulf's last speeches? There is no reference to fear of Hell or hope of Heaven. I suppose it might be argued that a Christ figure would have no need of any, but what does he suppose his death has done for others? He wishes to gaze on the treasure he has won "so that by reason of the wealth of treasure I may leave life more calmly and the people I have ruled so long." If it is sought to evade the inadequacy of this by some theological interpretation of the treasure, then how to explain Wiglaf's conduct and his very different interpretation of the fate of Beowulf's people? The hero gives us a catalogue of his achievements. No other king made him afraid: he did not pick treacherous quarrels: he swore no unjust oaths: he never murdered his kinsfolk. His dying prayer is one of thanks for being able to win the treasure for his people before the day of his death. It seems to me we are rather a long way from "My God why hast thou forsaken me?" It is noticeable that Dr. Goldsmith has seen the force of this and very rightly does not identify Beowulf with Christ. But, as Professor Tolkien has shown so clearly, one of the certain things about the poem is that its central theme has something to do with Beowulf fighting monsters. If Beowulf is not Christ, and even if Dr. Goldsmith's alternatives, which she hints at but does not press (St. Martin or St. Anthony), were acceptable—they are not—it still seems to me the impossibility of finding a Christ figure in the poem, that does not distort either the text or the basic *données* of theology, ruins the allegorical approach.

From a wider point of view the allegorical approach makes a basic mistake about context. Most followers of this school see *Beowulf* as more or less part of the world of medieval chivalry. In Dr. Goldsmith's bibliography, for instance, Miss Tuve's *Allegorical Symbolism* is listed, but nothing of Chadwick. At one point in his lively and dangerous translation of the poem, the late Professor Garmonsway speaks of "the chivalry of the Danes." Basic to this line of approach are some remarks of Professor Tolkien:

> The men of these legends were conceived as knights of chivalrous courts, and members of societies of noble knights, real Round Tables. If there be any danger of calling up inappropriate pictures of the Arthurian world, it is a lesser one than the danger of too many warriors and chiefs begetting the far more inept picture of Zulus or Red Indians. The imagination of the author of *Beowulf* moved upon the threshold of Christian chivalry, if indeed it had not already passed within.[27]

It is perhaps worth pointing out that Round Tables are fiction by definition: that probably centuries after *Beowulf* was written even the kings of England were not knights in any sense, and neither *miles* nor *cniht* denoted a person of any importance or status: that the biography of that *nonpareil* of English fighting men, William the Marshal, written when the world of Christian chivalry was indeed upon us, hardly suggests that it had influenced the English court of the late twelfth century very far. With the licence of such high authority, it is not surprising that Dr. Goldsmith should offer Beowulf as a model member of the *militia Christi*. She wishes to show that Beowulf's war-like profession can readily be interpreted in a Christian sense, and need not be evidence of residual pagan sentiment. She, therefore, takes the obvious step, on the chivalric view of the poem, of citing the early medieval *topos* of the *militia Christi* by way of proof. Had she read Chadwick, old-fashioned as some suppose him, she must have realized that *militia Christi* is wholly unmilitary in its connotation: it meant, of course, monks.[28] I do not find the idea of Beowulf as the model monk very persuasive. It is noticeable that students of *Beowulf* in my experience do not seem to read the late Carl Erdmann's fundamental study of the origins and ideology of the Crusade.[29] Erdmann showed that the notion of the profession of arms as a Christian vocation is intimately connected with reforming circles close to the reform movement of the late tenth and eleventh centuries. In the period in which *Beowulf* was written, on whatever view of the date we take, the warrior was very much in a class with the publicans and sinners.

If we turn from the high Christian theses of the allegorical school to the plainer, and in the last resort more serious, defence of *Beowulf*'s Christianity in Professor Dorothy Whitelock's *The Audience of "Beowulf,"* we are on very different ground. Dr. Whitelock makes no use of analogies from chivalric literature written centuries later. Drawing partly on Professor Girvan's remarkable study,[30] she shows how Christian things were taken for granted in a wealth of casual allusion. The sun is heaven's candle: candle being an ecclesiastical loan word that cannot ante-date the coming of Christianity to the Anglo-Saxons. It is assumed that the audience will detect in the line: "the flood, the pouring ocean, slew the race of giants," an allusion to Genesis 6:4. Nones or *non* is used, not as a reference to a church-service, but as a mere time reference like teatime. It is obvious, then, that *Beowulf* presupposes a society in which Christianity had had time to make its mark, and that in some sense the poet and his audience were Christian. But does it follow that we need make more of this than Chadwick or Blackburn did in their now rejected arguments?

I do not think we need to. Let me take a simple analogy. I may live in a bungalow and sit on my verandah, call for a bowl of mulligatawney, without the faintest notion that these words are all Indian loan words, the product of the former Anglo-Indian connection. Bungalow and verandah have been common English words for more than a generation but I doubt if more than a tiny minority know their origin. What is more, even fewer could tell you why an Indian would fail to recognize the term bungalow as appropriate for what Englishmen normally describe as such. How many people, of whatever standard of education, know, when they are faced with a bottle of tomato ketchup that what they have is a descendant of the Malayan *kechup,* a pickled fish sauce in which, for obvious reasons, tomatoes were never included? In other words, quite a lot of Far Eastern culture has been absorbed by Englishmen without anyone being aware of it. Did the men of Beowulf's world feel more in touch with classical Rome when they talked of candles than modern Englishmen feel with imperial India when they talk of bungalows? It is perfectly possible, of course, that they did, as it is equally possible they did not. What will not do is to assume an answer to the question and build on it as on a foundation of certain knowledge. What *was* obvious, what *was* typical, in that world is precisely what we ought to be seeking.

In most books on *Beowulf* we are told a great deal more about medieval Christianity than we ever are about Anglo-Saxon paganism. But to say that *Beowulf* is a Christian poem is to deny that it is a pagan poem. It seems to me obvious that in this case it is important to know the notion of paganism with which the writer is implicitly comparing his poem.

Now, there are important intellectual obstacles to answering this very difficult question. In modern times Christianity was the religion of a dominant group possessed of overwhelming economic, political, and social strength compared with the recent pagans they were converting. But, when the Germanic peoples were converted, it was the conquerors who adopted the religion of the vanquished; and that must have made a difference. Social anthropologists have shown us that religion is at least as much a matter of rituals and social structures as it is of doctrines and moral rules.[31] But because it seems improbable that Germanic paganism could be compared with early medieval Christianity, either as an intellectual force or, in the Christian sense of the word, a moral force, scholars have largely neglected to make any very close enquiries. The late Max Weber in his classic study of the *Sociology of Religion,* which was so grossly misrepresented by the late R.H. Tawney, has some penetrating remarks on the *ethos* of the warrior *élite:*

> As a rule, the class of warrior nobles, and indeed feudal powers generally, have not readily become the carriers of a rational religious ethics. The life pattern of a warrior has very little affinity with the notion of a beneficent providence, or with the systematic ethical demands of a transcendental god. . . . It is an every-day psychological event for the warrior to face death and the irrationalities of human destiny. Indeed, the chances and adventures of mundane existence fill his life to such an extent that he does not require of his religion (and accepts only reluctantly) anything beyond protection against evil magic or such ceremonial rites as are congruent with his caste, such as priestly prayers for victory or for a blissful death leading directly into the hero's heaven.[32]

This remarkably penetrating, though over-generalized, comment is by and large sustained by Professor Turville-Petre's essay on the *Myth and*

Religion of the Pagan Norse. We have now an attempt at a comparative study of one aspect of pagan Germanic religion and contemporary Christianity. This cannot be ignored by the students of *Beowulf* when the problems of the poem's religious ambience are so central to the discussion. It seems to me that there was something of an overlapping margin between the radically different centres of the two religions. Clearly these centres are as different as religions can be, but the history of Christianity surely shows how different men of different times and social groups have opted for the margins rather than the centre. The late Carl Erdmann, who first, I think, pointed to this overlapping margin and illuminated its importance for the development of the Christian doctrine of the just war, made a case for thinking that the early popularity of St. Michael is to be explained because he was a kind of baptized Woden: Woden's part in Germanic eschatology has a resemblance to that of Michael in Christian. It follows that we must not assume that what seemed central to the Christian religion to the *Beowulf* poet is necessarily what seems so to us: the radical discontinuity between the pagan and Christian *Ideenwelt* of the eighth century, so commonly assumed, needs testing.

Let us take the Old Testament ethos of the poem which no commentator can afford to ignore. It seems to me, in the light of the foregoing, that we assume too readily a rapid dissemination of biblical knowledge and we fail to realize that the Bible of the early Middle Ages may not have been our Bible. I do not mean to point to textual variants or whatever, but to the fact that the Bible is a very large book and even its most devout readers tend to select some things and neglect others. Now this process of selection is primarily socially and historically conditioned; personal predilection is a secondary matter. This is particularly evident when it comes to quotation. Even these days a writer might quote the Gospels and rightly assume his point would be taken. But how often, even in specialist gatherings or journals, is Numbers or Maccabees quoted? Recently Dr. Mary Douglas has pointed out[33] that it is the limitations of our culture, not that of the Old Testament authors, that makes the ritualistic passages boring and unrewarding. Now the educated person's selection of passages that adds up to "our" Bible is not the product of random reading and aesthetic taste. It is part of being English and it was created by many different channels: pamphlets like *Pilgrim's Progress* and oratorios like Handel's *Messiah* have created the English-speaking man's *Bible*. It does not seem to me safe to assume that any intelligent reader left to his own devices would make the same selection, let alone an early medieval man living on the edge of a pagan world, in which Christianity was the loser's religion to a much greater extent than it seems now.

I have already cited the line of *Beowulf* that shows its author expected his audience to be familiar with Genesis 6:4. I wonder, if one read a translation of the poem to an audience of professional theologians, how many would catch the allusion? Giants and monsters and devastating floods were much more part of the thought-world of the Anglo-Saxons than they are of ours. It is not unnatural that the passages of the Bible which struck a response in their own experience, real or imaginative, should have appealed to them in a way they cannot to us. The only passage in the Bible cited twice is that referring to Cain and Abel. The manuscript certainly, and the poet probably, got Cain's name wrong. He is called Cham, by confusion with one of the sons of Noah. Now the story of Cain and Abel is one of those stories that have become an integral part of the English-speaking *ethos*. No man who knew the Bible at all well could make this kind of mistake. I shall be told that the confusion is or was a tradition—as though an error made by a number of persons is any the less an error—which only proves that early knowledge of the Bible was derived more from spoken or written commentaries than from the study of the actual text. The error was, of course, made by Alcuin: this is a world in which a man of Alcuin's learning and stature could make such an elementary mistake.

We are dealing with new Christians learning to read a massive and complex text and having to acquire one alphabet and two languages to do so. We have no grounds for supposing that the means of doing so were numerous: there must have been more schools than the sources reveal, but even allowing generously for their silence there cannot have been many and, what is worse, we cannot assume that necessary continuity of endowment and resources continuing from generation to generation. A man like Bede is an exception (I am sure a very lonely one) but *Beowulf* scholarship too easily takes him as the rule, the norm. Consequently, when the author of *Beowulf* quotes or alludes a good deal to the Old Testament and hardly, if at all, to the New Testament, it is assumed that he must have the same kind of knowledge of the Bible that any right thinking readers, i.e. we ourselves, have. Consequently he is quoting for a purpose and he may be assumed to have had quotations from the New Testament at his finger-tips if only he chose to use them.[34] It seems to me, on the contrary, that he quoted what was for him and his audience their Bible: it is a warrior's Bible not a scholar's. Is it, then, strange that the Old Testament should appeal to warriors more than the New? I cannot think the Virgin's words about the lowly being exalted and the mighty humbled would have found more of an echo in the hearts of *Beowulf*'s audience than they would in the chapel of an English Public or American private school. I do not think that turning the other cheek was much of a medieval virtue. But Moses and David, Saul and Samuel they could understand and, as we now know, they served as themes for political thinking and action of the highest importance. Nor do we have to rely on *Beowulf* and conjectures about social influences for evidence that early medieval Christianity was unusually Old Testament centred. M. Fountain has pointed to evidence for a fairly wide-spread interest in the Old Testament. Mr. Mayr-Harting has pointed out, or is just about to, how St. Wilfrid's biographer presents him as an Old Testament prophet revived. Professor Hanning has noted the very Old Testament view of history that informs Gildas and Bede.[35]

Putting all this together and reading the evidence in the light of its world, not ours, we can, I think, see that this world is the world of the *Heerkönig*—that is what Beowulf, Scyld Scefing, Hrothgar, and Hygelac were, as was the undoubtedly historical St. Guthlac, who points the moral by returning one-third of his loot to the victims upon conversion. Guthlac's biographer Felix thought this admirable, praiseworthy, and thoroughly saintlike conduct, yet he was writing in the middle of the Mercian hegemony and was, to judge by his sources, a learned and cultivated man. It seems to follow that we cannot make easy or safe inferences about the poet's silences from assumptions that would be sound enough in a different world. It is clearly much more difficult to solve the riddle of the Christian and pagan elements in the poem than has usually been supposed. Above all, nothing of this can be done simply by attending to the words on the page: we shall get nowhere by asking what the words mean; what we need to know is how in this world were they used.

This seems to me a point worth labouring because *Beowulf* is a poem in the margins of English literature and cannot be studied like, say, *King Lear*, which is at the centre. Even the language and diction of the poem have their mysteries. Professor Tolkien has remarked: "If you wish to translate, not rewrite, *Beowulf*, your language must be literary and traditional: not because it is now a long while since the poem was made, or because it speaks of things that have since become ancient; but because the diction of *Beowulf* was poetical, archaic, and artificial (if you will) in the day that the poem was made."[36] Professor Tolkien seems to assume that the mode of the "archaic" is as fixed and concrete a thing as the French language. Fixed and concrete, that is, so far as to allow any sensible person to say with precision and truth when and when not somebody is speaking "archaic" in the way it is possible to determine whether someone is speaking French or not. But this is not true. Take

the opening of the translation Professor Tolkien is commending: "Lo!
We have heard of the glory of the kings of the people of the Spear-Danes
in the days of yore how these princes did valorous deeds." This sounds
distinctly Wagner period to me. Let us compare it with something of
which it is certainly true that its language and diction were artificial and
archaic on the day it was made:

> After this it was noised abroad that Mr. Valiant for Truth was taken
> with a summons, by the same post as the other; and had this for a
> token that the summons was true, that his pitcher was broken at the
> fountain. When he understood it, he called for his friends, and told
> them of it. Then said he, I am going to my fathers and with great
> difficulty I am got hither, yet now I do not repent me of all the
> trouble I have been to arrive at where I am. My sword I give to him
> that shall succeed me in the pilgrimage, and my courage and skill, to
> him that can get it. My marks and scars I carry with me, to be a
> witness for me, that I have fought his battles, who now will be my
> Rewarder. When the time that he must go hence was come, many
> accompanied him to the riverside, into which as he went he said
> Death where is thy sting? And as he went deeper, he said, Grave
> where is thy victory? So he passed over, and the trumpets sounded for
> him on the other side.

There are, in fact, as many kinds of archaism as there are authors who try
out the mode. Bunyan is successful, and the revised Clark Hall a failure,
because the one has its roots, makes its appeal, to a readership steeped in
King James's Bible and the solemn ritual occasions so many of the
allusions recall, whilst the other has no roots in anything at all other than
a vague sense that tradition is best expressed in outlandish locutions and
a vocabulary used only by the authors of children's books of a generation
ago. This is not the translator's fault. A prose-style has its roots in a way
of life and this is just as true of the style of a narrative poem such as
Beowulf. But the way of life of *Beowulf*'s audience is at least partly lost to
us and with it some, perhaps the major part, of the poet's intentions and
the poem's point.

This may be illustrated by considering the following piece of death-
less prose composed for the occasion: "Then a bird in her Mary Quants
awaited her escort in front of the Hilton. Across the street another bird
tarted up to the nines in her C and A Modes came out of the Vault of the
King's Head, waved to a young man on the pavement, stepped into his
E type and drove off. A moment later the first bird's expected turned up
in a Beetle. She took one look, turned on her heel and swept into the
King's Head." Even to most Americans of the present time the point of
the episode would be incomprehensible. You would need to know the

status difference between clothes from Mary Quant and clothes from C and A Modes: you would need to know that well-conducted girls do not drink in the Vaults of public houses and you would need to know the status difference between E Type Jaguars and Volkswagens. No one in England, unlike the United States, would drive a Volkswagen if he could afford something better. Thus not even in the "common" language of the English-speaking world would such a trivial piece of drivel be intelligible. Suppose that the passage were to be translated into a language that had only one word for automobile, and belonged to a people that did not use clothes as status symbols. Translation would simply not be possible and understanding could only be conveyed by a commentary, and such a commentary requires an author familiar with the ways of life of both societies.

If we bear this in mind and return to *Beowulf,* we can guess, though many authors who have written on the poem have not, that in a world where survival depended to large degree on swords, men would have special feelings about them. The text of *Beowulf* tells us, if we look at it with this question in mind, that certain kinds of swords were status symbols, particularly swords of pedigree, and this is supported by the *Wills,* but we cannot know what a man would feel about a sword if his life and fortune depended on it. Swords and other weapons are the subject of an intricate vocabulary in the poem: the late Dr. Harmer, who was one of the few Old English scholars whose command of the "historical" sources and literature equalled her command of the literary, always maintained that many of the so-called synonyms conceal a variety of differences amongst the actual weaponry at which we can only guess. It is obvious that feelings about swords are important in *Beowulf.* Beowulf refuses to use one against Grendel. Against Grendel's mother, whose inferior strength is emphasized, he uses a sword that fails him, as does his sword in his last fight with the dragon. Yet Grendel's mother is killed by a sword in the end. This theme must have a point and one that we can reasonably suppose was intelligible to an audience who shared the poet's attitude towards swords, but how can we ever hope to know exactly what this point, based on lost feelings, was? We are in the same case as the man who has only one word to render E Type and Beetle. We cannot, therefore, without more ado, read the poem against a generalized background of medieval chivalry and courtly love, looking up the words we do not understand in a glossary. We must constantly look outside the poem into the poet's world for guidance as to how the words were actually used. If I am right, it is obvious that some, and perhaps, much, of the life-style—and the feelings that style entailed—are lost irretrievably, but it is possible from the poem itself to get some kind of guide lines that can be followed up outside the poem. That is, we must follow up the themes of the feud and loot.

Chadwick, years ago, pointed to the importance of loot in the poem: if we count the references to "rings" and feuds, or weigh them according to the importance of the episodes in which they occur, it is obvious that *Beowulf* is just as much about feuds and loot as it is about fighting monsters. By following out these themes we can, I suggest, get something of the "feel" of the poem's world and a rather more precise idea of what sort of man he was and what his religious attitudes were.

If we follow up the theme of loot we can see immediately how realistic the poet is about the economic basis of the social group to which all its characters belong. The opening episode has Scyld Scefing taking tribute and property from others in its first lines. When he dies (26 ff.) he is put to sea in a boat laden with treasures and the artistic unity of the episode, if that is the right word, is in the contrast between Scyld's beginning—he was disposed of as a child by being put to sea in a boat—and his ending with his ceremonial funeral voyage and his treasures. The sense of the passage seems to me to be that dying prosperous and famous, with prosperity and fame duly recognized by the funeral rites, was a fitting consummation to a successful career. If there were rewards and judgement to come, there is no allusion to them. The episode is complete as it stands. Scyld Scefing is succeeded by a son called Beowulf, who appears to have no connection with the hero of the poem, unless there was a connection obvious to the audience but lost to us. The poet approves of him in the following lines: "So ought a young man to compass by noble deeds, by liberal gifts in his father's possession, that afterwards in later years, willing companions may stand by him— that men may come by service when war comes." One could not get a franker statement of the commercial side of the war band—"the local chivalry"—than this. Unless, that is, one rates Wiglaf's closing speech even franker: "Now shall the receiving of treasure and the gift of swords, all joy of ownership and comfort be wanting to your race: each man of your family will have to wander, shorn of his landed possessions, as soon as the nobles far and wide hear of your flight, your despicable act."

The theme recurs not only frequently but at crucial points in the action. When Hrothgar is introduced to the audience and is planning the building of Heorot, the scene of Beowulf's triumphs, it is on the occasion of a considerable distribution of what the context suggests was the spoils of war. We are told without question approvingly: "He did not break his promise, but gave out rings and treasure at the banquet." But, most significant, here is the motivation of Beowulf's visit to Heorot and his endeavours to dispose of Grendel.

Nothing is said about Beowulf's reasons for going to Hrothgar's help when he first appears. He would seek Hrothgar's court and sensible men do not dissuade him but consult the omens—a practice that would have been anathema to an instructed Christian. When he returns and tells his story to his kinsman, it is frankly admitted that he had been thought of previously as somewhat slack and Hygelac had given him little, withholding what seems to have been his father's land. Now Beowulf gets 7,000 hides and a proper status. It seems to me that this is not the conventional theme of an apparent sluggard proving himself. It is rather something the poem's audience would have been well-acquainted with: a young warrior proves his right to *folcland,* to "warrior's land":[37] and I think they would have taken it for granted that this was Beowulf's intention in fighting Grendel in the first place. Beowulf gathered a small band of companions to help him, as did the historical St. Guthlac, and Beowulf's actions seem to parallel precisely Bede's account of the typical warrior's career of his own day, who likewise entered a foreign lord's service if there was no endowment for him at home.[38] Again, Beowulf's reward has the flavour of reality. We are told that Hygelac: "gave him the rank of chief. To both alike was there land by natural right, an estate, a patrimony: but a great kingdom belonged rather to the one who was higher in rank."[39] This land amounted to 7,000 hides. It looks as though Hygelac had conferred on Beowulf a sub-kingdom[40] and its rating corresponds to the valuation of real provinces if we may believe the Tribal Hidage. It is noticeable, too, that Beowulf first handed over his treasures before he got his preferment. It is possible to read the poem as meaning he gave up his valuables out of pure affection for his lord, but I do not think the original audience would have taken this view. In this poem, valuables are given for consideration, for favours done and benefits expected. I think we are meant to understand that, Hygelac being willing at last to hand over the land which is in some sense Beowulf's patrimony, Beowulf preceded the gift in the usual fashion by paying a heriot. If we read the poem in the light of early medieval accounts of energetic warriors and the companions with whom they surrounded themselves, especially Bede's valuable insight into the normal career of the youthful warrior,[41] Beowulf's conduct makes complete and quite unromantic sense from beginning to end. From the first his motive was to rise in the service of his kinsman and earn his "patrimony," and through his deeds he did just that. These motives would have been perfectly acceptable to contemporaries and the values they imply unquestioned. It is difficult if one reads the poem and remembers how real people behaved at this time to miss the strictly economic aspects of lordship and vassalage, especially if we do not start out with the assumption that a ring bestowed is somehow heroic where a cheque earned is not. It seems that being brutally frank about the economic basis of his age's heroism is one of the characteristics of this poet and is what marks him off from the poets of chivalry, with whom he is so misleadingly compared.

The second basic theme is the feud, and there cannot be much doubt that here we are very close to the mind and heart of the poet. There are twenty-five references to feuds according to my calculation: the poet is obsessed by them. In his account of the building of Heorot his thoughts turn immediately to the feud, though there is nothing in the narrative at that point which requires this. "Nor was the time yet near at hand that cruel hatred between son-in-law and father-in-law should arise, because of a deed of violence" (83–85). This is the first reference to a feud and, interestingly, it is one between kinsmen. Unferth is said "in the play of sword blades" to have "shown no mercy to kinsmen" (1167–68). In line 2167 the poet observes that kinsmen should not lay snares for others. In Beowulf's farewell speech he reminisces about the killing of one brother by another in his own family. "For the eldest a bed of slaughter was prepared—and not as might befit him—but through his own kinsman's deed . . . brother slaying brother with a bloody shaft" (2435 ff.). His comment on this is interesting too: "that was a slaying for which there could be no blood money, an act of guilty violence . . . the noble prince had to lose his life unavenged." In this world the feud was the principal form of protection for the individual, and an institution that must have had some deterrent value.[42] The feud is a serious and unromantic institution, much as the police force is to us. Beowulf continues to reflect on this tragic event and implies that the man's father died of a broken heart, sorrowing for the son he could not avenge. "He could never make the killer pay the price of his bloody deed, nor could he show his hatred for that warrior by hostile acts, although he was far from dear to him." The section is one of the gravest in the poem and deeply touched by that sense of the tears of things which is such a prominent ingredient of the tone of the poem.

We may notice here that nothing can be done about the killing of one kinsman by another. The feud simply does not work if the kin is divided. We may guess that sometimes something was done and kinsman fought kinsman, and part of the poet's horror at the killing of kinsmen was due to the disastrous social consequences of such unappeasable feuds. We have, after all, the recorded history of the Merovingian family to show us an actual historical example.[43]

We might ask how the poet's theology affected his view of the feud. The obvious point is that the story of Cain and Abel is quoted twice in the poem: it is easy to see why this story had such force for a man of *this* world. But by and large the poet's religion affects his view of the feud very little. In the passage already cited at the end the bereaved father dies too. "So then in his sorrow which had fallen all too bitterly upon him, he forsook the joys of men and chose the light of God; when he deserted this life he left his sons land and the stronghold of their people, as a wealthy man does." It is a little reminiscent of "When he died the little port had seldom seen a costlier funeral," is it not? But it is noticeable how utterly inadequate is the context as a means of giving meaning to the phrase "light of God." The poet's religion is hardly brought to bear at all on the feud: it is in quite a separate compartment.

Beowulf proses on about old feuds and the farewell speech concludes with yet another, this time Beowulf's own: "I will once more seek a feud and a deed of glory" (2512–14). This refers to his intention to fight the dragon. In his dying speech he yet again reverts to the theme: "the Ruler of Men will have no cause to accuse me of a murderous slaughter of any kinsmen." Wiglaf, in his role of Cassandra, envisages a future feud consequent on the death of Beowulf at the very end of the poem.

The feud appears at every crux in the story. When Grendel is introduced he is having a feud with Hrothgar, and it is a sign of his fiendish nature that he will not pay compensation for the men he has killed; the payment of wergeld is one of the objects of the feud or threat of it. Grendel is also described as waging a feud with God (811). When Grendel is killed Hrothgar himself pays wergeld for the last of his men Grendel slew. Grendel's mother appears as seeking vengeance for her dead son (1278), and, as I have already pointed out, Beowulf himself claims to be waging a feud against his last monster. It is the feud, not the Fathers, that offers the key to this poem. The poet's imagination is filled with the idea and the whole poem is simply a series of feuds working themselves out. The poet's attitude is plainly ambiguous. It is clear that he considered some feuds right and proper for the men who took part in them and he says so without mincing words. In line 2618 King Onela did not speak of the feud when Weohstan killed his nephew; I think the poet implies criticism of Onela here. This is understandable: a man depended on his kinsmen, especially the powerful ones, for his protection and security. But when in pursuance of her feud Grendel's mother carries off a warrior from Heorot, the poet does not criticize her but says: "No good barter was this, when those on both sides must pay with the life of friends" (1304–06). The comment is generalized and does not seem meant for Grendel's mother alone. It appears to me not unreasonable that men of feeling had mixed reactions to the feud. In their world,

the feud was so important, and they might well have confused reactions
to it, as in our world many of us have towards the automobile.

If we try to understand what a society in which the feud was a basic
institution was like, it follows, I think, that we cannot take the three
monsters as evil in the same way and on the same level. Grendel's
mother is up to a point doing her duty, and it seems to me that the poet
would expect his audience to have somewhat different reactions to her
than they had to Grendel. The last dragon seems a very different case
and it is hard not to conclude that Wiglaf and, I think, the audience,
would see Beowulf as guilty of a display of empty *machismo*, reprehen-
sible because of the consequences to which it laid the innocent open. It
seems to me that a glance outside the poem to its world strongly
reinforces Professor Leyerle's powerful argument for a much more
critical view of Beowulf's conduct.[44]

Putting the themes of treasure and feud together, and taking them
from the realm of fairy-tales to the serious business of everyday life,
which is just what they were to the original audience, we can see the
beginning of the ideology of feudalism. This is not the settled world of
the feudalism of the High Middle Ages, when the social order was
strong enough, bureaucratic enough, sufficiently unfeudal in other
words, to afford the delights of litigation and the luxury of legal definition. But feudal it is none the less. The political order depicted in
Beowulf was fragile and dependent on the lives of kings, but it was also
an order in which the relationship of lord and man was *the* political
order. There are no *ministri*, no career officials, no police, no formal
legal profession, nothing of the bureaucratic order whatsoever. The lord
is several times equated with the senior kinsman, as when Hrothgar paid
wergeld for Grendel's victim. Wars between different lords and their
respective bands of retainers are treated as feuds, as in the war Wiglaf
expects when: "the Swedish folc attack us when they hear our lord has
lost his life" (3001–03). It seems clear that by and large the bond of lord
and man was stronger than that between kinsmen—this is implied in
places by the very loose use of the word "feud," which seems applicable
to any war-like activity engaged in by a lord and his companions.[45] Men
got away with the murder of kinsfolk easily enough but their posture
before their lord is one of utter subordination. Lords (the classic case is
Heremod) sometimes slaughtered their own vassals. "He would cut
down companions who feasted at his table and the comrades who
feasted at his side" (1713–14).[46] No one seems able to call him to account
and the poet notes the climax of his villainy: his refusal to give treasure
to the Danes. The poet has to content himself and us with the news that
at last Heremod died unhappy. Beowulf by way of contrast never kills

his vassals, even when in his cups; and this is a comment by the poet, not an extract from one of Beowulf's interminable speeches, unlike the parallel remark that Beowulf never killed kinsfolk.

This is why I call the poem feudal. These bands, in spite of the translators' use of modern words like "comrades" or "bosom friends," are not free and easy, overgrown troops of boy scouts. They are social groups, strictly authoritarian and hierarchical in structure, in which the so-called companions depend for their livelihood and their lives on their lord's pleasure. The men called kings have a very exalted status indeed and are apparently less vulnerable to trouble than common mortals. Even a really bad one like Heremod met no worse fate than a miserable death-bed. If we read the poem as a sort of early Public School story, as I think many commentators do, it is hard to feel that Beowulf's companions deserved the hard things that Wiglaf said about them at the end. They only did as they were told. But this is not a game and the failed vassal was in a terrible position. This is a world in which Alcuin could truly remark that the death of kings brought great sorrow. As Wiglaf puts it: "Now the acceptance of riches, the bestowing of swords, and all the delights of your own land and your beloved homes—all this must come to an end for your race. Every man within the circle of your kindred will have to become a wanderer, stripped of all right to hold land, once high born nobles far away have heard of your flight" (2884 ff.). The famous inalienable Anglo-Saxon family land appears unknown to this poet. There is an extreme, if not legally defined, connection between holding one's land and fighting for one's lord. It is because of the consequences of Beowulf's death, in part inevitable however it happened, that it is difficult to avoid the implication that the poet, very gingerly it is true, intends criticism of Beowulf. His attitude to the treasure is quite different from that attributed to Beowulf. He did not incur the curse out of greed but, I think, it is implied that he should have left it alone just the same. Beowulf's dying wish is to look on the treasure he has won for his people, but Wiglaf, and the poet, I think, rejected the treasure and buried it again: "They left the wealth of nobles to the earth to keep—left the gold in the ground where it still exists, as unprofitable to men as it had been before" (3166 ff.). This is a comment made by the poet himself and is totally at variance with the sentiments he makes Beowulf utter about the hoard.

The poem, then, seems essentially a feudal poem shot through with the values of a warrior society, and a very insecure one at that. It seems to me to have no affinities whatsoever to the sentimentalizing literature of high medieval chivalry. It has affinities to the high medieval world certainly, but to the realities of that world, to the ethos and institutions of what we call bastard feudalism; but none, it seems to me, to the rationalizations and fantasies of chivalry and courtly love. It seems too me, also, to be a religious poem and, what is more, a Christian poem of uncommon power and feeling quite other than the Fathers or the kind of books that Bede, for instance, read. Nothing in the poem—as distinct from the analogies scholars have claimed to find—compels us to assume that its author had a profound knowledge of theology. There is a good deal of traditional paganism there: taking the omens, the funeral ceremonies that would have been devil's rites to a man like Alcuin—the very worldly concern for reputation shown by the good characters on their death-beds and the very feeble signs of any hope of Heaven or fear of Hell. But for all that, the ethos of the poem is very far from that of the religion of Woden. Thanks to Professor Turville-Petre we have now more idea of what being a follower of Woden implied. The quality his followers seem to have attributed to Woden, and admired in him, was simply *chutzpah,* and *chutzpah* is exactly the quality that the poet has eliminated from his poem, replacing it with a very strong sense of duty and restraint, and unlike Bede, for example, refusing to present success and *fortuna* as the rewards of virtue. I would say that the religious sentiments of the poet were like those of the unnamed man at King Edwin's court, who compared human life to the flight of a sparrow through a lighted hall. I would argue that neither this man nor the author of *Beowulf* had much formal theological knowledge and little concern with the great questions of patristic theology, but that they did have questions of their own and these were not negligible.

To illustrate this let me take a work that might have been known to the poet, at least at second hand, the first *Life* of Gregory the Great. It would be absurd to compare this jejeune piece of spiritual biography with the masterpieces of an Augustine. But for all that, its author could raise a theological point of the first importance that never occurred to Augustine and would have become him if it had. In the story of the Emperor Trajan and St. Gregory, the problem of the good pagan, who died unbaptized through the accident of time and place, is raised for the first time. One of the miracles in Adomnan's *Life of Columba*[47] suggests that the problem had been raised at Iona—or possibly Iona was the source of the questioning—but Adomnan plays safe and evades the issue. The *Life* of Gregory does not. It is interesting that a fundamental question such as this should have been raised on the margin of the classical world by new Christians with as yet little knowledge of the metaphysical profundity of classical thought. It is to this climate of thought that I think *Beowulf* belongs. It is a new Christian poem by a man still deeply affected by an older way of thinking and feeling, but a man capable of comparing the two and wholly on the side of the new ways. But he is still sufficiently aware of the power of the old ways to attempt what is in effect a radical critique of them from a Christian point of view. Since, removed from the cult of Woden, these warrior-like values accommodated themselves comfortably to the cult of Christ, the poem had a continuing relevance but not, perhaps, a very agreeable message.

It is a common social experience with the bonds of lordship and vassalage; with the feud; with constant and frequent social collapses; with the enormous importance of the conduct of a few highly-placed individuals, that prompted the spiritual directions the new Christians were to take, quite as much as the book-knowledge that came in with the Conversion. Not surprisingly in a world of lords and vassals, feuds and murderous brawls, it is the transitoriness of human life that is of more immediate concern than the pleasures of salvation. Equally obviously, the Old Testament is of much more obvious relevance than the incomprehensible and strange doctrines of the New Testament. The poet of *Beowulf* is not on the same comparatively easy terms with his God as was Bede, and not necessarily the worse for that. We too easily assume that the pagan Anglo-Saxons were incapable of any moral or spiritual reflection until they learned it from books in strange tongues, when they then acquired the habit with remarkable rapidity. I suggest that a consideration of the religion of Woden and its interaction with the religion of Jesus would throw some light on *Beowulf,* and that the poem in its turn has something to tell us about the *Ideenwelt* of the early Anglo-Saxons.

It seems to me that the poem has nothing of the hallmark of the learned clerk in it. It seems to me impregnated with the social and personal experience of the retainer. I take it the poet has plenty of experience of actual fighting—or so I would interpret his concern for the physical experience of battle and the abundance of the references to weapons. I should say that his sense of the constant imminence of feuds, his feeling that decisions are made from above him and from outside his competence—Beowulf's decision to fight the dragon, the way it was made, its contempt for the vital interests of his dependants, and above all the delicately critical treatment it gets, illustrates this very well—his sense of the precariousness of the vassal's life and his social existence; all point to a man who came himself from the class of retainers. It is noticeable that he has a sense of the powerlessness of the retainer faced with even a drunken and murderous lord, and he always gives the impression of utter helplessness in this kind of situation. Yet in practice we know that some checks were available on the conduct of lords, because vassals would and could defect; sometimes vassals murdered lords and the poet must have known it, but he never admits it. It is essentially a poem, it seems to me, written from, about, and too, the class of retainers: at any rate, if one reads the poem looking at the feuds and the loot as well as the monsters that is how it seems to read.

Having said this, I must leave the problem in the air. A mere historian cannot do more than point to a direction for studies he cannot undertake himself. I have sought to suggest that we complete the revolution begun by Professor Tolkien's famous lecture. He rightly pointed out that you cannot push the monsters aside, since they are what the poem is about. I wish to suggest that the poem is scarcely less obviously about swords, feuds, and loot. We need, I think, to rest the theological *Beowulf* for a while, and try out a less familiar sociological *Beowulf.* At the same time we must realize, in my view, that some of the poem, including the qualities that would really enable us to make secure judgements on its literary merits, has been lost irretrievably. It is obvious that we ought to know just how good a knowledge of weapons and fighting the poet had: did his first audience approve his acumen or deride his ignorance? We shall never know. I do not mean loss in the sense that a manuscript might be lost, but the much more profound sense in which only the meaning of the words has remained whilst the knowledge of how and when to use them, and the feelings that went with them, have quite escaped us.

NOTES

1. I have taken some passages from another article, "Beowulf and the Limits of Literature," which appeared in *New Blackfriars* 52 (1971), by kind permission of the editor. Earlier versions of this paper were read to the Sixth Conference of Medieval Studies at the University of Western Michigan and the Medieval Seminar at Columbia University. I am particularly indebted to Professor Hanning and his pupils for a stimulating discussion that greatly improved the paper.

2. Kenneth Sisam, *The Structure of "Beowulf"* (Oxford, 1965); Margaret E. Goldsmith, *The Mode and Meaning of "Beowulf"* (London, 1970).

3. H.M. Chadwick, *The Heroic Age* (Cambridge, 1912). *The Origin of the English Nation* (Cambridge, 1907) is also relevant and deserves to be read more often than it is.

4. Cf. the Introduction to Fr. Klaeber, *Beowulf* (Boston, 1922).

5. "An Echo of *Beowulf* in Athelstan's Charters of 931–933 A.D.?" *Medium Ævum* 24 (1955): 101–03.

6. J.R. Clark Hall, trans., *"Beowulf" and the Finnesburg Fragment*, rev. ed. by C.L. Wrenn (London, 1940), 12.

7. Kenneth Sisam, "Anglo-Saxon Royal Genealogies," *Proceedings of the British Academy* 39 (1953): 287–348.

8. Dorothy Whitelock, *The Audience of "Beowulf"* (Oxford, 1951), 34.

9. *Aldhelmi Opera,* ed. R. Ehwald, Monumenta Germaniae historica, Auctores antiquissimi no. 15 (Berlin, 1919), 509.

10. *The Audience of "Beowulf,"* 33.

11. Dean Ware, "Hisperic Latin and the Hermeneutic Tradition," *Studies in Medieval Culture* 2 (1966): 43–48.

12. Eric John, *Land Tenure in Early England* (Leicester, 1960), 68 n. 1.

13. Rosemary Cramp, "*Beowulf* and Archaeology," *Medieval Archaeology* 1 (1957): 57–77.

14. H.L. Hargrove, ed., *King Alfred's Old English Version of St. Augustine's Soliloquies,* Yale Studies in English no. 13 (New York, 1902).

15. Eric John, *Orbis Britanniae* (Leicester, 1966), 64 ff.

16. W. Schlesinger, "Das Heerkönigtum," in *Das Königtum: seine geistigen und rechtlichen Grundlagen,* Vorträge und Forschungen no 3 (Lindau, 1956), 105–42.

17. John, *Land Tenure,* 53.

18. J.R.R. Tolkien, "*Beowulf:* The Monsters and the Critics," *Proceedings of the British Academy* 22 (1935): 245–95.

19. *The Heroic Age,* 47 ff., reprinted in L. Nicholson, *An Anthology of "Beowulf" Criticism* (Notre Dame, 1963), 23–25.

20. "The Religious Principle in *Beowulf,*" *PMLA* 61 (1946): 309–30; reprinted in Nicholson, *Anthology,* 105–35.

21. *Orbis Britanniae,* 5 ff.; "The Social and Political Problems of the Early Church," *Agricultural History Review* 18 (1970): 39 ff.

22. *The Structure of "Beowulf."*

23. The comparative bulk of Bede's output; the great difference in learning and latinity between Bede and any of his contemporaries, including Aldhelm; the very small number of men who can be shown to have written anything; the very small number of genuinely "academic" schools that are known to have existed, all warn us against taking Bede as typical. It has recently been pointed out how limited were the intellectual resources of even so famous a monastery as Whitby (Bertram Colgrave, "The Earliest Life of St. Gregory the Great, Written by a Whitby Monk," in Nora K. Chadwick, ed., *Celt and Saxon* [Cambridge, 1963], 130).

24. *The Structure of "Beowulf,"* 27.

25. "St. Gregory's Intention in the Stories of St. Scholastica and St. Benedict," *Revue Bénédictine* 75 (1965): 145–51.

26. John Leyerle, "Beowulf the Hero and King," *Medium Aevum* 34 (1965): 89–102; cf. "The Interlace Structure of *Beowulf,*" *University of Toronto Quarterly* 37 (1967–68): 1–17.

27. Clark Hall, *Beowulf,* 22.

28. Cf. Adomnan's description of Columba's career, 46: "Per annos xxxiii insulanus *miles* conversatus" (*Life of Columba,* ed. and trans. A.O. Anderson and M.O. Anderson (London, 1961).

29. *Die Entstehung des Kreuzzugsgedankens* (Stuttgart, 1935).

30. R. Girvan, *"Beowulf" and the Seventh Century,* rev. ed. (London, 1971).

31. Some social anthropologists would dismiss the study of doctrines and the actions of individuals as pointless, explaining everything in terms of social structure and the pressure of social institutions. An historian is unlikely to accept this: but it does not follow that because some sociologists abuse their methods they cannot

teach historians anything. The kind of study I have in mind is E. Evans-Pritchard's classical work on magic and witchcraft amongst the Azande (*Witchcraft, Oracles and Magic among the Azande* [Oxford, 1937]) which establishes beyond question the existence of connections between rituals and social structure, and the importance of offering explanations that take this into account. The same author's *Theories of Primitive Religion* (Oxford, 1965) shows how critical of over-generalization, and sensitive to the contingent and inexplicable, social anthropologists can be.

32. *The Sociology of Religion,* trans. Ephraim Fischoff (London, 1965), 85.

33. *Purity and Danger: An Analysis of Concepts of Pollution and Taboo* (London, 1966).

34. The dangers of assuming that a practice or institution in a marginal situation or society may be safely interpreted by analogy with a later one have recently been illuminated by philosophers. The late Ludwig Wittgenstein's "Remarks on Frazer's Golden Bough," together with Mr. Rush Rhees's commentary, are worth consulting (*The Human World* 3 [1971]: 18–41). Professor Peter Winch's *Idea of a Social Science* (London, 1958) is relevant, and see especially his paper "Understanding a Primitive Society," *American Philosophical Quarterly* 1 (1964): 307–24.

35. *The Vision of History in Early Britain* (New York, 1966).

36. Clark Hall, *Beowulf,* xvii.

37. John, *Orbis Britanniae,* 120 ff.

38. *Epistola ad Ecgberctum* (*Venerabilis Baedae Opera Historica,* ed. Charles Plummer [Oxford, Clarendon Press, 1896], 1:405–23). This is true not only of a warrior's career. The element of seeking a place in life, if necessary in far away places, is to be found in the career of the great Wilfrid; see John, "Social and Political Problems," passim.

39. I have softened the traditional translation of lines 2197 and 8. This is because natural rights and hereditary rights do not have the same, strict, force they have in later societies, as any study of the lawsuits will show. The loose force of *lond gecynde* is shown by a surprisingly late source. The *Chronicle,* s.a. 1086, in its obituary of the Conqueror says: "Normandige þæt land wæs his gecynde." This is meant to contrast with the lands he conquered, but William, being a bastard, had less natural right than Beowulf, and likewise had to fight his way into his right.

40. It is very easy to interpret, or rather misinterpret, the relations between over and under-kings in the early Middle Ages by later analogies that do not hold. For a penetrating discussion of such a relationship at the turn of the ninth century, between the Emperor Arnulf and his son Zwentibold, king of Lotharingia, see E. Hlawitschka, *Lotharingien und das Reich,* Schriften der Monumenta Germaniae historica no. 21 (Stuttgart, 1968), 158 ff.

41. *Epistola ad Ecgberctum.*

42. Cf. the important discussion by J.M. Wallace-Hadrill, "The Blood Feud of the Franks," in *The Long Haired-Kings* (London, 1962), 121–47. A pope of the period might expect to take part in a feud (*ibid.,* 127). The most extreme example of a Christianized view of the feud is Gregory of Tours: "he visualises (divine vengeance) as nothing less than God's own feud in support of his servants, who can have no other kin" (*ibid.,* 127). It seems to me that, a comparison between *Beowulf* and Gregory's *History,* which here treat of the same topic in the same mode, shows that

the poem's religion is a good deal less classical and a good deal more Germanic than the *History's*.

43. Wallace-Hadrill (*ibid.,* 135) has an important comment on this: "it was the wrong kind of feud; not feuding but feuding within the kin was what led to pointless bloodshed that stopped nothing and offered few of the normal opportunities for compromise and settlement." The poet's attitude to the feud is then reasonably historical and was likely to be common to him and his audience.

44. "Beowulf the Hero and King."

45. Wallace-Hadrill (*ibid.,* 125–26) points out that it was not easy in practice to separate the claims of kindred and lord in the business of the feud. The famous story of Cynewulf and Cyneheard shows that for one writer at least it was right and proper to prefer the claims of one's lord to one's kin. It is interesting that no such notion can be attributed to the *Beowulf* poet.

46. Clark Hall's "boon-companions" and "bosom friends" in his translation of this line are most unfortunate: they quite fail to convey the sense of inferiority, the status distance, that separated lord and retainer.

47. *Life of Columba* 1.33, 275.

Elements of the Marvellous
in the Characterization of Beowulf:
A Reconsideration of the Textual Evidence

by FRED C. ROBINSON

This essay first appeared in Old English Studies in Honour of John C. Pope, *ed. Robert B. Burlin and Edward B. Irving (Toronto: University of Toronto Press, 1974), 119–37. The present reprint incorporates some revisions by the author.*

ELEMENTS of the marvellous are not uncommon in *Beowulf.* A fire-breathing dragon, sea monsters, and magically protected ogres from the race of Cain are but some of the fabulous wonders that the poet has admitted to his story. But in general the wonders are carefully restricted to the devil's party. Against these superhuman (as well as many human) adversaries the hero Beowulf can pit only his man's strength and his man's courage.[1] True, he is not an average man—"se þe manna wæs   mægene strengest / on þæm dæge þysses lifes" (789–90)[2]—but he is *only* a strong man, and the poem thus reveals how the best of human beings might comport themselves in their struggle against the hopeless odds of the enemy. If the poet had been indiscriminate in his use of the supernatural, if he had lavished fabulous powers on ogre and champion alike, then the hero would have become a kind of monster himself, and *Beowulf,* instead of being a heroic poem, would have been a romantic fable describing the conflict between good monsters and bad monsters.

The poet's concern to portray Beowulf as a man rather than as superhuman is revealed in his repeated allusions to the hero's physical limitations and vulnerability. Most memorable, perhaps, is the account of Beowulf's suffering and death in the last part of the poem, a subject which is discussed with characteristic eloquence in John C. Pope's essay for the Meritt Festschrift.[3] But there are earlier reminders of human fallibility. In lines 739 and following we see that Beowulf is incapable of preventing Grendel from killing and devouring the Geatish warrior Hondscioh, and later he confesses to Hrothgar (960–62, 967–70) that he lacked the strength to hold the monster in the hall and kill him there,

79

as he wanted to do. The poet tells us that Beowulf all but died in his struggle with the hag (1500 ff.), a fact which the hero himself acknowledges in his reports to Hrothgar (1655–57) and to Hygelac (2140 ff.). In the dragon fight, only Wiglaf's intervention saves Beowulf from an instant and ignominious death.[4] The inadequacy thus demonstrated was sensed by the hero earlier when he apologized for having to use a sword and armour in his last adventure (2518 ff.). Here as elsewhere in his closing speeches, "the sense of his own vulnerability seems to draw him closer to the period of boyhood dependency,"[5] and we are reminded that throughout the poem he has been portrayed as a man, not a demigod.

But is it true that in characterizing Beowulf the poet systematically eschews elements of the marvellous? Doesn't he in fact sometimes allow the hero's physical powers to grow embarrassingly far beyond human dimensions? Beowulf remains underwater for hours—or perhaps for an entire day—as he descends to the bottom of Grendel's mere. Alone, he carries thirty suits of armour from the battlefield in Frisia and swims with them through the North Sea and the Skagerrak to Geatland, a distance of some five hundred miles. In early life he swam for five to seven days with his companion Breca, slaying sea monsters by night. At these points in the narrative it would seem that the distinction between the powers of men and the powers of his supernatural adversaries becomes quite indistinct.

At least two critics of the poem have perceived just how important these lapses are for our understanding of the nature and meaning of *Beowulf.* Citing the three episodes just mentioned, Rodney Delasanta and James Slevin point out that such feats temporarily remove Beowulf from the category of "high mimetic hero" and mark him instead as a "romance hero," one who is superior not only to other men but also to his environment.[6] By applying Northrop Frye's terms to *Beowulf,* Delasanta and Slevin bring into clear focus the tensions between epic and romance qualities which seemed to trouble W.P. Ker: "There was a danger that Beowulf should be transformed into a sort of Amadis," he muses, and concludes uncertainly, "this danger is avoided, at least in part."[7]

It is my purpose in the present essay to argue that, if we return to the text of *Beowulf* and examine each of the three occasions where Beowulf seems to be temporarily endowed with supernatural powers, we will discover a strange insubstantiality in the evidence for such endowments. In fact, I am convinced that the supposed evidence for a superhuman Beowulf is largely a fiction of editorial interpretation and comment and that Beowulf throughout is conceived of as a heroic man and not as a romance hero. The reason for the supernaturalizing interpretations, I shall further suggest, is that in reading the poem scholars may have been excessively influenced by its folktale analogues and so have sometimes read back into the sophisticated text of the poet a wild extravagance which he had carefully purged from the material he adopted.

✗ The Descent into Grendel's Mere

In his account of Beowulf's fight with the ogress the poet is at some pains to explain that the conflict does not take place under water but rather in a dry chamber where no water could reach the combatants:

> Ða se eorl ongeat,
> þæt he [in] niðsele   nathwylcum wæs,
> þær him nænig wæter   wihte ne sceþede,
> ne him for hrofsele   hrinan ne mehte
> færgripe flodes.   (1512–16)[8]

[Then the warrior perceived that he was in some hostile hall, where no water harmed him at all, and because of the roofed hall the sudden grip of the current could not touch him.—P.S.B.]

Thus localized, Beowulf's exploit is one which we could imagine a human being performing, and as the fight progresses and he begins to lose ground, we are prepared to believe that the hero is indeed fighting desperately for his life.

This careful circumscription of the hero's power is completely undercut, however, by the standard interpretation of the lines describing Beowulf's descent through the water:

> brimwylm onfeng
> hilderince.   Ða wæs hwil dæges,
> ær he þone grundwong   ongytan mehte.
>   (1494–96)

The surging water closed over the warrior. Then it was *the space of a day* before he could see the bottom of the mere.

This is the sense supplied by early editors and translators. Later editors, apparently embarrassed by the hero's holding his breath and swimming downward for an entire day, endeavour to reduce the time spent sinking to the bottom: *hwil dæges,* says Klaeber (186), means "'a good part of the day,' not 'the space of a day,'" and most modern scholars have agreed.

But it is strange that there is no mention elsewhere of the hero's fantastic ability to travel underwater for hours on end, and stranger still that the poet proceeds immediately to contradict himself by depicting the distance from the surface of the mere to the bottom not as a day's journey but as a very short space. For in lines 1588 and following, when

Beowulf beheads the monster, spilling his blood into the water, we are
told that men standing above the mere immediately (*sona*) see the gore
churn up to the top:

> Hra wide sprong,
> syþðan he . . .
> hine þa heafde becearf.
> Sona þæt gesawon   snottre ceorlas,
> þa ðe mid Hroðgare   on holm wliton,
> þæt wæs yðgeblond   eal gemenged,
> brim blode fah.   (1588–94)

[The corpse sprang far, after he . . . cut off his head. Immediately the
wise men who, with Hrothgar, were staring at the water saw that the
surging waves were all mingled, the water discolored with blood.—
P.S.B.]

And the hero's own ascent to the shore seems a matter of moments
(1618–24) rather than a day's journey. Such apparent inconsistencies
certainly justify R.W. Chambers' exasperation: "We may render this
phrase [i.e., *hwil dæges*] either 'a large part of the day' or 'the space of a
day,' as we will . . . unreason like this is possible in *Beowulf,* though one
wonders how so farfetched an idea ever occurred to anybody."[9]

But is the farfetched idea really in the text, or is it only in the minds
of the commentators? *Hwil dæges,* I believe, does not mean either "the
space of a day" or "the large part of a day" but simply "daytime," and all
the poet is saying is that by the time Beowulf reached the bottom of the
mere it was already daylight. S.O. Andrew suggested this interpretation
briefly in his *Postscript on "Beowulf"* (Cambridge, 1948, 99), but E.V.K.
Dobbie dismissed the idea without argument,[10] and so far as I am aware
it has never been advocated since. An examination of the phrase *dæges
hwil* in its occurrences throughout Old English poetry, however, suggests that Andrew was almost certainly correct:

> þa wæs on þam ofne,   þær se engel becwom,
> windig and wynsum,   wedere gelicost
> þonne hit on sumeres tid   sended weorðeð
> dropena drearung   on dæges hwile,
> wearmlic wolcna scur.   (*Daniel* 345–49)

Then, when the angel came, it was airy and pleasant in the furnace,
most like the weather in summer, when the dropping of rain, the
warm shower from the clouds, is sent in the daytime.

> . . . þonne on sumeres tid   sended weorðe
> dropena dreorung   mid dæges hwile.
> (*Azarias* 63–64)

[From the same context as *Daniel* 345–49] . . . when the dropping of
the rain is sent during the daytime.

> hord eft gesceat,
> dryhtsele dyrnne ær dæges hwile.
>
> (*Beowulf* 2319–20)

He [i.e., the dragon, who flies only at night] returned to his hoard, his
secret dwelling, before daylight.[11]

A parallel phrase is used in the poet's statement indicating that the
dragon flies by night:

> lyftwynne heold
> nihtes hwilum   (*Beowulf* 3043–44)

he held sway in the joyous air by night.

The manifest meaning of the phrase *dæges hwil* (and *nihtes hwil*) in
these passages would seem to indicate that the only reasonable interpretation of *Beowulf* 1495–96 is "Then it was daytime before he could get
to the bottom." This reading not only preserves the human dimensions
of the hero but also conforms with the poet's carefully marked time-
sequence throughout the episode. Grendel's mother raids the hall at
night, and Hrothgar is notified immediately (1279–1309). Beowulf is
summoned, and he reaches Hrothgar's chamber *samod ærdæge* (1311)—
that is, in the early hours of the morning before daybreak.[12] It is growing
light as the warriors proceed toward the mere, for they are able to see the
bloody track of the ogress over the moor (1402–04). In 1495 the poet says
it was broad daylight (*hwil dæges*) when Beowulf plunged to the bottom
of the lake. The struggle is arduous, and the Danes seem to wait a long
time before giving up their watch at *non dæges,* that is, at mid-afternoon
(1600). It is just then, however, that Beowulf overcomes the hag and
beheads Grendel. He swims quickly to the top of the mere, rejoins his
comrades, and they repair to the Danish hall, where Beowulf's triumph
is celebrated until night falls and the banquet ends (1789–90). The poet's
marking of the passage of time is exceptionally clear—

1311–12	Samod ærdæge / eode eorla sum . . .
1495	Ða wæs hwil dæges . . .
1600	Ða cwom non dæges . . .
1789–90	Nihthelm geswearc / deorc ofer dryhtgumum . . .

—provided we understand *hwil dæges* to mean "daytime" and not "the
space of a day" or "the large part of a day."

The contextual relevance of the statement that it is daylight when
Beowulf reaches the bottom of the mere is made clear by the ensuing
clause in 1497–1500. Indeed, if we assign to *þa* in 1495b the sense "as"

(which it seems to have in *Beowulf* 201, 723, 967, 1103, 1621, 2550, 2676, etc.), we may read the two clauses as one long sentence: "As it was daytime before he [Beowulf] could get to the bottom, the grim and ravenous one who, furiously greedy, had guarded the watery region for fifty years immediately perceived that some man was exploring the alien creatures' domain from above." The fact that it was now daytime explains why the ogress detected Beowulf's presence so quickly.[13]

Once these factors are all taken into account, the meaning "daytime" rather than "space of a day" seems so inevitable that one wonders what could have given rise and longevity to the erroneous interpretation. The answer, I suspect, is implied in the comment with which Klaeber annotates the passage:

> 1495. hwil dæges, "a good part of the day," . . . A long time is required
> for the same purpose in several corresponding folk-tales, see Panzer
> 119.[14]

Panzer does indeed provide examples of such descents requiring twenty-one days, a year, and even three years. But neither here nor in other parts of *Beowulf,* so far as I am aware, does the poet show himself to be such a slave to folktale sources that he cannot alter an inappropriate detail when he wishes. I suspect that it is not so much his judgment as the judgment of modern scholars which has been overmastered by the folktale sources.

THE RETURN FROM FRISIA

Lines 2359b–68 of *Beowulf* are generally supposed to tell the story of an astounding *geste* performed by the hero after Hygelac's defeat in Frisia:

> Þonan Biowulf com
> sylfes cræfte, sundnytte dreah;
> hæfde him on earme (ana) þritig
> hildegeatwa, þa he to holme (st)ag . . .
> Oferswam ða sioleða bigong sunu Ecgðeowes,
> earm anhaga eft to leodum.

R.K. Gordon, who fairly represents all the translations of this passage which I have seen, renders the lines, "Beowulf came thence by his own strength; swam over the sea. Alone he held on his arm thirty suits of armour when he set out on the sea . . . The son of Ecgtheow swam over the stretch of the gulfs, the hapless solitary man back to his people."[15]

Several years ago I published a study of this passage in which I argued that the actual words of the manuscript (before editorial intercession) say less than has been generally assumed. In particular I was concerned to show that there is no clear statement that Beowulf held thirty suits of armour on his arm when he set out or that he leapt into the sea with whatever it is that he *was* holding in his arm. The most that can be gathered from the transmitted text, I suggested, is that he was in possession of an unspecified amount of war-gear when he left the field of battle.[16] Recently Karl P. Wentersdorf has carried this analysis further, arguing that not only is there no basis for assuming that Beowulf swam to Geatland with thirty suits of armour; indeed, there is no evidence that he swam anywhere at this time.[17] The unique phrase *sundnytte dreah,* he points out, can be pressed into no more specific meaning than "he made the sea trip,"[18] and the verb *oferswimman* clearly did not have the meaning "swim over," as a speaker of Modern English would expect, but meant to pass over the water by any one of various possible means of locomotion. This broad semantic range of Old English *swimman* is recognized in the standard dictionaries and is amply illustrated in Bosworth-Toller, *Dictionary* and *Supplement.* Among documentations of the verb referring to a ship's movement through the water, a particularly clear specimen is that in Vercelli Homily XIX, which is not represented in the dictionaries:

> þa sona swa þa men þe on þam scipe wæron ut on þære sæs dypan gesegled hæfdon, þa onsende God mycelne ren 7 strangne wind 7 grimme yste on þa sæ, swa þæt þæt scip ne mihte naþer ne forð swymman ne underbæc . . .[19]

> [then as soon as the men who were on the ship had sailed out upon the deep of the sea, God sent a great rain and strong wind and fierce tempest onto the sea, so that the ship could sail neither forward nor backward . . . —P.S.B.]

A conflation of Wentersdorf's conclusions with my own would yield this interpretation of the verses quoted above: "From there [i.e., from the battle] came Beowulf by means of his own physical strength— undertook a journey on the sea. He had held battle-gear[20] on his arm when he moved toward the sea . . . Then, alone and wretched, the son of Ecgtheow crossed the expanse of the ocean, returning to his own people." This cautious translation is better founded, I believe, than previous ones based on the old editorial reconstructions and ad hoc interpretations of word-meanings. There is nothing in this translation about fantastic swimming feats, it will be noted, although there is no dearth of them in Panzer's collection of parallels (262–70).[21]

❧ The Swimming Feat with Breca

The story of Beowulf's exploit with Breca differs in kind from the two events discussed above. It does not take place in the poem's present time but is reported as something which occurred years earlier. This temporal distance gives the adventure a slightly different valence from that of the central narrative actions, one linking it as much with the remembered deeds of Hrethel, Heremod, and Scyld Scefing as with those of the mature Beowulf.[22] In another sense too the Breca episode is different: it never comes to us with the direct authority of the poet's own voice but is reported in two contrasting versions by characters within the poem—first by Unferth after he had drunk deep of the beer and wine (531, 1467) and then by the indignant Beowulf. Either the hostile circumstances of the telling or the temporal remoteness of the events described leads to a curious inconsistency and vagueness in the reports. Beowulf's counter-version plays down certain aspects of Unferth's initial account. He and Breca were together on the sea for five, not seven nights; they wore protective arms, and although the winds were cold, Beowulf does not say it was winter. Also, whereas Unferth makes it appear that the two contestants set out swimming ("eagorstream   earmum þehton . . . mundum brugdon"), Beowulf uses the verbs *rowan* ("to go by water, row, sail"),[23] and *fleotan* ("to float, drift, flow, sail").[24] (The only other occurrence of *fleotan* in the poem clearly has the meaning "sail": "fleat famigheals   forð ofer yðe," 1909). It is only during the last night of the Breca episode that Beowulf describes himself as actually being in the water (553 ff.), and that is when he grapples with the *merefixas*. But even here the possibility of a raft or boat being present cannot be completely ruled out, although I consider this unlikely.[25] The setting is also somewhat unclear in Beowulf's account. Usually he agrees with Unferth in locating the action on the open sea, but in line 568 he indicates that the monsters he fought were denizens of the fords.[26] Perhaps there is a rationale for these variations: Unferth exaggerates the dimensions of the episode in order to emphasize Beowulf's foolhardiness in undertaking it, and so Beowulf, in rebuttal, represents it as a somewhat less prodigious undertaking. But whatever the reason, Beowulf's version, which, I presume, we are expected to credit more seriously than we are Unferth's, presents the events of the swimming feat in terms less imposing and more noncommittal than is the case with Unferth's jeering account.[27]

However problematical these details may be, such local probings ignore the great overriding uncertainty of the Breca episode—the mystery as to who Unferth is and what is the nature of the entire exchange between Beowulf and the *þyle*. It is this enigmatic quality of the "Unferth Intermezzo" that leaves scholars undecided as to whether the tale of Beowulf and Breca should be interpreted as sober history, a boisterous flyting, or "whopping lies."[28] Therefore, in the remaining pages of this paper I shall turn to the problem of Unferth, trying to determine afresh what we know and do not know about his character and how we are to interpret the story which his report introduces into the poem.

Although interpretations of Unferth's character have been richly diverse, in general they fall into two broad categories, those which conceive of the *þyle* as a serious and powerful figure and those which see him as essentially a source of diversion or an object of ridicule in the Danish court.[29] Critics who view him as serious or sinister usually assume that the contest with Breca is to be taken more or less at face value. Those who view him as playing a lighter role often interpret the tale of the Breca swim as an exaggeration or a joke. Neither view has been firmly established or is like to be. Quite possibly the *þyle* represented for the audience of the poem some social role involving a combination of grave and playful elements which is now beyond our ken, the institution itself having eluded precise record. Recently, however, it seems to me that increasing evidence has come to light which gives support to the less serious interpretations of Unferth and weakens the case for the sombre readings. I shall review and supplement that evidence here.

Most critics have assumed that the designation *þyle* marks Unferth as holder of the solemn office of king's spokesman or counsellor, but the entry for *þyle* in Bosworth-Toller, *Dictionary,* points out that the gloss *ðelum* to *scurris* suggests rather that "his [Unferth's] function was something like that of the later court jester, and the style of his attack on Beowulf hardly contradicts the supposition."[30] Recent studies have added force to this suggestion.[31] Another fundamental datum for the advocates of a serious Unferth is his sinister name, for if we assume a certain amount of distortion in the letters and sounds, it can be construed as *Unfrið,* "discord, un-peace."[32] But, as I have suggested elsewhere,[33] the meaning of the name in its attested form without distortion has at least as much to recommend it: *un-ferð* to the unbiased eye would seem to mean "unintelligence" or "folly" rather than "discord." (Cf. *leasferhð(nes)* ["levity, folly"], *ungemynd* ["distraction or confusion of mind"], *ungewitt* ["folly"], *ungeræd* ["folly"], *unræd* ["folly"].) Unferth's name and his official title point at least as much in the direction of a jeering, risible performer as they do of a serious one.

But is such a role consonant with the motivation which the poet gives for Unferth's railing attack?

wæs him Beowulfes sið,
modges merefaran,   micel æfþunca,
forþon þe he ne uþe,   þæt ænig oðer man
æfre mærða þon ma   middangeardes
gehede under heofenum   þonne he sylfa.

(501–05)

Surely this clear statement justifies Bonjour's inference that Unferth is
"jealous of his own glory" and that only a man "of his prominent
position," "a distinguished and glorious thane," would harbour such
concern for his martial reputation?[34] So it would seem, but the cited
passage will bear scrutiny before the point is granted. As quoted, the
passage says that Unferth was unwilling to admit that "any other man on
earth should perform glorious deeds." But this meaning is achieved only
by means of an emendation of the verb *gehedde* to *gehede*, which is then
interpreted as preterite subjunctive of *gehegan* and assigned the unique
meaning "to perform (deeds)." Elsewhere in Old English the verb
always occurs with *þing, seonoð, spræc,* or *mæðel* as its direct object and
means "to hold (a meeting)." Left in its original manuscript form,
gehedde would be preterite of *gehedan* ("heed, care for") (see Klaeber's
glossary s.v. *hēdan*). If the sentence is read this way, then Unferth
emerges as a character with a most unheroic, Falstaffian attitude toward
heroic deeds: he did not want to grant that other men cared for glory or
for deeds of glory (*mærða*) any more than he himself did. This is not an
inappropriate sentiment for a man who, the poet later tells us, willingly
"forlcas ellenmærðum" (1470–71). Perhaps there is more than a little of
the swaggering coward in Unferth, and the speech reminding Beowulf
of a past failure is motivated by a desire to scare the hero out of his
commitment to face Grendel. If the speech is successful, then Unferth
will have shown the Danes that he is not alone in his distaste for derring-
do. Thus Unferth may very well be what Klaeber (lxii) long ago said he
was: "that singular personality of the 'Thersites' order."

The accusation of fratricide (587 ff., 1167 ff.) has widely, though not
universally, been taken as a charge of cowardice against Unferth, and it
is this interpretation that consorts best with the reading *gehedde* just
advocated. Unferth was such a craven that he would not even fulfil the
thane's duty to fight alongside his closest kin when they were in desperate straits. But if this is so, how are we to justify the vehemence and
gravity of Beowulf's statement, "þæs þu in helle scealt / werhðo
dreogan"? More than one critic has been troubled by the apparent
excessiveness of this dark curse. Chambers suggested that Beowulf's
taunt may be merely a "countercheck quarrelsome" to the abusive *þyle*.[35]

Charles Donahue says, "It is unlikely that Beowulf is referring here to a Christian *infernum*" since the hero who is elsewhere characterized as a pious pagan could hardly have knowledge of damnation in Christian terms.[36] He translates *helle* as "in the [pagan Germanic] realm of the dead." Donahue's point is well taken, and his translation, which mollifies Beowulf's taunt considerably, may be right.

Before interpreting the text, however, it is instructive once again to look at the words as they appear, or do not appear, in the manuscript. An examination of the facsimiles of Cotton Vitellius A. xv will show no trace of a word *helle* in the manuscript, and the commentaries of Zupitza and Malone confirm that the only vestige of a word at this point is a final -*e*, which is now covered by the leaf binding. Modern editors have inserted the word *helle* solely on the authority of the Thorkelin transcripts, and these too merit scrutiny. Looking at Thorkelin's own copy (Thorkelin B), we find that the word *helle* has been inserted "on an original blank in another ink."[37] Evidently Thorkelin was unable to make out anything in the manuscript at this point and so left the space blank; later, he must have copied the word from Transcript A into his own transcription. It is likely, then, that Thorkelin A constitutes the sole authority for this reading.

The testimony of Thorkelin's copyist is not to be treated lightly, of course, and yet this is a peculiarly delicate case. Except for the covered -*e*, there is no sign of a word *helle* in the manuscript today, and when Thorkelin examined the manuscript there was not enough there for him to make anything out. Surely the copyist, whose transcript preceded Thorkelin's "by a few months or weeks only,"[38] must have based his reading *helle* on manuscript evidence which was already quite deteriorated. Considering how much difficulty the copyist had in transcribing accurately even those words which are perfectly clear in the manuscript today (especially in the first part of the poem where he was struggling with an unfamiliar script), we might reasonably think of his *helle* as little more than a game try at reconstructing lost characters from the vestiges which he descried at the crumbling edge of the folio leaf.

One of the chronic errors in A's transcription is the adding or omitting of letters in a diphthong. Only four words after the moot *helle* he writes *þeaeh* for the manuscript reading *þeah*. Conversely, he writes *halle* for *healle* in line 89 and *hald* for *heald* in line 2247. He sometimes miswrites the *ea* diphthong as *e*, as in *bedwa* for *beadwa* (709) and *begas* for *beagas* (3105), and he starts to write *þelhþeon* for *wealhþeon* (629) but "corrects" this to *þealhþeon*. In the light of this latter tendency and of his earlier misreading of the diphthong in *healle*, I conceive the disturbing possibility that the original word was *healle* rather than *helle* in line 588, in which case the passage would read "þæs þu in healle scealt / werhðo dreogan": "for that you must endure condemnation in the hall." It is not my concern here to promote this reading, although some might find it preferable on several counts to the *helle* of the transcripts. I want only to illustrate the tenuity of the hitherto unquestioned *helle,* which has been thought to introduce such seriousness into Beowulf's retort to Unferth.[39]

How then are we to interpret Unferth's character? If pressed insistently for an opinion, I would say that he seems to be a blustering, mean-spirited coward who does not enjoy the respect of his comrades[40] and who seeks to bolster his self-esteem by decrying Beowulf's past performance and present qualifications. Beowulf imperturbably answers his hostile jibes, first by giving a more modest and convincing version of the boyhood experience which Unferth recounted and then by alluding pointedly to the cowardice of the *þyle* and to his deficient *wit, hige,* and *sefa* (589–94). The Danes are amused and impressed by the hero's perceptiveness in seeing Unferth for what he is, and they rejoice that such a resourceful champion is prepared to assist them (607–11: "Ða wæs on salum   sinces brytta . . . Ðær wæs hæleþa hleahtor"). Unferth resumes his accustomed state of disesteem in Heorot. But as the narrative progresses, Beowulf gradually regenerates the worthless Unferth into a man of some dignity and value in the court (an act of generosity which has been remarked by more than one student of the poem). By allowing Unferth to supply the sword needed for his second fight, the hero imparts a measure of reflected glory to the lesser man, whose pusillanimity nonetheless stands in effective contrast to the valour of Beowulf. Later, when he refuses to blame Hrunting for its failure and returns it to Unferth ceremoniously and with high praise (1659–60, 1807–12), Beowulf confers the most dignity he can upon the *þyle,* who is no longer called *Unferth,* but only *sunu Ecglafes.*[41]

This hypothesis as to what Unferth's character and his relation to Beowulf may be would accord with my reading of the Breca-tale as a semi-serious affair and also has a certain inner consistency. Moreover, the relation I suggest here between hero and poltroon is much like that described in another narrative of the Danish court in Hrothgar's time—the *Hrolfs saga kraka,* chapter 23. There we are told that the royal house at Leire is plagued by a nocturnal monster, and when the bear-like hero Boðvarr Bjarki arrives on the scene prior to doing battle with the monster, he encounters the despised coward Hottr. Boðvarr treats Hottr roughly, but eventually, in the course of purging the Danish court of the monster, he regenerates the coward, just as Beowulf regenerated Unferth. In an incident involving the lending of a sword called *Gullinhjalti* (which scholars have noted is cognate with the *gylden hilt* of *Beowulf* 1677), Boðvarr contrives to gain some esteem for Hottr from the monster-slaying, and the erstwhile buffoon gains a new reputation and a new name. Conceivably we have here a remote echo of the interplay between Beowulf and Unferth.

The characterization of Hottr in the saga demonstrates that a Germanic author could conceive of a relation such as I have suggested for Beowulf and Unferth, but it should be apparent from the sceptical treatment which I have given to analogues in the first part of this paper that I would be unwilling to regard the parallel as probative evidence of the Old English poet's intentions. Indeed, as I have said before, I find the data insufficient to warrant any definitive interpretation of Unferth. He may be, as some have thought, a serious, sinister character, but the evidence for this is weak, and it is at least as likely that he is a kind of jester, as Bosworth-Toller suggests, or that he is a fellow of low reputation in the court like Hottr in the saga. Given the uncertainty as to his character, it is impossible to argue with much conviction from the evidence of the swimming-tale which he introduces into the poem. It is conceivable that the Breca story is serious, but it could also be a wild yarn spun by the envious *þyle,* or a flyting, or Unferth's effort to start a lying match.

The undue importance which has been accorded the Breca episode in the past is in part a legacy of the early mythologizing critics like Müllenhof and Sarrazin, who viewed the swimming feat as a slightly veiled *Naturmythus* and hence thought it comparable in importance to the dragon fight and the contests with the Grendel kin.[42] The predisposition to see the Breca adventure as much bigger than life may have been nurtured by Panzer's carefully collected saga-parallels. Troubling aspects of the Unferth episode as a whole could always be shrugged off with the explanation that "they must be looked upon as an inheritance from the older legends which had come down from a ruder age,"[43] and this attitude may have discouraged close scrutiny of the textual mainstays of the received interpretation—such as the name and office of Unferth as well as his motivation, the precise terms in which Beowulf describes his own feat, and the manuscript evidence for his threat of hell in his retort. If the earlier interpretation of these matters have not been replaced here with indubitably surer and superior ones, I believe they have at least been shown to be less certain than scholars had previously assumed. If so, this must qualify one's interpretation of the evidence for astounding feats in the Breca episode, just as the textual realities of lines 1494–96 and 2354–68 must be taken into account in assessing the supposedly marvellous elements earlier in the poem.[44]

NOTES

1. Of course this does not mean that he was ineligible for divine favour. Just as Achilles enjoys the patronage of Athene and Hera, Beowulf occasionally receives the support of a God whom he but little knows or understands. In a Christian view such favour would not set him apart from other men.

2. All quotations from *Beowulf* are from Klaeber's edition, *Beowulf and the Fight at Finnsburg*, 3rd ed. (Boston, 1950), except that I have dispensed with Klaeber's macrons and other diacritics. Quotations from other Old English poems are taken from *The Anglo-Saxon Poetic Records*, ed. G.P. Krapp and E.V.K. Dobbie (New York, 1931–53).

3. "Beowulf's Old Age," in *Philological Essays: Studies in Old and Middle English Language and Literature in Honour of Herbert Dean Meritt*, ed. J.L. Rosier (The Hague, 1970), 55–64.

4. Wiglaf's speech in 2663–68 is a fitting emblem of the poet's tactful merging of Beowulf's pre-eminence with his human limitations:

> Leofa Biowulf, læst eall tela,
> swa ðu on geoguðfeore geara gecwæde,
> þæt ðu ne alæte be ðe lifigendum
> dom gedreosan; scealt nu dædum rof,
> æðeling anhydig, ealle mægene
> feorh ealgian; ic ðe fullæstu.

Invoking the king's youthful boasts as a means of urging him on to a last desperate effort is fine, but best is the lexical play by which Wiglaf emphasizes that even in his own youth he is inferior to the mighty king: only Beowulf can "perform"; Wiglaf can but "supplement the performance" ("læst eall tela . . . ic ðe fullæstu"). Klaeber's note here that "there is a singular lack of propriety in making young Wiglaf administer fatherly advice to Beowulf" seems to me to overlook the studiously respectful tone of the speech.

5. Pope, "Beowulf's Old Age," 60.

6. "*Beowulf* and the Hypostatic Union," *Neophilologus* 52 (1968): 409–16. I disregard a fourth element of the "marvellous" which the authors mention ("his voyage from Geatland to Denmark, although not miraculous, is surrounded by an aura of wonder and majesty") since this is a matter of interpretation. I also disregard here the main concern of the article, which tends toward theological explication. What I have found valuable is the authors' perceptive formulation of the apparently mixed quality of the characterization in the narrative.

7. *Epic and Romance*, 2nd ed. (London, 1908), 175. Cf. Frank Beaumont, "*Beowulf*," *Proceedings of the Royal Philosophical Society of Glasgow* 38 (1906–07): 201–33, especially 210–17.

8. Comparable settings are indicated in Norse analogues, of course; cf. R.W. Chambers, "*Beowulf*": *An Introduction*, 3rd ed. (Cambridge, 1959), 52–53 and 451–85.

9. *Ibid.*, 465.

10. *Anglo-Saxon Poetic Records* 4:196.

11. Dobbie's suggested translation of *dæges hwile* as "a [good] part of the day [had passed]" (196) must have been arrived at without reference to the passages here cited from *Daniel* and *Azarias* and in the hope of offering some support for the traditional interpretation of 1495b in *Beowulf.* All the translations I have consulted agree in rendering *Beowulf* 2320b "before daytime / the time of day / daybreak / daylight / dawn" rather than "before a [good] part of the day [had passed]."

12. *ærdæg* appears to be equivalent to *uhta* (Beowulf 126: "on uhtan mid ærdæge"; cf. *Andreas* 235, 1388; *Elene* 105) and both words are used to translate Latin *matutinus.* In the Cleopatra Glossary appears the explanation "Matutinum, uhttid, siue beforan dæge" (Thomas Wright, *Anglo-Saxon and Old English Vocabularies,* 2nd ed. by Richard Paul Wülcker [London, 1884], 450:3). Cf. F. Tupper, *Anglo-Saxon Dæg-mæl* (Baltimore, 1895), 37. The phrase *somod ærdæge* occurs again at *Beowulf* 2942, referring, presumably, to the pre-dawn hour at which Hygelac's troops arrived and saved the Geatish raiding party from being destroyed by the Swedes *on mergenne* (2929).

13. See S.O. Andrew, *Postscript on "Beowulf"* (Cambridge, 1948), 11–12 and now (1992) Bruce Mitchell, *Old English Syntax* (Oxford, 1985), 2:255.

14. Friedrich Panzer, *Studien zur germanischen Sagengeschichte,* 1, *Beowulf* (Munich, 1910).

15. *Anglo-Saxon Poetry,* selected and trans. R.K. Gordon (London, 1954), 47.

16. "Beowulf's Retreat from Frisia: Some Textual Problems in Ll. 2361–2362," *Studies in Philology* 62 (1965): 1–16.

17. Wentersdorf, "Beowulf's Withdrawal from Frisia: A Reconsideration," *Studies in Philology* 68 (1971): 395–415.

18. *Ibid.,* 402–03. That *sund* in *sundnytt* means "sea" rather than "swimming" seems to me particularly likely when we note that in every other nominal compound with *sund-* attested in the poetic corpus (*sundbuend, sundgebland, sundhelm, sundhengest, sundplega, sundreced, sundwudu*) the first element means "sea" and not "swimming." Further, in the other two Old English nominal compounds with *nytt,* the first element is in both cases a noun denoting the location of the act, not an abstract noun of means: *cyricnytt, weoroldnytt. Sundnytt,* then, would appear to mean "use of the sea" and the poetic phrase *sundnytte dreah* "he made use of the sea" or, as Wentersdorf suggests, "he made the sea trip."

19. Paul E. Szarmach, "Three Versions of the Jonah Story: An Investigation of Narrative Technique in Old English Homilies," *Anglo-Saxon England* 1 (1972): 186. The use of "swim" to refer to the progress of a boat over the water continues in Middle and early Modern English. (See Wentersdorf, "Beowulf's Withdrawal," 403–07.) Shakespeare uses the word in this sense in *Julius Caesar* 5.1.67, and in *As You Like It* 4.1.40 ("you have swam in a gondola").

20. As I point out in "Beowulf's Retreat from Frisia," the customary translation of *hildegeatwe* as "suits of armour" and the emendation *ana* are incorrect, and the numeral XXX is not to be trusted. See especially 2–7.

21. Wentersdorf's linguistic critique, to which I have referred here, is but a part of his argument. His article subsequently explores analogues in Old English and cognate literatures which suggest that the *Beowulf* poet probably conceived of his hero as making his way from Frisia through the Skagerrak by ship.

22. This may seem a shadowy distinction, but I believe it is a real one. Many readers would have been troubled, for example, if the author had introduced giants and the fabulous Weland as royal smiths at Hygelac's court, but it does not seem unfitting that Beowulf's heirloom armour is "Hrædlan laf, Welandes geweorc," or that he wields an ancient sword called "the work of giants" (1558, 1562, 1690, etc.; cf. 2616, 2979). So long as they do not intrude into the poem's present time such fabulous elements seem to leave undispelled our sense that the characters are human beings.

23. C.L. Wrenn, in his edition of the poem (195), notes that "*Rowan* 'swim' does not occur *in that sense* in poetry outside *Beowulf.*" In his glossary he defines the word "*row,* hence *swim.*"

24. Bosworth-Toller, *Supplement,* records two prose occurrences of *fleotend* used specifically to modify *fisc* in the formula "fleotende fixas and fleogende fugelas," but there are no instances of the word being used to describe men swimming.

25. The earliest editor of the poem conceived that a vessel was present in the adventure—not through one of his many misunderstandings of the text but through retention of the manuscript reading *wudu weallendu* in 581, which he translates "*lignis spumantibus.*" See G.J. Thorkelin, *De Danorum rebus gestis . . .* (Havni, 1815), 46. Julius Zupitza ("*Beowulf" Reproduced in Facsimile from the Unique Manuscript, British Museum MS. Cotton Vitellius A. xv.,* 2nd ed., EETS os 245 [London, 1959], note to 581) says, "*wudu* not *wadu* without the least doubt; an *a* open at the top does not occur so late in English MSS." Subsequent editors uniformly emend to *wadu weallendu* in order to bring the line into conformity with 546a, although the formula occurs nowhere else. Syntactical considerations and the similarity of phrases like *brim weallendu* (*Beowulf* 847) seem to me to argue strongly for the traditional emendation *wadu.* But it should not be forgotten that it is an emendation.

26. Alistair Campbell, "The Use in *Beowulf* of Earlier Heroic Verse," in *England before the Conquest: Studies in Primary Sources Presented to Dorothy Whitelock,* ed. Peter Clemoes and Kathleen Hughes (Cambridge, 1971), 284, calls attention to the odd appearance of *ford* in this context and questions whether it should be emended to *flod.* Campbell also remarks the odd application of *rowan* ("row") to swimmers. Unferth (512) as well as Beowulf uses *rowan* in describing the feat.

27. Beowulf's only heightening of the details of the episode would seem to be his introduction of the sea-monsters, and such prodigies, as we have seen, are a given in the poet's portrayal of the hero's adversaries. A further departure from Unferth's account, one which I have not mentioned above, is Beowulf's statement in 541-3 that he would not swim far from Breca, nor could Breca swim far from him. Prevailing opinion has it that this is an explicit contradiction of Unferth's statement that the adventure began as a race. Possibly, but there is a simpler explanation: perhaps the gallant hero intended to remain close to the weaker Breca until they were near their goal, at which time he would outstrip him and win the race without ever being beyond call if his companion should need help. Once again, the cryptic mode of the narrative here does not permit certainties.

28. The last phrase is that of Norman E. Eliason, "The Þyle and Scop in *Beowulf,*" *Speculum* 38 (1963): 272. This article is a valuable and provocative re-examination of the entire question of Unferth's character.

29. It is generally agreed, of course, that Unferth serves an important purpose within the economy of the poem in that he tests the hero at a crucial point in the narrative. This function is served whether he is a statesman or a poltroon.

30. The gloss occurs in the Cleopatra Glossary as "de scurris · hof ðelum." I agree with Bosworth-Toller that *hof* represents *of* (with inorganic *h-*) rendering Latin *de*. The association of *scurra* and *þyle* in Old English are expertly treated in James L. Rosier's "Design for Treachery: The Unferth Intrigue," *PMLA* 77 (1962): 1–3.

31. See especially the articles by Rosier and Eliason.

32. The most persuasive and influential statement of this view is that of Morton W. Bloomfield, "*Beowulf* and Christian Allegory: An Interpretation of Unferth," *Traditio* 7 (1949–51): 410–15.

33. "Personal Names in Medieval Narrative and the Name of Unferth in *Beowulf,*" in *Essays in Honor of Richebourg Gaillard McWilliams,* ed. Howard Creed (Birmingham, Ala., 1970), 43–48.

34. Adrien Bonjour, *The Digressions in "Beowulf"* (Oxford, 1950), 17–22. See further the important modifications of Bonjour's analysis in his *Twelve "Beowulf" Papers* (Neuchatel, 1962), 129–33.

35. Chambers, *"Beowulf": An Introduction,* 28.

36. "*Beowulf* and Christian Tradition: A Reconsideration from a Celtic Stance," *Traditio* 21 (1965): 92.

37. Zupitza, 29.

38. *The Thorkelin Transcripts of "Beowulf" in Facsimile,* ed. Kemp Malone, Early English Manuscripts in Facsimile no. 1 (Copenhagen, 1951), 4. But see now (1992) Kevin S. Kiernan, *The Thorkelin Transcripts of "Beowulf,"* Anglistica no. 25 (Copenhagen, 1986), esp. 29–30.

39. A.G. Brodeur, *The Art of "Beowulf"* (Berkeley, 1959), 155, speaks for many when he observes that "no one can . . . ignore the weight of Beowulf's assertion that the penalty Unferth must pay for his brothers' death is damnation in hell."

40. The statement in 1165–66 that the men in the hall trusted in Unferth's *ferhþ* (probably a pun on his name) and *mod* means, I take it, that in the joyous atmosphere of the victory celebration good will was extended to even the meanest of the company. The statement is preceded by the allusion to the temporary good will between Hrothulf and Hrothgar and followed by the reminder that Unferth had failed his brothers *æt ecga gelacum.*

41. Whether it was the Danish courtiers who conferred the demeaning name *Unferth* on the *þyle* or whether he acquired it elsewhere cannot be determined from the text. It is to be noted that Beowulf's sympathetic concern for rehabilitating Unferth takes on special poignancy when we recall that the hero himself was once held in low esteem by his fellow men (2183 ff.).

42. See W.W. Lawrence, *"Beowulf" and Epic Tradition* (Cambridge, Mass., 1928), 151–52. Cf. Klaeber, *Beowulf,* 147 n. 2.

43. Lawrence, *"Beowulf" and Epic Tradition,* 153.

44. I wish to thank Professors Stanley B. Greenfield and Edward B. Irving, Jr., for reading this essay and offering suggestions for improvement.

INDEX OF TEXTUAL INTERPRETATIONS

The Authenticating Voice in *Beowulf*

by STANLEY B. GREENFIELD

This essay first appeared in Anglo-Saxon England *5 (1976): 51–62. Translations in square brackets have been supplied by the editor.*

TWO major concerns of recent *Beowulf* criticism have been (1) to establish the extent to which the poet used his pagan heroic narrative to shadow forth Christian meaning and (2) to establish the exact attitude of the poet towards his hero and towards the social institutions and *mores* of his hero's day—which, as we know, was several centuries before the poet's own.[1] A nexus of such considerations has been the last word of the poem, *lofgeornost*: in the concluding lines the poet reports that the mourning Geats said that

> ... he wære wyruldcyning[a]
> manna mildust ond mon(ðw)ærust,
> leodum liðost ond lofgeornost.   (3180–82)[2]

[... of all earthly kings he was the mildest of men and the gentlest, the kindest to his people and the most eager for praise.]

There have been arguments on the basis of other contextual uses of *lofgeorn* that this word for "most eager for praise" must have an unfavourable connotation here in *Beowulf* and hence carry the implication of a moral flaw in the hero, though these arguments have not, in my opinion, been convincing.[3] But even if we accept a favourable connotation in this instance, since Beowulf's warriors would hardly be speaking ill of their fallen chieftain during his funeral rites, we still have the problem of deciding whether the poet himself was being sympathetic towards the warriors' view, or whether he was taking an ironic stance or attitude towards that praise from his undeniably Christian outlook.

Such concerns about Christian meaning and authorial stance are not unrelated; and even back in 1936, in his important essay on the monsters, J.R.R. Tolkien was not unaware of a distinction to be made between the authorial voice and the sentiments expressed by the poem's characters.[4] This distinction has been considered and explored in various ways since then, and my analysis of what I venture to call "the authenticating voice" is but a continuation of such efforts. It is my hope in some measure to clarify, even if not to resolve, these related issues.[5]

97

I should like to begin by quoting a paragraph from an essay by Paull F. Baum who, twenty-five years after Tolkien's article, felt some uneasiness over the several directions interpretation of the poem had taken:

> One of the "intentions" attributed to the poet is the portrayal of a virtuous pagan who might be said to manifest some of the high qualities inculcated by the new religion [of Christianity] . . . Or perhaps, as Gang conjectures, "*Beowulf,* so far from being a Christianized epic, is an attempt at a sort of secular Saint's Life," as though to prove that the heathen legends contained, latent, "a great deal of sound doctrine and Christian morality." Perhaps; or, since the divine guidance of the world, though prepotent, evidently . . . leaves room for family and dynastic distress . . . the poet's aim might be a warning to his contemporaries, pointing a deadly parallel to the local wars he saw all about him and their inevitable outcome. Or, even more narrowly, he might mean to show that the supernatural forces which threaten mortal man can be overcome—Grendel driven off and finally beheaded, his Mother killed in her hidden haunt, the Dragon tumbled lifeless over the cliff—but the human conflicts, treachery and cowardice against loyalty and bravery, bring ineluctable doom. But if so, the poet has left these inferences to our ingenious interpretation. He was too much the artist to certify a "palpable design."[6]

Baum evidently felt that these different theories about authorial intention—semi-didactic Christian preaching of one sort or another, sociological or political allegory, or moral lesson—were incompatible with each other; but more recent research suggests that this need not be the case. Further, we can question whether interpretation can or should be restricted to a "palpable design"; for the language of the poem—its imagery, its form and even its formulas—can produce legitimate designs that are part of its essence even if they are not part of the poet's conscious literary intention.

But Baum's *caveat* about ingenious interpretations is worth taking to heart, even more so today, some fifteen years and more than 500 critical articles and books later. For since Baum wrote we have been bombarded with suggestions, both ingenious and over-ingenious, about authorial intention and, additionally, about the historical audience's presumed eighth- or ninth-century responses to the poem. These hypotheses in the main follow either from Dorothy Whitelock's important study of the audience of the poem, or from the oral-formulaic investigations of F.P. Magoun, Jr, or from the "historical criticism" of D.W. Robertson, Jr.[7] It is interpretation stemming from the last that has been in the van of critical engagement most recently—the several allegories that have been put forth as the core of meaning in the poem and the various locations of sources for allegorical readings in the liturgy and, particularly, in patristic exegesis. Most such readings and source locations have certainly enriched our understanding of the Anglo-Saxon intellectual and literary milieu, although they have not necessarily, in my opinion, done likewise for our comprehension of Old English poems, especially *Beowulf.* In this regard we may note that even Whitney Bolton, a staunch advocate of allegoresis and of patristic exegesis as a tool for unlocking the Old English *scophord,* has cautioned us, in his revision of Wrenn's edition of *Beowulf,* that no one has as yet provided a consistent reading of the whole poem as a consecutive narrative in the light of his or her particular allegorical model.[8] Perhaps some attention to the "voice" in *Beowulf* may do more than exegesis can to identify the poem's design to man.

A word here about my key term, "authenticating voice." I have arrived at it after several false starts and am moderately happy with it. For, on the one hand, I do not think we can talk about a *persona* in *Beowulf* as we can in reference to later medieval literature. Nor can we, on the other hand, properly talk about the "poet" in the poem, since the heavy use of formulas, even in such phrases as *ic gefrægn* [I learned] and *ic hyrde* [I heard], has the effect of depersonalizing the "I." "Voice," it seems to me, fits the narrative situation of *Beowulf* rather nicely. By the attributive adjective "authenticating" I mean to suggest that the voice not only relates the events it has "heard," but in reporting them validates the way or ways in which it understands and wishes its audience to understand them. The term thus subsumes or embraces both the intentional and affective assumptions of much interpretative criticism.

In what follows, I shall attempt to demonstrate that this authenticating voice responds to the narrative events and characters it presents in four major ways: first, by historicizing or distancing them from its own and its immediate audience's time and way of life; second, contrariwise, by contemporizing them, suggesting a continuity between the past and the present; third, by commenting on the morality involved in the actions of the characters; and fourth, by putting the accidents and eventualities of human existence into a perspective which emphasizes the limitations of human knowledge. Taken together, these responses of the voice should give us some insight into the *Gestalt* of the poem itself.

Emphasis on the pastness, the historicity, of the events of the narrative is rather obvious. The poem begins by calling attention to the "other voices, other rooms" aspect of its presentation:

> Hwæt we Gardena   in geardagum
> þeodcyninga   þrym gefrunon   (1–2)

[Lo, we have heard of the Spear-Danes, of the nation's kings, in days of yore];

and on sixteen other occasions the voice uses the formulaic system *ic gefrægn / ic hyrde* [I learned / I heard] or its variant *mine gefræge* [according to my information] to bring its material into reportorial focus.[9] The variety of circumstances under which it does so is interesting. For one, the voice employs the formula simply to describe explicit narrative action, as when Wiglaf plunders the dragon's hoard on the dying Beowulf's command:

> Ða ic on hlæwe gefrægn   hord reafian,
> eald enta geweorc   anne mannan.   (2773–74)

[Then I learned that one man plundered the hoard, the old work of giants, in the mound.]

For another, it makes a more general, comparative observation upon an action already completed, as in its comment on Beowulf's death at the hands—or rather the teeth—of the dragon:

> Huru þæt on lande   lyt manna ðah
> mægenagendra   mine gefræge,
> þeah ðe he dæda gehwæs   dyrstig wære,
> þæt he wið attorsceaðan   oreðe geræsde.
> (2836–39)

[Indeed, few of the men in that land (according to my information), few of those possessed of strength were good enough (though he was daring in every deed) to rush against the breath of that poisonous foe.]

A third use of the formula occurs in general character reports, again in a comparative way, as in the description of King Offa as "the best of all mankind, *mine gefræge,* between the seas" (1955–56). And a fourth appears in the comparative description of objects, as in that of the splendid neck-ring Wealhtheow gives to Beowulf, "the greatest of neck-rings of those which I have heard about on earth" (1195b–96). This repeated and varied use of the "I have heard" formula suggests something of an antiquarian atmosphere: the story material has moved into the body of things told and been handed down from generation to generation. It is part of the storehouse of memory and literally true, the voice assures us, as action or value from the past.

In other ways, too, the voice dissociates its narrative from its contemporary scene. For example, three times it uses the formula *on þæm dæge þysses lifes,* "on *that* day of this life": twice (lines 197 and 790) to remark on the immense strength of the hero, and the third time (806) to refer to the imminent death of his adversary Grendel, whose "separation from life on that day of this life was destined to be miserable." A somewhat different kind of distancing occurs when mention is made of the hall thane who is to guide Beowulf to his night's repose after he has emerged victorious from his fight with Grendel's mother: the thane is said to have attended to all the hero's needs "such as in *that* time war-journeyers were accustomed to have [cared for]" (1797b–98).

But perhaps the most forceful distancing of the story's action from the time of the poet and his audience occurs at the end of fitt 2 in reference to another custom, the worship of the *gastbana* [soul-slayer] in heathen temples by the Danes in their distress (178b ff.): "Such was their custom, the hope of heathens; they remembered hell in their hearts, they did not know God, the judge of deeds . . ." Indeed, this reference and the relatively high concentration of Christian references in the prologue and first two fitts as compared with the rest of the poem has led Hakon Ringbom, in his book on the narrative techniques of the poem, to postulate that the poet was deliberately distancing his narrative in consideration of its heathen nature, as an attempt "to establish beyond doubt his true Christian faith."[10] This may well have been part of the poet's intention, but Ringbom is so obsessed with this idea of the "poet's awareness of the time factor, and his wish to stress temporal differences," that he even sees another repeated formula, *swa nu gyt deð* [as it still does now], as indicating "the contrast between fictional past and actual present" or "between the past of paganism and the present of Christianity."[11] Surely, this particular formula rather *merges* time past with time present and authenticates the relevance of those events of an heroic age for the poet's and his audience's own time. Let us look, therefore, at this contemporizing effect in the voice's presentation, an effect that complements the historicizing one.

The distancing of past from present, as we have just seen, is concerned with customs, literal actions or comparative observations about objects or human behaviour. The merging of past and present, on the other hand, operates in a somewhat different realm, in statements concerning control over the actions of men and the operation of the seasons. These statements make an interesting pattern in the poem as a whole and are worth closer observation.

Just before the hero's fight with Grendel, after explaining that none of the Geats expected ever to see his homeland again, the voice says, "But the Lord granted [them] success, comfort and help, so that they all overcame their foe through the strength and might of one man only"; and it immediately adds

Soð is gecyþed,
þæt mihtig God   manna cynnes
weold wideferhð.   (700b–02a)

[The truth is made manifest that mighty God has forever ruled
mankind.]

A second appearance of this God-ever-governs-mankind topos, indica-
tive of the very same attitude, comes after the fight with Grendel, when
Hrothgar pays wergild for the Geat slain by the monster, "as he
[Grendel] would have [slain] more of them,"

nefne him witig God   wyrd forstode
ond ðæs mannes mod.   Metod eallum weold
gumena cynnes,   swa he nu git deð.   (1056–58)

[had not wise God and that man's courage hindered fate. God ruled
all of the race of men, as he still does now.]

A third, slightly different appearance of the topos, but one which also
utilizes the *swa nu gyt deð* formula, occurs shortly thereafter in the
account of the Finn Episode; it refers to nature's renewal of itself by
unlocking the icy bonds of winter—

winter yþe beleac
isgebinde,   oþ ðæt oþer com
gear in geardas,—   swa nu gyt deð   (1132b–34)

[winter locked the waves in an icy bond, until the next year came to
men's dwellings, as it still does now]—

an unlocking that leads ironically, as Robert B. Burlin has recently
observed, to the bloody resolution wherein Hengest avenges Hnæf's
death.[12] Closely related to this expression of seasonal continuity from
past to present times, and linking it directly to the "God rules mankind"
idea by the *wealdan* formula, is the description at the end of Beowulf's
fight with Grendel's mother, when the sword melted "most like to ice,
when the Father releases the bond of frost, unbinds the water-fetters,"

se geweald hafað
sæla ond mæla: þæt is soð Metod.   (1610b–11)

[who has control of seasons and times: that is the true God.]

(It is interesting to note in passing that this instance also links up with
the first expression of this sort in its use of *soð* ("truth is made manifest";
"that is the true God") and with the second instance in its use of the
word *Metod* for God.) A fifth and final appearance of this particular kind
of commentary comes at the end of the dragon fight, in the description
of the futility of Wiglaf's attempt to rouse the dead Beowulf by sprin-

kling him with water: "he could not, however he might well wish to, hold life on earth in that chieftain,"

> ne ðæs Wealdendes wiht oncirran;
> wolde dom Godes dædum rædan
> gumena gehwylcum, swa he nu gen deð.
>
>   (2857–59)

[nor change anything of God's; the judgment of God would rule the deeds of every man, as it still does now.]

I wish to make two comments on these expressions of assurance about the controlling power over man and nature, one relative to them taken sequentially, the other relative to the collective account they furnish of the perspective of the authenticating voice. Concerning the former, we may note that the first occurrence, that which foreshadows Beowulf's victory over Grendel, associates a *mighty* God with the *might* of a single man; the second, concluding this victory, instead couples a *wise* God with the man's *mod,* that is, his wisdom or courage or spirit; the third and fourth instances do not explicitly refer to God's contribution to human achievement, either through might or wisdom, but are concerned, rather, with his control over the natural rounds of the seasons; and this disjunction leads to the final expression in connection with Wiglaf's failure to turn aside the *dom* of the ruler who controls the *dæde* of men—to that disjunction, in other words, where men's actions, spirit and might no longer concur with the will of the controlling judge. Viewed sequentially in this way, these comments *vis-à-vis* men's successes in this world, on this earth, seem to emphasize a movement from strength to wisdom, to a natural confluence of men's desires and seasonal turnings, to ultimate total dependence upon God's decree. It is a movement that puts human capabilities for accomplishment in harmony with seasonal change and with the progress of man from youth to age—all within the providence of God.

And this movement, when the passages are taken collectively, is seen as just as viable in the poet's own day as it was in the *geardagum* setting of his heroic characters. And why not? The specific customs and deeds of the past may indeed be distanced from the voice's own time, but the nature of man and the universal context of his actions remain the same, are as valid to the voice's (and the poet's) contemporaries. Surely the recurring formula *swa nu gen (git) deð* in these passages (and *wideferhð*) contemporize the past; and I find it hard to understand why Ringbom, in his extended analysis of voice and point of view, should have considered the formula as distancing. For the voice is saying that God—his might, his wisdom, his judgement—controlled Beowulf's success, controlled nature's appointed rounds, controlled Wiglaf's failure, even as he controls their counterparts in these latter days.

But the contemporizing of the past also occurs at the level of simple human behaviour through many gnomic statements, perhaps most notably in the verses immediately following Beowulf's victory over Grendel: "Therefore," says the authenticating voice, "forethought is everywhere best: much must he endure of good and evil who long here in *these* days of strife (*on ðyssum windagum*) makes trial of the world" (1059–62). (Such an observation, it must be noted, is categorical and not comparative, as were those described above in connection with the "I have heard" formula.) Although gnomic advice of this sort bridges the distance between past and present, it and similar remarks are so pervasive a response of the voice that they deserve consideration as a third *kind* of authentication.[13]

Most commonly in this sphere the voice expresses its approval of the behaviour of the characters in a particular sequence of narrative action, frequently by means of *swa sceal* formulas. Thus we find, for instance, approval of the liberality of Scyld's son while a young man:

> Swa sceal (geong g)uma   gode gewyrcean,
> fromum feohgiftum   on fæder (bea)rme,
> þæt hine on ylde   eft gewunigen
> wilgesiþas,   þonne wig cume,
> leode gelæsten;   lofdædum sceal
> in mægþa gehwære   man geþeon.   (20–25)

[So should a young man bring it about by his liberality, by splendid gifts of treasure while still in his father's bosom, that in his age his dear retainers will remain with him, his people stand by him when war comes; in every nation one must prosper by praiseworthy deeds.]

A similar approbation, equally valid for the narrating present, is implied in the remark on the hero's trusting in his own strength and not caring about his life when the sword Hrunting fails him:

> Swa sceal man don,
> þonne he æt guðe   gegan þenceð
> longsumne lof;   na ymb his life ccarað.
>   (1534b–36)

[So should one do, when he means to gain long-lasting praise in battle: he does not care about his life.]

Again, we find approval of Beowulf's loyalty and generosity to Hygelac when the former presents to the latter the treasures he had received in Denmark:

> Swa sceal mæg don,
> nealles inwitnet oðrum bregdon
> dyrnum cræfte, deað ren(ian)
> hondgesteallan.   (2166b–69a)

[So should a kinsman do—not weave a net of malice for others with secret cunning and prepare death for his close companions.]

Here the praise is deliberately contrasted with a kind of contrary behaviour, that of deceit and killing of kinsmen or close companions—a negative pattern that has been counterpointed in various allusions throughout the preceding first part of the poem: allusions to Heremod's past betrayal of *his hondgesteallan*; to Unferth's behaviour in the past with his kinsmen, with possible suggestions of future betrayal; to Hrothulf's future disloyalty. We find, finally, in a slight variation of the *swa sceal* formularization, the voice's authentication of Wiglaf's behaviour in coming to Beowulf's aid: "Swylc sceolde secg wesan, / þegn æt ðearfe" [So should a warrior be, a thane at a moment of need] (2168b–69a). In this last instance we may wonder at the past tense: only in those days? Such a limited time significance seems improbable, however, in the light of all the other time-extended approbations of the heroic ethos: for example, "ne bið swylc earges sið" [such is not the way of a coward] (2541b), of Beowulf's self-appointed undertaking against the dragon;[14] or "sibb' æfre ne maeg / wiht onwendan þam þe wel þenceð" [nothing can ever set aside the tie of kinship, for him who thinks rightly] (2600b–01), of Wiglaf's constancy towards Beowulf in the face of adversity; or "swa hit gede(fe) bið, / þæt mon his winedryhten wordum herge" [as it is proper, that one should praise his lord with words] (3174b–75), of Beowulf's followers praising their fallen leader. But we must be careful not to over-simplify the perspective of the narrating voice. While it can and does explicitly approve of heroic values, it simultaneously recognizes their limitations at the far side of human existence; and it expresses its eschatological concern in other pieces of gnomic wisdom. For example, it comments on Grendel's despairing flight: "Not at all is it easy to flee death—let him try who so desires—but he must seek out the place made ready for all living souls, for all children of men, etc." (1002b ff.). And it is particularly concerned when it comments, in the so-called Christian Excursus, on the kinds of behaviour separating the damned from the saved *after deaðdæge*:

> Wa bið þæm ðe sceal
> þurh sliðne nið sawle bescufan
> in fyres fæþm, frofre ne wenan,
> wihte gewendan! Wel bið þæm þe mot

æfter deaðdæge   Drihten secean
ond to Fæder fæþmum   freoðo wilnian!
                                      (183b–88)

[It is ill for him who, because of dire affliction, must thrust his soul
into the fire's embrace, and can expect no relief, or change anything!
It is well for him who, after the day of his death, may seek the Lord
and ask for protection in the Father's embrace!]

This concern for what lies beyond this human existence leads us to a
consideration of the fourth area in which the authenticating voice
operates. The view it expresses, that human knowledge is limited, seems
to provide a framework which contains or sets off the other three
responses it gives voice to.

The first occurrence of this recognition of human limitations is near
the beginning of the poem, in the description of the giving of Scyld's
burial ship to the sea:

                    Men ne cunnon
        secgan to soðe,   selerædende,
        hæleð under heofenum,   hwa þæm hlæste onfeng.
                                      (50b–52)

[Men cannot say with certainty—not hall-counsellors or heroes beneath the heavens—who received that cargo.]

The second profession of ignorance about something in the universe
beyond mortal ken comes a little later, in the description of Grendel's
twelve-year persecution of the Danes:

        (ac se) æglæca   ehtende wæs,
        deorc deaþscua,   duguþe ond geogoþe,
        seomade ond syrede,   sinnihte heold
        mistige moras;   men ne cunnon
        hwyder helrunan   hwyrftum scriþað.   (159–63)

[but the marvellous creature, the dark death-shadow, was persecuting
both old and young; he lay in wait and ambushed, and in perpetual
night ruled the misty moors; men do not know where hellish demons
go in their wanderings.]

There has been a suggestion recently that the phrase in the last verse,
hwyrftum scriþað, is meant to indicate a circling motion in hell, a
punishment of the wicked—a suggestion based on patristic exegesis;[15]
but I have argued, in an as yet unpublished paper, against the likelihood
of this interpretation. The phrase, it seems to me, is in the same spirit as
the previous *men ne cunnon* use, designed to express that sense of
mystery over the course of such movements, another kind of limitation
of human awareness. Later in the poem, in connection with Beowulf's

death, the voice expresses again a sense of awe, of wonder, at the mystery as to "where a brave warrior may meet the end of his destined life, when a man can no longer inhabit the meadhall with his kinsmen" (3062b–65). It is of some interest, and not accidental I believe, that these three professions of a sense of mystery at the limits of human knowledge involve, in the instance of Scyld's burial, a reference to a definitive action in the past that is expressed in terms of continuing ignorance in the present: "men *do* not know who *received* that burden"; in the instance of Grendel and the *helrunan,* a reference to a durative action from the past continuing to the narrator's present time: "men *do* not know whither such creatures *move* . . ."; and in the last case, that of Beowulf's death, a reference to a durative action extending from the past through the present and into the future, to the end of life for every man. This arching time-concern of the authenticating voice with respect to the indeterminacy and limits of human knowledge is perhaps not surprising in a poem whose thematic centre, on other grounds, has been seen, for example, as one of beginnings and endings, or as one of typological relationships that unite "the poem's chronological scene, its symbolic mode, and its historiographical outlook," or as one whose larger structural patterns of narrative "contribute powerfully to a sense of the mysterious shaping of human events."[16]

Space does not permit examination of all the explicit manifestations of the authenticating voice (for example, such statements as "that was a good king" or "God decided it rightly"), let alone consideration of implicit conveyance of its attitudes (as, say, through the choice of epithets or other descriptive terms). But I think I have given a fair sampling of the variety and range of its responses. Let me summarize briefly, and then make an observation on the significance of these responses for the interpretation of the poem as a whole.

We have seen that the voice of the poem authenticates the temporal distance of the story it narrates from its own time, making it history; but that simultaneously it contemporizes that story by expressing its relevance to the poet's and his audience's own time. Third, it authenticates men's moral behaviour on a continuing basis from past to present, crystallizing its concern in maximic forms and formulas. Fourth, it evinces an epistemological-eschatological concern for the limits and limitations of human knowledge and capabilities and a concomitant awe at the unfathomable beyond. These perspectives on time, behaviour and knowledge are not discrete; they interlace, even as do various other elements of the poem, as Leyerle and others have recently shown.[17] But they are suggestive of an historiographic mode of human experience which shows a continuity and contiguity with the voice's contemporary mode of existence, and a mode of experience beyond human ken that is mysterious even if not necessarily mystical. Further, these perspectives suggest a pattern of moral behaviour extending from man's involvement with the storied past, to his actions in the known present, to his disposition in the ineluctable and unknowable future.

Now, these concerns or responses of the authenticating voice may well call to mind the several levels of traditional Christian allegory: the historical, the allegorical, the anagogical and the tropological. Are they really the same? Does this analysis lend support to those allegorical and patristic critics who would find, on other grounds, various specific Christian meanings in the poem? I do not think so. Though there is a resemblance, perhaps even an interrelationship, the voice of the poem authenticates a *literalness* of meaning; it insists on the value of *what is there,* concretely. It does not invite symbolic or typological or allegorical value-adding.[18]

A similar literalness operates in other areas of the poem's metaphysic. Just one illustration. Though many critics have tried to abstract the nature of the evil that Grendel represents, the poetic voice seems to have no trouble visualizing Grendel *at one and the same time* as a *literal* historical monster, claw and all, with a consummate passion for human fodder; as a *literal* enemy of God descended in the race of Cain and hence *literally* a *feond on helle*; as a social outcast, a *wonsæli mon,* who cannot receive the ordinary benison of thaneship and who will not accept the sanctions of *comitatus* custom, such as wergild; and yet again as something more nebulous than any of these, a *literal* dark shadow of death who holds at night the misty moors, whose mysterious turnings are beyond the pale of human cognition.

But I have hinted at a resemblance between such literal perspectives and those more abstract significations derived from exegetical interpretation; and I should like, in concluding, to advance the hypothesis that the patristic exegetical mode of thought and analysis is but a sub-species of a more universal way of viewing human experience, a way that is embedded in the narrative mode itself, a way that is especially suited for, but not limited to, the epic genre. The review I have given here of the *voice* of the poem and its literal narrative perspectives provides, I think, some support for such a supposition, a supposition that would explain why, with changing critical zeitgeists and different individual critical sensitivities, *Beowulf* has been seen variously as embodying mythological representations, symbolic values and Christian allegorical meanings.[19]

NOTES

1. But hardly antediluvian, as L.E. Nicholson suggests ("The Literal Meaning and Symbolic Structure of *Beowulf,*" *Classica et Mediaevalia* 25 (1964): 151–201).

2. All quotations are from Fr. Klaeber's 3rd ed. of *Beowulf* (Boston, 1950).

3. See my discussion in *The Interpretation of Old English Poems* (London and Boston, 1972), 39–43.

4. "*Beowulf:* The Monsters and the Critics," *Proceedings of the British Academy* 22 (1936): 244–95, n. 20.

5. This paper, substantially in its present form, was delivered as a lecture at the University of Cambridge under the sponsorship of the Department of Anglo-Saxon, Norse and Celtic on 7 March 1975. Footnotes have been added.

6. "The *Beowulf* Poet," *Philological Quarterly* 39 (1960): 389–99; the passage is cited from the reprint in *An Anthology of "Beowulf" Criticism,* ed. L.E. Nicholson (Notre Dame, 1963), 356.

7. Dorothy Whitelock, *The Audience of "Beowulf"* (Oxford, 1951); Francis P. Magoun, Jr, "Oral-formulaic Character of Anglo-Saxon Narrative Poetry," *Speculum* 28 (1953): 446–67; and D.W. Robertson, Jr, "Historical Criticism," *English Institute Essays 1950* (New York, 1951), 3–31, and "The Doctrine of Charity in Medieval Literary Gardens: A Topical Approach through Symbolism and Allegory," *Speculum* 26 (1951): 24–49.

8. *Beowulf,* ed. C.L. Wrenn, rev. W.F. Bolton (New York, 1973), 87.

9. On this formula, see Thomas C. Rumble, "The *Hyran-Gefrignan* Formula in *Beowulf,*" *Annuale Mediaevale* 5 (1964): 13–20.

10. *Studies in the Narrative Technique of "Beowulf" and Lawaman's "Brut"* (Åbo, 1968), 18.

11. *Ibid.,* 26.

12. "Inner Weather and Interlace: A Note on the Semantic Value of Structure in *Beowulf,*" *Old English Studies in Honour of John C. Pope,* ed. R.B. Burlin and E.B. Irving, Jr (Toronto, 1974), 81–89, at 83.

13. Peter Clemoes has recently called attention to the contemporizing effect of the *Beowulf* narrator's references to permanent values and to permanent conditions of human life such as the seasons or God's power ("De quelques articulations entre présent et passé dans la technique narrative Vieil-Anglaise," *Actes du Colloque de l'Association des Médiévistes Anglicistes de l'Enseignement Supérieur sur les Techniques Narratives au Moyen Âge,* ed. André Crépin (Amiens, 1974), 5–21 at 17–19). Professor Clemoes's essay appeared after I had written this paper.

14. On the significance of this verse, see my *The Interpretation of Old English Poems,* 19–20.

15. Thomas D. Hill, "'Hwyrftum Scriþað': *Beowulf* line 163," *Mediaeval Studies* 33 (1971): 379–81.

16. Respectively, Tolkien, "*Beowulf:* The Monsters and the Critics," Nicholson, "Literal Meaning and Symbolic Structure," as summarized by Bolton, in his revision of Wrenn's ed., 87; and Burlin, "Inner Weather and Interlace," 84.

17. John Leyerle, "The Interlace Structure of *Beowulf,*" *University of Toronto Quarterly* 37 (1967): 1–17.

18. Cf. the remarks of Bennet A. Brockman on *Genesis A* ("'Heroic' and 'Christian' in *Genesis A*: The Evidence of the Cain and Abel Episode," *Modern*

Language Quarterly 35 (1974): 115–28, esp. 117), that even with a religious poem of this type, the concrete, secular, social meaning probably dominated the audience response, and that the poet had a "concrete, human interest in legendary material" rather than an "intellectual interest in theological allegory."

19. A similar observation by Derek Brewer in connection with Chaucer ("Towards a Chaucerian Poetic," *Proceedings of the British Academy* 60 (1974): separate reprint, 7) came to my attention after this was written.

The Great Feud:
Scriptural History and Strife in *Beowulf*

by Marijane Osborn

This essay first appeared in PMLA: Publications of the Modern Language Association of America *93 (1978): 973–81.*

BEOWULF is the story of a culture hero who fights in succession three monsters that threaten the fabric of his society. Each fight takes place at a farther remove from the lighted center of that society—in darkened hall, cave-hall, and barrow—and each antagonist is more nonhuman than the last. The primary concern of the poet is with the heroic response to the encroachment of an unformed, non-human outer darkness upon the formal grace of life in the hall.[1] But there is an element in *Beowulf* beyond this primal encounter. There is history.

The history in *Beowulf,* which makes up most of the famous digressions in the poem, is chiefly concerned with feuds. Dorothy Whitelock remarks that the historical Scandinavian feuds are

> referred to so frequently that it is obvious that the poet wishes them to be present in his hearers' thoughts as he tells his tale. The tragic stories of family strife within the Scylding dynasty, and of the wars fought by the kings of the Geats against the Swedes or Franks, attain almost to the position of sub-plots to the two parts of *Beowulf* respectively.[2]

The heaviest reference to these Scandinavian feuds comes in the second half of the poem. But in the first half of the poem, the mythic beginnings of the Scyldings, of Heorot, and of strife in Heorot evoke a series of "historical" references to feuds of quite a different order—the feuds of sacred history. While Scandinavian history is accessible within the world of the poem (sometimes as political prophecy),[3] this scriptural history is of course unknowable to the ancient Scandinavians in *Beowulf,* for Christianity has not yet penetrated to their lands. With decorum and subtlety the Christian poet introduces a perspective inaccessible to his protagonists, in such a way that it will enhance, but not interfere with, his tale of noble (and in some sense ancestral) pagans. He establishes two complementary frames of reference, one heroic and one cosmic. The former aligns us, the audience, with the native Germanic world within the poem, while the latter aligns us with the Christian world of the poet.

The poet distinguishes between the heroic and the cosmic frames of reference primarily by assigning to the monsters who attack Heorot a scriptural history recognizable only to his audience. But even before introducing Old Testament referents for the archetypically evil monsters, he has distinguished between two levels of knowledge, that bound by the secular world of the poem and that perceived from our initiated Christian perspective.

I. Scyld's Destiny

A recent critic remarks that the "before and after" of the hall world is not a major concern of the poem (Haarder, 241); yet it is very much a central theme in the Scyld episode that sets the stage and the tone for the story about Beowulf to follow. The episode is presented in two passages of nearly equal length, each concluding with a statement about Scyld's destiny after death. These two statements offer contrasting views, one certain and the other uncertain.

The first half of the episode deals with Scyld's glorious reign, establishes the beginning of dynastic history, which is the beginning of "time" in the story, and concludes with Scyld's death. Within these twenty-four lines the poet makes three almost casual references to God (*God, Liffrea,* and *Wealdend*), so that it is hard to interpret the destination described for Scyld at the end of the passage as anything but favorable, if not as Heaven at least as the bosom of some Germanic Abraham:

> Him ða Scyld gewat   to gescæphwile
> felahror feran   on Frean wære.

> Then Scyld went forth at his destined time,
> very old, to go into the Lord's keeping.[4]
>   (26–27)

Although the concept itself is formulaic—when St. Andrew dies his spirit goes *on Godes wære* (*Menologium* 218a) and Beowulf's own spirit goes *on ðæs Waldendes wære* (3109)—the poet uses it to make a firm authorial statement about Scyld's destiny directly to us, the audience outside the story. The Danes in *Beowulf* perceive Scyld's fate differently, as the second passage tells us.

The second half of the episode, concerned with the burial at sea, emphasizes the people's adoration of Scyld and their adornment of his "comely ship." This personal involvement sets the elegiac tone for the secular history to follow and presents, as it were, a closeup view of life in the poem, bringing us down into that world. Scyld's *swæse gesiþas* 'dear companions' place him in the treasure-filled ship and finally give him to the sea with mourning hearts, but their view of his destiny is in contrast to what the poet, as omniscient narrator, has already told us. The passage concludes:

> Men ne cunnon
> secgan to soðe,   selerædende,
> hæleð under heofenum,   hwa þæm hlæste onfeng.

> Men do not know how
> to say for certain, hall-councillors,
> heroes under the heavens, who received that load.

(50–52)

Pagan Danes and Christians alike would know that the important part of that ship's cargo was neither body nor treasure, but spirit. The death ship was a familiar metaphor in both ecclesiastical and secular traditions; the native tradition is attested by folklore, by excavated ship burials, and by such stone carvings as the magnificent Götland picture stones (often arranged much like the Scyld sequence, with battle and victory scenes above and a death ship below). Those who launched Scyld's ship had some concept of the soul setting forth to the Land of the Dead; but the most significant feature of Scyld's departure in *Beowulf* is that, while the poet assures us of his precise (and safe) journey's end, within the world of the story that destination is not known. Hall-councillors, heroes under Heaven, have only pagan knowledge, like Edwin's councillor as recorded by Bede: "This life of man appears but for a moment; what follows or indeed what went before, we know not at all."[5]

This double point of view in *Beowulf*—what they know in the poem and what we know outside it—has been noted in passing by previous scholars, two of whom take the audience specifically into account. Donahue mentions that the poet is "playing the limited hope of his protagonists against the fuller Christian knowledge of his audiences,"[6] and Renoir astutely observes that this disparity in knowledge is the chief source of dramatic tension in the poem. This tension, he says,

> is not exclusively intrinsic to the action, but is primarily due to a divergence in points of view between audience and the participants in the action. From our position outside the poem, we know far more about the participants than they do about each other, and we have access to information necessarily unavailable to them. . . .[7]

This disparity in knowledge, most striking in connection with Grendel's scriptural ancestry, occurs throughout those three passages that a recent commentator, Greenfield, has called "explicit scripturizing": "having the scop in Heorot paraphrase Genesis, the placing of Grendel in the race of Cain, and Hrothgar's sermon."[8] Surprisingly, what has not been remarked at all is that in these passages *the explicitly scriptural element is carefully kept separate from the perception of persons in the poem and is presented solely as a gloss for the audience.*

It must be noted, however, that the poet is not concerned about suppressing Christian doctrine, as opposed to scriptural history, in Beowulf's world. Concepts like judgment (see ll. 978 and possibly 2330 and 2820) and damnation (588–89) are elements of an inherent moral understanding known theologically as "natural knowledge," the law inscribed upon the hearts of righteous pagans (Rom. ii.15). Scriptural history, like any other history, is intellectual knowledge, conveyed by human instruction and hence unavailable to even the noblest pagan in the world of the poem.

II. The Creation Song in Heorot

The distinction first introduced in the Scyld episode between what those of us outside the story can perceive and what those within it can know is further elaborated by the first of the three "scripturizing" passages, the creation song in Heorot together with what follows it. The passage known as the creation song (92–98) has often been cited as evidence for the essentially Christian character of Hrothgar's court; the scop is said to paraphrase Genesis. But this observation misses the poet's point completely. For those listening in Heorot the song cannot be a paraphrase because they do not know Genesis. For us it is a paraphrase because we do know Genesis—but the echoes we hear extend beyond the song.

The creation song is not much more "Christian" than the hymn of Iopas in Book 1 of the *Aeneid,* to which Klaeber compares it (131); the chief difference is the presence of the Creator himself in the *Beowulf* song (as in the Scyld passage). In the *Aeneid,* "long-haired Iopas" makes the hall ring with his cithara, then

> Hic canit errantem lunam, solisque labores,
> unde hominum genus et pecudes, unde imber et ignes . . .

> He sang of the wandering moon, and the sun's labors,
> whence came the creation of men and beasts, of rain and fire . . .
>
> (1.742–43)

In Heorot the scop sounds his harp, says that the Almighty made the earth, then

gesette sigehreþig   sunnan ond monan . . .
> lif eac gesceop
cynna gehwylcum   þara ðe cwice hwyrfaþ.—

set victorious the sun and moon . . .
> and also made life
for every kind of being that moves.—

(94, 97–98)

The song ends here for those listening in Heorot. But for those of us outside the story it does not precisely come to an end at all. Rather, it dissolves back into the hall scene where it is being sung:

Swa ða drihtguman   dreamum lifdon,
eadiglice,   oð ðæt an ongan
fyrene frem(m)an,   feond on helle.

So the noble beings dwelt in joy,
happily, until a certain one began
to do wicked deeds, a fiend from Hell.

(99–101)

C.J.E. Ball would have the song in Heorot end after these three lines, with the scop in the hall having sung from the creation of the world into the story of Adam and Eve.[9] But these lines, hovering between the song in the hall and the scene in the hall, are an example of the classical figure of *synchysis,* liquid syntax, where "we do not know," explains Bede, "whether the thought ends with the words which have preceded . . .or with the words which follow."[10]

If we read the song as continuing from the creation of the world into the story of Adam and Eve, those "noble people" who "lived happily until a certain adversary from Hell began to perform wicked deeds" (as Ball translates), then we fully expect to hear next of Satan's arrival in Eden. What we get is:

Wæs se grimma gæst   Grendel haten.

That grim spirit was called Grendel.   (102)

With this pronouncement the fictive world of the creation song modulates conclusively back into that of Heorot, even from our alerted point of view. By following the song with explicit scriptural allusions, the poet reinforces our sense of it as a paraphrase, and we hear in it much more than the Danes can. But most important, through the synchysis that introduces the adversary of Heorot in a scriptural context, the poet has offered an archetypal referent for Grendel that is accessible to us but not to those in the story.

III. Grendel and the Race of Cain

Tolkien urges the importance of considering

> how and why the monsters become 'adversaries of God,' and so begin
> to symbolize (and ultimately to become identified with) the powers of
> evil, even while they remain, as they do still remain in *Beowulf,* mortal
> denizens of the material world, in it and of it.[11]

The poet contrives this dual vision by carefully presenting the monsters
and their attack upon Heorot within a context of cosmic history. After
the creation song and the introduction of Grendel, the allusions to
Genesis are continued until the end of the first fit, providing us with
much we need to know about the Great Feud, the cosmic battle between
good and evil that controls the three main actions of the poem in a
manner barely glimpsed by its chief protagonists. Early scholars of
Beowulf proposed that the scriptural allusions were interpolated, but
here one could almost say that the poet "interpolates" Grendel himself,
at lines 102–05, into his scriptural summary. As we have seen, however,
his method is not to interpolate but to interweave. The introduction of
Grendel is thematically interwoven with the creation song and the Cain
passage (86–114), so that he is totally identified with the Adversary of
Mankind.

But all this background information from Genesis is given only to
the poet's audience, those who have the understanding to grasp it; the
Danes who are beset by a monster have no notion of this cosmic setting.
They have what may be described as a sense of myth and the idea of
reversal: within the world of Heorot light challenges darkness, and it is
felt that the bright hall of friendship and harp song calls up the envious
grimma gæst from his misery. But after twelve long years of sorrow the
Danes *know* only that Grendel is openly feuding against Hrothgar and
that he will not abide by their legal codes (146–58). In the world of the
poem this most evil of monsters, though he dwells by night in Heorot,
cannot approach the *gifstol,* the center of giving and fellowship in that
hall; this too makes mythic sense, just as it follows (within the logic of
paradox) that the Devil cannot approach an altar.

The lines stating the inability of the demonic being to approach the
hall's numinous center are probably the most discussed crux of the
poem:

> No he þone gifstol   gretan moste,
> maþðum for metode,   ne his myne wisse.
>
> He could not approach that gift-throne,
> the treasure (before/on account of) the lord,
>   nor know his love.   (168–69)

C.L. Wrenn believes that these lines "probably have been misplaced in the MS. from their proper position between 110 and 111"[12]—an opinion that Kevin Crossley-Holland tacitly follows in his translation.[13] These interpreters would "restore" the lines about the *gifstol* to the end of the account of the banishing of Cain in the first fit. Wrenn translates the passage as follows, inserting the *gifstol* lines 168–69 between lines 110 and 111:

> He (Cain) had no joy of that act of enmity, but the Creator banished him afar off from mankind because of that wickedness. He (Cain) could not draw near to God's throne (as he could have done before his slaying of Abel), that precious thing (bejewelled as in *Ezekiel* or the *Apocalypse*), in the Creator's presence, nor did he feel his love. (69)

A reorganization of the received text is not necessary, however, once we are alerted to the double vision that is carefully being prepared for us. In neither line 109 nor line 168 does the *he* that Wrenn glosses "Cain" refer exclusively to an individual. The Danes know that Grendel (*he,* 168) cannot approach their *gifstol*; the audience outside the poem can observe that the direct antecedent of the pronoun *he* is *feond mancynnes* 'mankind's enemy' (164) and that Grendel is thus once more identified with the Antagonist of scripture.

Lest we miss the dual perspective at this point, the "crux" is bracketed between narrative comments about the ignorance of the Danes concerning cosmic matters: "Men do now know whither hell-creatures go in their wanderings" (162–63), but what is worse, "the Danes did not know the Lord" (180); they understand neither the demonic nor the holy. (This is clearly not true of those Danes who, like the scop in Heorot, know God through his creation.) The word for Lord here, *Metod* (180), appears also in the *gifstol* passage (169) and firmly establishes the dual focus of that passage.

Through this use of dual focus, the limited knowledge of the Danes in Heorot (their understanding of Grendel's strife against Hrothgar in terms of Germanic feud) is encompassed within the larger history of the Great Feud. When the Danes, not knowing how to worship the Lord, seek help from the "slayer of souls" (177), they are unwittingly aligning themselves with those adversaries of God enumerated at the end of the first fit. At the end of the second fit the poet follows his account of the most overtly heathen ritual in the poem (the Danes' devil worship) with strong Christian admonition, in language recalling the Feud:

> Wa bið þæm ðe sceal
> þurh sliðne nið sawle bescufan

> in fyres fæþm,   frofre ne wenan,
> wihte gewendan!   Wel bið þæm þe mot
> æfter deaðdæge   Drihten secean
> ond to Fæder fæþmum   freoðo wilnian!

> Woe be to him who must
> through terrible hostility shove his soul
> into the fire's embrace; he may not expect comfort
> or change at all! Well it will be for him who may
> seek the Lord after the day of his death
> and in the Father's embrace ask for peace!
>   (183–88)

On the whole the poet maintains his two frames of reference less overtly than this. When he again "scripturizes" the lineage of Grendel (1261b–67a), he first puts the warriors in Heorot to sleep, secure in their faulty knowledge that no "demon created of old" will move upon Heorot to bring "reversal to men." As in the first fit, he then interweaves the introduction of the monster, now Grendel's mother, with scriptural commentary to evoke the perspective of cosmic archetypes. Grendel's mother, at the heroic level of the Scandinavian feud, comes only to avenge her son (1276–78), but the coming of the Grendel kind at all is part of a feud more ancient and malicious.

IV. THE GIANT HILT AND HROTHGAR'S SERMON

This vision of evil intention is, like the scriptural history, an element added to the heroic level of the story; more hangs on the impeccability of the warrior than he can possibly realize. To the Germanic concepts of blind fate (*wyrd*) and the disaster that strikes the unwary, the poet adds the malice of a supernatural agent, first by recalling to us the ancient beginnings of the recurrent feud that exploded upon the Danes as they slept, then by associating this feud with Hrothgar's evocation of the soul-slayer who comes upon men asleep in spirit.

The third and last of the "scripturizing" passages in *Beowulf* moves again into the ancient history of the Grendel kind, but it does not concern them personally. It gives the "lineage" of the giant sword hilt that Beowulf brings back from the mere. When the hilt is given into Hrothgar's hand, the poet tells us more or less parenthetically that it came to Hrothgar after the "fall of devils," specifically after the deaths of Grendel and his mother (1679–83). The poet then completes the rhetorical figures of envelope pattern and variation by delivering a two-line eulogy to Hrothgar. He finally says that "Hrothgar spoke" (1687a)—but the speech does not in fact begin until fourteen lines later (1700). The delay, as we watch Hrothgar looking at the hilt, is significant.[14] It may be compared to the long look that occurs later when the poet stops all action to give the pedigree of the sword that Wiglaf has just drawn against the dragon. Attached to Wiglaf's sword is a tradition about ordinary feuding in the world of the poem, like that attached to the swords in the Hengest and Ingeld digressions; the political history of Wiglaf's sword will have repercussions after the dragon lies dead. But the golden hilt of Grendel's mere, the work of wondersmiths, gives information of a different order. Hrothgar "looks upon the hilt"—and while Hrothgar gazes, considering what to say, the poet tells *us* what is written on the hilt.

There are two inscriptions: the first refers to the beginning of the ancient fight; the second gives the name of the first owner of the sword, in runes. The latter is archeologically quite credible; there is a rune-inscribed sword pommel in Liverpool City Museum.[15] What is written about the ancient fight suggests that the poet has in his mind's eye a combination of runic and nonrunic inscriptions, which is quite possible in his own time but improbable in Beowulf's. Hence Klaeber notes the suggestion that the writing about the ancient fight was a graphic illustration.[16] But a fifth-century Scandinavian weapon would be unlikely to document, either in pictures or in writing, "the ungodly acts of the giants which preceded the deluge" (Klaeber), and one mode of inscription would be as unintelligible as the other to a reader with no knowledge of scriptural history. But we are not told that Hrothgar reads what he is looking at. He gazes upon the hilt, and the information with which the poet provides *us* during this pause gives a scriptural context for the wisdom that Hrothgar subsequently reveals about the recurrent feud with mankind's enemy within the human breast. This context is chiefly what makes his speech seem like a Christian homily.

Even quite recently an exclusively secular interpretation of Hrothgar's speech has been proposed:

> Hrothgar concerns himself with the duties and proper conduct of Germanic lords, and with the glory which they may lose if they fail to fulfill the ideals upon which that glory is founded. The speech is not a Christian homily, even though it may contain echoes of the poet's Christian background. . . . Hrothgar's "sermon" is important, perhaps central to the poem, not because it reveals a Christian view of life, but because it gives expression to secular ideals which control the conduct of Germanic heroes.[17]

But surely the speech is most relevant to the poem as a whole because it shows, through contextual allusion, how the highest conduct of Germanic heroes is not in opposition to that of any hero aligned with God's forces in the Great Feud. The speech reveals Hrothgar's character and perhaps relates to Beowulf's motives at the end of the poem, because it shows, again through contextual allusion, how the Germanic ethos of wise magnanimity supports the will of God. From the first, Hrothgar has been presented to us as more concerned with the binding social function of ring-giving than with the performance of heroic deeds; his purpose in building Heorot was to provide a hall in which to imitate God's generosity with his own. This "cosmic" connection is stressed both in the introduction of Hrothgar (70–73) and in his speech, for Hrothgar has a vision of giving as a kind of stability in the world of change, the world where *wyrd* strikes against honor and dignity and, as a matter of course, against avarice, the miserly hoarding of that treasure which is the lifeblood of Germanic society.

Hrothgar's vision reaches beyond the bounds of the heroic world until he seems able to accept (if not precisely to imagine) a generous God superior to *wyrd*, a Boethian ruler of the universe. Though Hrothgar is not, as Klaeber maintains he is, "depicted as a good Christian" (135; cf. 21), he may be compared to Augustine's pagan philosophers who have recognized God: "Whoever they may have been, we rank such thinkers above all others and acknowledge them as representing the closest approximation to our Christian position."[18] Snorri Sturluson, too, recognizes such minds among his pagan ancestors. God granted men earthly gifts, worldly wealth and prosperity, Snorri explains in the Prologue to his *Prose Edda*, "and he also bestowed on them wisdom so that they understood all earthly things, they guessed that there must be someone who ruled the stars. . . . They understood everything in a material sense, however, since they had not been given spiritual understanding."[19] Hrothgar is among those Danes who guessed (like his scop) that "there must be someone who ruled the stars." He is grateful to Beowulf, with whom he promises to share treasures, but he thanks God, not Beowulf, that he may now look on Grendel's severed head after his "ancient struggle" (1791).

In the context of the inscribed hilt and the meditation it inspires, this struggle has a meaning beyond the hero fight that we have witnessed in the story. But, as with the creation song, it is the accompanying scriptural allusions that lend Hrothgar's discourse a special meaning for us, different from the meaning it has for those listening in Heorot, who have not "been given spiritual understanding." It is what we are told of the sword's biblical history that elevates the ensuing discourse on generosity, *wyrd*, and vigilance to the level of a "sermon" for our Christian understanding and alerts us to the homiletic allusions throughout. The speaker himself, however, does not recognize that level in the words he speaks.

V. Levels of Knowledge in Beowulf

The poet controls his two perspectives simply by distinguishing between the natural wisdom possible to pagans and the revealed knowledge he shares with us. "In the persons of Beowulf and Hrothgar," writes A.D. Horton, "the poet is setting before us examples of noble pagans, virtuous in the practice of a natural religion."[20] He suggests that Paul's letter to the Romans, describing the ways in which pagans can know God and the degree to which they are culpable for their sins of ignorance, was influential in the *Beowulf* poet's time because it offered a means of justifying one's valued pagan ancestors that did not conflict with Germanic *pietas*. The line between what the ancient Scandinavians of Beowulf's world can and cannot have known may be charted from the Pauline doctrine expressed in Romans I and II. First, all men can know the Creator through his works. Certain persons in *Beowulf* give evidence of this knowledge, just as Snorri Sturluson acknowledges that some pagans have guessed at theistic truth. Second, all men have the natural law written in their hearts; so the freedom of right choice is not unduly affected by limited knowledge. The Danes are therefore culpable for deciding, in their despair, to worship the "soul-slayer." Both these kinds of knowledge, the principles of deity and of ethics, are said by Paul to be the "natural" knowledge available to pagans.

What is not available to the pagans in the story is revealed knowledge: eschatology and the scriptures. The destiny of the soul is of concern to the Danes, but it remains a mystery to them, as the Scyld prologue makes clear. The value of the scriptural references is to point to a cosmic history of feuds that a postrevelation audience may see repeated in the action of the story and may align with pre-Christian native tradition. For an audience in a royal hall, the biblical overtones would reaffirm the native culture, whose values had been called into question by the arrival of Roman Christianity; for a cloister audience, the archetypal reflection of scriptural history in Beowulf's fights with demonic monsters would serve to "redeem" the native past.[21]

There is a patristic precedent for the nonallegorical method by which the *Beowulf* poet fuses the native historical and folklore materials of his story with the scriptural history of the beginnings of good and evil among mankind. Augustine "scripturizes" Romulus in much the same way as the *Beowulf* poet does Grendel, but with an entirely different purpose:

The first founder of the earthly city was, as we have seen, a fratricide; for, overcome by envy, he slew his own brother, a citizen of the Eternal City, on pilgrimage in this world. Hence it is no wonder that long afterwards this first precedent—what the Greeks call an *archetype*—was answered by a kind of reflection, by an event of the same kind. . . . For this is how Rome was founded, when Remus, as Roman history witnesses, was slain by his brother Romulus.[22]

Augustine is using his theory of archetypes to defend his religion against the charge that it has corrupted his culture; the *Beowulf* poet is using a similar method to redeem his native and pagan culture by reconciling secular history to sacred "by a kind of reflection."[23] The text demonstrates that the poet had a firm grasp of this idea. His curiously unmedieval concern with anachronism, with what may be known "now" (in Christian England) but not "then" (in pagan Scandinavia), is necessary if he is to present Christian and secular themes as fused for us, as a kind of reflection of the archetype, while keeping these themes carefully separated, with the Christian element suppressed, for those in the story.

There is no need for further scriptural references after the two kinsfolk of Cain have been destroyed. We have had Hrothgar's warning that calamity continues to come unexpected upon mankind: strife is *always* renewed. "That feud with mankind has been going on since the earth first swallowed Abel's blood," proclaims the *Exeter Book* maximist, "that is not the hostility of a single day."[24] The advent of another adversary of mankind is inevitable. But the dragon's awakening is unexpected and misunderstood within the world of the story[25] because men there have little or no understanding of the Great Feud, continuous in cosmic history from Cain's blow until the monster fight of the apocalypse.

There is no pagan-Christian "problem" in *Beowulf,* as scholars have argued for over a century and a half, usually showing their prejudices by taking one side or the other. Rather than being in opposition, these two elements form an epistemological scheme embracing both secular and spiritual understanding like that presented more traditionally in *The Wanderer.*[26] Whereas some movement from the secular level toward the spiritual occurs within the Wanderer's experience, no such progression occurs within Beowulf's world, where the two levels are used for a different purpose. Our scriptural knowledge of the Great Feud gives us a framework within which to set particular feuds (both historical and monstrous) and to estimate men's valor. This cosmic dimension does not detract from, but instead supports, the native grandeur of the human soul as it is understood by the noblest pagans in *Beowulf.* By carefully maintaining two separate frames of reference, the poet allows us to "look down as if from a visionary height upon the house of man in the valley of the world" (Tolkien), and thereby to understand something more than may those heroes under Heaven, without intruding our Christian knowledge into Beowulf's world, where it is not relevant.

NOTES

1. Andreas Haarder's view of the poem is representative of that of many scholars:

> *Beowulf* presents a picture of a hall-life that is forever at stake, confronted as it is by the threat of the monster-world. . . . The hall of *Beowulf* is the basis of man's existence and the motivation of his actions. The hall is in focus, not the before and after that the Christian preacher will point to. . . . The monster is man's existential problem which has to be solved again and again. (*"Beowulf": The Appeal of a Poem* [Viborg, 1975], 239, 241, 279)

Such a description is accurate so far as it goes, but it does not go far enough.

2. Dorothy Whitelock, *The Audience of "Beowulf"* (Oxford, 1951), 34.

3. Even as Beowulf saves the Danes and the Geats from monsters, secular history, in the form of retribution for feuds, is working against these two nations. But this drama is not "in" the story; it is in the future of the story, implied by the poet or guessed by perceptive characters. Kenneth Sisam casts doubts upon the importance of such historicity in the poem and upon the interpretations that modern historians put upon the passages of foresight, in *The Structure of "Beowulf"* (Oxford, 1965), 51–59. For the counterargument that it is thematically important for these two sets of feuds to end tragically see Stanley J. Kahrl, "Feuds in *Beowulf*: A Tragic Necessity?" *Modern Philology* 69 (1972): 189–98.

4. All quotations from *Beowulf* are from Fr. Klaeber, ed., *Beowulf and the Fight at Finnsburg*, 3rd ed. (Boston, 1950). The translations are my literal renderings and do not represent the style of my forthcoming *"Beowulf": A Verse-Translation* (Los Angeles, 1978). [This translation appeared as *"Beowulf": A Verse Translation with Treasures of the Ancient North* (Berkeley, 1983). — P.S.B.]

5. *Ecclesiastical History of the English People*, ed. Bertram Colgrave and R.A.B. Mynors (Oxford, 1969), 185. Bede's story of the conversion of Edwin and his vivid symbol of pagan ignorance were probably as well known in the *Beowulf* poet's time as in our own, and perhaps the poet was counting on his hearers' having the image of the fleeting sparrow in the backs of their minds, or perhaps he himself was inspired by it in his account of Scyld. But there is an important difference between Scyld's departure and the sparrow's: in *Beowulf* it is not the horror of not knowing but the mystery that is stressed. The image of Scyld emerging from the unknown and fading back into it at his death is romantic rather than frightening.

6. Charles Donahue, "*Beowulf* and Christian Tradition: A Reconsideration from a Celtic Stance," *Traditio* 21 (1965): 81.

7. Alain Renoir, "The Heroic Oath in *Beowulf*, the *Chanson de Roland*, and the *Nibelungenlied*," *Studies in Old English Literature in Honor of Arthur G. Brodeur*,

ed. Stanley B. Greenfield (Eugene, Ore., 1963), 245.

8. Stanley B. Greenfield, *The Interpretation of Old English Poems* (London, 1972), 158.

9. "*Beowulf* 99–101," *Notes and Queries* 18 (1971): 163. When I first mentioned the transitional nature of these lines, in *Thoth* 10 (1969): 26–27, I did not comment on what now seems the most important point about this transition, mentioned by Ball: "Lines 90–114 of *Beowulf* thus contain a rapid summary of the main points of Genesis chapters i–vi."

10. Bede, *De Schematibus et Tropis, Patrologia Latina,* ed. J.P. Migne (Paris, 1844–65), 90:175–86.

11. J.R.R. Tolkien, "*Beowulf*: The Monsters and the Critics," *Proceedings of the British Academy* 22 (1936): 20.

12. C.L. Wrenn, ed., *"Beowulf" with the Finnesburg Fragment,* rev. ed. (London, 1958), 188.

13. Kevin Crossley-Holland, trans., *Beowulf* (New York, 1968), 35.

14. The technique of stopping the story is superficially reminiscent of the Homeric technique discussed by Erich Auerbach in *Mimesis* (trans. Willard R. Trask [Princeton, 1953]) in the chapter "Odysseus' Scar." But whereas (according to Auerbach) in Homer everything, including digressions, is equally "foregrounded," in *Beowulf* the two major digressions about swords introduce additional historical perspectives, scriptural in the passage about the golden hilt and Scandinavian in the one on Wiglaf's sword. Both confirm a perspective outside the sphere of awareness of the actors in the story, to whom the larger moral context of the monster rights and the future of their own continuing tribal identity are equally mysterious.

15. The inscription is reproduced by R.I. Page in *An Introduction to English Runes* (London, 1973), 170.

16. Klaeber, 189. Wrenn assumes that the story of the flood is graphic and runic, in a combination of "Christian and pre-Christian styles which reminds one of the Franks Casket" (56). "It is worth noticing," he adds, "how the Biblical story has been used in exactly the same way as the Germanic legends proper." That this is *not* so is precisely what I am trying to show.

17. Michael D. Cherniss, *Ingeld and Christ: Heroic Concepts and Values in Old English Christian Poetry* (The Hague, 1972), 149. In *The Mode and Meaning of "Beowulf"* (London, 1970), Margaret Goldsmith argues precisely the opposite: "There is a discernible Augustinian pattern of thought throughout Hrothgar's speech" (188).

18. Augustine, *City of God,* trans. Henry Bettenson (Harmondsworth, Eng., 1972), 311 (VIII, 9).

19. *The Prose Edda,* trans. Jean I. Young (Berkeley, 1964), 24.

20. "Religious Attitudes in *Beowulf,*" in *Essays and Poems Presented to Lord David Cecil* (London, 1970), 10.

21. Two such divergent experiences are still offered to the audience of the poem today, allowing one scholar to find the "meaning" of *Beowulf* "already complete within the Germanic heroic ethos" and another to read the poem as "the first great medieval allegory of human life and death based on the beliefs of the Western Church." The first is G.W. Smithers, quoted by Greenfield, *Interpretation,* 156; the second is Goldsmith, viii.

22. *City of God*, 600 (xv, 5). This concept of the archetype may well have been familiar to influential thinkers among the Anglo-Saxons. J.D.A. Ogilvy, in *Books Known to the English 597–1066* (Cambridge, Mass., 1967), says, "The *Civitas Dei* was one of the most popular, if not the most popular, of Augustine's works among the English. . . . The fifteenth book seems to have been especially popular, being used almost as much as all the other books combined" (82).

23. Citing Augustine's *City of God*, but not this passage, Marie Padgett Hamilton advances much the same interpretation in "The Religious Principle in *Beowulf*," *An Anthology of "Beowulf" Criticism*, ed. Lewis E. Nicholson (Notre Dame, 1963): "One is tempted to surmise that the author of *Beowulf*, in the manner of Bede and Augustine, envisioned the race of Cain in its timeless as well as temporal state . . ." (124). When she goes on, however, to ascribe to the poet a deep concern with Augustine's doctrine of Grace, she seems to me to be overreading the poem.

24. *The Exeter Book*, ed. George Philip Krapp and Elliott Van Kirk Dobbie, Anglo-Saxon Poetic Records 3 (New York, 1936), 163 (*Maxims I*, ll. 192–93).

25. When the dragon burns the gift-throne of the Geats, Beowulf wonders whether this is divine retribution for some crime he has unwittingly committed (2327–32); curiously, Margaret Goldsmith takes this as proof of Beowulf's "worldly outlook" (226), which, through a misreading of the text of the poem, she sees as culminating in avarice (239) and ultimately damnation (262 et passim). There is in fact a great difference between Grendel's attack upon Heorot and the dragon's upon the Geats: whereas Grendel cannot approach the gift-throne of Hrothgar, the dragon burns Beowulf's. In heroic terms this is equivalent to the murder of a kingdom, and in such circumstances the dutiful hero-king has little choice: he must avenge the kingdom and obtain an honorable *eðelgyld* (my word).

26. See Marijane Osborn, "Classical Meditation and *The Wanderer*," *Comparison* 1 (1975): 67–101, reprinted (condensed) as "Toward the Contemplative in *The Wanderer*," *Studia Mystica* 1.3 (1978), 53–69.

The Germanic Context
of the Unferþ Episode

by Carol J. Clover

This essay first appeared in Speculum *55 (1980): 444–68.*

THE idea that the Unferþ episode in *Beowulf* is related to the Norse flytings is hardly a new one. It has seldom progressed much beyond the stage of suggestion, however, and even the few longer discussions have failed to make much of the connection.[1] The problem seems to lie on the Norse side of the equation—in large part in reaching a consensus on just what constitutes a "flyting" so that we know what to measure the Unferþ episode against. From this point of view, scholarly discussions of the Norse material have been particularly unsatisfactory, being for the most part narrowly historical and lexical in their orientation. Despite the fact that the Norse flyting is a readily identifiable compositional unit, it has never been subjected to a systematic formal analysis. A recent dissertation by Joaquín Martínez Pizarro locates early Germanic examples of the flytings in Middle Latin sources and delineates the evolution of its scene and narrative context from Paul the Deacon to the late *fornaldarsǫgur,* but stops short of organizing themes and analyzing structure.[2] What may strike the outsider as the puzzling absence of a morphology for such an obvious category may have at least in part to do with the traditional and perhaps excessive respect paid by Scandinavianists to inherited native terminology—in this case the terms *senna* and *mannjafnaðr,* which, together with *níð,* have from the outset conditioned and inhibited scholarly discussion of the topic.

Senna (related to *sannr* 'true') is an uncommon word in Norse which seems to mean 'quarrel.' *Mannjafnaðr* ('man-comparison'), also uncommon, refers to a social practice involving the matching of two men's reputations. Both terms are thought to have legal origins: *senna* as a verbal effort on the part of one person to prove the guilt of another, and *mannjafnaðr* as an effort on the part of surviving relatives to assess the cash value of slain men.[3] Largely on the evidence of two attestations (the title of the Eddic poem *Lokasenna* and the explicitly labelled *mannjafnaðr* between the kings Eysteinn and Sigurðr in the historical tradition), the terms have been elevated by modern scholars to literary categories, the *senna* generally defined as a formal exchange of insults and threats and the *mannjafnaðr* a formal exchange of boasts. The difficulty is that neither category has a pure representative. One searches the corpus in vain for an unambiguous example. Certainly neither *Lokasenna* nor the Eysteinn-Sigurðr episode observes the distinction. The situation is further complicated by *nið*, that vague but spectacular category of sexual defamation for which Norse literature is justly infamous. The making of *nið* is supposed to have been proscribed in real life, but it clearly flourished in the literary underbrush and attached itself to the insult-boast tradition at a very early date.[4]

The *senna-mannjafnaðr* confusion is nowhere more apparent than in the scholarly literature, where the terms are applied inconsistently and with qualification.[5] It may well be that there once existed distinct forms, one an exercise in downgrading the opponent and the other an exercise in upgrading oneself. But by the time Norse documents appear, they are indistinguishable. Thus while the native terms may reflect a bifurcated prehistoric development and point to certain internal tendencies (the relative proportion of insults to boasts), they have no distinctive force as generic indicators. Descriptively the picture is clear: we have not two classes but one, itself a distinct category which English scholarship long ago labelled a flyting.

The Norse flyting may be mythological or heroic and is represented over the full literary range: Eddic poetry, Saxo Grammaticus's *Gesta Danorum*, the *þættir*, the major saga classes (including historical texts), and skaldic poetry. As a compositional unit it may stand alone (e.g., *Lokasenna* and *Hárbarðsljóð*) or be embedded in and subordinate to a larger context (e.g., the Sinfjǫtli-Guðmundr exchange in the Helgi poems or, in German tradition, the "ferocious ferryman" episode in the *Nibelungenlied*).[6] It consists of an exchange of verbal provocations between hostile speakers in a predictable setting. The boasts and insults are traditional, and their arrangement and rhetorical form is highly stylized.[7] No single example stands as an epitome (certainly *Lokasenna* is not the prototype it is commonly taken to be) for the simple reason that the form is traditional and hence subject to the usual thematic and motival variation. Any individual flyting is thus a unique combination of clichés and only approximates the general definition.[8] Yet the form itself is easily identified, in part because the clichés themselves are telltale markers. A characterization of the flyting thus necessarily involves an inventory of its commonplaces. What follows is a step in that direction: a brief catalogue, based on nearly forty examples,[9] of recurrent features of setting, contenders, dramatic situation, content, and outcome. As a survey of the generic territory it is not exhaustive, but strikes a compromise between the form as a whole and the particular properties of the Unferþ episode in order to suggest the extent of the common ground.

Setting. There are two standard settings, one outdoors over what Phillpotts called "the sundering flood" (a body of water separating the contenders),[10] the other indoors in the hall—at drinking, often at court (or, in Iceland, at the Alþing). The debate may arise spontaneously (as in *Þorgils saga ok Hafliða*) or it may be introduced as an entertainment, as in *Magnússona saga,* where it is specifically said to be a drinking custom (*ölsiðr, ölteiti*) to enter into verbal contests—a literary reflex of what we assume to have been actual banquet practice in the Germanic world.[11] Whether by accident or design, the debate typically begins on friendly, or at least calm, terms and then degenerates into angrier tones, with the severity of the provocations increasing accordingly. From *Eyrbyggja saga* comes the following report:

> Þar var ǫlteiti mǫrg; var þar talat um mannjǫfnuð, hverr þar væri gǫfgastr maðr í sveit eða mestr hǫfðingi; ok urðu menn þar eigi á eitt sáttir, sem optast er, ef um mannjǫfnuð er talat. . . .

> There was great ale-drinking; people spoke of a man-comparison, of who might be the most splendid man there in the district, or the greatest chief; and people did not agree, as is most often the case when there is talk of a man-comparison. . . .

Likewise the account of the historical Reykjahólar bridal (*Þorgils saga ok Hafliða*):

> Þeir drukku nú ákaft, ok fær á þá alla nökkut; gerask nú málgir, ok má kalla, at hverr styngi annan nökkuru hnœfilyrði, ok er þó fátt hermt af þeira keskiyrðum í þessarri frásögn.[12]

> They [the men] now began to drink heavily and grew somewhat intoxicated. They became voluble and (it may be said) taunted one another with insults—though few of the gibes are recorded in this account.

A seldom mentioned but striking parallel is found in the Exeter Book poem *Vainglory* ("Bi manna mode"), which suggests the existence in English social life of something very much like a hall flyting:

> . . . Monige beoð   mæþelhegendra,
> wlonce wigsmiþas   winburgum in,
> sittaþ æt symble,   soðgied wrecað,
> wordum wrixlað,   witan fundiaþ
> hwylc æscstede   inne in ræcede
> mid werum wunige,   þonne win hweteð
> beornes breostsefan.   Breahtem stigeð,

cirm on corþre,   cwide scralletaþ
missenlice.   Swa beoþ modsefan
dalum gedæled,   sindon dryhtguman
ungelice.   Sum on oferhygdo
þrymme þringeð,   þrinteð him in innan
ungemedemad mod;   sindan to monige þæt!
Bið þæt æfþonca   eal gefylled
feondes fligepilum,   facensearwum;
breodað he ond bælceð,   boð his sylfes
swiþor micle   þonne se sella mon,
þenceð þæt his wise   welhwam þince
eal unforcuþ . . .
Wrenceþ he ond blenceþ,   worn geþenceþ
hinderhoca,   hygegar leteð,
scurum sceoteþ . . .
Siteþ symbelwlonc,   searwum læteð
wine gewæged   word ut faran,
þræfte þringan   þrymme gebyrmed,
æfestum onæled,   oferhygda ful,
niþum nearowrencum . . .   (13–44a)[13]

. . . There are many men holding a meeting, proud war-makers in the
wine-halls. They sit at the feast, composing true songs, exchanging
words; they try hard to find out what battlefield may remain among
men inside the hall, when wine makes a man's heart excited. Noise
increases, the hubbub of the company, and voices ring out competing
with each other. In the same way minds are divided into types, for
men are not all alike. One sort presses on violently in his pride, an
immoderate spirit swells within him; of these there are too many. He
is filled by the devil's flying arrows of envy, by deceitful temptations.
He bawls and shouts, boasts about himself far more than does the
better man, thinks that his behavior must seem absolutely irreproach-
able to everybody. . . . He tricks and cheats, he thinks of many barbed
devices, he lets fly with premeditated shafts, he snipes continuously. . . . Sitting proudly at the feast, overcome by wine, he lets his
words stream out maliciously, pushing for a quarrel, swollen with
violence, inflamed by spite and hostility and tricks to cause trouble,
full of pride. . . .

In its immediate homiletic context the passage is nothing more than a
negative description of social drinking practices. But in its Germanic
context the scene falls in line as a version, complete with martial
metaphors, of the "indoor battlefield" commonplace. Particularly characteristic are its progressive sharpening of focus and darkening of tone:
from the larger crowd to certain envious and spiteful individuals within
it, from the jocular to the hostile, and from the general conversational

hubbub to a more specific sort of verbal combat. Just what form the *præft* ('quarrel, dispute, contention'; cf. OIcel *þrapt* and *prætta* 'dispute, wrangle, litigation') takes we are not told, though the Norse analogues permit us to make an informed guess.

The atmosphere of heavy drinking, unanimously stressed in the sources, is the context of such references to drunkenness as Egill's in chapter 44 of *Egils saga* (especially stanzas 9 and 10) and Heimdall's to Loki in *Lokasenna* 47:

> "Ǫlr ertu, Loki,   svá at þú er ørviti,
>   hvé né lezcaðu, Loki?
> Þvíat ofdryccia   veldr alda hveim,
>   er sína mælgi né manað."[14]

> "Drunk you are, Loki, out of your mind; why do you not cease? For overdrinking causes every man to be reckless with his tongue."

Drinking may itself be part of the contest, as in *Örvar-Odds saga,* where two brothers challenge Oddr to a match requiring each man to drink off a horn of beer before reciting an insult stanza. At the end of the 24-stanza contest, Oddr had emerged the victor, having outdrunk, out-recited, and outinsulted his opponents. There are numerous synoptic references to such combined drinking/slandering matches in the sagas (e.g., *Egils saga,* ch. 49), but their actual verbal content is seldom recorded (sometimes a sample stanza is included to suggest the tone of the whole). The particular value of the flyting in chapter 27 of *Örvar-Odds saga* is its complete scenic and procedural detail.

Contenders and dramatic situation. The contenders are in most cases male/male or male/female.[15] Female/female flytings appear to be linked with the "quarrel of the queens" of the Brynhildr tradition.[16] One on one is the rule, although sequential forms (one vs. two or several in turn) are found in *Lokasenna, Ǫlkofra þáttr, Bandamanna saga, Örvar-Odds saga,* and *Njáls saga.* There is also a pattern of delegates, whereby secondary figures (usually younger) speak on behalf of or instead of major figures (usually older). Thus Skírnir speaks for Freyr in *Skírnismál,* Sinfjǫtli for Helgi in *Helgakviða Hundingsbana I,* and Atli for Helgi in *Helgakviða Hjǫrvarðssonar.* The use of delegates is, as Martínez Pizarro shows, an old and persistent feature of the flyting.[17] The contenders may or may not know each other. The latter case typically involves a travelling hero entering unfamiliar territory and hence subject to hostile interrogation. Emphasis is on a margin or threshold: a new shore, or a gate or door of the hall.[18] Flytings of this sort (between unknown or unrecognized persons) open with an identification: an exchange of stylized questions and answers which establish name, paternity, and credentials. Although the greeting may be polite ("What heroes have come to Hatafjord . . . the name of their king I would know"; "Helgi is his name . . ."), it more typically takes the form of a baiting provocation, as in the opening of *Hárbarðsljóð*, the serial identifications of Skarpheðinn as he proceeds from booth to booth at the Alþing (*Njáls saga*), Grep's greeting of Ericus in Book V of Saxo ("Fool, who are you? What is your idle quest? Tell me, whence or whither do you journey? Which is your road? What your intention? Who your father? What your lineage?")[19] and the following exchange from *Helgakviða Hundingsbana I*:

> Frá goðborinn   Guðmundr at því:
> "Hverr er landreki,   sá er liði stýrir,
> oc hann feicnalið   fœrir at landi?"
>
> Sinfiotli qvaþ   —slong up við rá
> rauðom scildi,   rond var ór gulli;
> þar var sundvorðr,   sá er svara kunni
> oc við oðlinga   orðom scipta—:[20]
>
> "Segðu þat í aptan,   er svínom gefr
> oc tícr yðrar   teygir at solli,[21]
> at sé Ylfingar   austan komnir,
> gunnar giarnir,   at Gnipalundi."   (sts. 32–34)

Highborn Guðmundr asked: "Who is the king who heads the warriors and leads the great army to land?"

Sinfjotli said—raising on a sail-yard a red shield with a rim of gold; he was a coastguard who knew how to answer and to converse with kings—

"When tonight you swill your swine and call your bitches to their mush, say that the Ylfings have come from the east, eager for battle, to Gnipalundr."

The exposure of newcomers to mockeries and challenges ("I am baited with the jeers of the court-folk. . . . I am assaulted with harsh gibing, and stung with battling taunts")[22] is so common a feature in the literature that we may wonder whether it does not in fact reflect actual Germanic etiquette.[23]

The characterization of Sinfjotli as a coastguard "who could converse with kings" reminds us that the single most important attribute, and perhaps the only shared one, of flyting contenders is their verbal skill.[24] The Ericus toward whom Grep directs his contentious questioning is in fact Ericus Disertus (Eiríkr inn málspaki, Eric the Eloquent), a man "better spoken than all other people," "superior in words," "stronger in tongue," and "champion in argument" (*altercationum athleta*). His opponent Grep is likewise gifted, but his eloquence, Saxo explains, is "not so much excellent as impudent, for he surpassed all in tenacity of speech." Loki (*Lks*) is "auðigr í andsvorum" (rich in rejoinders), and Ófeigr, the flyting artist of *Bandamanna saga,* is characterized at the outset as "spekingr mikill ok ráðagørðar maðr" (a great sage and counselor), both appellations understood in the saga idiom as referring to verbal skills. King Eysteinn (*Magnússona saga*) claims to be "miklu sléttorðari" (more fluent of speech) on every topic than his brother Sigurðr; and Starkaðr is able "eigi seinna yrkja en mæla" (to compose verses as fast as he can speak). It is worth noting that Starkaðr, the grand master of Norse poetic invective, is specifically called a *þulr* (cf. Unferþ the *þyle*) in *Gautreks saga.*[25]

What is meant, of course, is not pure but applied eloquence: words used as ammunition in verbal warfare. Flytings are won by the articulate marshalling of superior evidence, and combat is the working metaphor. Saxo's Ericus is "as valorous in tongue as in hand," and King Fridleif (Saxo VI) is advised that a certain adversary who cannot be made to yield to physical force can be overcome by words. Likewise, Grep goes to meet Eric "intending to assault [him] with chosen and pointed phrases," but as it turns out Grep himself is "vanquished with words" (uerbis . . . uictus) and loses the "voice war" (certamen uocis). Of Gotwar (Saxo V) it is said that "words were her weapons" and that she "could not fight" but "found darts in her tongue instead." *Orðom bregðask* (to battle with words) and *sakask sáryrðom* (to fight with wound-words) are the flyting terms of *HHI* and *Lks.* The reciprocal notion is expressed in a number of kennings of the type *sverða senna* (quarrel of swords) for battle. The use of martial terms and images (apparent even in the homiletic *Vainglory*) and the emphasis on winning and losing make it clear that the flyting is not just a prelude to violence but itself the oral equivalent of war.

Structure. The structure of the flyting is conditioned by the terms of debate and has as a standard sequence a Claim, Defense, and Counterclaim.[26] The Claim and Counterclaim consist of insults and boasts (past) and threats, vows, and curses (future). The Defense typically involves concessive clauses ("that may be, but"). Longer multiplications of this sequence seem to be a peculiarly Norse development, and we may speculate that they were conditioned by the stanza (stanzaic features may be discerned even in prose flytings).[27] The format of the exchange is highly stylized and is characterized by logical and syntactic parallelism: questions and answers, counterposed speeches, recurrent phrases, and symmetrical reasoning. Familiar repetitions are *þegi þú* ("be quiet") + (name) and *veiztu* ("you know") in *Lokasenna* (17 and 6 times respectively); *þar sitr þú* ("there you sit") + (name) in *Bandamanna saga*; the formulaic identifications and balanced speeches of *Njáls saga* 119–120; *hvat vanntu meðan* ("what did *you* accomplish in the meantime?") + (name) in *Hárbarðsljóð* (9 times); and (name) + *vart eigi þar meðan* ("*you* weren't there while") in *Örvar-Odds saga* (12 times). Two features are particularly conspicuous: the use of the opponent's name in direct address, and the emphatic pronoun contrasts (I/you).[28] The last two examples are versions of the same challenge: What were *you* doing while *I* was doing thus and so? This query forms the rhetorical substructure of about half the Norse flytings and, we will see, the Unferþ-Beowulf exchange as well.

    Content. Most flytings consist of boasts and insults in varying proportions, with an admixture of threats, curses, or vows. The threat implies physical violence (and, for women, sexual degradation). "Hrungnis bani / mun þér í hel koma / fyr nágrindr neðan" ("[I] will send you to Hel, down to the gate of death"), Þórr says to Loki in *Lks,* and likewise to Hárbarðr in *Hbl* "ec mynda þic í hel drepa, / ef ec mætta seilaz um sund" ("I would smite you to Hel if I could reach over the sound"). The curse, which may be metrically indicated in *galdralag* (as in *Skírnismál*), is a threat in more pointed, formulaic form: "Farðu nú, þars þic hafi allan gramir!" ("Go now where the devils shall have you!") and "deili grǫm við þic!" ("may devils take you!"), both from *Hbl.* Boasts have to do with manly virtues: defeat of mighty adversaries, participation in military campaigns, victory in contests of strength, and rape. Vows promise positive action and may also take competitive form (as in the escalating sequence of oaths in *Jómsvíkinga saga.*)

    The repertory of insults reduces to a few major categories: appearance, acts of cowardice (deserting a battle), heroic failure (losing a battle), trivial or irresponsible behavior (pointless escapades, domestic indulgences, sexual dalliance), failings of honor (unwillingness or inability to extract due vengeance, hostile relations with kinsmen), alimentary taboos (eating corpses, drinking urine), and sexual irregularities (promiscuity for women; castration, bestiality, and passive homosexuality for men; incest for both).[29] From this list crimes of kinship emerge as a central theme: incest, failure to avenge a slain father or brother, strife with or slaying of a father or brother, and, for a woman, sex with the slayer of her father or brother. "You have laid your bright arms around your brother's murderer (*bróðurbani*)," Loki charges Iðunn in *Lks* 17.[30] Starkaðr unleashes a contemptuous diatribe against Ingeld, who is hosting his father's slayers at a banquet: "What strong heir or well-starred son would have sat side by side with such as these. . . . Why do you vex me with insolent gaze, you who honor the foe guilty of your father's blood, who are known to take your vengeance with loaves and warm soup?" (Saxo VI).³¹ Skarpheðinn says to Þorkell: "I, at least, never threatened my father's own life, as you once did, nor ever fought with him, as you once did" (*Njáls saga*). Atonement is the chief issue of the quarrel in *Eyrbyggja saga*. In *HHI*, Guðmundr charges Sinfjǫtli: "[Þú hefir] brœðr þínom at bana orðit" ("You have been your brother's bane"), and again, "[þú] brœðr þínom / brióst raufaðir") ("You broke your brother's breast").³² It should be remembered that fratricide and parricide are frequently mentioned in Germanic tradition and that some of its greatest heroes are "not free from the stain."³³

It is not, however, the most flamboyant provocations that win the flyting, but the most accurate ones. Inferior contestants (Þórr, Byggvir, Grep, and Sinfjǫtli) tend to be random and excessive in their remarks, while the first-rate performances of Ófeigr, Hárbarðr, Ericus Disertus, and Skarpheðinn are carefully proportioned, use classic rhetorical techniques, and build on a few standard oppositions: action vs. talk, hard life vs. soft life, adventurer vs. stay-at-home, etc.

> Snorri mælti: "Hverr er sá maðr, er fjórir ganga fyrri, fǫlleitr ok skarpleitr ok glottir við tǫnn ok hefir øxi reidda um ǫxl?" "Heðinn heiti ek," segir hann, "en sumir kalla mik Skarpheðinn ǫllu nafni, eða hvat villtú fleira til mín tala?" Snorri mælti: "Mér þykkir þú harðligr ok mikilfengligr, en þó get ek at þrotin sé nú þín in mesta gæfa, ok skammt get ek eptir þinnar ævi." "Vel er þat," segir Skarpheðinn, "því at þá skuld eigu allir at gjalda. En þó er þér meiri nauðsyn at hefna fǫður þíns en spá mér slíkar spár." "Margir hafa þat mælt áðr," segir Snorri, "ok mun ek ekki við slíku reiðask."

> Snorri said, "Who is that man, fifth in the line, the pale, sharp-featured man with a grin on his face and an axe on his shoulder?" "My name is Heðinn," he replied, "but some call me Skarpheðinn in full. Have you anything else to say to me?" "I think you look very ruthless and formidable," said Snorri, "but my guess is that you have not long to live." "Well and good," said Skarpheðinn, "for death is a debt we all have to pay. But you would be better employed avenging your father than prophesying my future." "You are not the first man to tell me that," said Snorri, "and I won't be baited."³⁴

This exchange is repeated five times in remarkably similar form (some lines verbatim) in *Njáls saga* 119–120. To the initial enquiry into his identity ("who is that man, fifth in line?"), with its insulting remarks about his appearance, Skarpheðinn responds with a rhetorical concession ("that may be, but") designed to reverse the direction of the argument. Thus on the offensive, he proceeds to discredit his opponents by producing some disagreeable facts from their past (Skapti's involvement in an ignominious murder and escape, Hafr's failure to retrieve his kidnapped sister, Þorkell's civic and familial irresponsibility, certain "unpleasant tales" about Guðmundr inn ríki). The sarcastic formulation "you would be better employed avenging your father (fetching back your sister, etc.) than prophesying my future" realizes the common opposition between words and deeds expressed succinctly in *HHII*:[35]

> Þér er, Sinfjǫtli,   sœmra myclo
> gunni at heyia   oc glaða ǫrno,
> enn ónýtom   orðom at bregða . . ."   (st. 23)

"It would better beseem you, Sinfjǫtli, to give battle and gladden eagles than to fight with words . . ."

The opposition between adventurer and stay-at-home is the basis of the magisterial flyting of the *Magnússona saga* in *Heimskringla* (found in fuller form in *Morkinskinna*), in which the royal brothers Sigurðr and Eysteinn engage in a debate of epic proportions to determine who is the better man. They begin with boyhood accomplishments—diving, skating, swimming:

> Þá mælti Sigurðr konungr: "Mantu, hversu fór um sundit með okkr? Ek mátta kefja þik, ef ek vilda." Eysteinn konungr segir: "Ekki svam ek skemmra en þú, ok eigi var ek verr kafsyndr. Ek kunna ok á ísleggjum, svá at engan vissa ek þann, er þat keppði við mik, ok þú kunnir þat eigi heldr en naut."

Then King Sigurðr said: "Do you remember how we fared at swimming? I could hold you under if I wanted." King Eysteinn replied: "I didn't swim less far, and I was no worse at diving. And I was so good on skates that no one could compete with me, and you could no more do it than an ox."

Then they proceed to manly qualities: strength, prowess with weapons, appearance, legal knowledge, eloquence, a just nature. When Sigurðr plays his trump card, Eysteinn has a ready answer:

> Sigurðr konungr segir: "Þat hefir verit mál manna, at ferð sú, er ek fór ór landi, væri heldr hǫfðinglig, en þú sazt heima meðan sem dóttir fǫður þíns." Eysteinn konungr svarar: "Nú greiptu á kýlinu. Eigi mynda ek þessa rœðu vekja, ef ek kynna hér engu svara. Nærr þótti mér hinu, at ek gerða þik heiman sem systur mína, áðr þú yrðir búinn til ferðar."

King Sigurðr says: "It is commonly thought that my expedition abroad was rather princely, while you in the meantime sat at home like your father's daughter." King Eysteinn answers: "Now you've hit the sore spot. But I wouldn't have started this discussion if I didn't have an answer for that. To my way of thinking, I had to dower you like my sister before you could leave on that journey."

Sigurðr persists:

> "... I went to Palestine, and I came to Apulia, but I did not see you
> there. I won seven battles, and you were in none of them. I was at our
> Lord's grave, but did not see you there. I went all the way to Jordan,
> where our Lord was baptized, and swam across, but I did not see you
> there. ..."[36]

He concludes this I/you opposition with a summary insult: "... ek
hygg, at eigi hafir þú hleypt heimdraganum" ("it seems to me that you
still haven't broken away from home" [lit. "stopped home-dragging"]).
Eysteinn's reply, however, is long and crushing: while his brother was
out seeking glory, he stayed home and governed Norway—built hos-
pices, churches, roads, harbors, towers, beacons, a royal hall, founded a
monastery, and annexed Jämtland. This victory coda ends the flyting,
and they both sink into silence.

The form, rhetoric, and opposition of the *Magnússona saga* flyting is
strictly conventional (particularly in its pre-Snorri form). Only the bias
is uncharacteristic, but this is of course a deliberate reversal: Eysteinn's
particular success lies in having upended the traditional terms.[37] Travel
and adventure are otherwise unanimously favored over domestic pastimes.[38] "Sigr hafða ek, sazt kyrr meðan" ("While you were sitting still, I
had victory") is the central premise of the flyting in *Örvar-Odds saga* (ch.
27), here represented by two stanzas:

"Sjólfr, vart eigi,	"Sjólfr, you weren't
þar er sjá máttum	there when we watched
brynjur manna	men's mail-coats
blóði þvegnar;	washing in blood;
hrukku oddar	spear-points probed
í hringserkjum,	into chaincoats,
en þú höll konungs	but all you explored
heldr kannaðir."	was the king's hall."
(st. 10)	
"Sigurðr, vart eigi,	"Sigurðr, you weren't there
er á Sælundi felldak	on Zealand when I felled
bræðr böðharða,	the battle-hard brothers
Brand ok Agnar,	Brandr and Agnarr,
Ásmund, Ingjald,	Ásmundr and Ingjaldr,
Álfr var inn fimmti;	and Álfr was the fifth;
en þú heimi látt	you were lying at home
í höll konungs,	in the king's hall,
skrökmálasamr,	full of tall stories,
skauð hernumin."	a captive gelding."[39]
(st. 13)	

The last two lines recur in variant form at the end of st. 17: "Hrókr hernuminn, / hví þegir þú nú?" ("Big-talking captive, why so silent now?"). Hanging about telling stories and "exploring" the king's hall (an ironic formulation) are just two items in Oddr's typical catalogue of inferior alternatives to heroic action: lying around the kitchen, consorting with farmers, wandering as a beggar, cavorting with slave girls, etc. The sarcastic reconstruction of these lowly activities is standard insult procedure.

The method, then, is for one contender to bring up what Axel Olrik termed a "preliminary incident"[40] from the life of his opponent—a specific event, with detailed information on place, duration, and names of other persons involved. But are such claims true or false? This is in fact a central question, with respect not only to the origin of the flyting, but to the understanding of its function in a literary context. If the flyting refers to actual events or behavior, it constitutes a major and serious plot event in which the moral character of the participants is at stake, and it is, further, an important source of historical information about the prehistory of the plot and characters (i.e., Unferþ's fratricide and the Breca episode). If on the other hand the flyting has no basis in reality, it constitutes nothing more than an entertaining digression in which only the participant's verbal wit is at stake, and it has no historical value. Chambers's view that Norse insults are "unfounded taunts" and "outrageous charges assuredly not meant to be taken literally"[41] has found recent analogic support in such investigations as that of William Labov into "ritual" sounding (that is, traditional and nonspecific verbal duelling) among ghetto youths.[42] But Labov's analysis of a living insult tradition, suggestive as it is, cannot be applied, at least in unmodified form, to the Germanic material. While there do exist numerous fantastic insults in Norse, it is clear from the strong responses they provoke that they cannot be "ritual" in Labov's sense. It seems more likely that their metaphoric diction is a function of their subject matter (male sexual irregularity) and is to be explained as a circumvention of legal injunctions against *níð*. Such insults are in any case irrelevant to the Unferþ episode and may be put aside as a special case. What we find in the majority remainder is a type of insult which bears little if any resemblance to Labov's formulation: charges which are not only eminently plausible, but in a surprising number of cases actually documentable, either by virtue of authorial explanation or corroboration in other sources. Sinfjǫtli's fratricide (*HHI*) is substantiated in *Vǫlsunga saga*. The narrator of *Þorgils saga ok Hafliða* confirms that Þórðr did indeed have halitosis (the result of a poor stomach condition), as the lampoons charge. The claims of the royal brothers Sigurðr and Eysteinn did in fact represent received history. Magnus Olsen has cogently demonstrated that Þórr's claims in *Hbl* reflect older legendary traditions.[43] Even the apparently bizarre charges of the mythological flytings may work this way, as in the sequence in *Lks* where a) Njǫrðr accuses Loki of having given birth to children; b) Loki counters by saying that the giants held Njǫrðr hostage; c) Njǫrðr concedes this but points out that it was the gods' gain, for it was then that he fathered Freyr, now esteemed by the Æsir; d) but Loki objects that Freyr is the product of incest, and so on. Again, all this rests, largely but not exclusively on the authority of Snorri, on what we take to be mythological fact: Loki did give birth (the Svaðilfari episode), Njǫrðr was held hostage and did beget Freyr with his sister, and so forth.

The best evidence, however, comes from the texts themselves—from the fact that the "preliminary incident" itself is never disputed, even by the offended partner. Skarpheðinn's charges at the Alþing are not denied; they are acknowledged, one after the other, tacitly or directly, by the men in question. This is perhaps the most striking characteristic of flytings: they argue interpretations, not facts. The following passage from *Magnússona saga* epitomizes both the method and the rhetoric:

> Eysteinn konungr segir: "... Kann ek ok miklu betr til laga en þú, ok svá hvat sem vit skulum tala, em ek miklu sléttorðari." Sigurðr konungr svarar: "Vera kann, at þú hafir numit fleiri lǫgprettu, því at ek átta þá annat at starfa. En engi frýr þér sléttmælis, en hitt mæla margir, at þú sér eigi allfastorðr ok lítit mark sé, hverju þú heitr, mælir eptir þeim, er þá er hjá, ok er þat ekki konungligt."

> King Eysteinn says: "... I am moreover more knowledgeable in law than you, and no matter what the subject, I am more eloquent." King Sigurðr answers: "It may be that you know more legal tricks, for I have had other things to take care of, nor will anyone deny you a smooth tongue; but there are many who say your words are empty, that what you promise cannot be trusted, and that you tailor your talk to those who are nearest—and that is not kingly."

In an exemplary blend of concessive clauses, sarcastic formulations, and insulting counterclaims, Eysteinn challenges not the substance of Sigurðr's boast—this he concedes at the outset—but its significance or practical value. It is not, in other words, a question of factual true and false, but of moral plus and minus. Far from being "unfounded taunts," flyting charges are, at least in the hands of the chief practitioners, deadly accurate: the art of the boast lies in creating, within the limitations of the facts, the best possible version of the event; and the art of the insult lies in creating, within the limitations of the facts, the worst possible version of the event. This particular kind of wrangling, with its use of miniature stories from the past, its contest form, and its almost legalistic method, is a defining characteristic of the flyting and distinguishes Germanic practice from similar traditions.[44]

Outcome. Critics seem uniformly attached to the idea that flytings end in violence.[45] This is not so; posturings and threats to that effect are commonplace, but they belong to the genre and are not to be taken literally as prefatory remarks. In *Bandamanna saga,* Ófeigr simply tongue-lashes his opponents in turn and that concludes the episode. In *Magnússona saga* the contenders lapse into angry but permanently peaceful silence. In the otherwise extravagantly violent *Örvar-Odds saga,* the drinking flyting ends with a victory coda—an extended boast of grandiose proportions on Oddr's part—upon which all three contestants go to bed. *Hárbarðsljóð* ends with Hárbarðr wishing Þórr to the devil. In Saxo's Book I, Gróa actually falls in love with her flyting opponent the minute he drops his disguise. These are just some of the nonviolent endings: the list is sufficiently long and various to lead us to the conclusion that we are dealing not with the outcome of the flyting itself but with its upshot, and that is conditioned by the requirements of the story. Even where there is a question of violence, the flyting is usually one episode in a causal series—in which it does not *per se* result in battle any more than Skarpheðinn's insults at the Alþing can be said to result in the burning at Bergþórshváll. The flyting is conceived, as we have shown, as a verbal combat complete in itself, with its own logic, rules, winners and losers. If a loser decides to seek redress in battle, that is a new phase of the story and may be treated independently as a revenge episode.

To an audience familiar with the literary conventions of the flyting, the *Beowulf* poet's intention is abundantly clear well before Unferþ opens his mouth. Lines 491–501a set the traditional scene: in a hall, at a banquet, over drinking, with emphasis on an arrival and a threshold. Hroþgar has received the newcomer Beowulf and invited him to sit and tell of his famous victories—of which, of course, he has already boasted at some length. Unferþ is stationed at Hroþgar's feet; however ambiguous that may be with regard to his court status, it does presume a special association with the king, and from this we can deduce the familiar delegate function.[46] Unferþ is the extension or agent of the king and court, and through his offices the newly arrived hero is interrogated in a manner whose conventional nature is designated in the prefatory words "Unferþ maþelode . . . onband beadurune" (Unferþ spoke . . . unbound war-words"). Like *sakask sáryrðom* and *orðom bregðask,* the phrase *on-*

bindan beadurune labels the flyting with the familiar battle metaphor.[47]

The apparent contradiction between Unferþ's belligerence and the decorous behavior of Hroþgar has long been regarded as a puzzle. As Brodeur saw it, Unferþ, acting on his own behalf, "dared to violate his official duty and flout the plain intention of his lord."[48] But Hroþgar's intention is not so plain as it seems. He at no time acts like a flouted lord: he does not intervene in the debate, and when it is over, he neither chastises Unferþ nor apologizes to Beowulf. That his silence must indicate sponsorship, or at least "lie in the presumption that Unferþ's behavior is expected,"[49] seems clear. In other words, his cordiality and Unferþ's hostility are not contradictory but complementary, with the former in fact predicated on the latter: secure in the knowledge that Unferþ will put the alien through the necessary paces, Hroþgar can afford to play the gracious host. The relation is a classic one and amounts to a "simple poetic analysis of government."[50]

Like his flyting counterparts, Unferþ is a man of words (this much at least can be safely deduced from the term *þyle*) whose wit is keen (589b). His opening words identify the newcomer by name and introduce the "preliminary incident" ("Eart þu se Beowulf, / se þe wið Brecan wunne"—"Are you that Beowulf who contended with Breca?") which he then proceeds to discredit before the gathered court. His speech drips with irony, starting with mock admiration for a man who would actually risk his life in such a trivial affair for the sake of *wlenco* (pride, daring) and *dolgilp* (foolhardy boasting)[51] and continuing with a description of the episode in "vivid and violent figures designed to stress and ridicule the vehement efforts in the sea of two young men frantically striving to make good a foolish boast":[52] "þær git eagorstream / earmum þehton, / mæton merestræta, / mundum brugdon, / glidon ofer garsecg" ("There you embraced the sea-streams with your arms, measured the sea-ways, flung forward your hand, glided over the ocean"). Since Unferþ did not after all witness the event, this can only be a sarcastic reconstruction for rhetorical effect in the familiar style of, e.g., *Lks, Hbl, Ǫlkofra þáttr,* and *Ǫrvar-Odds saga* (ch. 27). He then turns to specific charges: the contest took too long, Beowulf was worsted in the effort, and Breca covered himself with glory and came into possession of the land of the Brondings. He concludes his speech with a concessive clause ironically embedded in a grim prediction:

> "Ðonne wene ic to þe   wyrsan geþingea,
> ðeah þu heaðoræsa   gehwær dohte,
> grimre guðe,   gif þu Grendles dearst
> nihtlongne fyrst   nean bidan."   (525–28)

"Therefore I expect the worse results for you—*though you have prevailed everywhere in battles, in grim war*—if you dare wait near Grendel a night-long space."

The Claim thus amounts to a double charge of frivolous behavior and heroic inadequacy, to which Beowulf responds with a paradigmatic Defense and Counterclaim. That he is prepared to meet Unferþ on his own sarcastic terms is obvious from his first words:

> "Hwæt, þu worn fela,   wine min Unferð,
> beore druncen   ymb Brecan spræce,
> sægdest from his siðe."   (530–32a)

"Well, my friend Unferþ, drunk with beer you have spoken a great many things about Breca—told about his adventures."

Beowulf returns apostrophe with apostrophe; and after the familiar reproach of drunkenness, he rehearses the episode from his point of view: the contest was undertaken on a boast as an act of youthful exuberance, he was the stronger, they parted only because a storm drove them apart, and it took as long as it did because he had to subdue sea monsters.

To say that Beowulf "refutes Unferth's charges"[53] or "corrects him by telling the true story of the incident"[54] misses the point. What is remarkable about Beowulf's reply, after all, is that it concedes the issue. His own additions to the story are minor, more by way of clarification. The disagreement lies not in the facts, which are mutually acknowledged, but in their interpretation: was the Breca contest a harmless adventure with a heroic conclusion, as Beowulf claims, or was it brash with an ignominious outcome, as Unferþ claims? The significance of this aspect of the exchange was appreciated by Larry Benson, who concluded that Beowulf's failure to deny Unferþ's story confirms the existence of an earlier tale about a swimming match known to the *Beowulf* audience.[55] His proposition is buttressed by the analogous evidence of the flytings, where plausible claims based on accepted facts are, as is repeatedly seen in examples where documentation exists, "real" references. Flytings of this sort are predicated on the renegotiation of history, not its invention. There is little doubt that this is the sense of the Unferþ episode, and the story of Breca can likewise be assumed to reflect a preexisting tradition.[56]

This concludes Beowulf's on the whole well-mannered Defense. As Brodeur notes, "thus far he has merely justified himself, and has spoken with marked restraint."[57] In his Counterclaim he tries to turn the matter to his advantage by appealing to the paradigm "Where were you when I was doing heroic deeds?":

"No ic wiht fram þe
swylcra searoniða   secgan hyrde,
billa brogan.   Breca næfre git
æt heaðolace,   ne gehwæþer incer,
swa deorlice   dæd gefremede
fagum sweordum   —no ic þæs [fela] gylpe—"
(581b–86)

"I have not heard say of *you* any such hard matching of might, such
sword terror. Breca never yet in games of war—neither he nor you—
achieved so bold a deed with bright swords—not that I much boast of
it."

The opposition between Beowulf the adventurer (sword-wielder, warrior) and Unferþ the hall-dragger, coward, and *þyle* locates the exchange
squarely in the tradition of the *mannjafnaðr* flyting, with close parallels
in *Magnússona saga* and *Örvar-Odds saga*. Stanza 13 of the latter may be
recalled as especially apt, given the association of the OE *þyle* (ON *þulr*)
with speaking and entertainment in court: "You weren't there when I
felled the battle-hard brothers . . . you were lying at home in the king's
hall, full of tall stories." Equally familiar is the sarcastic reversal in the
form of a concessive clause: "Neither you nor Breca achieved so bold a
deed with bright swords, although you *did* kill your *brothers*" ("þeah ðu
þinum broðrum / to banan wurde").[58] Recourse to the Norse context
brings into sharper relief Beowulf's charge of fratricide, long the subject
of scholarly questions. Kinship crimes, we have shown, form a major
theme in the genre, and it is a rare flyting that does not exhibit at least
one such accusation. It may furthermore be concluded by extrapolation
from documentable examples that such insults tend as a group to be
true—true at least with respect to received tradition. The duplicate
charge in *HHI* ("[Þú hefir] þínom brœðr / at bana orðit") is verified
elsewhere. The Norse sources thus appear to substantiate Unferþ's
fratricide, and there is no reason not to take the *Beowulf* poet at face
value when he later says that Unferþ was "not honorable to his kinsmen
at sword play" (his magum nære / arfæst æt ecga gelacum—ll. 1167b–
68a).

Just as the Norse flytings combine curses with boasts and insults, so
Beowulf concludes his accusation of fratricide with a malediction (followed by a sarcastic concessive clause):

". . . þæs þu in helle scealt
werhðo dreogan,   þeah þin wit duge."
(588b–89)

"For this you will suffer punishment in hell, though your wit is keen."

This has been thought either excessively dark or an "unfortunate lapse into religious cliché,"[59] and Robinson has tried to temper it by reading *healle* for *helle*: "for that you must endure condemnation in the hall."[60] The suggestion is both attractive in context and eminently justified on manuscript grounds, yet the frequency of similar imprecations in Norse (go to Hel, be taken by devils) argues in favor of the traditional interpretation *helle*.[61] The inclusion of a curse in the context of boasts and insults, the drastic tone, and the specific vocabulary are thus fully consonant with flyting practice.

Beowulf clinches the argument by pointing out that Grendel's continued presence is unequivocal proof of Unferþ's heroic deficiency— Unferþ would presumably have been "better employed" putting his muscle where his mouth is—and he reaffirms his oath to meet the monster and so succeed where Unferþ has failed, putting his case in comparative terms to the very end. To this he adds, in the style of Oddr and Eysteinn, a grandiloquent coda in which he evokes a vision of a monster-free future in which all men may walk glad to the mead hall in the morning sun.[62]

It has often been remarked that the speeches of Unferþ and Beowulf stand rhetorically apart. They are "rather ornate considering the occasion"[63] and "gehören zu den Glanzstücken des Beowulfepos."[64] The exchange between eloquent contenders is in the best tradition of the flyting, and Unferþ and Beowulf may be seen as striking adumbrations of Grep and Ericus Disertus: both men are eloquent, but because Unferþ's talent is "not so much excellent as impudent," it is Beowulf who wins the oral victory. By deploying the full rhetorical arsenal of flyting tradition he has beaten the keen-witted *þyle* at his own game, thereby passing with flying colors the "hostile test of his *sapientia*"[65] and establishing his worthiness to "converse with kings."

The persistent notion that flytings end in violence has contributed to the opinion that the Unferþ episode is inconclusive. Klaeber considered the lack of a battle challenge to be an "obvious, inherent defect" in the poem,[66] and Brodeur on similar grounds concluded that "one can hardly regard this interchange as a mere flyting: flytings are either exchanges of crude wit, rough games, or invective preceding a fight. Here no fight can conceivably occur, since Beowulf is the honored guest of the king; and the encounter between Beowulf and Unferþ is simply no game."[67] Relying on Brodeur's incomplete understanding of the flyting, Norman Eliason argues that the Grendel episode constitutes the desired violent outcome and that Unferþ is an articulate stand-in for the mute monster.[68] But violence is of course not a requisite ending of the flyting; it is just one of several optional consequences which the poet did not choose.

What he *did* choose is equally conventional: Unferþ falls silent. He is not mentioned again in this episode, and the poet later comments:

> Ða wæs swigra secg,   sunu Ec[g]lafes,
> on gylpspræce   guðgeweorca . . .   (980–81)

Then was the warrior more silent in boasting speech of warlike deeds, the son of Ecglaf . . .

As Brodeur pointed out, the sentence as a whole has a deliberate thrust: "if he was ashamed,[69] it was not for his initial discourtesy, but because of his now proved inferiority to Beowulf."[70] Being silenced is of course of a particularly appropriate form of defeat in a battle of words. Silence is often threatened or urged in the flytings, and it is moreover clear that having the last word is equivalent to winning the contest. The chieftains in *Bandamanna saga* are unable to answer Egill's insults: "nú þagnar Styrmir" (now Styrmir becomes silent); "Þórarinn sezk niðr ok þagnar" (Þórarinn sits down and becomes silent); and, finally, "Þorgeirr þagnaði. En þeir Skegg-Broddi ok Járnskeggi vildu engum orðum skipta við Egil" (Þorgeirr became silent. And Skegg-Broddi and Járnskeggi wished to bandy no words with Egill).[71] A psychology of the silent ending is suggested in the concluding words of the *Magnússona saga* flyting:

> Eptir þat þǫgnuðu þeir báðir, ok var hvárrtveggi reiðr. Fleiri hlutir urðu þeir í skiptum þeira brœðra, er þat fannsk á, at hvárr dró sik fram ok sitt mál ok vildi hvárr vera ǫðrum meiri, en helzk þó friðr milli þeira, meðan þeir lifðu.

> Thereupon both were silent, and there was anger on both sides. More things passed between the brothers, from which it appeared that each of them would be greater than the other; however peace was preserved between them as long as they lived.

By the rules of the flyting, Unferþ's failure to respond to Beowulf's palpable victory coda is both a conventional and conclusive outcome. Like Eysteinn and Sigurðr, Unferþ and Beowulf survive the episode to enjoy strained relations for the duration.[72]

Blame literature appears to be a very nearly universal phenomenon, attested in living traditions (e.g., among Turkish youths, Eskimos, and in Black English Vernacular) as well as earlier ones (e.g., Sumerian, Indic, Irish, and Greek).[73] Dumézil has proposed that Indo-European society operated on the principle of counterbalancing praise and invective, primarily through the medium of poetry.[74] Certainly verbal combats involving invective and self-praise are to be expected in heroic societies operating on what Gouldner calls the "contest system," in which the broad range of human behavior (including the production and performance of literature) is realized in competitive terms.[75] To this

extent critics have correctly sensed a relationship between the Unferþ
altercation and such scenes as that in Book VIII of the *Odyssey,* in which
Odysseus retorts sharply to Euryalus's demeaning remarks about his
appearance. But that is, as Albert Lord suggests, the sort of general
correspondence that arises out of the heroic sense of the plot.[76]

The relation of the Unferþ episode to the Norse flytings, on the
other hand, is immediate and detailed, both with respect to situation
(the hostile investigation into the reputation of a newcomer by a man
who stands in a delegate relation to the king and is explicitly known as a
man of words) and the nature of the speeches themselves: in form
(Claim, Defense, and Counterclaim); in tone (the blend of insult,
competitive boasting, and curse); in the use of sarcasm (most character-
istically in concessive clauses); in the emphatic I/you contrast and the
use of names in direct address; in the combat metaphor; in the matching
of personal histories and the exposure of dubious or shameful deeds
(and their sarcastic reconstruction); in the telltale preoccupation with
the moral negotiability of past events; in the use of familiar oppositions
and paradigms; and in such correspondences of detail as the charges of
drunkenness and fratricide and the Hel curse. The only conspicuous
incongruity is the absence of a sexual element—but then the *Beowulf*
poet is not known for developing the erotic dimensions of his gothic
tale.

Two misapprehensions in particular concerning the Norse flyting
have impeded identification of the traditional nature of the Unferþ-
Beowulf exchange. The first, that the flytings are mere games and that
their charges are "whopping lies,"[77] has already been rejected. The
second, that they consist only of crude insults "from a ruder age,"[78] is
similarly inaccurate, as should be clear from the preceding examples.
Just as the flytings display variation in dramatic situation, outcome,
mode (mythological or heroic), and formal properties (short or long,
prose or poetry, dependent or independent), so they vary in tone from
solemn to humorous, negative to positive, light-hearted to murderously
angry. The flyting is an adaptable form, in these and other ways the
obedient servant of its context. Again, in light of the larger category, the
Beowulf flyting is not an extreme or deviant case, but an eminently
typical one.

The recognition of the Unferþ episode as a flyting illuminates certain
of its puzzling aspects. It explains what to the modern ear is the un-
provoked and "shockingly offensive . . . impropriety"[79] of Unferþ's
behavior. It accounts, as we have suggested, for the otherwise odd fact
that Unferþ receives no reprimand and Beowulf no apology for rude
treatment in Hroþgar's decorous court. It offers a formal rationale for

the unusual rhetorical features of the speeches. The seemingly abrupt
and anticlimactic ending (Unferþ's silence) is likewise accounted for.
The Hel curse may be regarded as a traditional element requiring no
further explanation. Although the delegate convention does not explain
Unferþ's larger role in the poem as a whole, it puts in a traditional
context his function in his first and most dramatic appearance. It further
makes more comprehensible his subsequent camaraderie, which need
not be interpreted as a shame-induced *mea culpa* (as Bonjour believes)[80]
nor as an act of disguised treachery,[81] but simply as a resumption of
normal deportment after his temporary stint as formal interrogator.
(The job of flyting delegate appears to have been part-time, *ad hoc,* and
thankless.) Nor does the meaning of "Unferþ" need be regarded as
crucial. The nature and aim of the episode would have been fully
identifiable to a contemporary audience no matter what the name of its
promulgator. If "Unferþ" is meant as a significant abstract (un-peace,
un-wisdom), it is by way of embellishment, not explanation.[82] The word
þyle, whatever its other meanings, suggests some form of eloquence, the
explicit attribute of flyting contenders. (It is entirely possible that the
word, which is after all applied for the first time 559 lines after the fact—
ll. 1165 and 1456—refers neither to a court office nor to a perfidious
function, but simply to his earlier role in the poem as flyting provoca-
teur, the spokesman for the king on that specific occasion. The inciden-
tal use of epithets, particularly those for "big talkers" and the like, is well
attested in Norse tradition.)[83] Finally, the evidence of the flyting may
authenticate two points of content: the Breca episode and Unferþ's
fratricide. None of this detracts from the literary understanding of the
episode as a subplot which rehearses the past to intimate the future; it
merely allows us to tie together some notoriously frayed ends which
internal readings have left lying loose.

NOTES

1. Two recent treatments are: James L. Rosier, "Design for Treachery: The
Unferth Intrigue," *PMLA* 77 (1962): 1–7; and Norman E. Eliason, "The Þyle and
Scop in *Beowulf,*" *Speculum* 38 (1963): 267–84. Joseph Harris, in his unpublished
paper "The *senna*: From Description to Literary Theory," goes further in identifying some conventional features of the Unferþ episode.

2. Joaquín Martínez Pizarro, "Studies on the Function and Context of the
Senna in Early Germanic Narrative," Diss. Harvard 1976. General accounts include:
Andreas Heusler, *Die altgermanische Dichtung,* 2nd ed. rev. (Potsdam, 1941), 105–08;
Anne Holtsmark in *Kulturhistorisk leksikon for nordisk middelalder fra vikingetid til
reformationstid* (hereafter *KHL*), s.v. *senna* and *mannjevning*; Paul Herrmann, *Er-
läuterungen zu den ersten neun Büchern der dänischen Geschichte des Saxo Grammaticus,* Zweiter Teil: *Die Heldensagen des Saxo Grammaticus* (Leipzig, 1922); Bertha

S. Phillpotts, *The Elder Edda and Ancient Scandinavian Drama* (Cambridge, 1920), 156–59. For a discussion of the oral presentation of flytings, see Lars Lönnroth, *Den dubbla scenen: muntlig diktning från Edda til Abba* (Stockholm, 1977), esp. 53–80.

3. See especially Klaus von See, *Altnordische Rechtswörter*, Hermaea 16 (Tübingen, 1964), 226–35; and Anne Holtsmark, *KHL*, s.v. *mannjevning.*

4. The major treatises are: Erik Noreen, "Studier i fornvästnordisk diktning II," *Uppsala Universitets årsskrift. Filosofi, språkvetenskap och historiska vetenskaper* 4 (Uppsala, 1922); and Bo Almqvist, *Norrön niddiktning: Traditionshistoriska studier i versmagi*, 2 vols. (Uppsala, 1965–74).

5. To take just one pertinent example, Joseph Harris ("The *senna*," 4–6) concludes that the Unferþ episode is a *senna*; Lars Lönnroth came to the independent conclusion that it is a *mannjafnaðr* (*Den dubbla scenen*, 65–66); and Martínez Pizarro, also independently, located it somewhere between the two ("Studies," 59).

6. Joseph Harris suggests that the shift in meters in *Helgakviða Hjǫrvarðssonar* and certain scribal indications in *Helgakviða Hundingsbana I* imply recognition of the semi-independent status of the flyting. Joseph Harris, "Eddic Poetry as Oral Poetry: The Evidence of Parallel Passages in the Helgi Poems for Questions of Composition and Performance," in *Edda: A Collection of Essays*, ed. Haraldur Bessason and Robert Glendinning (Manitoba, 1983), 210–42.

7. The flyting impinges on two other categories. One is the *hvǫt* or formal incitement scene, which draws on a common stock of insults and shares certain rhetorical features (Starkaðr's castigation of Ingeld in Book VI of Saxo is an intermediate example). The second is the wisdom dialogue (e.g. *Vafþrúðnismál*), of which Frode's exchange with Ericus Disertus (Saxo V) stands as an intermediate example. The sapiential dimension of the flytings themselves should not be ignored; see Heusler, *Die altgermanische Dichtung*, 105–09.

8. The tendency has been to measure the Unferþ episode against individual, and hence by definition unrepresentative, examples, e.g., Klaeber's comparison with the Guðmundr-Sinfjǫtli exchange in *Helgakviða Hundingsbana I* and two rather inapposite saga episodes (*Gunnlaugs saga*, ch. 5, and *Hrólfs saga kraka*, chs. 33–34). Fr. Klaeber, ed., *Beowulf and the Fight at Finnsburg*, 3rd ed. (Boston, 1950), 149.

9. Eddic examples include: Loki vs. Æsir in *Lokasenna* (*Lks*); Skírnir vs. Gerðr in *Skírnismál* (*Skm*); Þórr vs. Hárbarðr in *Hárbarðsljóð* (*Hbl*); Sinfjǫtli vs. Guðmundr in *Helgakviða Hundingsbana I* (*HHI*) and *II* (*HHII*); Hrímgerðr vs. Atli in *Helgakviða Hjǫrvarðssonar* (*HHj*); and Guðrún and Gullrǫnd vs. Brynhildr in *Guðrúnarkviða I* (*GkvI*). Citations are from Gustav Neckel and Hans Kuhn, eds., *Edda: Die Lieder des Codex Regius nebst verwandten Denkmälern* (Heidelberg, 1962).

Examples from Saxo Grammaticus, *Gesta Danorum*, include: Gram and Bessus vs. Gro (Book I); Ericus Disertus vs. Grep (Book V); Ericus Disertus vs. Frode (Book V); Ericus Disertus vs. Gøtwar (Book V); Ericus Disertus vs. Olmar (Book V); Fridleif vs. giant (Book VI); Starkaðr vs. Ingeld (Book VI); and Knud Lavard vs. Henrik (Book XIII). Edition: *Saxonis Gesta Danorum*, ed. C. Knabe and Paul Herrmann, rev. Jørgen Olrik and H. Raeder (Copenhagen, 1931).

Classical saga examples include Skarpheðinn vs. chieftains in *Njáls saga*, chs. 119–20; Hallgerðr vs. Bergþóra in *Njáls saga*, ch. 35; Ólfeigr vs. chieftains in *Bandamanna saga*, ch. 10; Egill vs. chieftains in *Bandamanna saga*, ch. 10; Broddi vs. chieftains in *Ǫlkofra þáttr*, chs. 3–4; Egill vs. Ǫlvir in *Egils saga*, ch. 44; hall flyting in *Egils saga*, ch. 49; Gunnlaugr vs. Þorsteinn in *Gunnlaugs saga*, ch. 5; hall flyting in *Eyrbyggja saga*, ch. 37; the protracted exchange between Þórðr and Bjǫrn in *Bjarnar saga hítdælakappa*; and Sigurðr vs. Eysteinn in *Magnússona saga*, ch 21 (in *Heimskringla*, III). All citations are from *Íslenzk fornrit* (Reykjavík, 1933–), hereafter *ÍF*. Legendary saga examples include: Hjálmþér vs. troll-woman in *Hjálmþés saga ok Ölvis*, ch. 12; Ketill vs. Gusi in *Ketils saga hængs*, ch. 3; Ketill vs. troll-woman in *Ketils saga hængs*, ch. 5; Ketill vs. Böðmóðr in *Ketils saga hængs*, ch. 5; Grímr vs. troll-women in *Gríms saga loðinkinna*, ch. 1; Oddr vs. Sigurðr and Sjólfr in *Ǫrvar-Odds saga*, ch. 27; Oddr vs. priestess in *Ǫrvar-Odds saga*, ch. 29; two unnamed warriors in *Ragnars saga loðbrókar*, ch. 18. Citations from Guðni Jónsson, ed., *Fornaldar sögur Norðurlanda* (Reykjavík, 1959), 4 vols.

See also: Þórðr vs. men at banquet in *Þorgils saga ok Hafliða* (in *Sturlunga saga*), ed. Halldór Hermannsson in *Islandica* 31 (1945), ch. 10; Bishop Nikulás vs. the Birkibeinar in *Sverris saga*, ed. Guðni Jónsson in *Konunga sögur* (Reykjavík, 1957), ch. 131; the lampooning of Þorvaldr and the bishop in *Kristni saga*, ed. Bernhard Kahle, Altnordische Saga-Bibliothek 11 (Halle, 1905), ch. 4; the oath-swearing in *Jómsvíkinga saga*, ed. N.F. Blake (London, 1962), ch. 26 (compare prose before st. 31 of *HHj*); and the comparative oath-swearing in *Svarfdæla saga* (*ÍF* IX), ch. 16.

The "quarrel of the queens" is represented in: Karl Bartsch and Helmut de Boor, *Das Nibelungenlied*, 20th ed. (Wiesbaden, 1972), 14th Âventiure; R.G. Finch, ed., *Vǫlsunga saga* (London, 1965), ch. 30; Snorri Sturluson, *Edda: Gylfaginning og fortellingene av Skaldskaparmál*, ed. Anne Holtsmark and Jón Helgason (Copenhagen, 1950); and Guðni Jónsson, *Þiðreks saga af Bern* (Reykjavík, 1962), ch. 343. Flytings or potential flytings have also been discerned elsewhere in the *Nibelungenlied* (esp. adventures 25 and 29), the *Hildebrandslied*, the Walter cycle, and *Maldon*. Translations are my own except where otherwise indicated.

10. Phillpotts, *The Elder Edda and Ancient Scandinavian Drama*, 158. Martínez Pizarro discusses the water setting, represented most conspicuously in Norse in *Hbl* and the Helgi poems, in German in the 25th Âventiure of the *Nibelungenlied* (the ferocious ferryman), in English in *Maldon*, and in Latin in Widukind's *Res Gestae Saxonicae* and Paul the Deacon's *Historia Langobardorum*.

11. See Nils Lid, *KHL*, s.v. *drikkeseder*; for a discussion of the social practice of *mannjafnaðr*, and the significance of boasting, in the Germanic world, see L.L. Schücking, "Heldenstolz und Würde im Angelsächsischen," *Abhandlungen der sächsischen Akademie der Wissenschaften*, Philosophisch-Historische Klasse 42, 5 (Leipzig, 1933).

12. Compare Gregory of Tours's account of how Chramnesindus invited his close friend Sicharius to dinner: "Quo veniente, resident pariter ad convivium. Cumque Sicharius crapulatus a vino multa iactaret in Cramsindo. . . ." (He came and they sat down together for dinner. Sicharius got drunk with wine and made many boasts to Chramnesindus. . . .) The ensuing altercation has to do with Chramnesindus's failure to exact due vengeance for a slain kinsman, and it ends with the murder of Sicharius. Gregory of Tours, *Liber Historiae Francorum* 9.19, ed. Bruno Krusch, MGH SSrer Merov 2 (Hannover, 1888). On the passage see Erich Auerbach, *Mimesis*, tr. Willard Trask (New York, 1957), ch. 4.

13. George Philip Krapp and Elliott Van Kirk Dobbie, *The Exeter Book*, The Anglo-Saxon Poetic Records, 3 (New York, 1936). Translation adapted from T.A. Shippey, *Poems of Wisdom and Learning in Old English* (Cambridge, 1976), 55 and 57. Schücking discusses the social context of this and other such descriptions in

"Heldenstolz und Würde," 10–11.

14. *Hávamál* repeatedly enjoins against immoderate drinking as a threat to thought and speech. See also *Lks* 18, where Iðunn says "Braga ec kyrri / biórreifan . . ." ("I will calm Bragi, drunk with beer").

15. In the latter case, the woman always loses.

16. See Alois Wolf, *Gestaltungskerne und Gestaltungsweisen in der altgermanischen Heldendichtung* (Munich, 1965), esp. 179–96; and Klaus von See, "Die Werbung um Brünhild," *Zeitschrift für deutsches Altertum* 88 (1957): 1–20.

17. Martínez Pizarro, "Studies," 146–66.

18. See st. 1 of *Hávamál*:

> Gáttir allar,   áðr gangi fram,
>   um scoðaz scyli,
>   um scygnaz scyli;
> þvíat óvíst er at vita   hvar óvinir
> sitia á fleti fyrir.

> (Through all doorways,   before proceeding,
>   one should investigate,
>   one should look about;
> for it is uncertain   where enemies
> may be sitting in the room.)

19. Translations of Saxo are adapted from *The First Nine Books of the Danish History of Saxo Grammaticus*, tr. Oliver Elton (London, 1894).

20. After he has silenced Sjólfr and Sigurðr in the flyting, Örvar-Oddr says: "Þit munuð hvergi / hæfir þykkja, / Sigurðr ok Sjólfr / í sveit konungs . . ." ("Nowhere will you be considered worthy company for a king, Sigurðr and Sjólfr . . .").

21. A common imputation of unmanliness: such farm chores were women's work.

22. Starkaðr's comment on his reception into Ingeld's court (Saxo VI).

23. Examples are too numerous to list here. Ch. 34 of *Hrólfs saga kraka* has been referred to as analogous to *Beowulf*; see Guðni Jónsson, ed., *Fornaldar sögur Norðurlanda*, 1 (Reykjavík, 1959). Newcomers might also be asked to *segja sínar íþróttir* ("name their accomplishments") and even, on occasion, to demonstrate them before being accepted as guests. The *íþróttir* included feats of swimming, running, wrestling, poetic composition, etc. See Anthony Faulkes, "*Rauðúlfs þáttr*: A Study," *Studia Islandica* 25 (Reykjavík, 1966), esp. 46–57.

24. "Der Held soll seinem Gegner . . . auch im Zungenkampf durchaus gewachsen sein" (L.L. Schücking, "Heldenstolz und Würde," 38). For a recent discussion of eloquence as an aristocratic attribute, see Geoffrey R. Russom, "The Germanic Concept of Nobility in *The Gifts of Men* and *Beowulf*," *Speculum* 53 (1978): 1–15.

25. Guðni Jónsson, ed., in *Fornaldar sögur Norðurlanda*, 1 (Reykjavík, 1959), ch. 7. Starkaðr, lamenting his unwitting role in the sacrifice to Óðinn of Víkarr, calls himself a *þögull* ('silent' or 'silenced') *þulr*. Joseph L. Baird refers to this attestation in his effort to show that "Unferth seems to have been, somewhere back in the dark matrix whence the poem arose, a divine favourite, a Woden's man, a *pyle*; and vestiges of this Wodenism are still discernible in the poem as we have received it."

See his "Unferth the *þyle*," *Medium Ævum* 39 (1970): 9. Other recent discussions of the term *þyle* include Rosier, "Design for Treachery"; Eliason, "The Þyle and Scop in *Beowulf*"; J.D.A. Ogilvy, "Unferth: Foil to Beowulf?" in *PMLA* 79 (1970): 370–75; and I.M. Hollowell, "Unferð the *þyle* in *Beowulf,*" *Studies in Philology* 73 (1976): 239–64.

26. Sometimes multiple Claims, Defenses, and Counterclaims are consolidated in single speeches. In one example there is not a proper exchange at all, but unilateral invective, viz. Fridleif's verbal assault against a mute adversary (Saxo VI). Cf. Joseph Harris's characterization ("The *senna*," 2) of the form as "a Preliminary, comprising an Identification and Central Exchange, consisting of either Accusation and Denial, Threat and Counterthreat, or Challenge and Reply or a combination; these structural elements are realized through a more or less regular alternation of speakers, first in question and answer, then comment and reply."

27. See for example the verbal repetitions, syntactic parallelism, and the evenly blocked nature of the speeches in *Bandamanna saga* and *Njáls saga* (chs. 119–20).

28. N.F. Blake discusses the I/You contrast in "The Flyting in *The Battle of Maldon,*" *English Language Notes* 13 (1975–76): 242–45.

29. It is a rare flyting that does not contain an insult or threat of this kind. The presence of sexual innuendoes in the earliest Germanic flytings indicates that the practice is not idiosyncratically Norse. See Martínez Pizarro, "Studies," passim.

30. It has been noted that the *bróðurbani* in question may be Iðunn's own husband Bragi. Magnus Olsen regards Bragi as the delegate figure and "official entertainer" of *Lks* and hence a counterpart to the fratricidal *þyle* Unferþ. Magnus Olsen, *Edda- og Skaldekvad,* Avhandlinger utgitt av Det Norske Videnskaps-Akademi i Oslo, II: Hist.-Filos. Klasse, No. 2 (Oslo, 1960), 53–55.

31. Starkaðr associates Ingeld's moral degeneracy with his alimentary decadence (his taste for such foreign dishes as fowl and puréed vegetables).

32. The poetic sources have singular "brother" (*bræðr* is an uncommon alternative for Dat. sg. *bróður*), but *Vǫlsunga saga* has the plural "brothers" (*bræðr þína*) and tells how Sinfjǫtli kills his half-brothers at his mother's request (ch. 8).

33. R.W. Chambers, *"Beowulf": An Introduction to the Study of the Poem* (Cambridge, 1921), 28–29.

34. Translation adapted from Magnus Magnusson and Hermann Pálsson, *Njál's Saga* (Baltimore, 1960).

35. The stanza appears in variant form in *HHI* 45. For a satiric use of the same formulation, see *Hbl* 48: "Sif á hó heima, / hans mundo fund vilia, / þann muntu þrec drýgia, / þat er þér scyldara." (Sif [Þórr's wife] has a lover at home whom you might like to meet; your strength would be better employed on him.")

36. C.R. Unger, ed., *Morkinskinna* (Christiania, 1867), 186–87 (my translation).

37. His doing so is no doubt a reflection of received historical opinion on that regency. See Bjarni Aðalbjarnarson's comments on the favoring of Eysteinn in his introduction (lvi) to the *ÍF* edition of *Heimskringla,* III. See also Lönnroth, *Den dubbla scenen,* 69–80.

38. On the broadening effects of travel, see *Hávamál,* st. 18.

39. "Skauð hernumin" is difficult. *Skauð,* f. means either 'cunt' or the fold of skin into which a horse's penis retracts. Used as a term of abuse between males, it

implies castration (a common insult: see, e.g., *HHI* 40 and *HHj* 20). If *skauð* in this stanza refers to a castrated male (as I have taken it), *hernumin* may simply mean 'captive' or possibly 'tamed, domesticated'. If *skauð* is understood as 'cunt', *hernumin* may mean 'raped, ravished'. The phrase does not in any case mean 'a comical captive', as Edwards and Pálsson translate it (*Arrow-Odd: A Medieval Novel* [New York, 1970], 89), or 'poltroon', as Cleasby-Vigfusson has it (*An Icelandic-English Dictionary*), or 'fej, ussel, karl', as Finnur Jónsson suggests (*Lexicon Poeticum*).

40. Axel Olrik, *The Heroic Legends of Denmark*, tr. Lee M. Hollander (New York, 1919), 59.

41. Chambers, *Beowulf*, 28.

42. William Labov, "Rules for Ritual Insults," *Language in the Inner City* (Philadelphia, 1975). Joseph Harris takes a Labovian perspective on Norse insults in "The *senna*."

43. Magnus Olsen, *Edda- og Skaldekvad*, 1–88.

44. Although Latin debates were translated into Norse shortly after 1200 (in *Hauksbók*), it is generally agreed that they play little or no role in the development of the native flyting genre. Hermann Jantzen, *Geschichte des deutschen Streitgedichtes im Mittelalter*, Germanistische Abhandlungen 13 (Breslau, 1896); and H. Walther, *Das Streitgedicht in der lateinischen Literatur des Mittelalters*, Quellen und Untersuchungen zur lateinischen Philologie des Mittelalters 5 (Munich, 1920).

45. See, for example, Arthur Gilchrist Brodeur, *The Art of "Beowulf"* (Berkeley, 1959), 144; and Klaeber, lvi.

46. Magnus Olsen (*Edda- og Skaldekvad*, 2:53) equated the roles of Unferþ and Bragi (in *Lks*): "Brage er den som skal hilse gjester velkommen. Hann intar da i Ægirs hall en stilling som har tilsvarende i Beowulf 499ff."

47. All citations are from Klaeber's edition. Translations are adapted from E. Talbot Donaldson's text in *Beowulf*, ed. Joseph F. Tuso (New York, 1975). As for this verse, Klaeber (150) writes that probably "only the vaguest suspicion of ancient heathen belief . . . was lingering in *beadurun*." Hoops agrees: "Daß der Dichter noch eine klare Vorstellung des altgermanischen Glaubens an streiterregende Runenzeichen hatte, ist unwahrscheinlich." Johannes Hoops, *Kommentar zum "Beowulf"* (Heidelberg, 1932), 77. The phrase is best regarded as a frozen epithet, like its Norse counterparts inherited along with the form.

48. Brodeur, *The Art of "Beowulf*," 144.

49. Rosier, "Design for Treachery," 7.

50. Joaquín Martínez Pizarro, "Studies," 64.

51. Cf. Hárbárðr's mock admiration of Þórr in *Hbl* 36–39: "What deeds were you doing then, Þórr?" "Berserk giant-women I battled on Hlésey; they did their worst to bewitch all men." "Brave you are, Þórr, to battle women!"

52. Brodeur, *The Art of "Beowulf*," 146.

53. Edward B. Irving, Jr., *A Reading of "Beowulf"* (New Haven, 1968), 69.

54. Klaeber, 147.

55. Larry D. Benson, "The Originality of *Beowulf*," in *The Interpretation of Narrative: Theory and Practice*, ed. Morton W. Bloomfield, Harvard English Studies 1 (Cambridge, Mass., 1970), esp. 20–22.

56. For the opposite view, see Rosier, "Design for Treachery"; Eliason, "Þyle and Scop"; and Klaeber, 148: "But nothing points to an old tradition in which the Breca incident was connected with the person of Beowulf. It should be added that

the story of the swimming could not well have formed the subject of a separate lay."

57. Brodeur, *The Art of "Beowulf,"* 143.

58. On the objection that the fratricide charge is "in Beowulfs Mund unedel," see the salutary remarks of Sophus Bugge, "Studien über das Beowulfepos," *Beiträge zur Geschichte der deutschen Sprache und Literatur* 12 (1887): 89.

59. Howell D. Chickering, Jr., *"Beowulf": A Dual-Language Edition* (Garden City, N.Y., 1977), 303.

60. Fred C. Robinson, "Elements of the Marvellous in the Characterization of Beowulf: A Reconsideration of the Textual Evidence," *Old English Studies in Honour of John C. Pope*, ed. Robert G. Burlin and Edward B. Irving, Jr. (Toronto, 1974), esp. 129–30.

61. Rosier ("Design for Treachery," 3) has noted a coincidental correspondence in *Fáfnismál*—in a non-flyting context—where a Hel curse is applied to the *þulr* Reginn.

62. Irving finds Beowulf's conclusion ironic: "Even Unferth can be courageous in the bright morning sunlight, after the danger has been cleared away. We come full circle to the opening of the speech with its allusion to those who are brave over a few drinks." *A Reading of "Beowulf,"* 76.

63. Klaeber, 150.

64. Hoops, *Kommentar,* 77.

65. R.E. Kaske, *"Sapientia et Fortitudo* as the Controlling Theme of *Beowulf,"* *Studies in Philology* 55 (1958): rpt. in *An Anthology of "Beowulf" Criticism,* ed. Lewis E. Nicholson (Notre Dame, 1963), 278.

66. Klaeber, lvi.

67. Brodeur, *The Art of "Beowulf,"* 144.

68. Eliason, "Þyle and Scop," esp. 270–71.

69. The reference is to Fr. Klaeber, "Unferðs Verhalten im Beowulf," *Anglia Beiblatt* 52 (1942): 271: "er schämte sich."

70. Brodeur, *The Art of "Beowulf,"* 150.

71. Cf. the silencings in the Irish flyting in "The Story of MacDatho's Pig" in *An Early Irish Reader,* ed. and tr. N. Kershaw Chadwick (Cambridge, 1927).

72. The sequel, in which Queen Wealhþeow, "cynna gemyndig" (mindful of custom), steps forth and offers ornate cups of mead and cheering words to the king, retainers, and Beowulf, may be something more than the commonplace "appearance of noble ladies at a banquet" (Klaeber, 152). In the concluding stanzas of *Lks,* after Loki has castigated all of the gods and goddesses but Sif (the queenliest of the goddesses, Magnus Olsen argues) makes the same placating gesture: "Þá gecc Sif fram oc byrlaði Loca í hrímkálki mjǫð oc mælti: 'Heill ver þú nú, Loki, / oc tac við hrímkálki, / fullom forns miaðar . . .'" (Then Sif came forth and poured mead for Loki in a crystal goblet and said: "Hail to you, Loki, and take the crystal goblet, full of ancient mead . . ."). This was noted briefly by Magnus Olsen in *Edda- og Skaldekvad,* 2:54–55. The *Morkinskinna* version of the *Magnússona saga* likewise depicts the intervention of the queen with words and wine.

73. See especially William Labov, "Rules for Ritual Insults"; Alan Dundes, Jerry W. Leach, and Boro Özkök, "The Strategy of Turkish Boys' Dueling Rhymes," in *Directions in Sociolinguistics: The Ethnography of Communication,* ed. John J. Gumperz and Dell Hymes (New York, 1972), 133–160 and editors' introduction, 130–33; and Gregory Nagy, *"Iambos:* Typologies of Invective and Praise,"

Arethusa 9 (1976): 191–205 (with bibliography).

74. Georges Dumézil, *Servius et la Fortune* (Paris, 1943).

75. Alvin Gouldner, *Enter Plato: Classical Greece and the Origins of Social Theory* (New York, 1965).

76. Albert Bates Lord, "Beowulf and Odysseus," *Franciplegius: Medieval and Linguistic Studies in Honor of Francis Peabody Magoun, Jr.*, ed. Jess B. Bessinger, Jr., and Robert P. Creed (New York, 1965), 86–91.

77. Eliason, "Þyle and Scop," 272.

78. W.W. Lawrence, *"Beowulf" and Epic Tradition* (Cambridge, Mass., 1928), 153.

79. Brodeur, *The Art of "Beowulf,"* 142–43.

80. Adrien Bonjour, *The Digressions in "Beowulf"* (Oxford, 1950), 20.

81. See especially Rosier, "Design for Treachery."

82. For recent discussions on the meaning of Unferþ (MS Hunferþ), see Fred C. Robinson, "Personal Names in Medieval Narrative and the Name of Unferth in *Beowulf,*" in *Essays in Honor of Richebourg Gaillard McWilliams*, ed. H.H. Creed (Birmingham, Ala., 1970), 43–48; the same author's "Elements of the Marvellous"; Morton W. Bloomfield, *"Beowulf* and Christian Allegory: An Interpretation of Unferth," *Traditio* 7 (1951): 410–15, rpt. in *The "Beowulf" Poet*, ed. Donald K. Fry (Englewood Cliffs, N.J., 1968), 68–75; and M.F. Vaughan, "A Reconsideration of 'Unferð'," *Neuphilologische Mitteilungen* 77 (1976): 32–48.

83. Vaughan has recently stressed the literary difficulties posed by an allegorical understanding of the name "Unferþ." The critics who urge such readings "imply that the poet's conception of [Unferþ's] character is completely dominated or, at least, best represented by the meaning of his name. . . . The failure of such approaches to handle adequately [Unferþ's] fame and his 'spirit of generosity, courtesy, and sportsmanlike fairness toward Beowulf,' later in the epic, casts doubt on the consistent application of concepts of strife or discord to this complex character. If indeed [Unferþ] is more a personification than a person, then the poem should be read in such a way that this character does not change, develop, or act in any way inconsistent with the abstract quality he is supposed to embody" ("A Reconsideration of 'Unferð'," 34–35). The word *þyle* may be a similar case of lexical straitjacketing.

Skaldic Verse and the Date of *Beowulf*

by Roberta Frank

This essay first appeared in The Dating of "Beowulf," *ed. Colin Chase, Toronto Old English Series no. 6 (Toronto: University of Toronto Press, 1981), 123–39.*

WHEN after one hundred and fifty years of speculation we have reached no certainty regarding the date of *Beowulf*, certainty may not be attainable. Still, there is always the chance that one's own peculiar perspective may suggest new lines of inquiry, add something, however minuscule, to the small kernel of evidence that is safe to regard as the established fact of *Beowulf* scholarship. This kernel is even smaller today than it was thirty years ago when Dorothy Whitelock advanced the *terminus ad quem* of *Beowulf* from 750 to 825, halting before the viking incursions of mid-century. She cited "the high respect with which the poet speaks of the Danes and their rulers"; no Anglo-Saxon would praise people who were draining England's coffers and ale kegs and carving blood-eagles on Christian backs.[1] Nicolas Jacobs has recently reminded us that "from 927 onwards the Danes constituted a widely accepted element in English society, and an English poem complimentary to them is conceivable at least down to the resumption of raids in 980."[2] Only three generations separated Danish veteran from Benedictine reformer: Oda, bishop of Ramsbury under Athelstan and archbishop of Canterbury from 940–958, was the son of a Dane who came to England with the first settlers. Oda's nephew was the Fleury-trained St. Oswald, prominent founder and renovator of monasteries.[3] If Oswald's contemporaries thought well enough of *Beowulf* to preserve the poem, the two preceding generations were just as capable of responding to the poet's lonely fenland monsters, drunken thanes in army blankets, and golden pagan hero. No linguistic or historical fact compels us to anchor *Beowulf* before the tenth century; if we do so, it is more from our emotional commitment to an early date than from hard evidence. Our one secure terminus is the palaeographic dating of the manuscript to around the year 1000.

Attempts over the last century to show Norse influence on the language of *Beowulf* have produced interesting similarities, but "no proofs of imitation."[4] The absence of demonstrable Scandinavianisms in

155

an Old English poem, however, does not rule out a late date of composition. *The Battle of Brunanburh* from around 937 has one loanword (*cnear* [ON *knǫrr*], a name for a viking ship) and one Nordicism—the Old English word *eorl* "man" found in line 31 in its Norse sense of "ruler" (like *eorl Ongenþio* "king Ongentheow" in *Beowulf* 2951).[5] No Scandinavianisms appear in *The Capture of the Five Boroughs* (942), *The Coronation of Edgar* (973), *The Death of Edgar* (975), or *The Death of Edward* (1065). *The Battle of Maldon,* composed more than a century and a half after the first Danish settlements, has two loanwords (*grið,* 35; *dreng,* 149) and one Nordicism (*eorl* as a title).[6] Old English loanwords are equally difficult to detect in skaldic poetry, even that produced in England for English kings; and a number of suspected Anglicisms in early Norse verse are found in Old English only in *Beowulf,* creating some doubt as to which poetry is the borrower and which the lender.[7] Similarly, the fact that the Scandinavian names of *Beowulf* are English in form tells us little about the date of the poem: poets on either side of the linguistic frontier readily adapted each other's names to their own phonological systems: the skalds invariably assimilated Athelstan to Athalsteinn; the Old English poet just as automatically and correctly translates Halfdanr into Healfdene and Hugleikr into Hygelac.[8] If we are ever to trace *Beowulf* to its point of origin in the period between 700 and 1000, it will be essential either to catch the poet in a telling anachronism or to establish some kind of convincing typological sequence—the stylistic equivalent of a dated series of coins—into which the poem can be fitted. My goal in this paper is less ambitious: it is to see whether Old Norse skaldic verse can persuade us that the Old English poet's interest in and knowledge of things Scandinavian was the result of the Danish settlements in England and not part of a distant folk memory imported by the Anglo-Saxons from their continental homeland.

An extensive body of skaldic verse survives from the tenth and early eleventh centuries—over a thousand stanzas taking up some three hundred double-columned pages in Finnur Jónsson's edition. Many of these stanzas are datable, the work of known individuals composing for known princes. As a guide to the Danishness of *Beowulf,* the corpus has its limitations: skaldic verse emerges only in the late ninth century and what has been preserved tends to reflect purely West Scandinavian concerns; skaldic style is so intricate, allusive, and knotty that we are not always sure what a poet is saying; and, finally, skalds in later centuries were so fond of putting their favourite compositions into the mouths of viking heroes of the past that we must question the authenticity of every stanza that does not exist in a contemporary inscription. There are various imperfect methods at our disposal for making sense of the verse and for distinguishing genuine from spurious stanzas: philological and metrical tests, kenning and contextual studies, luck and intuition.[9]

Somehow enough material comes through the sifting process to provide historians with useful primary sources. Curt Weibull cited skaldic verse in 1917 to buttress his case for Geatish survival after the sixth century.[10] He was able to show that until the end of the tenth century all battles fought by Norwegian kings against Sweden and recorded in skaldic verse are against the Geats (ON Gautar), not the Swedes. Thórbjǫrn hornklofi around 900 calls Haraldr hárfagr "enemy of the Geats" (23, 21, 13), Guthormr sindri claims halfway through the century that Hákon the Good "made the Geats pay tribute" (62, 55, 34); Glúmr Geirason around 970 rejoices that Haraldr gráfeldr "reddened his sword in the blood of the Geats" (76, 66, 41); Einarr skálaglamm in the 980s reports that Earl Hákon not only "wanted to destroy the lives of the Geats" (130, 123, 69) but that he "trampled all Geatland" (130, 123, 69). Being a Geat in tenth-century skaldic verse may not have been much fun, but at least you knew that you were not extinct, something the standard editions of *Beowulf* still fail to acknowledge.[11] The fact that the Geats held together as a people into the eleventh century does not pinpoint the date of *Beowulf,* but it does suggest that they were as known and topical in the tenth century as in any preceding one—and perhaps more so. Skaldic verse can provide similar information about dynasties, political catchwords, and heroes in *Beowulf,* even, perhaps, about the origin of the Scyldings.

Unlike the Geats, who were known to Ptolemy, Procopius, and Jordanes, the Scyldings are surrounded by silence. Nobody mentions a single Scylding, let alone a nation swarming with them, until the *Beowulf* poet uses the name thirty-five times for his sixth-century Danish dynasty. Names like Healfdene, Hrothgar, and Heorogar, if they are found in England at all, are not documented before the tenth century.[12] Legends of the Scyldings in skaldic verse get off to an equally slow start. The first reference by a skald to an event associated with one of the Scyldings of *Beowulf* occurs around 965 when Eyvindr skálda-spillir calls gold "the seed corn of Fýrisplains" (73, 64, 39), alluding to the story of how Hrólfr kraki (OE Hrothulf) sowed those plains with gold to delay the Swedish horsemen pursuing him. The first mention of a royal residence on Zealand comes in 1062 when the skald Steinn Herdísarson identifies the Danish king Sveinn Estrithsson as "he who sits at Leire" (407, 377, 187). Old Norse dictionaries and the historians Sven Aggesen around 1187 and Saxo Grammaticus around 1200 all tell us that Norse poets use *skjǫldungr* (OE Scylding) as a general poetic term for king, and never as a dynastic title the way the *Beowulf* poet does, as in "the old Scylding" (1792, 2105).[13] This may be true for the twelfth century, at least by 1153 when Einarr Skúlason calls both God and the Greek emperor *yfirskjǫldungar* "over-Scyldings" (468, 439, 216; 471, 444, 218); but in the early eleventh century, Norse skalds appear to bestow the title in a specifically political way.[14] In the quarter century between 1014 and 1040, they use Scylding to designate three kings: Knútr the Great, ruler of an Anglo-Danish-Norwegian empire; his contemporary and defeated rival, Óláfr Haraldsson, king of Norway; and the latter's son, Magnús the Good, king of Denmark and Norway and later claimant to the English throne of Hǫrtha-Knútr. There seems to be a connection between a poet's use of the title and the English adventures of these kings. The skald Thórthr Kolbeinsson around 1014 describes Knútr's arrival in England: "The Scylding, Knútr, he who struck the waves, brought his longships in to the shallows by the gravel bank" (216, 205, 107). Around 1026, another skald, Óttarr svarti, records one of Knútr's English battles: "Mighty Scylding, you worked a deed of war under a shield at Ashington" (297, 274, 140). By 1038, the association of Scylding with Knútr, shields, and England was familiar enough for the poet Sighvatr to play on the etymology of the title, addressing the king as *hlífskjǫldr* "protecting shield" (250, 234, 121) of the Danes. Both Sighvatr and Óttarr associate the term Scylding with King Óláfr Haraldsson, but in a less precise way, perhaps because he had trouble holding his own kingdom, let alone an empire. Óttarr, relating around 1023 the early viking exploits and English battles of Óláfr, calls him *skjǫldunga popti* "rowing-bench mate of Scyldings" (294, 270, 139) and "he who holds the empire of *þjóðskjǫldunga*" (295, 272, 139), the power of "national-Scyldings"—the same word, *þeod-scyldingas*, used by the *Beowulf* poet for Hrothgar and Hrothulf (1019). Magnús the Good, whose kingdom almost matched Knútr's, is addressed "O Scylding" five times by his proud skald Arnórr (333, 306, 155; 335–6, 309, 157; 338, 311, 158; 343, 315, 160).

The relevance of these Scyldings to their sixth-century counterparts in *Beowulf* would be easier to demonstrate or disprove if skaldic verse on Danish rulers before Knútr had been preserved; all we have is one stanza on Haraldr blátǫnn, obscene and not certainly genuine (176, 166, 89). What is clear from the poetry that survives is that Knútr's skalds were eager to show their king's continuity with the Danish settlers of England in the ninth century. Sighvatr's *Knútsdrápa* opens with a reference to the victory of Ívarr at York in 867, thereby reminding eleventh-century Danes that they had inherited the English conquest of this viking chieftain and his brothers (248, 232, 120). Evidence that these brothers and their followers went under the name of Scyldings in the conquered territories comes from the anonymous *History of St. Cuthbert,* first compiled around 950 and based mainly on the charters and records of donation to the church of St. Cuthbert, then at Chester le Street.[15] The chronicler three times calls the Danes *Scaldingi,* the first occasion referring to Ívarr's battle for York in 867, the second and third to the subsequent ravages of Ívarr's brother Halfdanr.[16] We do not know how far back this usage goes, but we can be fairly confident that *Scaldingi* means *Scyldingas* "shieldmen" or "descendant of Scyld" and not "men of the Scheldt" or "men of the punted ship," the two other etymologies suggested.[17] By 1200, when Saxo wrote his *Danish History,* both Ívarr and Halfdanr, sons of the legendary Ragnarr Lothbrók, were entered into the royal genealogies as ancestors of the kings of Denmark, a line running from Skjǫldr (OE Scyld) to Gormr the Old and beyond.[18]

The skalds who acclaimed as Scyldings the three Norse kings who fought in, ruled over, or pressed rights to England between 1014 and 1040, may have been trying to confer legitimacy on their empire-hungry patrons by linking them to the earlier Danish conquerors of England. English documents from the 880s and 890s reveal, I think, similar attempts by the West-Saxon house to establish its right to rule over both peoples in England. The dynasty legitimized its present—the Alfredian design of Dane and Anglo-Saxon as equal partners in a united kingdom—by revising its past. The author of the Old English *Orosius,* for example, reporting Ohthere's account to King Alfred of his passage from the Oslofjord to Hedeby along the eastern coasts of Jutland, adds on his own the comment that the Angles lived in this area before they came to England.[19] Such a belief may lie behind the *Beowulf* and *Widsith* poets' special interest in Offa I, king of Angeln. Yet the Danish origin of the Angles has no early authority: Ptolemy places them well inland in north-central Germany.[20] If the Alfredian program to promote Anglo-Danish brotherhood could fill in a misty past, it could also outline a future: when the English king stood sponsor for Guthrum at his baptism, he gave the Danish king the aristocratic West-Saxon name of Athelstan.[21]

The West-Saxon regnal table that was compiled or reworked after Alfred's succession in 871 did not go back beyond Woden, the old stopping point for royal genealogies.[22] The name of Scyld, eponymous ancestor of the Scyldings, is first found, along with other Scandinavian names like Beaw, Geat, and Heremod, in the remotest part of the official royal pedigree, the genealogy of Alfred's father Æthelwulf, that was added to the *Anglo-Saxon Chronicle* around 892 and copied by Asser around 893.[23] If, in the period between 871 and 892 (and presumably not

before Alfred's peace with Guthrum at Wedmore), the house of Cerdic
suddenly found itself saddled with an ancestor named Scyld, it is likely
that there were people calling themselves Scyldings in the neighbour-
hood, recent arrivals who had to be assimilated. The new genealogy
reflected a new social reality.[24] In the course of the tenth century, the
West-Saxon royal house continued to develop its past in a Danish
direction. Alfred's great-grandnephew Æthelweard, whose *Chronicle*
ends in 975 at the close of the golden age of the dynasty, places Scef,
Scyld, and Beo in the same order followed by the Old English poet, tells
of a mysterious arrival by boat in Scani (although he attributes the
landing to Scef, not Scyld), and introduces even more Norse names into
the royal genealogies.[25]

What little Old English and Old Norse evidence there is suggests
that the Scyldings and their legends may have been an Anglo-Danish
innovation. By acquiring a founder named Scyld, the West-Saxons
strengthened their position in the Danelaw. By calling a Norse king
Scylding, a skald confirmed his patron's English heritage. The *Beowulf*
poet's incentive for composing an epic about sixth-century Scyldings
may have had something to do with the fact that, by the 890s at least,
Heremod, Scyld, Healfdene, and the rest, were taken to be the common
ancestors both of the Anglo-Saxon royal family and of the Danish
immigrants.[26]

The political geography of *Beowulf* fits comfortably into the period
between Alfred and Æthelweard. The Old English poem is almost
exclusively concerned with one particular corner of the Scandinavian
world, with relations between Dane, Geat, and Swede on the shores of
the Kattegat, the inland sea that separates present-day Norway, Sweden,
and Denmark. These coasts were for much of the ninth and tenth
centuries a Danish sphere of influence, and in later legend form the
backdrop for the youthful careers of Ragnarr Lothbrók and his sons.[27]
Beowulf the Geat is connected to each of the three major Scandinavian
peoples in the poem, as well as to the Wulfings and Wægmundings.[28]
Similar multiculturalism enters into the *Ynglingatal*, a genealogical
praise poem composed around 900 by Thjóthólfr, skald of King Haraldr hárfagr; he dedicates the eulogy to the king's cousin Rǫgnvaldr, a
prince of Vestfold on the northern shore of the Kattegat.[29] Like *Beowulf*,
the *Ynglingatal* speaks of Geats, Swedes, and Scylfings, Danes (but no
Scyldings), Jutes and giants, and even Vendill; the skald, however,
mentions Norway, a region the *Beowulf* poet studiously ignores.
Thjóthólfr apparently attached the six Vestfold dynastic names known
to him to twenty-one names from the royal house of Sweden, including
such *Beowulf* characters as Ohthere, Eadgils, and Onela. The Vestfold

line was new and probably of Danish origin; its royal house acquired not a little mythological depth and perhaps even some political legitimacy by this linkage with its neighbours. The *Beowulf* poet, too, seems to have been aware that the more peoples his hero could attach to himself, the more authentically representative of the culture and traditions of central Scandinavia he would be.

Ynglingatal gives the title *þjóðkonungr* (OE *þeodcyning*) "great" or "national king" to the first member of the Vestfold dynasty, one Half-danr (13, 12, 8). The Old English poet gives the same epithet to Hrothgar, Ongentheow, and Beowulf, and displays this political catchword prominently in his opening sentence: "We have heard of the splendour of the great kings of the Spear-Danes." In tenth-century skaldic verse, the title is used of only two kings, the Vestfold Halfdanr and his descendant, Haraldr hárfagr (23, 21, 13), the king who united all Norway before 900 and who apparently had diplomatic relations with Athelstan.[30] The term *þjóðkonungr* does not occur again in skaldic verse until the next viking age of England, the quarter century between 1014 and 1040, when the skalds restricted its use to the same three kings they called Scyldings: Knútr, Óláfr, and Magnús.[31] *Þjóðkonungr* has, if not imperial overtones, at least a suggestion of overwhelming power; in *Beowulf,* it is explicitly associated with regional overlordship of surrounding tribes. The *Beowulf* poet depicts the Danish nation's former glory in a time when powerful *þeodcyningas* had been able to unite the various peoples of the land, something that did not occur in Denmark, as far as we know, until the late tenth century.[32] He is probably imposing his own monarchic mentality upon the past, just as Thjóthólfr did when he called a petty eighth-century breaker-of-rings in Vestfold a *þjóð-konungr.* The vision of both poets seems to derive from contemporary politics and not from historic reality, from a need to establish in the present an ideological basis for a *rex gentium* and for national unity.

Skaldic verse can sometimes help to establish the chronological bounds of a heroic legend alluded to in *Beowulf.* Sigemund's dragon fight, for example, is often cited as proof either of the Old English poet's confusion and incompetence or of the great age of his poem. Wrenn's edition offers both explanations, affirming that "in *Beowulf* . . . the deeds of the son Sigurthr have been transferred to his father Sigemund, but it is quite as likely that the Old English, being set down several centuries before the Norse accounts, has the older tradition."[33] The evidence of skaldic verse suggests that the *Beowulf* poet could have been working very late indeed and still not have been acquainted with any of young Sigurthr's doings. No Norse skald alludes to that hero's dragon fight, dragon-heart roast, sword, horse, Brynhildr, Rhine gold, or any of the rest before the last half of the tenth century and in most cases not until the early eleventh.[34] A stanza from around 1030 by Thórfinnr munnr is the first to mention Sigurthr's fight with Fáfnir and the subsequent roasting of that dragon's heart (315, 292, 149). Scenes from the Sigurthr legend appear frequently on English and Manx sculpture— but only in the late tenth and eleventh centuries.[35]

There is, however, good skaldic evidence for the early existence of Sigemund and Fitela: the former's immunity to poison is alluded to in Bragi's *Ragnarsdrápa,* probably from the second half of the ninth century, while both heroes appear in the *Eiríksmál,* a pagan memorial eulogy composed shortly after 954 to commemorate Eiríkr Bloodaxe, Haraldr hárfagr's son and the last king of Northumbria. The poem depicts Eiríkr's reception in Valholl after his death on an English battlefield; the chief speaker is Óthinn, who bids the warriors Sigemund and Fitela go forth to welcome the king to their hall. A second pagan memorial eulogy, the *Hákonarmál* composed around 960 for Eiríkr's half-brother, King Hákon the Good of Norway, probably used *Eiríksmál* as a model.[36] The skald portrays the gods summoning Hákon to them; this time Óthinn sends Heremod (ON Hermóthr) with Bragi to greet the king who, as Athelstan's baptized foster son, is understandably apprehensive about his reception.[37]

There is general agreement that the *Beowulf* poet's coupling of Sigemund and Heremod as heroes of greatest renown springs from Scandinavian tradition; the two are paired again as Óthinn's heroes in the eddic *Hyndluljóð.*[38] The usual assumption is that whatever borrowing there was took place at some dark period in pre-viking-age England or even in the Angles' continental homeland. But if we start from the known—the fact that Heremod and Sigemund act as Óthinn's henchmen in two mid-tenth-century skaldic poems, one of which was probably composed in England while the other has English ties—we can test an alternative hypothesis, that the *Beowulf* poet had his sixth-century Danish scop sing of Sigemund and Heremod because contemporary Danes sang of them, because pagan skalds like the poets of *Eiríksmál* and *Hákonarmál* singled out these two men as Óthinn's favourites, Valholl's finest. If this is true, though, we must be able to explain why the *Beowulf* poet does not regard these heroes with the same esteem as the skalds do. Heremod, despite the fact that his name is registered in the West-Saxon royal pedigree of Alfred's time, is for the poet a blood-thirsty, blackhearted table-companion; the incestuous Sigemund is equally infamous for his feuds and crimes.[39]

Everyone recognizes that the *Beowulf* poet shares common narrative motifs and conventions with his Scandinavian counterparts; what has

not been sufficiently noted, perhaps, is that these conventions are sometimes used as literary borrowings, as familiar quotations from a set text
that the poet can then cap— *Waste Land* style—with a new and pointed
ending. A number of apparent Scandinavianisms in *Beowulf,* words or
idioms for which there are parallels in Norse poetry, seem to be inserted
by the poet in order to underline the traditional nature of an incident in
which Beowulf reacts in a most untraditional manner. As he lay dying,
Beowulf rejoiced over three things: that he never fomented strife, never
swore empty oaths, never murdered his kin (2738–42). The poet wanted
an uncommon hero and found him: the anti-Odinic, anti-Vǫlsung pagan
pagan champion.

For example, the poet tells of the tragic death of Hrethel's son
Herebeald, killed by his brother Hæthcyn when they were playing with
arrows: *miste mercelses* "he missed the target," says the poet, "and shot his
kinsman" (2439). The similarity between this accidental royal fratricide
and the myth of Baldr's death at his brother Hǫthr's hand has long been
noted.[40] But in addition to employing similar name elements (*beald:*
Baldr; *hæð:* Hǫthr), the *Beowulf* poet inserts what seems to be a Nordicism: *missan* (ON *missa*) "to miss, not hit" with a genitive of the object, a
usage common in Old Norse but otherwise unknown in this sense in
Old English. The idiom seems to mark the spot where pagan myth and
the poet's own reconstruction of northern history converge. The poet
goes on, however, to compare Hrethel's plight to that of a man whose
son is hanging on the gallows, a man who has no heart to wait for
another son, now that this one is gone; revenge was not to be had for an
executed criminal under Anglo-Saxon law, nor could a father take
vengeance on his own child. Beowulf seems to express admiration
(2470) for Hrethel's heroic resignation and restraint. Yet the myth tells
how Óthinn, Baldr's father, took swift vengeance on Hǫthr by begetting
another son for the sole purpose of slaying the former; this fratricidal
sequel to the Baldr story is alluded to by at least one tenth-century skald,
while the gods' revenge on the instigator Loki is portrayed on the early
tenth-century Gosforth cross from Cumberland.[41] Æthelweard's
Chronicle confirms that Baldr's affiliation to Óthinn was known in
tenth-century England.[42] The *Beowulf* poet's adaptation of the myth
diminishes and condemns Óthinn's role as reported in Norse story.

Unlike normal Odinic warriors, Beowulf insists on making friends
of potential foes. A set piece in Norse eddic poetry is the encounter
between a quarrelsome coastguard and a hero reaching the end of his
journey.[43] The *Beowulf* poet's strange observation as the Geats depart
from Denmark that the coastguard "did not greet the strangers with
insult" (1892) suggests some familiarity with this narrative cliché. Earlier

the coastguard, having directed Beowulf towards Heorot, opened the shortest speech in the poem, a farewell, with the Bogart tough-guy line *mæl is me to feran* "time for me to go" (316). The metre of the half-line is irregular, the only verse of its kind in *Beowulf* in which the noun in stressed position—*mæl*—does not alliterate.[44] Identical half-line types occur in Norse poetry: Helgi, Sigemund's son and Fitela's half-brother, departs abruptly for Valhǫll with the words *mál er mér at ríða* "time for me to ride" (*Helgakviða Hundingsbana* II, 49); the heathen thyle in *Hávamál* begins his chant just as abruptly with *mál er at þylja* "time to perform" (111). In all the eddic examples, as in *Beowulf,* the half-line opens a stanza of speech and the initial noun—*mál*—never alliterates. It is possible, though not provable, that the *Beowulf* poet introduced the phrase as a context marker, a kind of pagan Norse colouring to remind the hearer that the encounter between coastguard and champion here described had, traditionally, a far more violent outcome.

Beowulf also manages to avert strife in his subsequent flyting with the thyle Unferth, a stylized exchange with many parallels in Norse verse and prose.[45] Beowulf's countercharge that Unferth was a multiple fratricide (587) has a word-for-word parallel in the first Helgi poem, in Guthmundr's countercharge against Fitela, who actually had killed two of his brothers (*Helgakviða Hundingsbana* I, 36). Unlike the eddic combatants, however, Beowulf proves that he can contain his wrath: the Geat ends his rebuttal on a bright note, and eventually secures Unferth's friendship. Echoes of Norse poetry again serve as narrative moorings, pointers to a world of popular Odinic heroes against whom the Old English champion was to be measured.

Beowulf's nationality is not one that skalds would naturally associate with an anti-Odinic hero. Ninth- and tenth-century Norse poets regularly call Óthinn *Gauta Týr* "God of the Geats" (64, 57, 35), *Gauta spjalli* "counsellor of the Geats" (42, 37, 24), *Her-Gautr* "War-Geat" (2, 2, 1), *Val-Gautr* "Slaughter-Geat" (319, 295, 150), or simply and most frequently *Gautr* "Geat" (75, 66, 40; 79, 69, 42, etc.), what Beowulf is called four times in the Old English poem. Skaldic diction confirms place-name and other evidence that Gautland remained a centre of Óthinn worship into the eleventh century.[46] A fierce Odinic warrior named Hathagat (*Hathugaut* "Battle-Geat") leads sixth-century Saxons to victory in Widukind of Corvey's national history, the first version of which was composed by 967; the pagan Saxons hail Hathagat as godlike, and the tenth-century monk calls him *pater patrum* "founder of the tribe."[47] The Old English poet's choice of a Geat as his heathen prince of peace, his northern Good Samaritan, is perhaps the boldest manipulation of Scandinavian poetic convention in *Beowulf.*

It has recently been pointed out how the *Maldon* poet imparted Norse colouring to the speech of his viking messenger, in what may be the first literary use of dialect in English.[48] A number of syntactic oddities in *Beowulf* can also be explained as imitations of normal Norse word order. One construction not found in Old English outside *Beowulf* is the half-line consisting of a masculine compound in the accusative followed by the demonstrative pronoun *þone* "that"; such lines occur six times in the latter part of *Beowulf:* three times in connection with the dragon (*grundwong þone,* 2588; *eorðweard þone,* 2334; *goldweard þone,* 3081); twice in connection with the Swedish wars (*freoðowong þone,* 2959; *wælhlem þone,* 2969); and once when Beowulf, at home in Geatland, reminisces about Grendel's attack (*uhthlem þone,* 2007).[49] Since skaldic word order is notoriously skewed, the sporadic appearance in a verse of a demonstrative following its noun is not very significant. But the postpositing of the demonstrative "that" to its noun also occurs in Norwegian and Swedish runic inscriptions from the seventh century on, while "this" following its noun is a notable characteristic of viking-age runic monuments such as the Danish or Swedish gravestone from St. Paul's Churchyard, London.[50] Finally, the suffixing of the definite article to its noun (unless an adjective preceded) appears to have been normal Norse, especially Norwegian, practice by the end of the tenth century.[51] Whatever their origin, the postponed demonstratives of *Beowulf* might have sounded northern and darkly heathen to an Anglo-Saxon ear, the way the inversion in "Castle Dangerous" somehow calls up the atmosphere of a Gothic romance, and that in "Eggs Florentine" an elegant menu. The *Beowulf* poet may have copied a prominent linguistic feature of the Danelaw in order to colour the last third of his poem Geatish.

Sometimes the *Beowulf* poet seems to count on his listeners' familiarity with a contemporary skaldic genre, on their ability to recognize the changes he rings. In the final forty-six lines of *Beowulf,* we witness the building and kindling of a funeral pyre and hear a Geatish woman's song of lament as she predicts hard times ahead: "she sang," the poet says, "in memory of Beowulf a mournful song, said over and over that she greatly dreaded evil days, many slaughters, the terror of troops, shame and captivity." Then we watch the construction of a barrow on the headland and the deposition within of Beowulf's ashes and his gold. Twelve horsemen ride round and round the barrow, intoning a eulogy to their dead leader, enumerating his deeds and qualities. Each of the two physical rites—cremation on the pyre and deposition in the mound—is thus accompanied by a libretto, a chant that the poet twice describes as a *gyd.* The mourners' voices move from memory of past deeds to triumphant praise, focussed in the last three lines on the man himself: "They said that he was of earthly kings mildest to his men and gentlest, kindest to his people and most eager for fame."

This combination of personal lament and public eulogy, a prophecy of impending catastrophe joined with praise of a hero's deeds and goodness, is characteristic of tenth- and early eleventh-century skaldic memorial odes or *erfidrápur;* the sequence of laments that concludes *Beowulf* could have been put together with these Norse poems in mind.[52] In the pagan *Eiríksmál* and *Hákonarmál*, in Hallfrethr's Christian lament for Óláfr Tryggvason (159, 150, 82), and even in a 1076 stanza (416, 384, 191) by the last Norse skald we know of with direct English connections, the same balance is struck: only wars, humiliation, and terror after the death of the prince, but the glory of the man, his fame and goodness, will survive to the end. In the *erfidrápa*, as in *Beowulf*, at the moment of closure all attention is riveted on the fallen king. Lament as a genre has inevitably a certain sameness of content; but elegy— perhaps for this reason—has always been one of the most tradition-bound of literary forms, and the pattern of consolation found in *Beowulf* and the early Norse memorial eulogies is not easily paralleled. It is certainly not present in any of the analogues usually brought to bear on the ending of *Beowulf*.[53]

The last word of the poem, *lofgeornost* "most eager for fame," is a lexicographer's nightmare: the speakers clearly intend to praise (the word caps the Christian sequence "mildest," "gentlest," "kindest"), but it is found elsewhere in Old English only in a bad sense meaning "ostentatious, boastful."[54] *Lofgeorn* is documented in an unambiguously good sense in Scandinavian verse, however; Old Norse *lofgjarn* occurs in an eddic stanza praising the Vǫlsung hero Sigurthr as he passes through encircling flame.[55] Similar complimentary compounds ending in *-gjarn* abound in tenth-century skaldic poetry: *tírargjarn* "eager for glory" (159, 150, 82) occurs in the final stanza of Hallfrethr's praise poem on Óláfr Tryggvason, while *fremðargjarn* "eager for glory" (228, 216, 113) occurs in the final stanza of Sighvatr's *Víkingarvísur* in praise of Óláfr Haraldsson. The earliest example I can find is in the *Ynglingatal*, where a Swedish king—*Beowulf's* Eadgils in fact—is extolled as *dáðgjarn* "eager for great deeds" (12, 11, 7). The *Beowulf* poet makes sure that sixth-century pagan Geats and not he describe their fallen king as *lofgeorn;* "they said," he insists, forcing his audience to take the word in its secular, heroic sense, that of the skaldic cognate. A comparable distancing technique occurs in *Lycidas*, when Milton adds a coda to his final consoling vision: "Thus sang the uncouth Swain." In both cases, the poets go out of their way to separate themselves from the character and motives of the lamenters, thereby ensuring that the questions raised by the poem remain for Christian hearers far more compelling than the answers.

Both Old English poet and Old Norse skald are concerned with one particular group in society. The chief metre of the skalds was called *dróttkvætt,* the metre fit for the *drótt,* the king's band of retainers. The same élite and its aristocratic pastimes are a preoccupation of the *Beowulf* poet; his people act out elaborate rituals of greeting and drinking, boast and poetry, gift-giving and parting, the generative grammar of life in the hall.[56] The poet and the skald seem to be able to draw upon the same technical vocabulary. The benchplanks of Heorot, twice designated by the *Beowulf* poet as *bencþelu* (486, 1239), either stand dripping with blood after Grendel's depredations or are removed at nightfall to make room for the men to bunk down. The compound occurs only once again in Germanic poetry: in the mid-tenth century *Eiríksmál,* all *bekkþili* (175, 165, 89), all benchplanks within Valhǫll, creak noisiliy as the prince approaches.[57]

Like the skald, the Old English poet keeps a careful eye on where and how securely men park their weapons. The Geats march in armour to Heorot; they are instructed to leave their shields and stacked spears outside, but have explicit permission to enter the hall in helmet and mailcoat. In the mid-tenth-century *Hákonarmál,* the slain king urges his men to keep wargear on when entering Valhǫll, saying: "one must watch over one's helmet and mailcoat. It's good to be prepared" (67, 59, 37). The Geats in Heorot sleep with their helmets, mailcoats, and spears ready on a bench above them; the skald Sighvatr describes the similar interior decoration of Óláfr Haraldsson's court: "The king's retainers furnish the royal hall with helmets and mailcoats; I see a choice of both on the walls" (238, 224, 116). The skald associates meaddrinking and versemaking: poetry for him is Óthinn's precious mead;[58] the *Beowulf* poet also associates the two activities whenever the scop in Heorot is called upon to entertain the Geats (496, 1066). In *Beowulf,* Unferth has a place of honour at the king's feet; Wulfgar stands before the Danish king's shoulders: "he knew," the poet assures us, "the custom of retainers" (359). For the early skalds, the relevant royal bone was the knee: Egill Skallagrímsson delivers his poem "before the knee of the king" (45, 39, 25); Thórmóthr Bersason declares, "He who long stands before your knee, O king, needs courage" (282, 260, 134); and Sighvatr Thórtharson boasts: "Up to now I have had luck with all the good marshalls of the battlebold king, those who go before our king's knee" (267, 247, 128).

The *Beowulf* poet believed that the hall protocol and rituals he described were facts, whether they were familiar from literature or current practice; and he seems to have expected his audience to understand his aristocratic shorthand. When Beowulf tells Hrothgar that the latter will not need to "hide the head" (446) of his champion if Grendel eats him, no further explanation is offered. We need not, however, assume great age for this expression, tracing in it a memory of old Anglian funerary customs or even a reference to the cloth enfolding the seventh-century abbess mentioned by Bede (*Historia Ecclesiastica* 4.17). The same phrase—*hylja hǫfuð* "to hide the head" —occurs in an anonymous, mid-eleventh-century skaldic poem on the death of King Magnús the Good: "The king's retainers have hidden the head of the one who was the highest of princes" (425, 395, 196).[59] Nor need we assume that dim antiquity has caused the battle standard set high over Scyld's head, the one given to Beowulf by Hrothgar, and the one standing over the dragon's hoard, to be portrayed as "golden": *segen gyldenne* and *segn eallgylden*. King Edwin's seventh-century banners, standard, and *tufa* as described by Bede (*Historia Ecclesiastica* 2.16) and the royal standard (or lampstand) of Sutton Hoo have nothing of gold about them, nor do the war banners of Vergil, Statius, or the Bible; but when we reach the stanzas of Sighvatr we again encounter golden standards (*gyld stǫng*, 229, 218, 113; 258, 240, 124) lifted high in battle before the Norwegian king.

Sighvatr, who spent some time in England and who belonged to the first generation of Christian skalds, is the Norseman whose voice most reminds me of the *Beowulf* poet's. They share a fondness for sentiment, moral promptings, and the gentler pursuits of court such as horseback riding and diplomacy. Departing on a mission, Sighvatr recites a farewell that Beowulf might have directed at Hygelac: "Remain now in health in your hall, King Óláfr, until I come back to serve you, until we meet here again. I pray that the prince will hold his life and this land" (267, 247, 128). Reaching Knútr's court in England and left to cool his heels for a while, Sighvatr complains as Beowulf could have at Heorot: "I had to inquire outside the door of the hall before I could get a word with the lord of the Jutes; I saw the house barred before me" (241, 226, 117). To a royal officer who assists him, Sighvatr offers a careful compliment: "Often, Bjǫrn, you put in a good word for me with the prince. You give good advice, soldier, because you know a lot" (267, 247, 128). Like the *Beowulf* poet, Sighvatr takes time out to cast scorn on the ignorant heathenism of rural folk;[60] and he, too, seems to have a particular horror of kin-slayings. One verse rebukes a cousin-killer: "Áslákr has increased kinsman-guilt; the lord of the Hordalanders is killed; no one should start a conflict this way; a family-killing cannot be denied; born kinsmen should hold back from wrath; they should look to the old sayings" (246, 230, 119). Though working perhaps more than a century apart, Sighvatr and the *Beowulf* poet probably appear at the same moment in their respective literary traditions, a moment when learned Christian poets were being called upon to celebrate the roots of a new and only partly literate secular aristocracy.[61]

Our excursion through the skaldic landscape is almost at an end. This might be an appropriate moment to pause and recall what the exercise was all about. Nothing in the bits and pieces of information extracted from skaldic verse was found incompatible with a date for *Beowulf* in the late ninth or the first half of the tenth century; and some facts were more compatible with this period than with any other. I cannot prove that *Beowulf* was composed then; nevertheless, accepting that the poem came into existence between 890 and 950 solves far more problems than it poses. An Alfredian or post-Alfredian date means that the central fable of *Beowulf* could have come from the lips of English Scandinavians and not from the wellspring of folk memory;[62] it explains the poet's and audience's apparent acquaintance with Norse literary genres, his ability to manipulate Scandinavian legend and myth, and theirs to follow what he was doing. A late date accounts for the cumulative, allusive richness of the poem, and for the congruence of outlook, idiom, and theme in *Beowulf* and skaldic verse; it provides in Alfred and his successors a focus and an incentive for the production of court poetry. Even the similarity between the poet's description of Grendel's mere and the conclusion of the sixteenth Blickling homily becomes more explicable.[63] If, on the other hand, we assume that *Beowulf* is early, we also have to assume that for over three centuries Old Norse poetry remained static, that Sigemund and Heremod held their frozen paired pose like figures on a Grecian urn, that golden standards, bloodied *bekkþili,* and idioms like "to hide the head" belonged to Scandinavian hall-vocabulary as early as 700 or—conversely—were borrowed by tenth-century skalds from a static Old English verse. But this won't work: neither poetry remained the same for three hundred years. Between 900 and 1200, we observe skald after skald striving to outdo his predecessor, just as he must have done in the centuries that preceded; imitation for him meant making something different, taking stock of the tradition with an appreciative or cool eye. The *Beowulf* poet, too, took stock, and the material he seems to have weighed was that of the Danelaw skalds and storytellers. When the Old English poet inverts the character of a traditional Norse hero, changes the outcome of traditional Norse incidents, and modifies the ending of a traditional Norse memorial genre, all the while garnishing his epic with Norse names, colour, and decorative motifs, it is easy to imagine that he was composing not long after, or far from, the Danish skalds he was outdoing.

The effect on Old English poetry of decade upon decade of Anglo-Danish interaction—two peoples speaking closely related languages, living in the same area, praying to the same god, and working within similar political and ecclesiastical structures—has probably been rendered imperceptible to us by the very congruity of the two cultures, the way archaeologists in the Danelaw have not yet been able to distinguish a single Scandinavian farm or village from indigenous settlements.[64] For much of the tenth century, the Danes and the English do not seem to have formed discrete, mutually-hostile communities:[65] the coinage, inscriptions, and sculpture of the first Scandinavian settlers show them striving to be more Christian and English than the English;[66] native artistic traditions can be seen absorbing more and more Norse elements as time goes on.[67] The Anglo-Saxons did not "catch" Scandinavian taste from the vikings like a case of cultural measles. Nevertheless, between *Bede's Death Song* and *Maldon* something did happen to Old English poetry, whether we call this something rebarbarization or "conceiving Christian experience afresh in terms of Germanic heroic poetry."[68] Unlike Anglian stone crosses of the eighth century, English religious sculpture after the Danish invasions drew on pagan myth and heroic legend: Wayland in Leeds parish church, Thor in Gosforth church, Sigemund at Winchester Old Minster.[69] We have learned to recognize Scandinavian symptoms in much English sculpture and drawing from the Middleton crosses to the Cædmon manuscript; even in the heart of tenth-century Wessex, stones were carved with intricate Norse designs.[70] Not all Old English verse was immune to this taste. The *Beowulf* poet pondered his northern heathens and northern heroes, and raised to their memory a monument far more Christian and, at the same time, far more Scandinavian than the mound at Sutton Hoo.

NOTES

1. Dorothy Whitelock, *The Audience of "Beowulf"* (Oxford, 1951), 24–25.

2. Nicolas Jacobs, "Anglo-Danish Relations, Poetic Archaism, and the Date of *Beowulf:* A Reconsideration of the Evidence," *Poetica* (Tokyo) 8 (1977): 40.

3. See J. Armitage Robinson, *St. Oswald and the Church of Worcester,* British Academy Supplemental Papers no. 5 (London, 1919), 38–51. Oskytel, another kinsman of Oda, was the mid-tenth-century archbishop of York: less than eighty years after heathen invaders martyred Edmund, king of the East Angles, both archbishops of England were of Danish extraction.

4. Frederick Klaeber, ed., *Beowulf and the Fight at Finnsburg,* 3rd ed. (Boston, 1950), cxvii. The first editors of *Beowulf* believed that the poem was Scandinavian: Grímur J. Thorkelin subtitled his 1815 ed. *Poëma Danicum dialecto Anglo-Saxonica.* They differed, however, as to whether it was a 449 or 1016 import. John

M. Kemble (2nd ed., 1835) surmised that *Beowulf* was "written in Angeln and brought hither by some of the earliest Anglo-Saxon chieftains who settled upon our shores" (xx). Benjamin Thorpe (1855) decided that the poem was "not an original production of the Anglo-Saxon muse, but a metrical paraphrase of a heroic Saga composed in the south-west of Sweden . . . and probably brought to this country during the sway of the Danish dynasty" (viii). In 1885, Gregor Sarrazin tried to demonstrate that *Beowulf* was derived from an Old Norse (ON) original: "Der Schauplatz des ersten Beowulfliedes und die Heimat des Dichters," *Beiträge zur Geschichte der deutschen Sprache und Literatur* 11 (1885): 159–83; "Altnordisches im Beowulfliede," *Beiträge zur Geschichte der deutschen Sprache und Literatur* 11 (1885): 528–41. Philological objections were raised by Eduard Sievers, "Die Heimat des Beowulfdichters," *Beiträge zur Geschichte der deutschen Sprache und Literatur* 11 (1885): 354–62, and "Altnordisches im *Beowulf*," *Beiträge zur Geschichte der deutschen Sprache und Literatur* 12 (1887): 168–200. Sarrazin's translation theory informs his *Beowulf-Studien: Ein Beitrag zur Geschichte altgermanischer Sage und Dichtung* (Berlin, 1888).

5. On *eorlas Anlafes* = Óláfr's jarls, see John C. Pope, ed., *Seven Old English Poems* (Indianapolis, 1966), 162 s.v. *eorl* (b), and Dietrich Hofmann, *Nordisch-englische Lehnbeziehungen der Wikingerzeit*, Bibliotheca Arnamagnæana no. 14 (Copenhagen, 1955), 167. The first occurrence of Old English (OE) *eorl* as a Norse title is in the *Chronicle* entry for 871, where it is found in apposition to Scandinavian personal names: *Two of the Saxon Chronicles Parallel*, ed. John Earle (1865), rev. Charles Plummer (1892–99; reissued D. Whitelock, Oxford, 1952), 1:70. See also L.L. Schücking, "Die Beowulfdatierung: Eine Replik," *Beiträge zur Geschichte der deutschen Sprache und Literatur* 47 (1923): 305.

6. The first Norse loanword in *Maldon* occurs in the viking messenger's speech; the second, as a technical term. F.C. Robinson, "Some Aspects of the *Maldon* Poet's Artistry," *JEGP* 75 (1976): 25–28, detects additional Scandinavianisms in the viking's speech.

7. Hofmann, *Nordisch-englische Lehnbeziehungen*, 45–46, accepting Whitelock's pre-viking date for *Beowulf*, concludes that a tenth-century skald working in England must have borrowed the term *bekkþili* from OE poetry (but *bencþelu* occurs only in *Beowulf* 486, 1239). Suspected "Anglicisms" in Norse verse that (if *Beowulf* is dated late) could be regarded as "Danicisms" in the English poem include the pairs *glaðir Ylfingar* (*Helgakviða Hundingsbana* I, 49) and *glæde Scyldingas* (*Beowulf* 58); *dís Skjǫldunga* (*Helgakviða Hundingsbana* II, 51; *Brot af Sigurðarkviðu* 14) and *ides Scyldinga* (*Beowulf* 1168); *þjóðskjǫldungar* (Óttarr svarti 295, 272, 139) and *þeod-Scyldingas* (*Beowulf* 1019). On the supposed Norse borrowing of an OE kenning-type for ship (*Beowulf* 208, 226, 1906), see Hofmann, 80–81. The absence from *Beowulf* of the common kenning-type "seahorse" = ship (e.g. Alfred's *merehengest*, Cynewulf's *wæghengest*, *sæmearh*) probably tells us more about the poet's taste and sophistication than about his date (but see Peter Clemoes, "Style as the Criterion for Dating the Composition of *Beowulf*," *The Dating of Beowulf*, ed. Colin Chase (Toronto, 1991), 180). In ON, "horse of the sea" = ship seems to have been most popular in late (i.e., twelfth- and thirteenth-century), eddic, and Christian poetry, in verse that prized clarity, sincerity, and obviousness. On ship-kennings in ON poetry, see Rudolf Meissner, *Die Kenningar der Skalden: Ein Beitrag zur skaldischen Poetik*, Rheinische Beiträge und Hülfsbücher zur germanischen

Philologie und Volkskunde no. 1 (Bonn and Leipzig, 1921), 208–22. Citations of eddic poetry in this paper refer to Gustav Neckel, ed., *Edda: Die Lieder des Codex Regius nebst verwandten Denkmälern*, vol. 1, *Text*, 4th ed. rev. Hans Kuhn (Heidelberg, 1962). The three numbers following a citation from skaldic verse give its location in the first vol. of each of the standard eds. in this sequence: 1. *Den norskislandske skjaldedigtning*, ed. Finnur Jónsson, A. Tekst efter håndskrifterne (Copenhagen, 1908); 2. The same, B. Rettet tekst (Copenhagen, 1912); 3. *Den norskisländska skaldediktningen*, reviderad av Ernst A. Kock (Lund, 1946).

   8.   On heroic names in *Beowulf* that do not correspond exactly to their ON equivalents (e.g. Eadgils/Athils; Wælsing/Vǫlsungr), see Andreas Heusler, "Heldennamen in mehrfacher Lautgestalt," *Zeitschrift für deutsches Altertum* 52 (1910): 97–107. The fact that *Beowulf* does not employ Sconeg as the OE *Orosius* does (*King Alfred's Orosius*, ed. Henry Sweet, Early English Text Society, original series no. 79 [London, 1883], 19) or *Skáney* as skalds around 1000 do (75, 65, 40; 157, 149, 81; 250, 233, 121) but "retains" *Scedenig* (1686) and *Scedeland* (19) as names for Scandinavia is often cited as evidence for the pre-Alfredian date of the poem (see Whitelock, *Audience*, 26; R.W. Chambers, *"Beowulf": An Introduction to the Study of the Poem* [Cambridge, 1921], 323; Elliott V.K. Dobbie, ed., *Beowulf and Judith*, Anglo-Saxon Poetic Records no. 4 [New York, 1953], lvii). But a tenth-century Englishman, like his modern counterpart, no doubt distinguished between a single province within the Danish kingdom of his day (*Sconeg*, Swedish *Skåne*, German *Schonen*) and the larger region *in geardagum* known from classical and early medieval sources as *Scadinavia* (Pliny, *Naturalis historia* 13.96), *Scathanavia* (Fredegar, *Chronicon*, ed. B. Krusch, *Monumenta Germaniae historica, Scriptores rerum Merovingicarum* [1888], 2:65), *Scadan, Scadanan, Scandenan* (*Origo gentis Langobardorum*, ed. G. Waitz, *Monumenta Germaniae historica, Scriptores rerum Langobardicarum* [1878], 2), or *Scatenauge* (*Chronicon Gothanum, ibid.*, 8). OE *Scedenig*, corresponding to Prim. Norse *Skaþin-awjo* (or *Scedeland*, in the plural like *Scandiae*), could have survived into the tenth century and could reflect a ninth-century transposition into OE of ON *Skaðin-* (*Scedenig* is to *Skáney* as Hrothgar to Hróarr or Hrothulf to Hrólfr: see Adolf Noreen, *Geschichte der nordischen Sprachen*, 3rd rev. ed. [= Hermann Paul, ed., *Grundriss der germanischen Philologie* vol. 4] [Strassburg, 1913], 108, on the sporadic disappearance in ON of *ð* before *n*, a process only partly completed by the end of the ninth century). Indeed, it is easier to explain the *d* in OE *Scedenig* as a later (**Skaðin-*) rather than an earlier (**Skaþin-*) borrowing from ON: see Erik Björkman, *Namn och Bygd* 6 (1918): 166. Similarly, the *Beowulf* poet, recreating a past, calls Hrothgar's kingdom *land Dena* (242, 253, 1904) and not *Denamearc* (cf. *Wedermearc* "Geatland" in *Beowulf* 298), a neologism that first appears in the OE *Orosius* (19). See Josef Svennung, *Scadinavia und Scandia, lateinische-nordische Namenstudien*, Acta societatis litterarum humaniorum regiae Upsaliensis no. 44 (Uppsala, 1963).

   9.   For more on these methods and their limitations, see discussion and bibliography in E.O.G. Turville-Petre, *Scaldic Poetry* (Oxford, 1976), lxvi–lxxiv, and Roberta Frank, *Old Norse Court Poetry: The Dróttkvætt Stanza*, Islandica no. 42 (Ithaca, N.Y., 1978), 31–32.

   10.   Curt Weibull, "Om det svenska och det danska rikets uppkomst," *Historisk Tidskrift för Skåneland* 7 (1917–21): 351.

   11.   C.L. Wrenn, *"Beowulf" with the Finnesburg Fragment*, 3rd ed. rev. W.F. Bolton (London, 1973), 39, says that "the fact that the Geats are not heard of in

history after about the middle of the sixth century corroborates the implication in ll. 2999 ff. and 3015 ff. of the complete overthrow of the Geats by the Swedes after the death of Beowulf." Arthur G. Brodeur, *The Art of "Beowulf"* (Berkeley, 1959), 135, also speaks of "the downfall of the Danish and Geatish kingdoms," of "national catastrophes." On post-550 Geatish survival, see R.T. Farrell, "*Beowulf,* Swedes, and Geats," *Saga-Book of the Viking Society* 18 (1972): 256–71.

12.   See Gustav Binz, "Zeugnisse zur germanischen Sage in England," *Beiträge zur Geschichte der deutschen Sprache und Literatur* 20 (1895): 141–223. The name Healfdene first appears in an English document around 930; Heorogar, Hrothgar, and Heoroweard never occur; and Halga, Hrethric, and Hrothmund are heard of only after the Danish settlement. In contrast, Heathobard names like Ingeld and Froda are early.

13.   My ON lexicographical information comes from Johan Fritzner, *Ordbog over det gamle norske Sprog,* vols. 1–3 (1883–96; repr., Oslo, 1954), vol. 4 (supplement by Finn Hødnebø, Oslo, 1972); Richard Cleasby and Gudbrand Vigfússon, *An Icelandic-English Dictionary,* 2nd ed. with supplement by William A. Craigie (Oxford, 1957); Finnur Jónsson, *Lexicon poeticum antiquae linguae septentrionalis . . . af Sveinbjörn Egilsson,* 2nd ed. (Copenhagen, 1931; repr. 1966); Jan de Vries, *Altnordisches etymologisches Wörterbuch* (Leiden, 1961). Sven Aggesen speaks about the Icelanders' use of *skjǫldungr* in *Brevis historia regum Dacie,* ed. M. Cl. Gertz, *Scriptores minores historiae Danicae medii aevi* (Copenhagen, 1917–22), 1:96–97; Saxo in *Gesta Danorum,* ed. Jørgen Olrik and Hans Ræder (Copenhagen, 1931), 11.

14.   *Skjǫldungr* appears in two skaldic stanzas of doubtful authenticity assigned to the tenth century: Jórunn skaldmær (61, 54, 34) and the anonymous *Oddmjór* (177, 167, 90).

15.   *Historia de sancto Cuthberto* in *Symeonis monachi opera omnia,* ed. Thomas Arnold, Rolls Series no. 75 (London, 1882), 1:196–214. On the date see Edmund Craster, "The Patrimony of St. Cuthbert," *English Historical Review* 69 (1954): 177–99.

16.   *Historia de sancto Cuthberto* 7.10, 11, 12 (1:200, 202).

17.   The Scheldt etymology was proposed by Felix Liebermann, "Der Name Scaldi für Dänen," *Archiv* 148 (1925): 95, based on an entry in the *Annals* of Lindisfarne for 911: "Scaldi Rollo duce possident Normanniam." The equation Scaldis/Scheldt is made by G.H. Pertz, ed., *Annales Lindisfarnenses,* in *Monumenta Germaniae historica, Scriptores,* vol. 19 (1866; repr., Leipzig, 1925), 506. Erik Björkman, "Two Derivations," *Saga-Book of the Viking Society* 7 (1912): 132–40, derived Scaldingi from Old Saxon/Old Low Franconian **skalda,* a vessel propelled by a punting pole. But Scaldingi almost certainly reflects a ninth-century ON form **skealdur* or **skjaldur,* an intermediate stage after fracture of Prim. Norse **skeldur* but before the *o*-mutation to *skjǫldr* (*Skjǫldungr*). Cf. *skialti* (i.e. *skialdi*), the dat. sg. of "shield" on the Rök stone, Östergötland, ca. 900: Adolf Noreen, *Altschwedische Grammatik* (Halle, 1904), 314; Andreas Heusler, *Altisländisches Elementarbuch,* 4th ed. (Heidelberg, 1950), 25–26. On Scalding = Scylding, see William H. Stevenson, ed., *Asser's Life of King Alfred* (1904; repr., Oxford, 1959), 218; A.L. Binns, "The York Viking Kingdom: Relations between Old English and Old Norse Culture," *The Fourth Viking Congress,* ed. Alan Small (Edinburgh, 1965), 181–89; and Binns, *The Viking Century in East Yorkshire* (York, 1963), 49–50.

18.   Alfred P. Smyth, *Scandinavian Kings in the British Isles, 850–880* (Oxford,

1977), 12, charts the kings of Denmark from 800–1000, showing how Saxo grafted the line of Ragnarr Lothbrók onto a leading Danish dynasty. *Skjǫldunga saga,* from around 1200 but now known chiefly through a Latin abstract, probably contained a similar sequence of kings from Skjǫldr, son of Óthinn, to Gormr the Old. See Bjarni Guðnason, *Um Skjǫldungasǫgu* (Reykjavík, 1963), 114–32, and Jakob Benediktsson, "Icelandic Traditions of the Scyldings," *Saga-Book of the Viking Society* 15 (1957–59): 48–66.

19. Frank M. Stenton, *Anglo-Saxon England,* 3rd ed. (Oxford, 1971), 13, finds the Alfredian narrator's comment "the strongest evidence for the northern origin of the Angles" (Sweet, *Alfred's Orosius,* 19). The chronicler Æthelweard, working shortly after 975, is even more precise about a Danish homeland, reporting that English Anglia had its origin in "Anglia vetus": *The Chronicle of Æthelweard,* ed. Alistair Campbell (London, 1962), 9.

20. Herbert Jankuhn argues for the Danish origin of the Angles in "Zur Frage nach der Urheimat der Angeln," *Zeitschrift der Gesellschaft für schleswig-holsteinische Geschichte* 70/71 (1943): 1–43; "Siedlungs- und Kulturgeschichte der Angeln vor ihrer Auswanderung nach England," *Jahrbuch des angler Heimatvereins* 14 (1950): 54–132; and "Wirtschafts- und Kulturgeschichte Angelns in der Wikingerzeit," *Jahrbuch des angler Heimatvereins* 16 (1952): 25–75. Contra, see O. Scheel, *Die Heimat der Angeln,* Schriften der wiss. Akademie des NSD-Dozentenbundes der Christian-Albrechts-Universität Kiel (Kiel, 1939).

21. Plummer, *Saxon Chronicles Parallel* 1:82–83 (s.a. 890); trans. Dorothy Whitelock with D.C. Douglas and S.I. Tucker, *The Anglo-Saxon Chronicle: A Revised Translation* (London, 1961), 53: "And the northern king, Guthrum, whose baptismal name was Athelstan, died. He was King Alfred's godson, and he lived in East Anglia and was the first to settle that land."

22. Kenneth Sisam, "Anglo-Saxon Royal Genealogies," *Proceedings of the British Academy* 39 (1953): 287–346.

23. On the ascription of Æthelwulf's pedigree to the "Alfredian" annalist, see Sisam, "Royal Genealogies," 332; Whitelock, *Anglo-Saxon Chronicle,* xxii, xxiv. On the writing of the *Chronicle* in the 890s, see Peter H. Sawyer, *The Age of the Vikings,* 2nd ed. (London, 1971), 14–25. The occurrence of Æthelwulf's pedigree in the first chapter of Asser's *De rebus gestis Aelfredi* (Stevenson, *Asser's Life,* 2–4), which was given its present shape by 893, provides a *terminus ante quem.*

24. See David Dumville, "Kingship, Genealogies, and Regnal Lists" in *Early Medieval Kingship,* ed. Peter H. Sawyer and I.N. Wood (Leeds, 1977), 72–104, for a statement of the propagandist value of early medieval genealogies. Jack Goody and Ian Watt, "The Consequences of Literacy," in *Literacy in Traditional Societies,* ed. Jack Goody (Cambridge, 1968), 33, observes how chronicles are constantly changing and how they often serve "the same function that Malinowski claimed for myth; they act as 'charters' of present social institutions rather than as faithful historical records of times past."

25. Campbell, *Chronicle of Æthelweard,* xx, xxiv, lix–lx. Æthelweard introduces the names Balder (ON Baldr) and Withar (ON Vitharr), substitutes Iguuar (ON Ívarr) for Inwær and Guthrum for Godrum, and reports that viking leaders were known as *eorlas* and that Woden was a king who received divine honours after his death.

26. With Dane and Englishman now brothers, the falling out of Cain and

Abel—the *Beowulf* poet's paradigm for the kinslayings and civil wars that renew themselves throughout the poem—could be used to make a political point. Martin Biddle, "Excavations at Winchester 1965," *Antiquaries' Journal* 46 (1966): 308–32, interprets a sculpture (perhaps part of a stone frieze) from Winchester Old Minster that seems to portray a scene from the Vǫlsung legend (Sigemund and the wolf) as celebrating the common origin of the West-Saxon and Danish royal houses. Biddle would like the sculpture to belong to the reign of Knútr; but as Jacobs ("Anglo-Danish Relations," 40) observes, the slab — if contemporary with the rebuilding of the Old Minster (971–994)—is evidence for the period that probably preserved our poem.

27. See Smyth, *Scandinavian Kings,* 23–24.

28. Farrell, *"Beowulf,* Swedes, and Geats," 253, charts Beowulf's family connections.

29. *Ynglingatal* or "List of the Ynglingar" is a difficult poem with numerous textual cruces. See esp. W. Åkerlund, *Studier över Ynglingatal,* Skrifter utg. av. Vetenskaps-Societeten i Lund no. 23 (Lund, 1939); Walter Baetke, *Yngvi und die Ynglingar: Eine quellenkritische Untersuchung über das nordische Sakralkonigtum,* Sitzungsberichte der sächsischen Akademie der Wissenschaften zu Leipzig, phil-hist. Klasse no. 109 (Leipzig, 1964).

30. Thirteenth-century Norse accounts of the two kings' diplomacy can be found in Bjarni Aðalbjarnarson, ed., *Heimskringla,* Íslenzk Fornrit no. 26 (Reykjavík, 1941), 143–45, and Finnur Jónsson, ed., *Fagrskinna,* Samfund til udgivelse af gammel nordisk litteratur no. 30 (Copenhagen, 1902–03), 20–22.

31. *Þjóðkonungr* designates Knútr (284, 263, 135), Óláfr (228, 217, 113; 242, 227, 118; 260, 242, 125; 268, 248, 128; 325, 330, 152) and Magnús (274, 253, 131; 338, 311, 158).

32. Charlemagne's contemporary Gothfrith (800–810) seems to have been more than a petty or regional king, at least in the vocabulary of the Frankish annalists, but after his assassination the Danish kingdom seems to have been shared out among multiple rulers until the last half of the tenth century (with the possible exception of one brief period around 850–855). See discussion and bibliography in Horst Zettel, *Das Bild der Normannen und der Normanneneinfälle in westfränk-ischen, ostfränkischen, und angelsächsischen Quellen des 8. bis 11. Jahrhunderts* (Munich, 1977), 69–84. On West-Saxon hegemonial tendencies during the first half of the tenth century, see E.E. Stengel, "Imperator und Imperium bei den Angelsachsen," *Deutsches Archiv* 16 (1960): 15–72; J.L. Nelson, "Inauguration Rituals," in *Early Medieval Kingship,* ed. Peter H. Sawyer and I.N. Wood (Leeds, 1977), 68–70. In the 940s Archbishop Oda addresses "all peoples (*gentes*) everywhere subject" to the *regale imperium* of Athelstan's brother Edmund: Patrologia Latina 133, col. 952.

33. Wrenn, *Beowulf,* 47. But see William W. Lawrence, *"Beowulf" and Epic Tradition* (Cambridge, Mass., 1928), 321.

34. Heinz Hungerland, "Zeugnisse zur Vǫlsungen- und Niflungen Sage aus der Skaldendichtung (8–16 Jahrhundert)," *Arkiv för nordisk filologi* 20 (1904): 1–43; Fr. Kauffmann, "Zur Geschichte der Sigfridsage," *Zeitschrift für deutsche Philologie* 31 (1899): 5–23 ("Man wird festhalten dürfen, dass es vor der mitte des 10. jahrhunderts im norden weder eine Sigurdsage noch Sigurdlieder gegeben hat," 8).

35. H.R. Ellis, "Sigurd in the Art of the Viking Age," *Antiquity* 16 (1942): 216–36; J.T. Lang, "Sigurd and Weland in Pre-Conquest Carving from Northern

England," *Yorkshire Archaeological Journal* 48 (1976): 83–94.

36. For information on the relationship between the two poems, see Edith Marold, "Das Walhallbild in den *Eiríksmál* und den *Hákonarmál*," *Mediaeval Scandinavia* 5 (1972): 19–33; also Klaus von See, "Zwei eddische Preislieder: *Eiríksmál* und *Hákonarmál*," in *Festgabe für U. Pretzel* (Berlin, 1963), 107–17. Both poems are in a metre (mixed *fornyrðislag* and *ljóðaháttr*) which does not differ radically from that of *Beowulf*; unlike skaldic verse in court metre (*dróttkvætt*), their diction is relatively straightforward: *Eiríksmál* has only a single kenning (sword storm = battle); the kennings of *Hákonarmál* are more numerous and evocative (e.g. wound fires = swords; cf. wound gates = gashes, *Beowulf* 1121).

37. The tradition that Hákon the Good had been fostered at the English court is a commonplace in Norse histories compiled in the late twelfth and thirteenth centuries. Hákon's nickname *Aðalsteinsfóstri* first occurs in Sighvatr Thórtharson's *Bersǫglisvísur*, a skaldic poem probably from the 1030s.

38. Neckel, *Edda*, 288–96. The date of *Hyndluljóð* is not known: Einar Ól. Sveinsson, *Íslenzkar bókmenntir í fornöld* (Reykjavík, 1962), 351, places the poem between the late eleventh century and the end of the twelfth.

39. *Beowulf* 879: *fæhðe ond fyrene*. Heremod does not appear in Æthelweard's version (ca. 975) of the West-Saxon royal pedigree (Campbell, *Chronicle of Æthelweard*, 33–34).

40. See Klaeber, *Beowulf*, xli. Ursula Dronke, '*Beowulf* and Ragnarǫk," *Saga-Book of the Viking Society* 17 (1969): 322–25, points out that *Beowulf* contains human analogues for two additional mythological incidents recorded in Norse poetry.

41. Kormakr Ǫgmundarson (79, 69, 42). On the iconography of the Gosforth cross, see Knut Berg, "The Gosforth Cross," *Journal of the Warburg and Courtauld Institute* 21 (1958): 27–43.

42. Campbell, *Chronicle of Æthelweard*, 33.

43. See Carol Clover, "The Germanic Context of the Unferþ Episode," *Speculum* 55 (1980): 444–68.

44. On the unusual form of the line see E.G. Stanley, "Some Observations on the A3 Lines in *Beowulf*," in *Old English Studies in Honour of John C. Pope*, ed. Robert B. Burlin and Edward B. Irving (Toronto, 1974), 146.

45. See, e.g., Aage Kabell, "Unferth und die dänischen Biersitten," *Arkiv för nordisk filologi* 94 (1979): 31–41.

46. Jan de Vries, *Altgermanische Religionsgeschichte*, 3rd ed. [= Hermann Paul, ed., *Grundriss der germanischen Philologie* vol. 12] (Berlin, 1970), 2:52–54, 91–92, observes that the greatest number of place-names containing an Óthinn name come from the region in central Sweden occupied by the Gautar (OE Geatas). Also E.O.G. Turville-Petre, *Myth and Religion of the North: The Religion of Ancient Scandinavia* (London, 1964), 66. The skald Sighvatr journeyed through Västergötland around 1018 and found that some of the natives still "feared Óthinn's anger" (234, 221, 115). Ailnoth of Canterbury as late as 1100 contrasted the Danes among whom he resided, the good Christians, with the Swedes and Geats who in times of trouble would drive out the new religion: *Vitae sanctorum Danorum*, ed. M. Cl. Gertz (Copenhagen, 1908–12), 83. See Kenneth Sisam, *The Structure of "Beowulf"* (Oxford, 1965), 56.

47. *Rerum Saxonicarum libri III*, chs. 11–12. See Karl Hauck, "Lebensnormen und Kultmythen in germanischen Stammes- und Herrschergenealogien," *Saeculum*

6 (1955): 186–223. Hans Kuhn, "Gaut," in *Festschrift für Jost Trier zu seinem 60. Geburtstag* (Meisenheim/Glan, 1954), 417–33, compares the threat of Ongentheow in *Beowulf* 2940 (*getan* [*gautian*] . . . *on galgtreowum* "to sacrifice [men] on the gallows") with a boast by the mid-tenth-century skald Helgi trausti Óláfsson: *guldum galga valdi Gauts tafn* "I paid to the gallows-prince [Óthinn] Gautr's sacrifice" (99, 94, 55).

48. Robinson, "Aspects of the *Maldon* Poet's Artistry," 25–28. In "Syntactical Glosses in Latin Manuscripts of Anglo-Saxon Provenance," *Speculum* 48 (1973): 443–75, Robinson demonstrates the Anglo-Saxons' sensitivity to the strongly patterned word order of their language and, therefore, to deviations from normal syntax.

49. Alistair Campbell, "The Use in *Beowulf* of Earlier Heroic Verse," in *England Before the Conquest: Studies in Primary Sources Presented to Dorothy Whitelock,* ed. Peter Clemoes and Kathleen Hughes (Cambridge, 1971), 286, argues that this half-line type is evidence for the use in *Beowulf* of heroic lays on the Swedish-Geatish wars. Sarrazin, *Beowulf-Studien,* 69, cited the same construction to show that the poem was a translation from Old Norse.

50. E.g., a postposited "that" occurs on the stone from Istaby, Sweden, ca. 650, and on the whetstone from Strøm, Norway, ca. 600–650. The St. Paul's gravestone reads: "Ginna and Toki had *stone this* (*stīn pensi*) placed." The opposite order—e.g. *pena kirk* on the twelfth-century Pennington tympanum—is taken as proof of English influence or workmanship. See R.I. Page, "How Long did the Scandinavian Language Survive in England?" in Clemoes and Hughes, *England Before the Conquest,* 165–81; K.M. Nielsen, "The Position of the Attribute in Danish Runic Inscriptions," *Acta philologica Scandinavica* 16 (1942–43): 227–29.

51. See Finnur Jónsson, *Norsk-islandske kultur- og sprogforhold i 9. og 10. årh.,* Det Kgl. Danske Videnskabernes Selskab, hist-filol. Meddelser no. 3.2 (Copenhagen, 1921), 315.

52. See Roberta Frank, "Old Norse Memorial Eulogies and the Ending of *Beowulf,*" *Acta* 6 (1979): 1–19.

53. Jordanes (*Getica* pars. 256–58, ed. Theodor Mommsen, *Monumenta Germaniae historica, Auctores antiquissimi,* 5.1 [Berlin, 1882]) tells of horsemen at Attila's funeral who proclaim his deeds, but Jordanes stresses the mourners' gaiety: no one expresses apprehension, no one anticipates the end of the Huns. Hector's funeral in the *Iliad* (ch. 24) is well provided with wailing women, among whom Andromache, like the Geatish woman in *Beowulf,* predicts captivity and humiliation for herself now that Troy's protector is dead; but there is no formal praise of Hector, either before or after his cremation. For a general guide to the genre, see Claude Thiry, *La plainte funèbre,* Typologie des sources du Moyen Âge occidental no. 30 (Turnhout, 1978).

54. E.G. Stanley, "*Hæthenra Hyht* in *Beowulf,*" in *Studies in Old English Literature in Honor of Arthur G. Brodeur,* ed. Stanley B. Greenfield (Eugene, Oregon, 1963), 148. See also M.P. Richards, "A Reexamination of *Beowulf,* ll. 3180–3182," *English Languages Notes* 10 (1973): 163–67.

55. Neckel, *Edda,* 322 (*Vǫlsunga saga,* ch. 27). In a similar way, the word *oferhygd,* which in OE usually means blamable pride or mortal sin, in ON designates a desirable quality (*ofrhugi* "a daring man"; *ofrhugr* "high courage"). See Hans Schabram, *Superbia: Studien zum altenglischen Wortschatz,* vol. 1 (Munich, 1965),

39–40.

56. G.R. Russom, "A Germanic Concept of Nobility in *The Gifts of Men* and *Beowulf*," *Speculum* 53 (1978): 1–15, after examining the close match between *Gifts of Men* and ON literature on the one hand, and *Gifts* and *Beowulf* on the other, concludes that the attitude towards aristocratic society and its pastimes is the same in both literatures. See also B.S. Phillpotts, "*The Battle of Maldon:* Some Danish Affinities," *Modern Language Review* 24 (1929): 172–90, who observed that many of the resemblances she noted between *Maldon* and the Danish *Bjarkamál* were shared by *Beowulf*; Rosemary Woolf, "The Ideal of Men Dying with Their Lord in the *Germania* and in *The Battle of Maldon*," *Anglo-Saxon England* 5 (1976): 63–81.

57. See n. 7.

58. On the frequency and exclusiveness of this skaldic metaphor, see Carol Clover, "Skaldic Sensibility," *Arkiv för nordisk filologi* 93 (1978): 63–81; on the "myth" supporting the kenning system, see Roberta Frank, "Snorri Sturluson and the Mead of Poetry," in *Speculum Norrœnum: Norse Studies in Memory of Gabriel Turville-Petre*, ed. Hans Bekker-Nielsen, Ursula Dronke, Guðrún Helgadóttir, and Gerd Wolfgang Weber (Odense, 1980).

59. Ernst A. Kock, *Notationes norrœnæ: Anteckningar till Edda och Skalde-diktning*, Lunds Universitets Årsskrift, N.F. Avd. 1 (Lund, 1923–44) §1147, cites a parallel use of *hylja* "to bury." For bibliography on Anglian funerary customs and Bede's abbess, see Klaeber, *Beowulf*, 144, and Ferdinand Holthausen, "Das Verhüllen des Haupts bei Toten, ein angelsächsisch-nordischer Brauch," *Englische Studien* 54 (1920): 19–23.

60. See n. 46. Whitelock noted (*Audience,* 79) that the closest English parallels to the *Beowulf* poet's outburst against Danes who returned to their old superstitious ways (ll. 175–88) are post-viking. In addition to the Ælfric and Wulfstan passages, see the penalties imposed in the Edward/Guthrum treaty of 921 on those who abandon Christian for heathen customs: Felix Liebermann, ed., *Die Gesetze der Angelsachsen* (Halle, 1903–16), 1:130–31. Mere conversion like that demanded by the Alfred/Guthrum treaty is not enough a half-century later: Athelstan's treaty of Eamont (12 July 927) makes the suppression of idolatry a requirement. See Stenton, *Anglo-Saxon England*, 336.

61. C.P. Wormald, "The Uses of Literacy in Anglo-Saxon England and Its Neighbours," *Transactions of the Royal Historical Society*, 5th ser., 27 (1977): 113, reasserts the traditional view that restricted literacy predominated throughout the whole early English period. New supporting evidence is marshalled by M.T. Clanchy, *From Memory to Written Record: England 1066–1307* (London, 1979), 12–21.

62. The two main "fabulous" elements of *Beowulf* (Grendel and his mother the *merewif*; the dragon) have numerous analogues in thirteenth- and fourteenth-century Icelandic sagas of which the Sandhaugar episode in *Grettis saga* is only the best known. See George V. Smithers, *The Making of "Beowulf"* (Durham, 1961). The usual assumption is that both *Beowulf* poet and saga author drew on two very similar stories, ultimately stemming from a single (presumably Anglian) prototype. See L.D. Benson, "The Originality of *Beowulf*," in *The Interpretation of Narrative: Theory and Practice*, Harvard English Studies no. 1 (Ithaca, N.Y., 1970), 25–28; P.A. Jorgensen, "Beowulf's Swimming Contest with Breca: Old Norse Parallels," *Folklore* 89 (1978): 52–59, and "The Gift of the Useless Weapon in *Beowulf* and the Icelandic Sagas," *Arkiv för nordisk filologi* 94 (1979): 82–90.

63. The relationship between homily and poem has been explained by at least four different hypotheses: Richard Morris, ed., *The Blickling Homilies of the Tenth Century,* Early English Text Society, original series nos. 58, 63, 73 (1874–80; repr. in 1 vol., London, 1967), claimed (vii) that the homily was a "direct reminiscence" of the poem; Theodore Silverstein, ed., *Visio sancti Pauli: The History of the Apocalypse, Together with Nine Texts,* Studies and Documents no. 4 (London, 1935), demonstrated that the homiletic passage was much closer to a ninth-century redaction of the *Visio* than it was to the OE poem and concluded that the *Visio* was a common source for both (11); Carleton Brown, "*Beowulf* and the *Blickling Homilies* and Some Textual Notes," *PMLA* 53 (1938): 905–16, indicated that the description of the *mere* in *Beowulf* was independent and that the homily fused elements from both *Visio* and poem; R.L. Collins, "*Beowulf* and Blickling Homily XVI," an unpublished paper presented to the Modern Language Association in 1972, argued on the basis of specific verbal parallels that *Beowulf* was influenced by the homily and not vice-versa.

64. D.M. Wilson, "The Scandinavians in England," in *The Archaeology of Anglo-Saxon England,* ed. David M. Wilson (London, 1976), 400–01.

65. Recent scholarship tends to stress assimilation, the mutual tolerance and even attraction of the two peoples, and to support William of Malmesbury's claim (*De gestis regum Anglorum,* ed. William Stubbs, Rolls Series no. 90 [London, 1887–89], 2:125) that the English and Danes in Northumbria soon coalesced into one nation. See Binns, "York Viking Kingdom," 179–89; D.M. Wilson, "The Vikings' Relationship with Christianity in Northern England," *Journal of the British Archaeological Association,* 3rd ser. 30 (1967): 37–46, and "Scandinavian Settlement in the North and West of the British Isles: An Archaeological Point-of-View," *Transactions of the Royal Historical Society,* 5th ser. 26 (1976): 95–113. As for the south, the OE poem on the recovery of the five boroughs (942) indicates that at the very least the chronicler and his audience thought it conceivable that the Danish element in the Midlands would sympathize with English rather than Norse aspirations (see Jacobs, "Anglo-Danish Relations," 39–40), while the *Chronicle* entry for 918 envisages Dane and Englishman joining forces against the Northerners (Plummer, *Saxon Chronicles Parallel* 1:104). The earlier view that discerned "a racial cleavage" in pre-Conquest England is eloquently put in F.M. Stenton, "The Danes in England," *Proceedings of the British Academy* 13 (1927): 203–46, repr. in *Preparatory to Anglo-Saxon England,* ed. Doris M. Stenton (Oxford, 1970) at 161–64.

66. The coins that Guthrum began to circulate as soon as he became king of East Anglia bore the Danish king's new baptismal name, Athelstan; coins commemorating the slain English king Edmund were issued in Danish East Anglia as early as 890, twenty years after his martyrdom. See C.E. Blunt, "The St. Edmund Memorial Coinage," *Proceedings of the Suffolk Institute of Archaeology* 31 (1969): 234–55. Inscriptions produced in areas of heavy Danish settlement for people with Scandinavian names are in OE, not ON: see Elisabeth Okasha, *Hand-List of Anglo-Saxon Non-Runic Inscriptions* (Cambridge, 1971), 41, 47, 88, 114–15, 126–27, 131. OE is found on ornaments showing a strong stylistic influence from Scandinavia, such as the Sutton, Isle of Ely, disc-brooch: Okasha, 116–17; David M. Wilson, *Anglo-Saxon Ornamental Metalwork 700–1100 in the British Museum* (London, 1964), 50, 86–88. On the settlers' Anglophile tastes in stone sculpture see Binns, *Viking Century,* 181–89, and J.T. Lang, "The Sculptors of the Nunburnholme Cross,"

Archaeological Journal 133 (1977): 75–94, who traces a persistent Anglian conservatism, even in thoroughly Scandinavianized areas.

67. See J.T. Lang, "Continuity and Innovation in Anglo-Scandinavian Sculpture," in *Anglo-Saxon and Viking Age Sculpture and Its Context: Papers from the Collingwood Symposium on Insular Sculpture from 800 to 1066,* ed. James T. Lang, British Archaeological Reports, British Series no. 49 (Oxford, 1978), 145–72; C.D. Morris, "Pre-Conquest Sculpture of the Tees Valley," *Medieval Archaeology* 20 (1976): 140–46.

68. Peter Clemoes, "Late Old English Poetry," in *Tenth-Century Studies: Essays in Commemoration of the Millenium of the Council of Winchester and Regularis Concordia,* ed. David Parsons (London, 1975), 104.

69. See Richard Bailey, *Viking Age Sculpture in Northern England* (London, 1980).

70. Wilson, "Scandinavians in England," 400.

Beowulf, Bede, and St. Oswine: The Hero's Pride in Old English Hagiography[1]

by COLIN CHASE

This essay first appeared in The Anglo-Saxons: Synthesis and Achievement, *ed. J. Douglas Woods and David A.E. Pelteret (Waterloo, Ontario: Wilfrid Laurier University Press, 1985), 37–48. Translations in square brackets have been supplied by the editor.*

IN Book Three of his *Historia Ecclesiastica Gentis Anglorum,* Bede devotes most of one chapter (chapter 14) to the character and rule of Oswine, king of Deira until 651. The tone and emphasis which Bede adopts differ in some notable ways from his habitual style:

> In the first part of his reign, Oswy had a companion in royal power named Oswine, who was of King Edwin's line, a son of Osric whom we mentioned before and a man of outstanding piety and religion, beloved of everyone. He remained over the province of Deira in the greatest possible prosperity for seven years. But the man who was ruling over the other, northern, part of Northumbria, that is, the province of Bernicia, could not remain at peace with him; rather, after the points of contention grew between them, he put him to a very sad death. For when both of them had gotten an army together against one another, and Oswine saw that he would not be able to fight against Oswy, because he had a great many allies, he thought it more sensible to give up the idea of fighting for the present and to await a better chance. So, he disbanded the army he had gathered and commanded everyone to go individually to their homes from the place called *Wilfaresdun,* which is about ten miles northwest of the town of Catterick; and he himself went away with only one of his most loyal soldiers, named Tondhere, to hide in the home of his thane Hunwald, who he also felt certain was entirely loyal to him. *Sed heu! pro dolor! longe aliter erat!*; for betrayed by that same thane, he was killed by Oswy through the agency of his reeve, named Æðelwine, in a murder detestable to everyone. This occurred on the twentieth of August, in the ninth year of his reign, at a place called Gilling, where afterwards a monastery was built in reparation for this

crime, in which prayers were daily to be offered for the salvation of
both kings, the one murdered and the one who ordered the murder.[2]

"*Sed heu! pro dolor! longe aliter erat!*" This phrase has a strange ring for
Bede. Though Bertram Colgrave translates it, "But alas, it was quite
otherwise," the original seems less restrained. In Old English the equivalent would have been more like "ac hilahi, afæstla sarlic," to translate the
first phrase, and the parallel in *Beowulf* to the latter part would be "Ne
wæs þæt wyrd þa gen" (734) or "Him seo wen geleah" (2323). Almost
every chapter in Bede's history deals with someone's death, and yet to
my recollection, nowhere else is he driven to interjection, a facet of
language not in harmony with the usual moderation and control of his
restrained style. In fact, one of the chief ways in which a sense of the
divinely ordered nature of the universe suffuses Bede's work is in his
ability to impose a rounded phrase or polished period on incidents
which might otherwise be personal tragedies or national catastrophes.
Abbess Hild dies after a long and painful illness: "In the midst of her
words of encouragement she happily saw the approach of death; or
rather, to use the language of the Lord, she passed from death to life"
(4.23), or Britain, along with the rest of the Empire, undergoes the
terrible persecution of Diocletian: "At that time the greatest glory of a
devoted profession of faith in God also elevated Britain" (1.6). Such
phrases run, like a major key, through the whole work, rendering the
conventional artifice of declamatory rhetoric unnecessary.

This contrast between our small phrase and the tone of the whole
work makes Bede's momentary outburst very interesting. He seems to
recognize that this material needs to be treated differently from what he
has ordinarily encountered. One can rejoice with the martyrs in achiev-
ing a much-desired reward, and one can point to the justice in the
violent deaths of apostate kings, such as Osric and Eanfrith, Oswine's
father and uncle (3.1), but to describe without passion the deliberate
betrayal of a king by his trusted thane is quite another matter.

And yet, though the phrase disturbs the calm of Bede's habitual
attitude momentarily, nothing else in the passage or in the rest of the
chapter builds on the effect. In fact, there appears to be a consciously
controlled effort to inhibit any close or sustained identification with the
king's outraged innocence or any indulgence in the emotions appropriate to such identification. Principally, this is accomplished through the
structure of the narrative.

First, immediately after the bare facts of Oswine's betrayal and death
are narrated, we are told of the monastery built at Gilling in reparation
for the crime, where prayers are to be offered constantly for both Oswine

and Oswy. Before we have had time to dwell on the enormity of Oswy's and Hunwald's crime, we learn of an ultimate equilibrium established in the spiritual order.

Second, in a passage more than twice as long as the one which details Oswine's betrayal and death, Bede tells a story to exemplify the deep humility which characterized the king. The curious thing about this story is that, while the ostensible theme is Oswine's humility, at least to modern sensibilities, the tale seems a much more striking description of Bishop Aidan's detachment, for this is the well-remembered incident when the bishop gave to a beggar the horse with which Oswine had supplied him. The point to be made is that in the structure of the narrative, the story of Aidan's horse functions as a transition between a brief focus on the reign and fate of Oswine and a more sustained concern with the character of Aidan, for the three succeeding chapters are taken up exclusively with miracles worked through St. Aidan during his life. Again, the structure of the narrative averts attention from the outrageous deed done to Oswine.

Finally, the next time Oswine's slayer, King Oswy, appears in Bede's *History*, he is conforming to a far different role. In chapter 22, we are told that "at the instance of King Oswy, the East Saxons accepted the faith they had once rejected, at the time of Mellitus's expulsion" (3.22), and again in chapter 24, far from being the villain of the piece, under the pressure of the pagan King Penda's vicious attacks, Oswy turns "to God's mercy for help," vows to build monasteries and to consecrate his daughter to God, and defeats an army thirty times larger than his because, in Bede's phrase, he trusts in Christ as his leader. From villain, Oswy has become hero and saint of Bede's account.

One important effect of this treatment of the story of Oswine and Oswy is to prepare the reader for the role which Oswy was to play in the critical decision coming out of the synod of Whitby, a decision so central to the larger theme of Bede's work. Another effect, however, less important to Bede's overall concern, but more germane to my purpose, is to distract attention from the sort of questions and emotions that would inevitably have arisen from a fuller, more direct treatment of Oswine's story, at least if our usual description of early Anglo-Saxon culture is at all accurate. One might think, for example, of the story told in the *Anglo-Saxon Chronicle* under the year 755 and describing events climaxing in 786. One might contrast the sort of motivation that drove the swineherd in that story to push his *seax* into the deposed King Sygebryht's flesh, apparently a considerable time after Sygebryht's slaying of Cumbra. One might remember the attitude of the followers of the story's protagonists, Cynewulf and Cyneheard, their unwillingness to accept any kind of terms, and the fierce determination to avenge their lord which drove Cynewulf's men to ride to Merton through the early morning. One might recall the numerous parallel tales evoked by names such as Finn and Hnæf, Frodo and Ingeld, Ongentheow and Hæthcyn, Byrhtnoth and Byrhtwold. All this is commonplace in Anglo-Saxon studies and yet reflects an emphasis strangely missing from Bede's story of the murder of Oswine. Where is the revenge motive? What has happened to the idea that lord and thane are in competition to prove their valour on the battlefield? Where have Oswine's followers gone once he is dead? Were it not for Bede's momentary passionate exclamation, "Sed heu! pro dolor! longe aliter erat!" we would wonder if he belonged to the same culture.

In a recently published paper based on his 1973 Cornell lecture, Patrick Wormald noted similar differences between Bede's treatment of English history and the content of Anglo-Saxon vernacular poetry.[3] Identifying a "vast zone of silence"[4] separating Bede's world from Beowulf's, Wormald argues that *Beowulf* may legitimately serve to make up for this lack, since its author was in touch with values and attitudes apparently unimportant to Bede. Possibly, in Wormald's view, this was because he was an oblate to Monkwearmouth-Jarrow at the age of seven and had never had sustained contact with the aristocratic warrior class of his time. Though I am dubious about the methodology, since most of the explicitly heroic literary remains from Anglo-Saxon England are either late, like *The Battle of Maldon,* or of disputed date, like *Beowulf,* my intent in this discussion is to investigate the same "zone of silence" which appears to separate Anglo-Saxon history from the Old English epic, with a view not to filling out Bede's picture but to understanding *Beowulf.*

Though Oswine appears to have excited as little attention in the time immediately following his death as he excites in our own day, apparently in the years just before and after the Conquest, a cult arose on his behalf, owing first to the invention of his body in the ill-fated rule of Tostig as Earl of Northumbria (1055–65), and then, most probably, to the efforts of Ealdwine of Winchcombe and Reinfrid, the Norman knight turned monk, who joined together in a mission to the north to revive the ancient piety both had discovered in Bede.[5] Directly or indirectly, this activity must lie behind the desire to write a more extensive account of Oswine's life than could be found in Bede, a desire which bore fruit in an account surviving today in the Cotton manuscript Julius A. x. Though edited by James Raine in 1838, this anonymous *Vita Oswini* has attracted little attention either from historians or literary critics, probably because it adds neither information nor elegance to Bede's account.

For my purposes, however, what it does add is more important than either. The anonymous *Life* includes everything found in Bede's account, most of which is lifted verbatim and acknowledged with unusual care, but is more than six times longer. Much of the additional material is simply the kind of prolix rhetorical expansion illustrative of the difference in style and temper between Bede and his age and the tastes of the late eleventh and early twelfth centuries. But a large proportion of it reflects just the kind of emphasis missing in Bede but so strong in Anglo-Saxon heroic literature such as *Beowulf.*

For example, early in the story, when the author is telling about the death of Oswine's father, Osric, at the hands of Cædwalla and about the prince's ten-year exile among the West-Saxons, he feels he has to explain that "his relatives and followers took the blessed Oswine away because he was too young, and the tenderness of his years and his lack of means did not permit him to avenge the death of his father."[6] In a saint's life, such a detail is a little surprising and can serve as an early warning signal that it is dangerous to impose our own ethical system or our own reading of the Gospel even on a work explicitly identified with Christianity, though in the light of Dorothy Whitelock's massive evidence illustrating revenge as a positive value throughout the Anglo-Saxon period, few of us should need such a warning.[7]

A second detail, less important, perhaps, but still worth noting, occurs when the author comes to describe, in general terms, a two-year period during which Oswy first attempts to subvert Oswine's rule to himself and then despairs of the attempt: "When, therefore, he saw that the dragon's craft was doing him no good, he put on the ferocity of the roaring lion."[8] The only point to be made from this is that the *Vita Oswini* shares an imaginative context which includes Sigurd, Beowulf, St. George, and their respective dragons.

The most extensive expansions of Bede's work occur in the final section of the *Vita Oswini,* describing events leading up to the king's death. In Bede's account, Oswine's decision to turn from the fight against Oswy is dealt with in two sentences: "When Oswine saw that he would be unable to compete with Oswy, who had a large number of allies, he thought it would be more sensible to give up the idea of fighting at that time and to wait for a better chance. He therefore disbanded the army and sent his soldiers each to their own homes." For the author of the *Vita Oswini,* the motivation is not clear or explicit enough. He therefore both describes Oswine's motivation for us and gives him a speech in which he explains to his men why he has decided to avoid the fight against Oswy:

> The renowned and divinely favoured King Oswine, knowing that every law and right allow the meeting of force with force, and surrounded by his own troops, went to meet him [Oswy] at a place called *Wilfaresdun*. But King Oswine, the holiest of men, though he was aware that all his followers were not only willing to fight the enemy, but even prepared to lay down their lives for their king, began to reflect on the cold-blooded evil to which this crisis had given rise and that he alone was the reason for the commission of so much manslaughter, near and far, and becoming sincerely concerned rather to spare his men than himself, addresses them in the following words:
>
> "O faithful thanes and valiant soldiers, I am very grateful to you for your service to me in war and for your honour, and I give you thanks for your good will toward me. But far be it from me that you should meet the hazard of war only for my sake, after you made me your king at a time when I was a poor exile. I prefer to return to exile with a few of my followers, as I did once, or even by myself. In fact, I would prefer to die than that so many fine men should be endangered for my sake. For that is a cruel and disloyal man who would try to destroy many for his sake when he is unable to avert the judgment of God."[9]

The point the author is so anxious, perhaps too anxious, to make is that Oswine turns from the fight neither because of the treachery of his followers nor out of personal fear, but because he is concerned for the lives of his men. This is the reverse of the kind of heroic abandon Hamlet envies in Fortinbras, who sends to their deaths

> twenty-thousand men
> That for a fantasy and trick of fame
> Go to their graves like beds, fight for a plot
> Whereon the numbers cannot try the cause.
> (4.4.60–63)

This interpretation of the motives of King Oswine is interesting because it stands as a sort of literary commentary on Bede's work, for I think we can reasonably take it that the material added by the anonymous author would have been considered by Bede to be implicit in his original. The nature of the speech just quoted is doubly interesting because it relates so directly to current discussion of the central theme of *Beowulf.* In two separate, but related, studies of 1965 and 1967, John Leyerle described the "major theme of *Beowulf*" as a "fatal contradiction at the core of heroic society. The hero follows a code that exalts indomitable will and valour in the individual, but society requires a king who acts for the common good. . . ."[10] Though certainly not contemporary with *Beowulf*—however uncertain the date of composition of that poem is—the evidence of this speech does come from a cultural context demonstrably similar to, and modelled upon, that from which *Beowulf* arose. To that extent, it supports the notion that a conflict between the demands of the heroic code and the responsibilities of kingship would have been meaningful within that cultural context, and supports it perhaps more convincingly than the witness of St. Thomas Aquinas, the only author cited in Leyerle's articles who treats precisely this aspect of the issue.[11] If the author of the *Vita Oswini* ever did have an opportunity to turn the leaves of Cotton Vitellius A. xv, one feels sure that some of the darker implications of Beowulf's decision to fight the dragon alone would not have been lost on him.

In fact, the response of Oswine's men to his proposal that they disperse sounds remarkably like an inverted version of Wiglaf's speech to Beowulf's retainers, a version in which the retainers try desperately to avoid the sort of final judgment with which Wiglaf charges his comrades. Accordingly, Oswine is addressed in these terms:

> O remarkable king, O king worthy of the name of king, we beg you to be kind to us, though we are unworthy. Was there some time when we proved cowards or disgraces to our families, or did you find us too slow somewhere in going to battle? In fact, many a time we passed unscathed through the enemy lines. So we want you to let us fight against the enemy in this battle that is approaching, and to take the auspices of these evil times with iron, on the point of the sword. If things should go badly for us in the fight, it is better that we die in battle than that we become a byword for cowardice in the songs of the people, as deserters of our lord.[12]

These men would agree entirely with Wiglaf's judgment:

> Nu sceal sincþego   and swyrdgifu,
> eall eðelwyn   eowrum cynne,
> lufen alicgean;   londrihtes mot
> þære mægburge   monna æghwylc
> idel hweorfan,   syððan æðelingas
> feorran gefricgean   fleam eowerne,
> domleasan dæd.   (2884–90a)

[Now the receiving of treasure, the giving of swords, all the joys of home, indeed all comfort must cease for your people; every man of the family must wander, deprived of land-right, after princes hear from afar of your flight—your inglorious deed.]

Such a fate, say Oswine's soldiers to their reluctant captain, would be worse than death: "Deað bið sella / eorla gehwylcum þonne edwitlif!"

[Death is a better thing for every warrior than life in disgrace] (2890b–91).

But, of course, the author of the *Vita* is not free to change the main outline of the story, and the king remains firm. He assures his men that they have always been brave and unflagging in battle, but goes on to say that since Oswy pursues him and not them, "it is expedient that one man die for the nation rather than that a nation of so great size be destroyed for the sake of one man, especially when I know that a complete reward has been laid aside for me,"[13] this last a reference to bishop Aidan's prediction that the king would die a martyr's death.

Still, in spite of the unwavering front Oswine puts up before his men, as he concludes his speech and turns anxiously to prayer, we see that the issue is not nearly so clear to him as he pretends:

> Father of mercies, and God of all consolation, grant that under the pressure of such great distress I may choose the better way. For if I fight this battle, I appear in your eyes guilty of shedding blood. If I flee I stain my own honour and my family name. Fleeing, I displease men. Fighting I displease you.[14]

In this speech, which comes at the climax of the *Vita Oswini,* just as the king is to go off to meet his death, the central issue of the story is fixed in an unresolved conflict of opposed, and equally imperative, value systems. In Leyerle's description, these value systems involve the contradictory requirements of the heroic code and the responsibilities of royal office, and correspond, respectively, to Georges Dumézil's military ethic and ethic of sovereignty, two of the three fundamental ethical systems according to which any society may be described.[15] The fact that in the *Vita Oswini* this conflict is perceived but left unresolved is important. The fact that nowhere is Oswine's desire to protect his name, shun disgrace, and gain glory on the battlefield equated with pride is even more important. In this explicitly religious context, in which the hagiographer had every reason to depict what his hero chose not to do as evil, and what he chose to do as unalloyed good, it apparently never occurs to him to suggest that the impulse to fight against impossible odds was born of the sort of pride against which Hrothgar warns the young Beowulf.

While the *Vita Oswini* does support the identification of a conflict in *Beowulf* between the heroic code and royal responsibility, it does not support the further conclusion, espoused by John Leyerle, Margaret Goldsmith, John Halverson, James Smith, and others, that the hero is himself infected with the pride or avarice of which Hrothgar speaks.[16] In the *Vita Oswini,* an ethic of sovereignty and a heroic, military ethic not only coexist, but the tension arising from their coexistence creates the martyr-king's dilemma. Those who argue for Beowulf's moral failure do so, in my view, by subjecting the heroic code of which he is a perfect exemplar to the judgment of another value system, e.g., an ethic of sovereignty (Leyerle) or an ethic springing from Christian-monastic culture (Goldsmith). What the *Vita Oswini* helps us to do is to see that such value systems can exist in the same culture and in the same person, where they can, and will, produce dilemmas and tensions, but that one need not be invoked as a norm by which the other must be judged. Neither Oswine nor his author conclude that the generous spirit which makes the king's men want so much to fight his enemies is wrong or not to be admired, or that in determining to break off the fight, the king is resisting the blandishments of pride or cupidity. At the same time, the form of the story and its outcome tell that the king's concern for the life and safety of those who follow him is also an inescapable imperative.

Though Hrothgar does warn Beowulf against pride and avarice in the famous and extensive "sermon" before his friend's departure for home (1700–84), the hero clearly avoids the trap against which he is warned. In graphic terms, the old king had depicted the growth of pride as if it were a fatal disease or poisonous wound:

> Wunað he on wiste; no hine wiht dweleð
> adl ne yldo, ne him inwitsorh
> on sefan sweorceð . . .
> oð þæt him on innan oferhygda dæl
> weaxeð ond wridað; . . .
> þinceð him to lytel, þæt he lange heold,
> gytsað gromhydig, nallas on gylp seleð
> fætte beagas . . .   (1735–37, 1740–41, 1748–50)

[He lives in prosperity; neither sickness nor age leads him astray at all, nor does the sorrow of malice darken in his heart . . . until a portion of pride grows and flourishes within him . . . ; what he has long possessed seems to him too little; with hostile mind he grows covetous, does not, as he has promised, give ornamented rings . . .]

Presumptuous pride stifles generosity and leads to avarice, which prevents him from sharing with his followers, but Beowulf does not lapse into presumption and avarice. Rather, in his old age, he goes out to meet a deadly threat against his people and in his dying moments exults over the dragon's treasure, not for himself, but "þæs ðe ic moste minum leodum / ær swyltdæge swylc gestrynan" [because I could, before my dying day, acquire such (a treasure) for my people] (2797–98). In his dying moment, Beowulf has become, not like the Heremod against whom Hrothgar warned him, but like Sigemund, who had slain another dragon and "elne gegongen, / þæt he beahhordes brucan moste" [brought about with his valor that he could enjoy the hoard of rings] (893–94).

But the poem does not end with Beowulf's death. We hear from the messenger what the people are to expect as a result of his death: the renewed warfare of Franks and Frisians and Swedes (2911 ff., 2922 ff.); a life of violence, poverty, and frequent exile; and we hear from the poet what is to be the eventual destiny of the gold, buried in the funeral monument "þær hit nu gen lifað / eldum swa unnyt, swa hi(t æro)r wæs" [where it still remains, as useless to men as it was before] (3167–68). Beowulf's courage and generosity are to yield a harvest of bitterness and suffering. As with Oedipus, and as with Hamlet, the tragic effect lies precisely in the gap between intention and result, "between the idea and the reality." What the poem as a whole does is what John Leyerle begins by saying it does: it points to "the fatal contradiction at the core of heroic society," but that contradiction is not the soft, moral flaw of Hrothgar's sermon, but the harsh and unrecognized error in judgment which confuses a heroic military ethic with an ethic of sovereignty. In Aristotelian terms, *Beowulf* ends in a tragic reversal unattended by discovery, peripety without recognition. This is the kind of irony that overshadows the final lines of *Beowulf.* Neither the hero, nor Wiglaf, nor the messenger, nor anyone realizes "the fatal contradiction at the core of heroic society." Their silence is not simply poetic reticence or obscurantism, but the fact that they never understand why the courage and generosity of their leader has led so inevitably to violence, suffering, poverty, and exile. Structural juxtaposition has itself revealed the profound irony of Beowulf's story, an irony which finally transcends the political strategies of warring nations and the doctrinal differences of opposed creeds, in much the same way that Albany's speech at the end of *Lear* transcends the rivalries which trigger the action of that play:

> The weight of this sad time we must obey,
> Speak what we feel, not what we ought to say.
> The oldest hath borne most: we that are young
> Shall never see so much, nor live so long.

NOTES

1. Much of the material in this essay has been summarized for a different purpose in my "Saints' Lives, Royal Lives, and the Date of *Beowulf*," in Colin Chase, ed., *The Dating of "Beowulf,"* Toronto Old English Series no. 6 (Toronto, 1981), 161–71.

2. "Habuit autem Osuiu primis regni sui temporibus consortem regiae dignitatis, uocabulo Osuini, de stirpe regis Eduini, hoc est filium Ostrici, de quo

supra retulimus, uirum eximiae pietatis et religionis, qui prouinciae Derorum septem annis in maxima omnium rerum affluentia, et ipse amabilis omnibus, praefuit. Sed nec cum eo ille qui ceteram Transhumbranae gentis partem ab aquilone, id est Berniciorum prouinciam, regebat, habere pacem potuit; quin potius, ingrauescentibus causis dissensionum, miserrima hunc caede peremit. Siquidem congregato contra inuicem exercitu, cum uideret se Osuini cum illo, qui plures habebat auxiliarios, non posse bello confligere, ratus est utilius tunc demissa intentione bellandi seruare se ad tempora meliora. Remisit ergo exercitum quem congregauerat, ac singulos domum redire praecepit a loco qui uocatur Uilfaresdun, id est Mons Uilfari, et est a uico Cataractone x ferme milibus passuum contra solstitialem occasum secretus; diuertitque ipse cum uno tantum milite sibi fidissimo, nomine Tondheri, celandus in domum comitis Hunualdi, quem etiam ipsum sibi amicissimum autumabat. Sed heu! pro dolor! longe aliter erat; nam ab eodem comite proditum eum Osuiu cum praefato ipsius milite per praefectum suum Ediluinum detestanda omnibus morte interfecit. Quod factum est die tertia decima kalendarum Septembrium, anno regni eius nono, in loco qui dicitur Ingetlingum; ubi postmodum castigandi huius facinoris gratia monasterium constructum est, in quo pro utriusque regis, et occisi uidelicet et eius qui occidere iussit, animae redemtione cotidie Domino preces offerri deberent." The text is that of Bertram Colgrave and Roger A.B. Mynors, *Bede's Ecclesiastical History of the English People* (Oxford, 1969), 256.

3. Patrick Wormald, "Bede, 'Beowulf' and the Conversion of the Anglo-Saxon Aristocracy," in Robert T. Farrell, ed., *Bede and Anglo-Saxon England: Papers in Honour of the 1300th Anniversary of the Birth of Bede, Given at Cornell University in 1973 and 1974*, British Archaeological Reports no. 46 (London, 1978), 32–95.

4. *Ibid.*, 36. The phrase is adapted from Arnaldo Momigliano, "Pagan and Christian Historiography in the Fourth Century A.D.," in Arnaldo Momigliano, ed., *The Conflict between Paganism and Christianity in the Fourth Century* (Oxford, 1963), 96.

5. For Ealdwine and Reinfrid see, for example, F. M. Stenton, *Anglo-Saxon England*, 3rd ed. (Oxford, 1971), 677–80. The invention is established in the *Miracula* of St. Oswine appearing in British Library MS. Cotton Julius A. x., fols. 10–43 (see especially fol. 15r) and edited by James Raine, *Miscellanea Biographica*, Publications of the Surtees Society no. 8 (London, 1838), 1–59.

6. "Tuleruntque beatum Oswinum propinqui et fautores eius quia infra annos erat et etatis imbecillitas et facultatis tenuitas patris mortem uindicare non permittebat et cum eo apud occiduos saxones per decennium exularunt," Cotton Julius A. x., fol. 3r; Raine, *Miscellanea*, 2. The Latin text is taken from my transcription of a photocopy of the manuscript.

7. Dorothy Whitelock, *The Audience of "Beowulf"* (Oxford, 1951), 13–18.

8. "Cum igitur draconis insidias nichil sibi prodesse persensit, leonis rugientis feritatem induit," Cotton Julius A. x., fol. 7r; Raine, *Miscellanea*, 7.

9. "Praeclarus itaque Deoque acceptus Rex Oswinus, sciens quod uim ui repellere omnes leges omniaque iura permittent, suorum circundatus acie, loco qui Wilfaresdun dicitur ei obuius uenit. Sanctissimus autem Rex Oswinus, uidens suos cum aduersariis unanimiter uolentes non solum contendere uerum etiam pro suo rege paratus occumbere, uoluens in animo discriminis horrendum facinus seque solum homicidii hinc inde passim committendi in causa esse, suis potius quam sibi

parcendo pie consulens, sic eos alloquitur:

'Congratulor, quidem, o fidissimi principes et strenuissimi milites, uestre militie et probitati, et gratias ago bone erga me uestre uoluntati. Sed absit a me ut mei solius causa belli discrimen periculose quidem omnes incurratis, qui me quamquam iure dominum, pauperem tamen et exulem, regem uobis constituistis. Malo itaque, sicut hactenus, ubi ubi cum paucis uel solus exulare. Immo potius diligo mori, quam uos tot et tales mei solius causa contingat quoquomodo periclitari. Impius, enim, et inhumanus est, qui cum Dei iudicium nullo modo possit auertere, plures sui causa conatur euertere,'" Cotton Julius A. x., fol. 7r; Raine, *Miscellanea*, 8.

10. "Beowulf the Hero and King," *Medium Ævum* 34 (1965): 89; "The Interlace Structure of *Beowulf,*" *University of Toronto Quarterly* 37 (1967): 8–9.

11. That such a conflict would have been meaningful at an earlier date in the Anglo-Saxon period is also clear from Alcuin's citation of a situation for debate in his popular *Disputatio de Rhetorica et de Virtutibus* 13: "Conparatio est, cum aliud aliquod factum rectum aut utile contenditur, quod ut fieret, illud quod arguitur dicitur esse commissum, ut in illo exemplo, quod paulo ante posuimus. Cum dux Romanus ab hostibus obsideretur, nec ullo pacto evadere potuit nisi pacaret ut hostibus arma daret: armis datis milites conservavit, sed post accusatur maiestatis. Intentio est 'non oportuit arma relinquere': depulsio est oportuit: quaestio est 'oportueritne': ratio est: 'milites enim omnes perissent, si hoc non fecissem': infirmatio est 'non ideo fecisti.' Ex quibus iudicatio est, perissentne, et ideone fecisset. Conparatio, an melius esset ad hanc turpissimam conditionem venire, vel milites perire." Wilbur S. Howell, ed. and trans., *The Rhetoric of Alcuin and Charlemagne*, Princeton Studies in English no. 23 (Princeton, 1941), 82 and 84. This evidence establishes the existence of this line of thought in Anglo-Saxon legal and ethical tradition, but is less helpful than the *Vita Oswini* for illuminating the narrative concerns of works of a more literary character.

12. "O rex insignis, o regis nomine dignus, nobis indignus, petimus, esto benignus. Numquid nos ignauos aut degeneres aliquando repperisti, an apparuimus alicubi in conflictu bellico tardiores? Hostium profecto cuneos securi persepe penetrauimus. Liceat ergo nobis cum hostibus instantis certaminis inire conflictum, et in ore gladii peruersae aetatis rimari uiscera ferro. Si fortasse nobis in pugna sinistre cesserit, melius est nobis mori in bello quam apud uulgus domini desertores in prouerbio cantitari," Cotton Julius A. x., fol. 7v; Raine, *Miscellanea*, 8.

13. "'Expedit ergo ut unus moriatur pro populo' (John 11:50) quam ut populus tantae multitudinis deleatur pro uno, presertim cum mihi scierim mercedem plenam esse repositam," Cotton Julius A. x., fols. 7v–8r; Raine, *Miscellanea*, 8.

14. "Pater misericordiarum et totius consolationis Deus . . . da mihi in tantae anguistiae instantia meliorem eligere uiam. Quia si bello conflixero, fundendi sanguinis coram te reus appareo. Si fugam iniero et propriae dignitati et parentum nobilitati degener appareo. Et hominibus fugiens displiceo et tibi dimicans," Cotton Julius A. x., fol. 8r; Raine, *Miscellanea*, 9.

15. Dumézil's system is elaborated in *The Destiny of the Warrior*, trans. Alf Hiltebeitel (Chicago, 1970); *Archaic Roman Religion*, trans. Philip Krapp, 2 vols. (Chicago, 1970); *Gods of the Ancient Northmen*, ed. Einar Haugen, Publications of the UCLA Center for the Study of Comparative Folklore and Mythology no. 3 (Berkeley and Los Angeles, 1973).

16. Leyerle, see n. 10 above; Margaret Goldsmith, *The Mode and Meaning of "Beowulf"* (London, 1970); John Halverson, "The World of *Beowulf*," *English Literary History* 36 (1969): 593–608; James Smith, "*Beowulf*—I," *English* 25 (1976): 203–29 and "*Beowulf*—II," *English* 26 (1977): 3–22 (written ca. 1957, ed. by Martin Dodsworth).

The Legacy of Wiglaf:
Saving a Wounded *Beowulf*

by Kevin S. Kiernan

This essay was delivered as a lecture at the University of Kentucky on 9 December 1983; it was printed in The Kentucky Review *6 (1986): 27–44. For the present reprint the author has added annotations both supplementing and updating the text.*

TO try to dignify my fascination with the *Beowulf* manuscript, I will liken it to Wiglaf's attempt, at the end of the poem, to help Beowulf fight the fire-drake. As a *Beowulf* scholar, I fight like a loyal thane to save the poem from fire-damage and other forms of draconic emendation. In other words, I want to revive an Old English *Beowulf,* the one still surviving in the manuscript. I am depressed by the cosmetics of the mortuary, the neat and tidy but still rather stiff view of *Beowulf* I think we get in modern editions of the poem. What makes me a little nervous about my analogy is that all of Wiglaf's efforts were in vain. Beowulf died, and Wiglaf's whereabouts are unknown. Nonetheless, a modern-day analogous Wiglaf limps among you.

The single surviving medieval copy of *Beowulf* is in a hefty composite manuscript known as British Library manuscript Cotton Vitellius A. xv. It is called this because the book was owned by a seventeenth-century antiquary named Sir Robert Cotton who kept track of his manuscripts by their shelf position in bookcases surmounted by the busts of Roman emperors. Thus, Cotton Vitellius A. xv was the fifteenth book on the first shelf of the Vitellius case. If we look inside this big book we find that Cotton bound together two distinct and quite unrelated manuscripts. The first 90 folios are in a twelfth-century handwriting, and we call this part of Cotton's book the Southwick Codex, based on the notice of ownership—actually a chilling curse on anyone who stole the book—on the second folio. The last 116 folios are copied by two early eleventh-century scribes, and we call this part of Cotton's book the Nowell Codex, because a previous owner, Laurence Nowell, left his name in it in 1563.[1]

The Nowell Codex is the part of Cotton Vitellius A. xv we are interested in: it contains a fragment of the life of St. Christopher; a couple of treatises (one illustrated) describing the kind of monsters who live in the East; the apocryphal Biblical story of how Judith lopped off the head of Holofernes; and of course the true story of how Beowulf, among other things, lopped off the head of Grendel.[2]

We don't really know exactly when people began to study the poem in modern times. Perhaps it was Nowell in the sixteenth century who underlined some of the proper names in the manuscript, if indeed he ever attempted to read it.[3] But the seventeenth-century table of contents in Cotton's book leaves a blank for *Beowulf,* probably reflecting his librarian's utter bewilderment.[4] The first intelligible reference to the poem was in 1705, when Humfrey Wanley mistakenly described it as a story about Beowulf the Dane who fought with Swedish princes. At any rate the *Beowulf* manuscript survived intact, if virtually untouched, until 1731, when a disastrous fire decimated Cotton's Library and left the *Beowulf* manuscript badly scorched along its outer edges.[5]

Wanley's inaccurate description, making our hero a Dane instead of a Geat, can be indirectly credited for preserving a large part of the poem for us.[6] In 1786, Grímur Jónsson Thorkelin, an Icelander who worked in Denmark as an archivist, and who eventually became the Danish National Archivist, went to England to find Danish heroes in British archives. He learned about *Beowulf* in Wanley's description, and in 1787 he hired a professional scribe to copy the manuscript for him, and later made a second copy himself. The great value of these two transcripts is that they alone preserve nearly 2000 letters which subsequently crumbled from the scorched edges of the manuscript.[7] Thorkelin used his two transcripts to produce the first edition of the poem in 1815, and all modern editors use them, too, to fill in the gaps in the manuscript.[8]

Ten years before Thorkelin's edition appeared, and exactly one hundred years after Wanley's brief description of the poem, Sharon Turner, in his history of the Anglo-Saxons, took issue with Wanley, saying that his "account of the contents of the manuscript is incorrect. It is a composition more curious and important."[9] Turner should have stopped while he was ahead. He goes on to say, "It is a narration of the attempt of Beowulf to wreck the fæhthe or deadly feud on Hrothgar, for a homicide which he had committed." Turner was the first scholar to attempt to translate parts of the poem into English. He came up with the following excerpt from the celebrations after the building of Heorot, Hrothgar's great hall:

> There every day
> He heard joy
> Loud in the hall.

> There was the harp's
> Clear sound—
> The song of the poet said,
> He who knew
> The beginning of mankind
> From afar to narrate.
>> "He took wilfully
>> By the nearest side
>> The sleeping warrior.
>> He slew the unheeding one
>> With a club on the bones of his hair."

Turner remarks that "The transition to this song is rather violent, and its subject is abruptly introduced, and unfortunately the injury done to the top and corners of the MS by fire interrupts in many places the connections of the sense" (402). Fortunately the fire-damage to the manuscript is nowhere near as serious as Turner indicates. His main problem, in addition to a very rudimentary understanding of Old English poetry, was that the leaf containing Grendel's attack on Heorot was misplaced in the manuscript when Turner used it.[10] His translation, though, helps illustrate the state of *Beowulf* studies as late as 1805; and Thorkelin's Latin translation confirms that the discipline was not much further along as late as 1815.

Although *Beowulf* now plays a primary role in the history of English language and literature, it has played this role for a shorter time than (say) Wordsworth's *Lyrical Ballads,* about as long as the later Romantics. The study of *Beowulf* is, in other words, a relatively young discipline despite its formidably hide-bound aspect. English literary history was already well-established when *Beowulf* arrived on the scene, and there was no doubt at all where it belonged in the grand scheme.[11] The situation was somewhat like the posthumous publication of Hopkins's poetry in 1918. By then, scholars had characterized the nature of Victorian verse and it was perfectly clear that Hopkins had no place in the continuum. He became for a while a 20th-century poet.[12] I believe this is basically the way *Beowulf* became the earliest English poem.

The situation with *Beowulf* was, of course, far more complicated. It was an international phenomenon, not only the earliest English epic, but the earliest Germanic epic, an ancient record of a Germanic language, and a new window to the pan-Germanic heroic age, through which everyone eagerly peered. They saw Danes and Swedes, Geats and Goths, Angles and Jutes, Franks and Frisians, Finns, Norwegians, Vandals, and more, and heard from them all in an early Germanic dialect then known as Anglo-Saxon.[13] No wonder there was little interest in the unique manuscript, dating perilously near the conquest of Anglo-Saxon England. From the start the manuscript was dismissed as a late, corrupt copy, and scholars set to work trying to reconstruct the ruined original, or what they imagined it to be.[14]

The manuscript was so fully ignored, in fact, that until 1916 scholars with unrelated interests could still refer to the date of the *Beowulf* manuscript as around the year 1000, but to the preceding prose texts, in the same handwriting as the first part of *Beowulf,* as mid-eleventh and even twelfth century.[15] Needless to say, when the mistake was discovered the eleventh and twelfth century dates were quietly moved back to around the year 1000, with a quiet effect on literary history. Scholars had previously thought that two of the prose texts, *The Wonders of the East* and *Alexander's Letter to Aristotle,* were among the last books written in Late Old English.[16] They thought the new fascination with the East must have been imported from the Continent around the time of the Norman Conquest. Now the Anglo-Saxons had to be interested in this kind of romantic lore much earlier, around the year 1000.[17]

In fact, there is good linguistic evidence to date Alexander's Letter, like *Beowulf,* sometime after 1016—that is, after the Danish conquest and during the reign of Cnut the Great. We can apply this evidence to our dating of *Beowulf.* The letter exhibits clear, explicable cases of linguistic change, amelioration of the word *here,* "Danish army," and pejoration of the word *fyrd,* "English army." These words had definite connotations for the Anglo-Saxons. The Bosworth-Toller notes that *here* "is the word which in the Chronicle is always used of the Danish force in England, while the English troops are always the *fyrd,* hence the word [*here*] is used for *devastation* and *robbery.*" The same dictionary refines this statement in volume 2, by adding that "in the annals of the eleventh century *here* is used in speaking of the English."[18] Obviously it lost the connotations of devastation and robbery. The reason for the semantic amelioration is that, after Cnut's accession in 1016, the Danish *here* in word and deed was the English army.

How does this criterion affect our dating of *Alexander's Letter?* Alexander consistently refers to his special Greek forces as a *here,* the equivalent of the Anglo-Saxon "select *fyrd,*" and to his combined forces as a *fyrd,* the same as the Anglo-Saxon "great *fyrd.*"[19] He notably refers to his enemy's armies as a *fyrd,* the term the Anglo-Saxons reserved for themselves in both senses of the word. In this text, the linguistic pejoration of *fyrd* (the enemy) and amelioration of *here* (the good guys) can only be explained by assuming that the translation was made sometime after 1016, after the Danish conquest. It might well be added that the collocation of a *Greca* (or "Greek") *here,* in the sense of a select imperial guard, received its first historical warrant when Danish Vikings served as a *here* for the Greek emperors in the Varangian guard, which only came into existence in the closing years of the tenth century, just in time for our translation of *Alexander's Letter.*[20]

The usage of *here* in *Beowulf* falls in line with the usage in the *Letter.* Hrothgar's Danes are specifically singled out as a *þeod tilu,* "a good nation," because of their readiness for war both at home and in the *here* (1246–50). In nearly a score of *here*-compounds in *Beowulf,* not one carries a pejorative connotation. By contrast, Beowulf's cowardly thanes, the ones who run away at the end, are called *fyrdgesteallum,* "*companions* in the *fyrd*" (2873). The Anglo-Saxon *fyrd* earned a similar reputation in their late conflicts with the Danes. I mention this case here to allay any nagging doubts you may have that linguistic evidence precludes an early eleventh-century date for *Beowulf.* I have yet to hear of any linguistic evidence showing that *Beowulf* predates its manuscript. The pseudo-evidence always brought forth to bolster an early date is dubious, at best, perhaps because scholars never felt the need to make a strong case for something they deemed self-evident.[21] In any event, the preconceived notions of where *Beowulf* belonged in literary history had a profound effect on the text we read in the editions available today. At first, because of a romantic desire to put *Beowulf* into the pagan past, scholars had to explain all of the implicitly Christian elements, from Genesis to Doomsday, in the poem. That seemed easy. Christian scribes copied the poem over the centuries, and as they did so they merely interpolated Christian parts in precisely the same style as their pagan source.[22] This theory exploded when scholars began removing the supposed interpolations, leaving behind a poem in little bitty pieces. The only way to put it back together again without seriously disrupting literary history was to move it into the eighth century, as near to the pagan era and as far away from the manuscript as possible.

The move had many apparent advantages. We still had the earliest English epic, the earliest Germanic epic, an ancient record of a Germanic language, and at least a decent view of the pan-Germanic heroic age. So what if the poet was a Christian? At least he only quoted the Old Testament. Some readers, disturbed by the way *Beowulf* grew younger as the years wore on, seized on the absence of references to the New Testament as an indication of the Anglo-Saxons' recent conversion, as if they were first converted to Judaism before being persuaded to switch to Christianity. The real motive, I think, in this line of argument was to root *Beowulf* in the eighth century, where it could not get any younger.

A more gripping argument with the same motive closes off the ninth and tenth centuries, when the viking invasions traumatized the island.[23] No matter where they sailed from, the vikings were called Danes by the Anglo-Saxons, and it is hard to imagine a poet during these times creating peace-loving, home-body Danes more interested in sleek architecture than sleek warships. It was not a time to be admiring the stout Sea-Geats, either, those unabashed vikings who lost their king Higelac in a raid on the Rhineland. As long as viking raids continued in England, no Anglo-Saxon *scop* in his right mind would chant the opening lines of *Beowulf* before a live, beer-drinking audience: "Yes, we have heard about the glorious deeds of the Spear-Danes of the old days—how those noble ones performed deeds of glory; [how] Scyld Scefing deprived so many people of their beer-halls, terrified men . . . until everyone had to obey him and hand over their money. *That* was a good king!" (1–11).

Without the ninth and tenth centuries, editors were left with what everyone seemed to want, an early poem and a late manuscript. Editors could still make hundreds of changes in the text on the assumption that the late scribes, through laziness, ignorance, and indifference, contributed to the hundreds of blunders the poem accumulated as it lumbered through its supposed transmission.[24]

What the editors ignored was that the argument ruling out the ninth and tenth centuries for the composition of the poem also wiped out these centuries for the transmission of the text. If no Anglo-Saxon poet would create the poem, no *scop* recite it, and no audience listen to it, why would ninth and tenth century scribes copy it? The usual scribes of the time were the same monks whose rich monasteries were prime targets of the vikings. If *Beowulf* is an eighth-century poem, its transmission in Anglo-Saxon times must have been abrupt, from a time when Danes were not synonymous with viking marauders to a time when they ruled England and thus put a stop to the marauding. The regnal list of Danish Scyldings at the start of *Beowulf* would have been a compliment to Cnut, the latest member of the line, but it is hard to see it as anything other than an insult to any other king of England before him. In the ninth century, King Alfred, who for political reasons reasons seems first to have appropriated Scyld for his line of Anglo-Saxon Scyldings, would not have appreciated the enemy's version in the prologue of *Beowulf*.[25] And at the end of the tenth century, I am sure that Ethelred Unræd would have been ready to include our scribes in the St. Brice's Day massacre if he found out about it.[26]

Using political history to help date the poem early, but not to explain its preservation in a late manuscript, modern editors of *Beowulf* have always assumed that the ninth and tenth centuries participated in a long and complicated transmission of the text, which included corrosive copying through all the main dialect areas.[27] While they agreed that the extant manuscript preserves the poem in more or less standard Late West Saxon, they thought they found the linguistic residue of an ancient, multi-dialectal transmission in one defunct (and in fact imaginary) instrumental reading, an early West Saxon linguistic form here, a Kentish form there, a Mercianism hither, a Northumbrianism yon, with a dash of Saxon *patois* for good measure.[28]

But as scholars have increasingly come to recognize, the mixture of linguistic forms in *Beowulf* is not extraordinary. Most of the archaic forms are part of a poetic word-hoard used also in undoubtedly late poems like *Brunanburh* and *Maldon.* The mixture of cross-dialectal forms shows up in late prose, as well as verse, and so must be a reflection of copying conventions in some late scriptoria.[29] Keep in mind that Late West Saxon was a literary dialect used throughout England around the year 1000. When it was used in Mercian scriptoria, Mercianisms naturally crept into it; when it was used by a southerner in a Mercian scriptorium, both southern and Mercian features were likely to occur.

Think about our own literary dialect, used throughout the world now regardless of spoken dialects. It contains archaisms like "knight" (Old English *cniht*) and "should" (Old English *scolde*), Scandinavianisms like "they" (Old English *hi*) and "skirt" (Late Old English *scyrte,* which comes down to us as "shirt"), and a rich mixture of cross-dialectal forms, including those from other ancient and modern languages. A writer with a Mississippi accent today communicates in writing, at least, with readers in the Bronx. Yet even today some spellings differ from center to center. In Binghamton the word "center" in Center for Medieval and Renaissance Studies ends in "-er," while across the border in Toronto the same word in Centre for Medieval Studies ends in "-re." Across the same *campus,* at the Pontifical Institute of Mediæval Studies, the word at the Centre spelled "medieval" is at the Institute spelled "mediæval," another archaism. In short, if we wanted to, we could use the same linguistic criteria used to date *Beowulf* early to create long and complicated transmissions for texts written the day before yesterday in North America. Throw in an Eastern Kentucky scribe with a sense of humor and he might add an Old English relic like "hit," standard English "it," for us to ponder.

My first interest in the *Beowulf* manuscript had nothing to do with the date of the poem. I accepted the conventional dating. I only wanted to read the poem in its Old English version, freed from all of the modern emendations. In my view, modern editors had done to *Beowulf* precisely what they had accused the eighth, ninth, and tenth-century scribes of doing. They created a new poem from an ancient source. But whereas the editors could only imagine their pristine source emanating from the misty moors of prehistoric times, I had a hard copy of my ancient source in a photographic facsimile, and the ancient source itself at the British Library on a misty, but well-travelled street in modern London.[30]

For a long time, the facsimile alone served my purposes. I was mainly interested in verifying manuscript readings where the editions I used had changed them. I will try to give you some idea of the range of these editorial changes without driving you outside or into the arms of Morpheus. I want to show you, in particular, how seemingly innocuous emendations, based on alliteration and meter, have far-reaching conse-quences.

Theories about Old English prosody, the art of versification, invari-ably join forces with theories about the date of the poem to justify emendations.[31] The Old English verse line is divided in two main parts, called an on-verse and an off-verse. Each half-line has two heavily stressed syllables and a variable number of less heavily stressed or un-stressed ones. Sophisticated metrical studies have revealed that there are only 5 main patterns, or types, of metrical stress in the half-lines, though these types are by no means as regular as the iambs, trochees, dactyls, and anapests of later English poetry.[32] The two half-lines of *Old* English poetry are linked by alliteration, which can occur on the first or second stress (or both) of the on-verse, but only on the first stress of the off-verse, that is, on the third stress of the full line. So for a line of Old English verse you cannot have "Peter Piper picked a peck," but only "Peter Piper picked a bushel," "Ethelred Piper picked a bushel," or "Peter Cnutsson picked a bushel."

The problem is that not all of the lines in *Beowulf,* which was used to establish the rules of Old English prosody, follow these rules. Sometimes there is no alliteration; sometimes there are three stresses in a half-line; sometimes there is only a half-line and sometimes there are three instead of two; rather often an atypical metrical type surfaces. These aberrations naturally offend the sensibilities of metrists and alliterationists, and with all of the positive evidence they have amassed they have generally been able to persuade editors to get rid of the few bits of negative evidence.

According to the rules, any vowel can alliterate with any other vowel, but a particular consonant (including *h*) is strictly bound to alliterate only with itself. The fact that words beginning with *h* often alliterate with words beginning with vowels in *Beowulf* is a sure sign, according to the rules, of scribal corruption.[33] But the relentless application of this rule may be hiding some linguistic evidence from us. We would say that the alliterative phrase "honest Abe" alliterates vocalically with the phrase "heir apparent," but not with the phrase "hairy head." "Hairy head" alliterates for me with "humble Harry," but for some English speakers "'umble 'arry" alliterates with "honest Abe." In late Old English times the quality of *h* was protean, too. That's how Hroðgar and Hroðulf ultimately became Roger and Ralph.

Emending this kind of evidence out of existence can have a major impact on our interpretation of the poem.[34] According to our modern editions, there is a character in the poem named *Unferð*, whose name, the editors tell us, means "mar-peace" (*un* means "not" and *ferð*, actually *frið*, means "peace"). It seems like a good name for the troublemaker who quarrels with Beowulf on his first night in Heorot. One wonders, though, why his parents named him *Unferð*. Elaborate interpretations have evolved making the character an allegorical representation of Discord or Dissension.[35] Yet the name that four times appears in the editions as Unferð appears four times in the manuscript as Hunferð, a fairly common name in the Anglo-Saxon period. The first time it appears in *Beowulf,* the name begins a new section of the poem, and here the scribe went to special trouble drawing a large, unusually ornate, capital *H* for it.[36] Are we to suppose that an ignorant, lazy scribe made such a self-confident and industrious change, and kept his eye peeled for the three additional *uncapitalized* cases as he copied? As we have seen, the name Hunferð may have been pronounced "'unferth" in Old English times, but neither the poet nor his audience would be likely to interpret the pronunciation, just as we would not be inclined to interpret Cockney "'arry" to mean "light as air, delicate, or graceful."

Consider another far-reaching emendation involving alliteration. A line lacking it occurs in the manuscript at the point where Beowulf is greeted at Heorot. In the on-verse, the first half-line, Hroðgar tells his messenger to say that Beowulf and his men are welcome by *Deniga leodum*, "the people of the Danes." In the off-verse, the second half-line, *Word inne abead,* "he brought the message in." Editors have supplied the missing alliteration by creating a modern "Old English" off-verse to alliterate with the real Old English on-verse, and a modern "Old English" on-verse to alliterate with the authentic Old English off-verse. The most influential modern interpolation now reads, *þa to dura eode widcuð hæleð,* "then the famous warrior went to the door—and brought the message in."[37] While the manuscript forgiveably ignores the movements of the messenger, the editor puffs the messenger's walk to the door into epic proportions. In view of the high stakes, we ought to be able to tolerate a few lines in *Beowulf* that lack alliteration. Here the allure of alliteration allots a line of modern Old English to the poem. Some *Beowulf* scholars, who believe that the number of verse-lines in the poem was of special significance to the poet, have even been including such modern interpolations in their calculations.[38]

The metrists, like their cohorts the alliterationists, believe that an *ur*-text of *Beowulf* once existed whose meter unalterably followed their rules. As one metrist says in the opening sentence of his book, "Metrical studies of ancient poetry have at least two immediate aims, the establishment of the text and the recovery of the pleasure inherent in verse."[39] Metrists, to put it in a more skeptical way, aim to emend the manuscript. Their emendations, moreover, are circuitously linked to the belief in an early date for the poem, since the manuscript readings they change undermine their rules. Thus they change by deletion the off-verse in line 9, *þara ymbsittendra,* "of the neighboring peoples," to *ymbsittendra,* "of neighboring peoples," because *þara* ("the") would not be used in this way, they claim, in *early* poetry.[40]

A final example of how metrical theory and dating theory converge and collaborate can be seen in the on-verse of line 6. The manuscript reads *egsode eorl,* "terrified the man," but singular *eorl* is routinely emended to plural *eorlas* ("men") or to the proper name *Eorle* ("the ancient tribe of Erulians") because the metrical rules demand an unstressed syllable after it. However, if we do not change the manuscript, the word *eorl* may be seen as a roughly datable anachronism. Old English *eorl* took on the meaning of Danish *jarl* in Anglo-Saxon England after the Danish invasions, and survives today in the modern title of Earl.[41] Another plausible case occurs later in the poem in the phrase *eorl Ongenþio,* in reference to a king of the Swedes. Parts of what is now Sweden were ruled by Cnut's Danish *jarls* at the time of the *Beowulf* manuscript. In the context at the beginning of the poem, Scyld Scefing, among troops of his enemies, deprived many tribes of their meadhall benches, but his final victory was that he *egsode eorl,* terrified the ruling chief, or petty king.

The desired meter for the phrase can be achieved, moreover, without resorting to emendation by pronouncing *eorl* in two syllables—*eor-el.* We all know people who say both "athlete" and "ath-e-lete," or "twirl" and "twir-el" to cite a current "r-l" example, and distinguished poets such as Chaucer, Shakespeare, and Milton have been known to use side-by-side such forms as "Canterbry" and "Canterbury," "alarm" and "alarum," "sprite" and "spirit," solely on the dictates of meter.[42] The *Beowulf* poet uses, for example, *Dena* beside *Denia,* along with a host of other metrical variants.

In the light of this kind of evidence, I am not persuaded by the metrists' contention that certain contractions in *Beowulf* prove that the poem is early. True enough, in the old days the whiskey, Scotch, was Scottish and the people, Welsh, were Wealhish. But there is reason to believe that speakers of Late Old English would have naturally pronounced the contractions in *Beowulf* in two syllables, rather than one, despite the conventional spellings, particularly if the meter encouraged them to do so. There are only a few such contracted forms in *Beowulf* and one explanation can serve for all.

In Old English the ending for all verbs in the infinitive form was *-an*, but at an early stage the stem of the verb *do* (our "do") had contracted with this ending to produce the form *don* instead of *doan*. But native speakers would have recognized by analogy with all the other infinitives that this was a contraction. Native speakers of modern English recognize, with much less linguistic reinforcement, that "don't" is a contraction of "do not." We know, moreover, that in late Old English times the old pronunciation survived or revived in some dialects, for uncontracted spellings like *doan* re-emerge in some late texts, if not in *Beowulf*.[43]

Remember, though, that the *Beowulf* manuscript is written in the standard late West Saxon literary dialect, and that its spellings do not necessarily reflect the pronunciations of non-West Saxon poets.[44] Note that today in formal prose we always write "do not" even where we would naturally *say* "don't." If *Beowulf* is a late poem, the poet may well have decided to use a conservative spelling instead of a provincial one, since he knew that the word would be pronounced correctly in any case. Our standard literary dialect gives us an old, conservative spelling for the number 2, "t-w-o," but everyone I know now pronounces it [tu] "too," not [two] "two."

My quarrel (or quar-rel) with the metrists is not with their aim to recover the pleasures inherent in verse. They have surely hit the target, if not the bull's-eye, in their analyses. I think they are right that the few contractions in *Beowulf* usually need to be decontracted to sound like verse. I think they are quite wrong to assume that contractions thereby prove that *Beowulf* is an early poem preserved in a late, corrupt manuscript. My quarrel with them, with most textual critics of the poem, and with all modern editors of it, is their common aim to establish the text by making emendations to fit their theories.[45]

I was content to believe that *Beowulf* is an early poem preserved in a late, *reliable* manuscript, until I studied the manuscript at first hand at the British Library. What I found there was a hoard of evidence that had never been mentioned, much less taken into account, by the metrists, the textual critics, and the editors. Before giving you an inventory of its extraordinary features, I need to tell you what the *Beowulf* manuscript looks like today. The fire of 1731 destroyed Cotton's binding and left the outside edges of the manuscript crumbled and charred. In short, the fire had left behind what was essentially a big stack of separate vellum leaves, rather than a book. In the middle of the nineteenth century, in 1845 to be exact, the officials at the British Museum decided to rebind *Beowulf* and the other manuscripts of Cotton Vitellius A. xv, to make the stack of leaves a book again.

The officials realized that they could not simply slap a new cover around the stack and call it a book. Skilled bookbinders had to connect the leaves somehow, to recreate gatherings that could then be stitched together in a conventional binding. Morever, they had to come up with a way to protect the charred, crumbling edges of the vellum. The method they decided on was to mount each vellum leaf in a paper frame and to bind the paper frames. For each leaf they made a tracing on heavy paper and cut the center out, leaving a retaining space of 1–2mm around the edge. They put paste in this retaining space and then carefully pressed the vellum leaf into place. To secure the leaf from the front, they then pasted transparent strips around the edges. When the work was done they bound the paper frames in a brown-calf facsimile of the original covers.[46]

The new binding was a triumph of book preservation, for it stopped the crumbling of the vellum in its tracks. However, I think it is fair to say that the binders were more interested in the outside appearance of the book than with the inside preservation of the text and the physical features of its original manuscript. The retaining space of the paper frames covers hundreds of letters of the text. Moreover, the decision to mount each leaf separately meant that any vestige of the original vellum gatherings had to be sacrificed.

In 1882, Julius Zupitza attempted to record all of the covered letters for his facsimile edition by holding the manuscript up to the light. He did a great job for someone working before the days of the light bulb. In the summers of 1982 and 1983 I used fiber-optic light to check his work and found few mistakes, but over 300 letters and letter-fragments he had been unable to see.[47] It is symptomatic of the general neglect of the *Beowulf* manuscript that no one bothered to verify Zupitza's claims for a hundred years. And no one had *ever* tried to reconstruct the original gatherings of the *Beowulf* manuscript from any scraps of physical evidence that might remain of them.[48]

Any medieval manuscript, quite apart from the texts it preserves, tells a unique story. There are no two alike. Before Beowulf could slay his monsters, someone had to slay a lot of sheep. It was a costly proposition to copy a poem of the length of *Beowulf,* and someone had to believe that it was worth a small flock of sheep, and a large flock of precious time and labor. Once the sheep were slaughtered and skinned, the hides had to be washed, limed, unhaired, scraped, dried, washed again, stretched on frames, scraped again to remove blemishes, smoothed and polished with pumice, softened with chalk, and cut to size.[49] When the prepared sheets of vellum finally went to the scriptorium, more work had to be done before any copying could begin. Someone, presumably the scribe, had to rule the sheets of vellum for lines of text and margins, and arrange the sheets in small booklets called gatherings. The usual gathering at this time was made up of four folded sheets, providing eight leaves or sixteen pages to write on.[50]

The way booklets were put together in manuscripts sometimes tells us something worth knowing about the intended use of the texts. For example, in manuscripts of homilies, scribes often copied separate texts in single gatherings, small, irregular, self-contained units that could be removed from the manuscript for use in preaching.[51] Though the original gatherings of the *Beowulf* manuscript were permanently obscured by the fire and the new binding, anyone with my blind faith in this manuscript wanted to hear its hidden secrets. Part of its story was buried in those original gatherings.

My approach was to collect any extraordinary manuscript evidence that had been overlooked, ignored, or forgotten. For instance, I had to determine for each vellum leaf which side was the hair (or wool) side and which side was the flesh side of the animal skin. If I was going to reconstruct the original gatherings, I could not deduce an original sheet that had hair on one side of its fold and flesh on the other.[52]

I also had to make sure that the scribal rulings lined up properly. The scribes ruled the vellum for lines of text and margins a gathering at a time. First, they punched tiny holes through the stacked sheets of a gathering along both sides for lines of text, and along the top and bottom for the margins. Then they drew the lines with a ruler and an awl, using the holes as guide-marks. Although these guide-marks were destroyed in the fire, the writing-grids they helped create of course still survive. The awl left rulings in the form of furrows, or indentations, which show up in reverse on the other side of the sheet. I could not come up with a sheet that had furrows on one side of the fold and reversed markings on the other. Nor could I come up with a sheet that had 20 rulings on one side of the fold and 22 on the other, since the same sheet would have had the same number of guide-marks for the rulings.

By this simple process, I was able to establish the most probable construction of the original gatherings and definitely eliminate some alternatives that once had seemed more likely. I discovered that the two scribes of *Beowulf* had constructed their gatherings in completely different ways. The first scribe had made 4-sheet gatherings, ruled (with one exception) for 20 lines of text, and had consistently arranged his sheets with hair sides facing hair sides and flesh sides facing flesh sides, to obscure the contrast when the book was opened at any point. This arrangement was typical for early eleventh-century manuscripts. But the second scribe had made 5-sheet gatherings, ruled for 21 lines of text, and had invariably arranged his sheets with hair sides facing flesh sides, as if to highlight the contrast between hair and flesh wherever the book was opened in his part. It is a striking change in format.

Knowing this kind of information can have important consequences. I believe, for example, that I have been able to identify another manuscript from the same scriptorium on the basis of striking paleographical and codicological similarities. The manuscript is the famous Blickling Homilies codex in the Scheide collection at Princeton. A paleographical connection was noted long ago, but no one ever noticed that the Beowulf manuscript and the Blickling Homilies manuscript share the same odd features in the sheet arrangement of the gatherings and that the size of the writing grids are virtually identical.[53] What makes this discovery so exciting to me is that it explains in the best possible way why the description of Grendel's mere is so like the description of Hell in Blickling Homily 16.[54] The *Beowulf* poet had access to this manuscript of homilies, which is dated internally in the year 971. *Beowulf* must have been composed after that.

You can understand, then, my interest in the original gatherings of the *Beowulf* manuscript. Through my analysis of the sheet arrangement, I learned that the make-up of the first gathering in *Beowulf* was extraordinary. In 1705, when the original gatherings were still intact, Wanley had told us that *Beowulf* began a separate manuscript, but later scholars preferred to think that the poem had been copied continuously with the prose texts that precede it, and that copying of the poem began in the middle of the last prose gathering. Since they had no evidence to contradict Wanley, I think these scholars wanted to believe that *Beowulf* was copied mechanically and that its manuscript was in no way special to the scribes. The hair and flesh arrangement of the leaves supported Wanley's statement, while the rulings from the *Beowulf* leaves did not line up properly with rulings on the relevant prose leaves.[55]

There is a good deal of corroborating evidence that the first page of *Beowulf* originally served as an outside cover. I will mention only one aspect of this evidence. The page shows unmistakeable signs of unusual wear and tear that cannot be attributed to exposure in modern times. Most of the damage is in the lower right corner, where some of the text has worn off and is no longer legible. It looks like the result of excessive handling, as if the book had been repeatedly held by the corner. The damage presumably occurred in Old English times, since Wanley, in his transcript of the first page, copied one of the partly illegible words as it now appears and then stopped transcribing when he reached the other illegible words. The Thorkelin transcripts unequivocally show that the damage was as advanced in 1787 as it is now.

There was inarguable evidence, in addition, that the last page of *Beowulf* had also served as an outside cover, making the manuscript what appeared to be a special, self-contained unit. The most obvious evidence was that the scribe had to use a plethora of abbreviations in order to squeeze in the last lines of the poem on this page; that he later had to freshen up the ink where readings had worn off; and that a medieval bookworm feasted on the last pages of *Beowulf* before the *Judith* fragment became part of the codex.[56]

To make a long lecture somewhat shorter, I found some remarkable things going on in this newly separate, special manuscript. Those ignorant, lazy scribes had both carefully proofread their work and had made nearly 200 corrections of their mistakes. I can't believe they overlooked up to 350 additional mistakes, about one every ten lines, as the modern editions maintain. The second scribe had even proofread the first scribe's work, and in addition to making some corrections had made a few minor emendations.[57] There was no comparable evidence of proofreading, by either of the scribes, in the prose texts. This convincingly proved that the scribes were neither ignorant nor lazy, that they well understood what they were copying and that they worked uncommonly hard to provide a reliable text.

But there were more remarkable things going on. The second scribe, who took over copying in the middle of one of the first scribe's gatherings, ostentatiously ignored the rulings on four consecutive pages and between the first and last rulings adroitly inserted more lines of text than the rulings provided for. To appreciate his feat, try doing it yourselves in a lined notebook. In the immediately preceding gathering, the first scribe, who always ruled his gatherings for 20 lines of text, suddenly ruled one for 22 lines, before resuming his normal format. The second scribe, after squeezing in those extra lines in the first scribe's gathering, used a totally different format for his own gatherings, with more sheets, more lines of text per page, and wider margins.

The first leaf of his first gathering was a full palimpsest—that is, the original text on it had been completely eradicated, and a new, shorter text, written in a slightly different script with a few strange spellings, had replaced it. Parts of it were later erased, and a full restoration was never achieved. On the reverse side of the second leaf three lines had been deliberately erased, with no attempt to replace or restore them.[58] In the midst of all of these remarkable features, the first scribe, who numbered the sections of the poem after copying them, introduced an error in the number sequence. The second scribe sometimes forgot to leave space for numbers in his part, but otherwise continued numbering his sections based on the first scribe's erroneous sequence.[59]

It all seemed like the *locus Anglo-Saxonicus* of the right hand not knowing what the left hand was doing, or the mental breakdown of a schizophrenic manuscript. All of the traumas were clustered at the breaking point, where one scribe abruptly (in the middle of a verse) stopped copying and the second took over.[60] Moreover, they were all clustered in the section of the text known as "Beowulf's Homecoming," a loose transition that fuses the story of Beowulf's youthful exploits in Denmark with the story of his confrontation as an old man with the dragon in Geatland.[61]

For me, all of the evidence led to an unorthodox, but seemingly inescapable conclusion. Two separate stories and two separate manuscripts had been linked together in the same manuscript that has come down to us from the early eleventh century. The *Beowulf* manuscript was not a late copy of an early poem, but a revision-in-progress of a contemporary one. It was not planned in advance, to judge by the sudden breakdown in the format.

Both scribes copied parts of the new transitional text. The first scribe stopped where he did to go back and supply his share of the revision in the preceding gathering. The length of the new text did not permit him to use his normal-sized gathering ruled for 20 lines to the page. He was thus obliged to rule it for 22 lines to the page. If part of his new transition had deleted a former section of the poem it would explain how he messed up the number sequence. He recopied the old numbers, not remembering that one of the old numbers was now gone. Since the second scribe often forgot to leave space for numbers, it follows that he had no numbers to miscopy from his exemplar. This deduction explains why he innocently resumed the number sequence where the first scribe had erroneously left off.[62] The second scribe, moreover, was obliged to squeeze in extra lines of text, in disregard of the rulings, because he had already copied the last two gatherings, containing the dragon episode. It was not easy to link up two completely different stories in two different manuscripts.[63]

The palimpsest suggests that the second scribe many years later decided that the transition was not as it should be. After erasing all of the original text on the first folio (front and back) of the dragon episode, and three related lines on the reverse side of the next folio, he provided a new start for this episode. The current state of the text on this folio indicates that it was still in a draft stage when the poem's Old English history came to an abrupt halt.[64] It is well to remember that at this time Anglo-Saxon *history* was about to come to an abrupt halt, too.[65] The poem remains unfinished on this folio to this day, making the manuscript, at least in part, an early eleventh-century record of an early eleventh-century poem.[66]

NOTES

1. For a full analysis of the composite codex with illustrative plates (one in color) see Kiernan, "The History and Construction of the Composite Codex," *Beowulf and the Beowulf Manuscript* (New Brunswick, 1981), 65–169, hereafter referred to as *BBMS*. For the Nowell Codex alone, see also Kemp Malone, *The Nowell Codex, British Museum Cotton Vitellius A. XV. Second Manuscript*, Early English Manuscripts in Facsimile 12 (Copenhagen, 1963).

2. The *Judith*-fragment is itself headless, and scholars do not agree how much of the text is actually lost at the beginning, a head only or a torso too. Moreover, its concluding lines are only preserved by an early modern hand, suggesting that the rest of its original manuscript was still intact at the time, but for some reason was dismembered. I argue that the fragment was added to the Nowell Codex when its monastic library was dissolved in the Reformation in *BBMS*, esp. 59–60, 150–159. Kenneth Sisam first suggested that the Nowell Codex was conceived as a book of monsters in *Studies in the History of Old English Literature* (Oxford, 1953), 66; cf. Michael Lapidge, "*Beowulf*, Aldhelm, the *Liber Monstrorum* and Wessex," *Studi Medievali* 23 (1982): 151–192.

3. George Hickes made the earliest known reference to *Beowulf* when he replied in a letter to Humfrey Wanley on 20 August 1700, "I can find nothing yet of Beowulph" (*BBMS*, 133 note 44). The letter was recently printed in *A Chorus of Grammars: The Correspondence of George Hickes and His Collaborators on the 'Thesaurus linguarum septentrionalium'*, ed. Richard L. Harris, Publications of the Dictionary of Old English 4 (Toronto, 1992), 337.

4. See *BBMS*, plate 2, 75. This and two other early modern flyleaves in Cotton's binding unfortunately threw off the numbering of the manuscript leaves when in 1884 they were included in a count now regarded as "official," even though one of the three prefixed leaves is no longer in the codex. For students of *Beowulf*, the best recourse is to use the older foliation still visible on the manuscript leaves, as nearly all modern editors have done.

5. Sir Frederic Madden, Assistant Keeper of Manuscripts in the British Museum, 1828–37, and Keeper, 1837–66, began restoring the burnt Cotton manuscripts in 1839. His ledger book, *Cottonian MSS, Repairing and Binding Account,* is now BL MS Add. 62577.

6. Readers of translations may not know about Beowulf the Dane, who often shows up in them as Beow. In *The Norton Anthology of English Literature,* 5th ed. (New York, 1986), E.T. Donaldson asserts that "most scholars now agree" that the MS readings at lines 18 and 53 should be changed to "Beow" (note 2). An informal poll of Anglo-Saxonists on ANSAXNET, the computer network for Anglo-Saxonists, seemed to suggest the contrary, despite a spirited defence by Howell Chickering of his use of *Beow* in his dual-language edition. The discussion can be found in ANSAXDAT, <telnet mungate.library.mun.ca>.

7. For an account of his research trip see Kiernan, "Thorkelin's Trip to Great Britain and Ireland, 1786–1791," *The Library,* 6th series, 5 (1983): 1–21; and Part One of *The Thorkelin Transcripts of Beowulf* (Copenhagen, 1986).

8. *De Danorum Rebus Gestis Secul. III & IV. Poëma Danicum Dialecto Anglosaxonica* (Copenhagen, 1815). Editors have usually relied on Julius Zupitza's transliteration, which incorporates lost readings from the Thorkelin transcripts. Klaeber, for example, says in a note preceding the text that readings quoted from A and B are "from Zupitza's notes." "The Text," *Beowulf and the Fight at Finnsburg,* 3rd ed. (Boston, 1950), facing p. 1.

9. Sharon Turner, *The History of the Manners, Landed Property, Government, Laws, Poetry, Literature, Religion, and Language, of the Anglo-Saxons* (London, 1805), 4:402.

10. See *BBMS,* 137. In a recent study also citing Turner's blunder, Allen J. Frantzen refers to the misplaced leaf as "fol. 137" (*Desire for Origins: New Language, Old English, and Teaching the Tradition* [New Brunswick, 1990], 194–195). In the manuscript foliation the leaf was numbered 131 when it was out of place. Now that the leaf is back in place between folios 146 and 147, we can keep track of its former misplacement without disrupting the useful manuscript foliation by referring to it as fol. 147A(131).

11. After Thorkelin suggested in the title of his *editio princeps* that the poem derived from the third or fourth century, scholars slowly moved the date forward to a fairly firm consensus in the eighth century. For an overview see Colin Chase, "Opinions on the Date of *Beowulf,* 1815–1980," *The Dating of 'Beowulf',* ed. Colin Chase (Toronto, 1981), 3–8.

12. Hopkins died in 1889, but still seemed to belong to "The Twentieth Century" (between Thomas Hardy, who died in 1928, and Bernard Shaw, who died in 1950) as late as the 4th edition of *The Norton Anthology of English Literature* (New York, 1979), 2:1785–97. He is, however, referred to as a Victorian poet in the 5th ed.

13. J.S. Cardale reminds his readers at the start of the 19th century that Hickes in the early 18th century distinguished three Saxon dialects in England: Britanno-Saxon from the 5th-century Anglo-Saxon invasions until the coming of the Danes in 793; Dano-Saxon, until the Norman Conquest in 1066; and Normanno-Dano-Saxon after that. Cardale presumed that King Alfred spoke "pure Anglo-Saxon" (*King Alfred's Anglo-Saxon Version of Boethius De Consolatione Philosophiæ: with an English translation, and Notes* [London, 1829], no page numbers). Today most Anglo-Saxonists have forgotten all about the Dano-Saxon dialects that

must have been spoken in the vast Danelaw areas of Anglo-Saxon England.

14. J.M. Kemble set the prevailing tone in the English editions when he said, "All persons who have had much experience of Anglo-Saxon MSS. know how hopelessly incorrect they in general are. . . . we are yet met at every turn with faults of grammar, with omissions or redundancies of letters and words, which can perhaps only be accounted for by the supposition that professional copyists brought to their task (in itself confusing enough,) both lack of knowledge and lack of care." He adds that "A modern edition, made by a person really conversant with the language which he illustrates, will in all probability be much more like the original than the MS. copy, which, even in the earliest times, was made by an ignorant or indolent transcriber" (*The Anglo-Saxon Poems of Beowulf, the Travellers Song and the Battle of Finnes-burh* [London, 1833], xxiii–xxiv).

15. Stanley Rypins, ed., *Three Old English Prose Texts in MS. Cotton Vitellius A xv*, EETS 161 (1924), xi–xiv. As Rypins says, Sisam first pointed out in print the identity of the first hand of *Beowulf* with that of the prose texts. Madden had in fact sorted them out in his journals nearly a century earlier, as I mention in "Madden, Thorkelin, and MS Vitellius/Vespasian A. xv," *The Library* 8 (1986): 130.

16. As Richard Wülker says, "Dieses Stück [*i.e. Wonders of the East*] wie das vorige [*Alexander's Letter*] entstand wohl kaum früher als um die Mitte des elften Jahrhunderts" (*Grundriss zur Geschichte der angelsächsischen Litteratur* [Leipzig, 1885], 505).

17. The loose dating of the *Beowulf* manuscript "around the year 1000" or "*circa* 1000" has effectively prevented scholars from investigating the implications of Ker's paleographical dating of the script any time in the 50-year span from the last quarter of the 10th century through the first quarter of the 11th. Thus a recent book on Cnut, who ruled England during Ker's dating limits, avoids the issue by presuming that "the surviving manuscript of *Beowulf,* with its story of pagan Scandinavia," comes from the reign of Æthelred, who was deposed by Cnut's father in 1014 (M.K. Lawson, *Cnut: The Danes in England in the Early Eleventh Century* [Longman, 1993], 130–131).

18. J. Bosworth and T. Northcote Toller, *An Anglo-Saxon Dictionary* (Oxford, 1898), 532, and Toller, *Supplement* (Oxford, 1921), 537. For a review of opinions on these words, see Phillip Pulsiano and Joseph McGowan, "*Fyrd, here,* and the Dating of *Beowulf,*" *Studia Linguistica Posnaniensia* 23 (1990): 3–13.

19. As this use of *fyrd* shows, Pulsiano and McGowan misunderstand my position when they say that by my theory "*here* would have come to mean by the reign of Cnut the forces of the allies; *fyrd* the forces of the enemy" (11). Both words can be used with neither positive nor negative connotations in *Beowulf.* My point is that *fyrd* had pejorated to the extent that it was no longer reserved for English forces, and that *here* is used honorifically.

20. See Christine Fell, "The Icelandic Saga of Edward the Confessor: The Version of the Anglo-Saxon Emigration to Byzantium," *Anglo-Saxon England* 3 (1974): 179–196; and Sigfús Blöndal, *The Varangians of Byzantium: An Aspect of Byzantine Military History,* translated, revised and rewritten by Benedikt S. Benedikz (Cambridge, 1978). The most famous former Varangian guard associated with England at this time was Harold Hardråde, who died at Stamford Bridge trying to conquer England in 1066.

21. Ashley Amos provides a comprehensive analysis of these tests in *Linguistic*

Means of Determining the Dates of Old English Literary Tests (Cambridge, Mass., 1980). See also Angus Cameron *et al.*, "A Reconsideration of the Language of *Beowulf*," in *Dating of Beowulf*, 33–75, and Kiernan, "The Linguistic Tests for an Early Date," *BBMS*, 23–37.

22. Karl Müllenhoff, "Die innere Geschichete des *Beovulfs*," *ZfdA* 14 (1869): 193–244. Walter A. Berendsohn; *Zur Vorgeschichte des 'Beowulf'* (Copenhagen, 1935). Klaeber notes with exasperation that "even the exact number of lines credited to each one of the six contributors was announced by Müllenhoff," adding that "Ettmüller in his edition (1875) pared the poem in its pre-Christian form down to 2896 lines," while "Möller condensed the text into 344 four-line stanzas" (cii, n. 1).

23. Dorothy Whitelock, *The Audience of 'Beowulf'* (Oxford, 1951), 24–25.

24. For an historical overview of editorial changes, see Birte Kelley, "The Formative Stages of *Beowulf* Textual Scholarship: Part I" *Anglo-Saxon England* 11 (1983): 247–74, and "Part II," *Anglo-Saxon England* 12 (1984): 239–75. Cf. Tilman Westphalen, *Beowulf 3150–3155: Textkritik und Editionsgeschichte* (Munich, 1967).

25. See A.C. Murray, "*Beowulf*, the Danish Invasions, and Royal Genealogy," in *Dating of Beowulf*, 101–111.

26. See the Chronicle entry for 1002. Although Ethelred's order could not have had much effect in the Danelaw, there were massacres, as Ethelred himself makes clear in a charter renewal in 1004 for the monastery of St. Frideswide, Oxford. As one of his scribes records, "to all dwelling in this country it will be well known that, since a decree was sent out by me with the counsel of my leading men and magnates, to the effect that all the Danes who had sprung up in this island, sprouting like cockle amongst the wheat, were to be destroyed by a most just extermination, and this decree was to be put into effect even as far as death, those Danes who dwelt in the afore-mentioned town, striving to escape death, entered this sanctuary of Christ, having broken by force the doors and bolts, and resolved to make a refuge and defence for themselves therein against the people of the town and suburb; but when all the people in pursuit strove, forced by necessity, to drive them out, and could not, they set fire to the planks and burnt, as it seems, this church with its ornaments and its books" (*English Historical Documents, I, c. 500–1042*, ed. Dorothy Whitelock [London, 1955], nos. 127, 545).

27. Sam Newton attempts to resuscitate this theory in *The Origins of 'Beowulf' and the Pre-Viking Kingdom of East Anglia* (Cambridge, 1993), 10–11.

28. Thus Klaeber characterizes the spelling *ēo*, for instance, as variously reflecting Anglian, Kentish, Saxon patois, Northumbrian coloring, and even "partly" West Saxon dialects (lxxx). There is a full discussion of *wundini* (1382) in *BBMS*, 30–37. Wrenn called this form "the only certain evidence for dating *Beowulf* before *circa* 750 on purely linguistic grounds" (*Beowulf with the Finnesburg Fragment* [London, 1953], 21, note 2). The manuscript reads *wundmi*, as Thorkelin A records.

29. While she agrees with me that "the mixture of spellings does not necessarily mean a long history of textual transmission" (411, note 11), Janet Bately for dating purposes singles out the Early West Saxon shibboleth *ie* as phonological rather than orthographical evidence (411–415). She admits, however, that *ie* spellings occur even in 12th-century manuscripts (412). See "Linguistic Evidence as a Guide to the Authorship of Old English Verse: A Reappraisal, with Special Reference to *Beowulf*," *Learning and Literature in Anglo-Saxon England*, ed. Michael Lapidge and Helmut Gneuss (Cambridge, 1985), 409–431.

30. Both modern facsimiles use the same photographs. See Julius Zupitza, ed., *Beowulf: Reproduced in Facsimile*, 2nd edition by Norman Davis, EETS 245 (London, 1959); and Malone, *The Nowell Codex*.

31. The most recent proponent is R.D. Fulk, who defends the 19th-century theories of reconstruction in his exhaustive *History of Old English Meter* (Philadelphia, 1993).

32. In the Preface to *The Metrical Grammar of 'Beowulf'* (Cambridge, 1992), ix–x, Calvin Kendall confides, "I began this study many years ago in the fond hope of reducing to a neat system (neater than the systems of Sievers, Pope or Bliss, whose basic patterns kept dissolving, as it seemed to me then, into a welter of anarchic subpatterns) the seemingly endless varieties of rhythmic possibilities in *Beowulf*. . . . That goal," he continues, "now seems to me a will-o'-the wisp."

33. This is the only motivation for emending *handlean* to *andlean* 'retribution' (1541, 2094) or *hondslyht* to *ondslyht* 'counterblow' (2929, 2972). For an excellent discussion of the phonological value of *h* in *Beowulf*, see M.F. Vaughan, "A Reconsideration of 'Unferð'," *Neuphilologische Mitteilungen* 77 (1976): 32–48.

34. Historical linguists have traditionally preferred the diachronic reconstruction of a prehistoric stage of Old English to a synchronic analysis of unique or unusual manuscript forms, which may in fact give us important linguistic information if it is not hidden by emendation. For example, at *Beowulf* 2295, *þone þe him on sweofote sare geteode*, Klaeber notes without apparent motivation that "*sare* is an adverb, not the object of the verb, the fem. gender of the noun *sar* being more than doubtful" (210–11). He does not mention that at line 2468b the MS. reads *sio sar* (fem. nom. sg.), which he quietly emends to *to sar*. We may have here a late confusion of forms. Cf. the strong *scod* (1887b) and weak *scepede* (1514b), morphological variants of the verb *scepðan* 'harm', or the phonological variants *hraðe* (which usually alliterates with *h*, but sometimes with *r*) and *raðe* (724). Because of editorial emendation based on 19th-century interest in reconstruction, it will be necessary for linguists to return to Old English manuscripts to discover much of this kind of evidence.

35. Morton Bloomfield, "*Beowulf* and Christian Allegory: An Interpretation of Unferth," *Traditio* 7 (1949–50): 410–415.

36. Fol. 141r–15 (line 499). The fit numbers in the manuscript are also routinely ignored. For an excellent study, see Eamonn Ó Carragáin, "Structure and Thematic Development in *Beowulf*," *Proceedings of the Royal Irish Academy* 66 (1967): 1–51.

37. Lines 389–390. Although Birte Kelley, "The Formative Stages," does not mention it, Kemble began this radical line of emendation in his 1835 edition when he commented that "Probably two lines have been omitted, of which the second may have been Wulfgár maþelode" (28).

38. See, for example, T. Hart, "*Ellen*: Some Tectonic Relationships in *Beowulf* and Their Formal Resemblance in Anglo-Saxon Art," *Papers on Language and Literature* 6 (1970): 263–90; David Howlett, "Form and Genre in *Beowulf*," *Studia Neophilologica* 66 (1974): 309–325. Even if something is missing by haplography in lines without alliteration, it might just as well be three lines as one or four. The advantage of following the manuscript version is that we can be sure an Anglo-Saxon audience knew *Beowulf* in that form.

39. John C. Pope, *The Rhythm of 'Beowulf*,' 2nd ed. (New Haven, 1966), 3.

40. Klaeber was also bothered by the rare anacrusis in the off-verse of a Type D meter, but he omits *para,* he says, because it is "syntactically objectionable" (280). I would scan 9b without emendation as x x / / x x, Type C. As E.V.K. Dobbie observed, "the metrical arguments for the omission of this word are not as convincing as they once were, and the argument from syntax (the infrequency of *se, seo, pæt* as a definite article in the early poetry) is refuted by *ymbesittendra ænig ðara,* l. 2734, where *ðara* is required by the meter." *Beowulf and Judith,* Anglo-Saxon Poetic Records 4 (New York, 1953), 114.

41. See *OED,* sense 2, "In late OE: a Danish under-king (see JARL); hence (under Cnut and his successors) the viceroy or governor of one of the great divisions of England, Wessex, Northumbria, Mercia, etc."

42. After noting that the line as it stands in the manuscript might be metrically acceptable, Fulk objects to my suggestion of an intrusive vowel in *eorl* because of a lack of "orthographical evidence for such anaptyxis" in this word (*History,* 205, n. 70). See the variant spellings *erel, errel, erell, errille* of *Earl* in *OED,* which also cites the Old Norse runic spelling *erilaʀ.* Intrusive vowels are in fact most likely to occur in the environment of liquids *r* and *l,* even when spellings fail to reflect them.

43. A. Campbell points out that "analogical forms with the contraction eliminated quite often occur." Among his examples are Northern forms of the verb "to do," *dōa* for Southern *don* (*Old English Grammar* [Oxford, 1959], §239, p. 104). Both the *Dictionary of Old English,* ed. A. Cameron *et al.,* Fascicle *D* (Toronto, 1986), 509, and the *Microfiche Concordance to Old English,* ed. Antonette diPaolo Healey and Richard Venezky (Toronto, 1980), 211–213, list many uncontracted forms, including *doan* and the inflected infinitive *to doanne.*

44. C.L. Wrenn, "The Value of Spelling as Evidence," *Transactions of the Philological Society, London* (1933): 14–39, and, more recently, Angus Cameron et al., "A Reconsideration of the Language of *Beowulf,*" *Dating of Beowulf,* 33–75, and Joseph Tuso, "*Beowulf*'s Dialectal Vocabulary and the Kiernan Theory," *The South Central Review* 2 (1985): 1–9.

45. Kendall says he has "resisted the temptation to emend the text to suit my theories" (xv), but by "the text" he does not mean the manuscript, but Klaeber's edition, which is already heavily emended for metrical reasons.

46. Scholars sometimes talk about the manuscript without having seen it. For example, J.D.A. Ogilvy and Donald C. Baker wrongly assert that "Today each leaf of Vitellius A. 15 is encased in transparent plastic to protect it from further harm" in their chapter, "The Manuscript," in *Reading 'Beowulf': An Introduction to the Poem, Its Background, and Its Style* (Norman, Oklahoma, 1983), 4. Some of the mistakes in Leonard Boyle's "The Nowell Codex and the Poem of *Beowulf*" (*Dating of Beowulf,* 23–32) can be explained because he formulated it first in Toronto in April 1980, before he had ever seen the manuscript.

47. "The State of the *Beowulf* Manuscript, 1882–1983," *Anglo-Saxon England* 13 (1984): 23–42.

48. Neil Ker determined the hair/flesh patterns in the single quire of *Judith,* but for some reason did not try to ascertain them in *Beowulf,* where they can help establish the original construction of the dismembered gatherings (*Catalogue of Manuscripts Containing Anglo-Saxon* [Oxford, 1957], 282). Cf. Malone, *Nowell Codex,* 16.

49. There is a good introduction to these methods in Christopher de Hamel, *Medieval Craftsmen: Scribes and Illuminators* (Toronto, 1992). See also the section on "Materials and techniques" in Michelle Brown, *Anglo-Saxon Manuscripts* (Toronto, 1991), 46–53.

50. The characteristic methods mentioned below for arranging, folding, and ruling gatherings are based on Ker's findings, *Catalogue,* xxii–xxv; see also L.W. Jones, "Pricking Manuscripts: The Instruments and Their Significance," *Speculum* 21 (1946): 389–403, and the excellent guide by Alexander Rumble, "Using Anglo-Saxon Manuscripts," forthcoming in *Basic Readings in Anglo-Saxon Manuscripts,* ed. Mary P. Richards (New York: Garland, 1994).

51. P.R. Robinson, "Self-Contained Units in Composite Manuscripts of the Anglo-Saxon Period," *Anglo-Saxon England* 7 (1978): 231–38.

52. After describing them correctly as five- and three-sheet gatherings, Max Förster mistakenly describes the first two gatherings of the Nowell Codex as four-sheet quires. The hair/flesh patterns of the second proposed quire unequivocally show that only one set of folios could have been conjugate ("Die Beowulf Hand-schrift," *Berichte über die Verhandlungen der Sächsischen Akademie der Wissenschaften zu Leipzig, Philologisch-historische Klass* 71 (1919): 7–8 and 21–23). Cf. Ker, *Catalogue,* 282, and Boyle, *Dating of Beowulf,* 23–24, for the same mistake.

53. Scheide MS 71. For a full facsimile see Rudolph Willard, ed., *The Blickling Homilies (The John H. Scheide Library, Titusville, Pennsylvania),* Early English Manuscripts in Facsimile 10 (Copenhagen, 1960); the collation is more accurately presented in Donald Scragg, "The Homilies of the Blickling Manuscript," *Learning and Literature,* 299–316.

54. See Rowland Collins, "Blickling Homily XVI and the Dating of *Beowulf,*" *Bamberger Beiträge zur Englischen Sprachwissenshaft* 15 (1983): 61–69.

55. Wanley not only notes that Cotton Vitellius A. xv is a composite codex (*ex diversis simul compactis*), but also describes the prose texts alone as belonging to the Nowell Codex. For him *Beowulf* began a new book. I think the scribe, wishing to make *Beowulf* a self-contained unit for ease of access, pulled a sheet from the previous gathering when he began copying the poem. See my article, "A Long Footnote for J. Gerritsen's 'Supplementary' Description of BL Cotton MS Vitellius A. xv," *English Studies* 72 (1991): 493–496 and nn. 12–16.

56. In "The Place of *Judith* in the *Beowulf*-Manuscript," *Review of English Studies* 41 (1990): 470, n. 21, P.J. Lucas asserts that "Kiernan's claim (*Beowulf,* p. 151) that the depth of the ruled frame in Quire 14 [*i.e. Judith*] is half a centimeter less than that of the previous quires is not observable." Lucas was presumably observing Malone's facsimile, rather than the manuscript, where one can both observe and accurately measure the rulings. Boyle, whom Lucas cites as an authority on this manuscript (465), radically mismeasures them at the start of *Beowulf* when he says "the spaces between rulings 18 and 19 (giving line 19) and between 19 and 20 (giving line 20) are 9 mm. and 10 mm. respectively for each frame in folios [123–130], whereas the space ruled for folios [132–139] is the regular 7 mm. or so that one usually finds throughout this part of the Nowell Codex and for the rest of the lines in each frame in folios [123–130]" (23). If Boyle's measurements were correct, the usual text frames would measure only *c.* 133 mm. from top to bottom (7 mm. x 19 spaces between ruling 1 and 20 = 133), rather than *c.* 175 mm. for the written space, as Ker says (*Catalogue* 282).

57. See *BBMS*, 272–277. An example is the second scribe's emendation of the first scribe's customary spelling of *-scaðan* to *-sceaðan* at fol. 140v14.

58. Both Thorkelin transcripts single out these lines, A by leaving three lines blank in his transcript (67, lines 1–12), and Thorkelin himself by writing in the margin that they were deliberately deleted in the manuscript (104a). It is surprising that no modern editor, including the editors of the facsimiles, even mentions Thorkelin's comment.

59. For a full discussion see *BBMS*, 264–270.

60. To suggest that the first scribe may have abruptly stopped copying *Beowulf* because "he had taken ill, and died" (32), Boyle says he may have stopped, not at the end of line 3 of fol. 172v, but after writing *most-* of *moste* in the next line. Boyle's argument is paleographically untenable: the *st* ligature is distinctive of the second scribe, and is never used by the first. If he gave up copying because he died, we must place his demise at the end of line 3, not at the beginning of line 4.

61. See Levin Schücking, *Beowulfs Rückkehr* (Halle, 1905).

62. The evidence is somewhat obscured by the alterations someone made to fit numbers XXV–XXVIIII, which led editors to think (*e.g.* Klaeber, number [XXVIII–XXX] at line 2039) that two fits belonged after fol. 174v19, where the second scribe simply omitted [XXX] for lack of space. See *BBMS*, 264–270.

63. It is not unprecedented, however, as *Guthlac A* and *B* and *Genesis A* and *B* both attest.

64. See "The Palimpsest and the New Text of Folio 179," *BBMS*, 219–243.

65. In 1066 two Scandinavian warlords who thought they had claims to Cnut's Anglo-Danish descent invaded England from different directions when Edward the Confessor died. Harold Hardråde of Norway arrived first and died in battle at Stamford Bridge. William of Normandy landed at Hastings a few weeks later and defeated the exhausted English forces.

66. David Dumville seeks to restrict the dating of the script to the opening years of the eleventh century in "*Beowulf* Come Lately: Some Notes on the Palaeography of the Nowell Codex," *Archiv* 225 (1988): 49–63. Ker specifically cautions against this temptation. "The failure of Anglo-Saxon minuscule at the end of the tenth century," he says, "led to a period of some fifty years, approximately 990–1040, during which there was great variety in the writing of books and charters in England, with some good writing and, especially in the vernacular, much rather poorer imitative writing with no character of its own. In this period great differences are to be seen between the hands of scribes writing at the same time and in the same place, between, for example, the first and the second hand of *Beowulf*. . . . These examples illustrate the impossibility of dating script of this period at all closely, and in particular hands which are either dully imitative like our scribe's or which have gone some way towards Caroline minuscule, like the first hand of *Beowulf*. . . ." (*The Will of Æthelgifu* [Oxford, 1968], 45–46). If one follows Ker, there is no paleographical evidence for excluding the writing of the *Beowulf* manuscript during or even sometime after the reign of Cnut the Great, 1016–1035.

The Women of *Beowulf*:
A Context for Interpretation

by GILLIAN R. OVERING

This essay is based on the final chapter, "Gender and Interpretation in
Beowulf," *of* Language, Sign, and Gender in "Beowulf" *(Carbondale
and Edwardsville: Southern Illinois University Press, 1990). The author has
revised it for separate publication.*

> "An impossible dialectic of two terms, a permanent alteration: never
> one without the other. It is not certain that someone is capable of it
> ... Perhaps, a woman ..."
>
> Julia Kristeva, *About Chinese Women*

OTHER VOICES

ALTHOUGH my title indicates that I will discuss women in *Beowulf*, I want to attempt both more and less than this rather
sweepingly implies, and to pay considerable attention also to the
issues of critical context and interpretation.[1] I will look specifically at
only three of the women in *Beowulf*, but this critical activity occasions
an inquiry into how we have previously looked at women in this poem.
Gender and interpretation are interdependent issues both within and
without *Beowulf*; like the hero's glory, our critical selves are situated *on
þæm dæge þysses lifes*.[2] Critical views and explanations of male and female
behaviors in this Anglo-Saxon poem have much to do with our views on
these subjects as they are constructed historically and contextualized in
place and time. Gender as a critical category has been sometimes confined to feminist reexaminations of patriarchally defined social roles,
and analyses of marginality and oppression. This essay too will eventually focus on women, and I shall be discussing varieties of marginality,
but my broader aim will be to suggest a context for interpretation of the
poem in which the operation of desire—that of the characters within the
narrative and that of the critics without—may be acknowledged and
revalued.

To ask a question, Teresa de Lauretis suggests, is itself a question of
desire, but "a story too is always a question of desire" and we can ask
"whose desire is it that speaks, and whom does that desire address?"[3] If

we look at how desire operates within the narrative, at how or if it is given voice, at the ways in which desire is directed, redirected and conflicted in *Beowulf,* we also see how marginal desire, whether this is monstrous, feminine, or even heroic, continually intrudes upon and deflects the progress of dominant desire. The poem presents us with a polyphony of voices, an interplay of desires, which contribute to its restless complexity and dynamic irresolution. And this might explain, at least partially, why my students often tell me (and I agree with them) that it's so hard to keep this whole poem in your mind at the same time, but that this very difficulty is part of its particular power and appeal.

How, then, to characterize dominant desire in the poem in order to examine its restless dialectic with marginal desire? Who wants what in *Beowulf* and who gets it? At first, and even second glance, *Beowulf* seems to be a poem about death: how to die, how to seek out death, how to meet it head on, how to make it so commonplace that it becomes an old familiar, how to choose it, privilege it, embrace it. Everywhere in the poem this deathly embrace spawns a variety of forms of closure, a continual need for resolution, the notion that choice is heroic, inescapable and reducible to simple binary oppositions—one or the other. And the other always loses. *Beowulf* is also an overwhelmingly masculine poem; it could be seen as a chronicle of male desire, a tale of men dying. In the masculine economy[4] of the poem desire expresses itself as desire for the other, as a continual process of subjugation and appropriation of the other. The code of vengeance and the heroic choice demand above all a *resolution* of opposing elements; a decision must always be made. Consider the story Beowulf tells about his grandfather Hrethel: Hæth-cyn, his second son, accidentally kills Herebeald, his first son; vengeance is necessary—one death must pay for another—but impossible in this case; the old man cannot, will not, survive in the in-between of indecision; he gives up all joy in life (*gumdream ofgeaf,* 2469), withers away and dies himself. All "choice" leads to death.

In "Beyond the Pleasure Principle," Freud equates the logical end, the ultimate object of all desire with actual death.[5] A psychoanalytic understanding of desire as deferred death, of the symbolic nature of desire in action, is often not necessary in *Beowulf*; death is continually present, always in the poem's foreground: the hero says "I will do this or I will die." Resolution, choice, satisfaction of desire frequently mean literal death. On a less extreme level, the closure that desire-as-appropriation involves is just that: a shutting down of the dialectic of oppositions, of differences, of others; a foretaste of the grand closure of death.

Kaja Silverman characterizes the Freudian concept of desire as/for death as a "notion of pleasure as a zero-degree of tension,"[6] and though we must concede that there is a lot of death and need for resolution in *Beowulf,* we must also recognize that there is a great deal of tension. One can find places in the narrative where the poet actually *prefers* tension to resolution, the process of making the decision to the decision accomplished.[7] As the poem escapes closure and resolution in a variety of ways, it also escapes this "dead end" of masculine desire. I have argued that the metonymic mode of language in the poem is partially responsible for the poem's vibrant, immediate, and peculiarly life-related qualities, and I have also demonstrated how the poem's structure, or the ways in which the signs of the text cohere, embodies the restless, kinetic mode of interlace, an artistic mode alien to closure, where resolution is resisted by inherent dynamism and expansion.[8] There are other elements in the poem that speak for desire as life, elements of marginal desire that disrupt the dominant discourse, that escape appropriation and operate against resolution in a simple, binary sense. Who, what are these others, what is "other" in *Beowulf*?

A genuine "Other," in Hélène Cixous and Catherine Clément's terms, cannot be theorized, "it doesn't settle down." Nevertheless, they continue, historically "what is called 'other' is an alterity that does settle down, that falls into the dialectical circle. It is the other in a hierarchically organized relationship in which the same is what rules, defines, and assigns 'its' other."[9] In the byzantine tribal feuds, the repeated reconfiguration of enmity and alliance in *Beowulf,* we see the continual production of the other as reproduction of the same, of the master/slave dialectic. Such alterity is assimilated into the binary status quo, feeds on resolution, indeed demonstrates the "dreadful simplicity that orders the movement Hegel erected as a system."[10] The monsters, of course, as more seriously alien, hint at an unrealizable, genuine alterity; they temporarily disrupt, even confuse the apparently inexorable process of assimilation and reappropriation. But the dynamism of this poem is also a function of that which transcends, or rather resists, binary opposition and resolution, of an otherness that resides in paradox.

The elements of otherness, or of marginal desire, can be monstrous, feminine, and even heroic; the ambiguous "perhaps" in my introductory quotation from Kristeva suggests that the capacity to participate in an "impossible dialectic" is not limited to women. Although I cast a brief glance at the heroic, I will narrow my focus to the feminine, and more specifically to the human females in the poem, mainly because they use language. This is not to suggest that monsters and monstrous females do not communicate, but only to confine my discussion to the formal, if arbitrary, boundaries of human discourse. The otherness that is generated in paradox is most clearly located in the voices of those ongoing manifestations of paradox, the women of *Beowulf,* and in the related concept of the advent of, or cultural initiation into, language embodied in the poem. I should note here that by "voices" I also mean a more general idea of presence and function, including speech, gesture and silence; there are several profoundly silent women in this poem. Also, the concept of language, taken up in my examination of Queen Wealhtheow, will enter the discussion in its simplest sense, as the counterpart or opposite to the mute regime of violence and action, as speech versus non-speech.

There is no place for women in the masculine economy of *Beowulf;* they have no space to occupy, to claim, to speak from. The terms of psychoanalysis have a peculiar clarity and literality of application in this context. Lacan's construct, the Name-of-the-Father, engenders the Symbolic order, the Law, which is "an arbitrary order of abstraction whose power derives from the threat of castration as signified by the phallus."[11] The arbitrary nature of this order, the advent of which Freud saw as a "victory of spirituality over the senses," and "a declaration in favour of the thought-process,"[12] stems from paternal doubt: "The legal assignation of a Father's Name to a child is meant to call a halt to uncertainty about the identity of the father. If the mother's femininity ... were affirmed, the Name-of-the-Father would always be in doubt, always be subject to the question of the mother's morality. Thus the Name-of-the-Father must be arbitrarily and absolutely imposed, thereby instituting the reign of patriarchal law."[13] Lacan's construct "sustains the concept of desire with the structure of the law,"[14] and also serves to connect the father and his name as a means of associating patriarchy with language: "the patronym, patriarchal law, patrilineal identity, language as our inscription into patriarchy. The Name-of-the-Father is the fact of the attribution of paternity by law, by language."[15] Paternal identification becomes the necessary condition for the subject's identification and entry into the world, a condition that caused Lacan to state repeatedly that "woman does not exist."[16]

The Name-of-the-Father functions on several literal and symbolic levels in *Beowulf,* underscoring the elements of exclusivity and homosexuality—here I refer to love of the same as a means of developing solidarity against the other, a primary bond, which may be social, emotional or sexual, which is exclusively masculine.[17] (I am putting aside for the moment the issue of language as an inscription into patriarchy.) Most obviously there is a tremendous preoccupation with genealogy in *Beowulf;* the father always identifies the son and daughter; the son is then identified by name. Often the women in the poem are not identified other than as daughters, wives or mothers. Of the eleven women in the poem we know the names of five: Wealhtheow, Freawaru (both of which Eliason thinks are only nicknames[18]), Hygd, Hildeburh, and Modthryth/Thryth. These are, notably, all queens, with some titular power of rule. Beowulf's mother, a woman lauded as fortunate in her childbearing, remains nameless, in sharp contrast to his father Ecgtheow who is mentioned sixteen times. Healfdene's daughter (King Hrothgar's sister) is mentioned in a problematic, much-amended part of the manuscript; Eliason advises against contriving an emendation for her name based on two considerations: the poet's "usual avoidance of women's names and his apparent unconcern about daughters."[19] Hygelac's only daughter is given to Eofor, slayer of Ongentheow, as reward for his battle prowess, along with land and rings (2993–97). Ongentheow's wife is shuttled back and forth in the battle between the Geats and the Swedes; a nameless Geatish woman mourns at the end of the poem. And, finally, there is Grendel's unnamed mother; barely identifiable as human, she also makes a doubtful female: *Ðæra oðer wæs, / þæs þe hie gewislicost gewitan meahton, / idese onlicnes* (1349–51, one of them was, to the extent that they were able to make out with any certainty, in the likeness of a woman). Her son, too, is a doubtful male, not just because of his monstrous appearance but also because the human community don't know who his father is (*no hie fæder cunnon*, 1355). (The poet, of course, identifies them both as the misshapen progeny of Cain, 1265–66). The certainty of maternity, overwhelming in the case of this outraged dam, will not suffice to inscribe Grendel into the patriarchal symbolic order prevailing in the Danish court.

These fatherless monsters and nameless women have no place, no condition for entry into the symbolic order at the most literal level; the process of exclusion, moreover, operates with increasing complexity in the case of those named queens who speak and act, who have, ostensibly, a role to play in the poem. Acquiring a "place" through marriage does not guarantee identification; in fact, it can be a major force for exclusion. Fred Robinson has noted the absence of "love" or "romantic passion between the sexes" in *Beowulf,* and throughout most Old English poetry. The secondary nature of the emotional marital bond provides a possible explanation for the hero's apparent celibacy: while scholars have pondered Beowulf's marital status, or lack thereof, Robinson suggests that the poet might simply have considered "that Beowulf's marital status was of insufficient interest to warrant mention in the poem."[20] While we have no way of guessing at Beowulf's sexuality, or at the poet's or the hero's personal views on marriage, we cannot ignore the strength of expressed masculine desire in the poem. Intensity and passion are located in the bonds of loyalty and friendship forged between men, and marriage is valued as an extension of this larger emotional context. In *Beowulf* the marriage alliance is essentially an alliance of men; Deleuze and Guattari identify "the perverse tie of a primary homosexuality," a love of, even an obsession with the "same" as a means of avoidance of the other, in tribal negotiation for marriage partners: "Through women, men establish their own connections; through the man-woman disjunction, which is always the outcome of filiation, alliance places in connection men from different filiations."[21] That such filiation often fails in *Beowulf* as a result of incessant feuding does not change the fact that the woman given in marriage is perceived as the visible token of male alliance.

The role of "peace-weaver" is one of the most critically discussed roles for women in *Beowulf* and elsewhere in Old English poetry; it is also one of the most problematic, and I shall take it up at greater length in my discussion of Hildeburh. Here I want to emphasize that the most outstanding characteristic of the peace-weaver, especially as we see her in *Beowulf,* is her inevitable failure to *be* a peace-weaver; the task is never accomplished, the role is never fully assumed, the woman is never identified. The system of masculine alliance allows women to signify in a system of apparent exchange but does not allow them signification in their own right, that is, outside the system of signification; they must be continually translated by and into the binary language of the prevailing masculine symbolic order. It is, as we shall see, an essentially untenable position, predicated on absence; but it also breeds paradox, a major means of deflecting/redirecting desire away from death.

As peace-weavers, women enact *and* embody the process of weaving, they weave and are woven by the ties of kinship. The identification of women with the kinship system is made clear by a linguistic equation; James W. Earl points out that the "terms most used to denote these kindreds in Old English are *mæg* and *mægth,* which, not coincidentally, are homonymous if not identical with the words for 'woman.'" Earl also suggests that women as embodiments of kinship are simultaneously identified with its opposite, as "the warrior class . . . identified the prime source of internal violence as the kinship system and so justified its attack on the kindred."[22] Earl's Freudian argument, which develops the opposition of women/kinship/family to the masculine business of civilization, demonstrates the cultural process by which women become "other,"[23] underscoring the weaver's paradoxical complicity in the destruction of the web.

Enacting the ties of kinship, weaving the web of peace in *Beowulf* is a task of infinite regression, a never-ending process which finds an apt analogy in Derrida's concept of *différance.* In fact Derrida chooses the metaphor of weaving to describe the play of meaning and infinite substitution that is *différance*,[24] and provides a striking point of connection between post-modern and Anglo-Saxon modes of representation. The structure of the web allows a multiplicity of convergences and divergences, and invokes both movement and potential. The web of *différance*, like the peace-weaver's, involves the dual attributes of deferral and absence of resolution, and the attendant presence of a multitude of possibilities, a state of infinite potential. Taking the side of possibility and preferring to see this open-ended "glass" as half-full, I shall argue that these women weavers serve potential; they extend and revalue the multidirectionality of the web.

The women in *Beowulf*, whether illegitimate monsters or pedigreed peaceweaving queens, are all marginal, excluded figures; they resemble, to differing extents, the figure of the "hysteric" as this is employed by Cixous and Clément in their considerably expanded and revalued definition of Freud's term. The hysteric is one of society's anomalies, one of the "abnormal ones," a category encompassing "madmen, deviants, neurotics, women, drifters, jugglers, tumblers" (9), those who fall into the cracks of the symbolic system; to this list we could easily add monsters and heroes, especially if we recall the double sense of *wrecca* in *Beowulf* as "exile" and "hero." Their alienated status allows and invites society to make special demands on these anomalous individuals: in Levi-Strauss's terms, "the group asks and even compels these people to represent certain forms of compromise, unrealizable on the collective level, to simulate imaginary transitions, to embody incompatible syntheses." Women, in particular, are "all decked-out" in such contradictions: "more than any others, women bizarrely embody this group of anomalies showing the cracks in an overall system."[25] The hysteric's essential quality is that of ambiguity: is she a heroine or victim, does she dismantle or reinforce the structures that contain her? Throughout *The Newly Born Woman* (*La Jeune Née*), Cixous and Clément conduct a dialogue of definition which is not, cannot be resolved; Cixous asserts that "the hysteric, with her way of questioning others . . . is, to my eyes, the typical woman in all her force . . . a force capable of demolishing those structures" (154). Clément agrees that the voice of the hysteric "introduces dissension, but it doesn't explode anything at all"; it can never bring about change in the symbolic order. But the presence of the hysteric demands a continual confrontation with unresolvable ambiguity: "there is no place for the hysteric; she cannot be placed or take place. Hysteria is necessarily an element that disturbs arrangements" (156).

I want to suggest that in differing degrees of intensity the women of *Beowulf* provide such a disturbance, and that we can find in them the revalued feminist sense of the term "hysteria" as an affirmation of energy and potential. While they do not figure in, let alone overturn, the symbolic order in the poem, they embody Kristeva's "impossible dialectic," an insistent paradox that is part of the poem's affinity with life, and its eventual rejection of desire as death.

CRITICAL VOICES

Characterizing the women of *Beowulf* as hysterics not only allies them with ambiguity, but is also a means of avoiding a reductive critical approach. Before examining the "hysterical" potential of some of the poem's female characters, and their capacity to disrupt its binary dynamic, it would be customary and informative to look at some other critical views of women in *Beowulf* and in Old English poetry as a whole. But in this case it is also important to my argument to look at the operation of desire outside the narrative and to ask what critics want from this poem.[26] There has been a perhaps equally overwhelming binarism coming from without the poem. The push for definition and resolution, often resulting in reductive either/or classification, has in the past been reflected with most alarming clarity and rigidity in critical assessments of women, not only in *Beowulf,* but in Old English poetry in general.[27]

Following an examination of his initial generalization that "the women of Anglo-Saxon secular poetry endure something more than their rightful share of discomfort," Alain Renoir postulates the "existence of a tradition of suffering women," which gives rise to a degree of expectation on the part of the audience and compliance on the part of the poet. In other words, female suffering and passivity are forms of poetic givens, and the more or less casual nature of their acceptance is well described by Renoir's analogy:

> The principle invoked here is the same which applies to ethnic jokes in modern America: though the members of a given audience may never have been directly exposed to this particular brand of entertainment before, enough of them will have heard about it to lead the others tacitly into expecting the humor to be at the expense of some ethnic group and responding accordingly.[28]

Renoir posits one extreme, that of the passive, suffering victim, as the female norm in secular poetry,[29] and it is a critical view that has been developed in a variety of ways. Anne Klinck looks at several secular and Christian poems and finds "a definite pattern traceable through Old English poetry," in which "the female character is confined and restricted," literally, emotionally, and by convention. Klinck manages to transform this rather gruesome state of affairs into a happy, artistic accident; passivity is productive psychological material as one form of exploitation spawns another:

> Women characters can be exploited in subtler and more searching ways than male characters in the conventional heroic situations. Simply because women are debarred from action, their position becomes psychologically more interesting, . . . Because the poets are treating an area not provided for in the poetic conventions, they are forced back upon observation and intuition instead of literary precedent.[30]

Klinck makes a virtue out of what is perceived as a necessity, and discovers poetic virtue and vitality in the norm of female passivity. Elaine Tuttle Hansen takes yet another compensatory approach and emphasizes the moral function of this inevitable and pitiable, but nonetheless educational, passivity. She asserts that one of the aspects of the Germanic woman most emphasized in poetic tradition is her "greater share in human suffering and anguish," but that this extreme has a moral implication. In *Beowulf,* there is a "dramatic contrast between the feminine ideal, a civilizing, ordering force, and the underlying weakness of woman's moral and social powers in the face of the irrepressible evils in man and his society."[31] If female suffering functions as a moral directive on the one hand, it is also seen as totally ineffective on the other: one form of passivity spawns another.

No one can deny that women and, indeed, men suffer a great deal in Old English poetry. What I am objecting to in these arguments is the basic conceptual assumption of woman as passive, suffering victim which is then placed in binary opposition to, and measured against, male aggressivity. Men are violent, women are weak; the other is always destroyed, literal death or the closure of desire-as-appropriation will always prevail. This denies the power of the hysteric and the vitality of the poetry, especially of *Beowulf.* Many, perhaps all, of the women in *Beowulf* do not qualify as "civilizing, ordering" forces in the sense that they cannot be defined or even perceived in contrast to the masculine economy that negates them; they resist simple definition by contrast, by means of opposition. This point is made curiously clear in the case of Old English Christian poems, where the woman "disappears" completely, leaving no trace even in paradox.

The female saints and martyrs of the Christian poems are often seen as active rather than passive, their suffering transformed into an aggressive triumph: "for the first time we meet females who do not suffer as symbols of man's impotence in the face of *wyrd,* but who are triumphant saints and heroes fighting for the true faith and thus empowered to overcome the limitations of both their sex and their unaided mortality."[32] The almost ghoulish aspect of the series of distortions/contortions involved here is hinted at by Renoir; his generalization about secular female misery does not apply to this set of women: "There, the opposite principle applies more often than not, so that we may find a Juliana's disposition 'greatly cheered' (*micclum geblissad*) at the prospect of her own demise."[33] Desire for death, desire as death, annihilates these saintly women.

Jane Chance has demonstrated the ways in which both the heroic status and Christian approbation of women are absolutely attendant upon chastity: "The protagonists of the religious epics—Juliana, Judith, Elene—exemplify degrees of chastity from pure virginity (Juliana) to chaste widowhood (Judith) and chaste conjugality (Elene). Each illustrates heroic behavior through sanctity";[34] one becomes a condition for the other. This principle extends well beyond the poetry to the public domain. Women with public positions and political power, of whom there were a considerable number in the Anglo-Saxon period,[35] were "permitted an active political role in kingdoms as chaste rulers or strong abbesses, and some became saints who were even allowed to adopt heroic behavior (even masculine clothing) once their chastity and sanctity had been attested." Women who attempted to use power in any way without this "'armor' . . . were usually castigated as lascivious, immoral, and even diabolic."[36] The premise at work here is apparent; the escape from passivity may only be accomplished by a denial of sexuality, an obliteration of femininity. Chance's study makes this point clear, but the critical view of Christian women as aggressive, triumphant, or somehow vindicated overlooks the patristic invention of necessity for their absence (i.e. Eve as responsible for evil), and glosses over their complicity in their own disappearance. It reaffirms either/or binarism, while simply reconfiguring its elements: women may be not-weak as long as they are not-women.

Whether or not the patristic view of the evil of women leads eventually to their legal and social decline later in the Anglo-Saxon period, as some recent historians have suggested,[37] it does guarantee their very literal effacement in much of the Christian poetry. But the spectre of denied or repressed sexuality does not haunt the secular poetry with such finality and drastic oversimplification. A "trace," in Derrida's terms, of the woman (or woman *as* trace) may still be discovered, provided that one is prepared to find it through absence, and in the play of paradox: "the trace is not a presence but is rather a simulacrum of a presence that dislocates, displaces, and refers beyond itself. The trace has, properly speaking, no place, for effacement belongs to the very structure of the trace."[38] We can identify the trace of the women of *Beowulf* in this continual process of effacement ("one tracks down tracks"[39]), the very process denied those saints and martyrs, whose hysteric potential is absorbed and ratified, and who are so far assimilated into the patriarchal, Christian, symbolic order that they leave no trace whatsoever.

One other critical voice merits attention: that which seeks to reexamine the assumption of female passivity in the secular poetry. There have been several recent attempts to create a different context for the discussion of women and women's roles,[40] including Helen Damico's *Beowulf's Wealhtheow and the Valkyrie Tradition*. Rejecting traditional critical views of Wealhtheow as a tragic or ironic victim, idealized queen or ornamental figure, Damico argues for the literality of her position as a powerful political force in the poem; she identifies *Beowulf's* most important female as a valkyrie figure, and marshals historical and textual evidence to support her claim. This argument is initially attractive because it acknowledges and validates the sense one has of the power and enigmatic presence of this woman, the only one who actually speaks in the poem. Damico allows her the menacing, ambiguous authority of the valkyrie, the chooser of the slain and cup-bearer to the Gods; she interprets Beowulf and Wealhtheow's meeting in the Danish court as "the archetypal first encounter between a valkyrie and a hero."[41] In true valkyrie fashion, Wealhtheow charges the hero with his heroic destiny when she offers him the cup, and fulfills her own desire at the same time. She incites the hero to his own possible death in order to help him forge his heroic "immortal" identity.

Damico's interesting argument, to which I shall return in my own discussion of Wealhtheow, nonetheless raises some difficult questions. There is a reactionary backlash inherent in some aspects of this vision of the queen. Is Wealhtheow's power truly active and self-generated? The valkyrie offers death, embodies contact with death; her semi-religious, priestess function gives her tremendous power as the repository of men's fears and ambivalence. She represents a kind of "making holy" or mythologizing of the code of violence, self-destruction and desire-as-appropriation, and also provides an external focus for ambivalence; as death fulfills her own desire as well as that of the hero, she may be blamed or praised, despised or adored, feared or welcomed. The valkyrie essentially *participates* in the death-centred, male definition of power, and is finally a vehicle for its consummation—another variety of victim, another version of woman as death-and-salvation for men, another assimilated hysteric.

Renoir's vision of pathetic, inevitable female passivity may appear to contrast with Damico's vision of menacing, semi-religious power, but both views are subsumed by the premise of passivity on a much broader scale: that is, female participation in male, death-centred desire. Although the ambiguity of the valkyrie figure makes it difficult to net her in simple opposition, to claim conclusively or confidently that she is either/or, my point is finally whether or not she must be netted, or allowed to escape the limitations of binary definition. Whether or not ambiguity may be tolerated, even affirmed, as a condition for "tracing" Wealhtheow and her counterparts in *Beowulf* will be central to the following discussions. I shall limit my discussion to just three of the women in the poem, chosen for the variety and degree of disturbance they provide in their roles as hysterics. The profoundly silent Hildeburh is an interesting counterpart to the language-wielding Wealhtheow; both offer individual versions of hysteria as well as illuminating each other's function in the poem. Much of what can be said about these two women may also apply by implication to the poem's other human females, who are mentioned only in passing by the poet. I have chosen not to discuss Grendel's mother separately precisely because she is not quite human, or, rather, she has her own particular brand of otherness; her inhuman affiliation and propensities make it hard to distinguish between what is monstrous and what is female—an interesting complication, but one beyond the scope of my present argument. My third choice is Modthryth, the brevity of whose appearance in the poem is in surprising contrast to the extent and impact of her hysterical contribution.

THE HELENIZATION OF HILDEBURH

Queen Hildeburh, whom Renoir calls "by far the most unfortunate human being in *Beowulf*,"[42] is a victim *par excellence,* but her presence serves to indict the system which ostensibly champions her as its cause, and to expose its paradoxical demands. She has much in common with the legendary Helen as the designated female focal point of a masculine system of exchange, or more accurately, of appropriation:

> Men say that it is for her that the Greeks launched a thousand ships, destroyed, killed, waged a fabulous war for ten-times-ten years— among men! For the sake of her, yonder, the idol, carried off, hidden, lost. Because it is for-her and without-her that they live it up at the celebration of death that they call their life.[43]

Hildeburh's story is told to the Danish court by Hrothgar's scop, as part of the "entertainment in the hall" (*healgamen,* 1066) following Beo-

wulf's first victory over the monster Grendel. She is married to Finn, a
Frisian king, as a pledge of peace between Frisians and Danes. When her
brother Hnæf comes to visit her (or possibly to look for trouble) at
Finn's court, a fight breaks out and he is killed, along with her son by
Finn. In the next round of fighting, led by Hengest, Hnæf's faithful
retainer who cannot rest until he avenges the death of his lord, Finn is
killed off, and the sorrowful queen hauled victoriously back across the
sea to her people along with other prizes of treasure and war spoils.
Queen loses all. This is her story in a nutshell, though the poet's
narrative technique is a key factor in explaining its powerful, psychological effect.[44]

In the Finn episode Hildeburh has nothing to say; we hear the echo,
or follow the trace, of her speech when we are told that she gave the
order for her son to be burned on the same funeral pyre as her brother
(1114–16), and that she lamented with songs (*geomrode giddum,* 1118) as
the smoke wound upwards. Both gestures may seem to associate her
with passivity and/or death; one is a kind of acquiescence to the equa-
nimity of its embrace, the other connects her directly to the nameless
Geatish woman who laments with mournful song (*giomorgyd,* 3150) as
the smoke rises from Beowulf's pyre at the end of the poem. She thus
participates in a scarcely interrupted dirge of female sorrow and impotence. In addition to the loss of husband, brother, son and home,
Chance asserts that she also mourns her own failure, heaping self-blame
upon impotence in a positive conundrum of death and defeat:

> all she does, this sad woman, is to mourn her loss with dirges . . . In
> fact, she can do nothing, caught in the very web she has woven as
> peace pledge . . . the peace pledge must accept a passive role precisely
> because the ties she knots bind her—she *is* the knot, the pledge of
> peace. Her fate interlaces with that of her husband and brothers
> through her role as a mother bearing a son: thus Hildeburh appropri-
> ately mourns the loss of her symbolic tie at the pyre, the failure of her
> self as peace pledge, the loss of her identity. (100)

Chance's assessment of Hildeburh's situation may be at odds with a
point she stresses elsewhere—that of the basic untenability of the role of
peace-weaver—as well as overlooking the fact that Hildeburh cannot
lose an identity she never possessed in the first place.

Peace-weavers are assigned the role of creating peace, in fact, embodying peace, in a culture where war and death are privileged values.
Female failure is built into this system, as Chance clearly demonstrates
in an ostensibly different context. In her discussion of Eve in *Genesis B,*
Chance rationalizes her failure to withstand temptation on grounds that
resemble the recent sociolinguistic notion of "trained incapacity" in

female language use.[45] Satan represents eating the apple to Eve as part of an attempt to make peace between God and Adam, to avert the enmity between them which would ensue if Adam disobeys Satan, who poses as God's retainer. When Eve finally agrees, she is accepting her role as peace-weaver. "Thus Eve fails here not because she is unintelligent or inferior to Adam but because she has not been trained to resist, to fight, to remain strong against an adversary, and because this 'best of women' in an Anglo-Saxon society would have been trained instead to concede, to ameliorate, to harmonize."[46]

One of the less publicized but perhaps equally dire results of Eve's peace-weaving is that she persists in trying to assume the role, to do the impossible; later in the poem she weaves clothing for the naked pair, an act which prefigures the "heavenly weaving," or intercession, of the Virgin Mary. Eve, the Virgin Mary and the Germanic woman are all located in a continuum of perpetual aspiration to fulfill the role of peace-weaver; the Virgin's relative success may spur on "the peace-weaver who has failed but who will continue in succeeding centuries to toil for peace between family members and between tribes, weaving through words and offspring what the First Peace-weaver attempted through her disobedient eating of the fruit and her later weaving of leaves into suitable covering for the pair."[47] This sweeping vision of female failure[48] through the ages to come bears an uncanny obverse resemblance to Milton's prophesy concerning female "perverseness" in *Paradise Lost,* "Which infinite calamity shall cause to human life, and household peace confound" (10. 908–09).

Perversity is certainly one of the key elements in Hildeburh's situation, and is not unrelated to paradox. The inevitable failure and essential untenability of her female role is even affirmed by the hero himself. When he returns to Hygelac's court, Beowulf tells his lord of Hrothgar's attempt to make peace with the Heathobards by marrying his daughter Freawaru to Ingeld, prince of the Heathobards (2020–69). Beowulf constructs a scenario, visualizes the details of Freawaru's failure: at a scene of feasting in the hall presided over by the young couple, an old Heathobard warrior will become incensed at the sight of a young Dane flaunting battle gear stripped from dead Heathobard warriors; the old man cannot rest until Freawaru's thane (*se fæmnan þegn,* 2059) is dead, and the feud is renewed. Such bitter hatred, comments Beowulf, is bound to diminish Ingeld's love for his bride: *ond him wiflufan / æfter cearwælmum colran weorðað* (and his love for his wife, through such seethings of sorrow, will become cooler, 2065–66). Moreover, Beowulf generalizes, feuds are seldom settled by peace-weaving, whatever the individual worth of the woman involved: *þeah seo bryd duge!* (*however right the bride!* 2031. My italics, Klaeber's exclamation point).

Beowulf's story is interesting for several reasons. The sensitivity and accuracy of his understanding is remarkable in this scene as it is when he tells the story of his anguished grandfather, Hrethel. It is no small part of the poem's power and attraction that its hero is also a thinker, that he is polite (witness his tact with the Danish coastguard), and intelligent, (witness his strategic assessment of Grendel's method of attack), and that he suffers from recognizable neuroses (witness his wondering what he had done to deserve the scourge of the dragon). The most accomplished binarist in the poem (i.e. I will do "x" or I will die), Beowulf is also aware of the often agonizing circumstances of coming to a decision. This duality in the hero suggests some of his own potential as an hysteric; even as he functions as an epitome of the binary heroic standard, he is also calling it into question and pointing out its limitations.[49]

The hero himself is one of the most unsettling forces in the poem, and has long been recognized for the kinds of ambiguity he generates— about the value of pagan and Christian ideals or the value of treasure, for example. His power to disturb as an hysteric accrues throughout the poem; when Beowulf, the accomplished, one might say professional, binarist, finally chooses death fully understanding the terms of the choice, he calls attention to the illusion of choice and the illusion of the power of the subject to make it. Beowulf's barrow remains a profoundly ambiguous reminder of a life and a death. The important difference, however, between the hero as hysteric, and some of the women in the poem, is that he *does* choose death—unlike Hildeburh, or the nameless mourner who laments over the barrow.[50] He may question, disrupt or challenge the symbolic order, but eventually he opts for resolution. In this regard, he has something in common with Modthryth, who becomes, as we shall see, an assimilated hysteric—she rocks the boat, challenges the dominant symbolic order for a while, but then settles down. The hero's understanding of process must always culminate in resolution, the capacity for which is a condition of heroism in this binary, death-centred context, but the added complexity and hysterical potential of Beowulf's heroic character, while it is an unsettling force in its own right, also comments on the nature of binarism in the poem and women's paradoxical relation to it.

The hero's description and prophesy of Freawaru's failure is almost casually included in his account of his Danish adventures; it is one of those regular and regrettable facts of Germanic daily life, one which not only reveals the totality of female exclusion but diagrams the terms of their non-signification. The system of male alliance that negates Freawaru, Hildeburh *et al.* is one of appropriation, not exchange: "Desire knows nothing of exchange, *it knows only theft and gift,* at times the one within the other under the effect of a primary homosexuality."[51] The primary bond, in both social and emotional, and possibly sexual terms, is exclusively masculine, and therefore precludes any possibility of genuine exchange, which must take into account the other, the feminine, as an actual, realized entity. As these female peace-weavers are taken and given, stolen or discarded, their potential currency, their function, their power to signify is removed. I have argued that elsewhere in the poem there is a peculiar interchangeability of words, deeds and things,[52] but this flow of signification stops short of, or with, the women in the poem. The sword may recall the boast that may assure the deed; objects have an almost palpable presence. But even the gold adorning the queen will not translate *her*; it may point inevitably to renewed strife, that is, it may translate into war, into the currency of the masculine economy, but her meaning as peace-weaver is *untranslatable.* The "language" of women is not spoken here.

With this argument for the silence, the utter non-signification of the woman as peace-weaver, to some extent revealed and authorized by the hero himself, I return to the "unfortunate" Hildeburh. Her spectacular failure evokes far more than pity. Her silence and absence create an even more profound silence within the poem. Into the noisy merriment, the *sang and sweg* of Hrothgar's court, her story falls like a solitary pebble; the focus of the beginning, center and conclusion of the poet's song is the queen. She is immediately introduced by name, her father's name mentioned several lines later as a secondary means of identification. The story begins from her vantage point, and describes what she saw, what she may have thought and felt:

> Ne huru Hildeburh   herian þorfte
> Eotena treowe;   unsynnum wearð
> beloren leofum   æt þam lindplegan
> bearnum and broðrum;   hie on gebyrd hruron
> gare wunde;   þæt wæs geomuru ides!
> Nalles holinga   Hoces dohtor
> meotodsceaft bemearn,   syþðan morgen com,
> ða heo under swegle   geseon meahte
> morþorbealo maga,   þær heo ær mæste heold
> worolde wynne   (1071–80)

Indeed Hildeburh had no need to praise the good faith of the Jutes. Guiltlessly, she was deprived of her loved ones, son and brother, at the play of shields; they fell fated, wounded by the spear. That was a sad woman! Not without cause did Hoc's daughter lament the decree of fate when morning came, and she was able to see beneath the sky the slaughter of her kinsmen, where before she had held most of her worldly joy.

After the first round of fighting the poet returns to her, to report her gesture of conciliation, a kind of peace-weaving in the face of death—indeed, an affirmation of connection via death. Her affirmation of connection, of the ties of kinship, between the life-severed bodies of her kinsmen, prefigures the eventual paradox she embodies and exposes, and provides a reported trace of her presence as a weaver of *differance*. As she gives the command to burn her brother and son on the same pyre, she is identified by name; a few lines later, she has become a woman mourning (*Ides gnornode*, 1117), identifiable with the anonymous woman who mourns Beowulf's death. Following the second round of hostility, the poet concludes the song with a reference to Hildeburh, now a nameless queen among a list of war trophies, all of which are "ferried" (*feredon*, 1154, 1158) back to Denmark. But this time it is a completely passive image; we watch her as she is moved across the chessboard, given and then taken. She has become an object, like the precious swords and cups elsewhere in the poem; like these objects, she too is ambiguous, translated into the chain of signification as an emblem of both death and victory, but the woman has disappeared:

> Ða wæs heal roden
> feonda feorum, swilce Fin slægen,
> cyning on corþre, ond seo cwen numen.
> Sceotend Scyldinga to scypon feredon
> eal ingesteald eorðcyninges,
> swylce hie æt Finnes ham findan meahton
> sigla searogimma. Hie on sælade
> drihtlice wif to Denum feredon,
> læddon to leodum.   (1151–59)

Then the hall was stained with the life-blood of enemies, likewise Finn was slain, the king among his troop, and his queen taken. Scylding warriors brought to the ships all the house possessions of the king of the land, such jewels and treasures as they could find in Finn's home. They brought the noble woman on a sea-journey to the Danes, led her back to her people.

To her people? Who, or what are they? Hasn't the poet just described the annihilation of everyone that this woman has any real connection with? Although her "people" await her, we might suspect that Hildeburh has nowhere to go, no space or place to be. The poet's story has, in effect, chronicled the stages of her complete disappearance. She has become the figurehead Helen, whose war is waged "for-her and without-her." If silence may be said to resound, that is what happens at the end of this story. The idea or the image of Hildeburh exists only through our apprehension of her absence, who she is or was is only discernible as an echo or a "trace," which continually effaces itself. The silence at the end of her story is that of a kind of paralysis of understanding, a momentary point of standoff when the play of paradox is revealed. It is an uncomfortable silence for the reader (perhaps also for the Anglo-Saxon hearer), a silence that argues persuasively for permission for the other, that demands recognition of the "other" as brother or son or husband, as the closest of kin. The trace of Hildeburh does not lurk passively, as the vision of a failed peace-weaver impotently spinning and enmeshed in her own web of paradox; the silence she creates affronts, forces a confrontation with unresolvable ambiguity, *declares* paradox. This woman weaver, unlike the weaver in Freud's construct who weaves out of shame to conceal her own lack,[53] makes present the trace of the absence which is imposed upon her: *she images the lack which is defining her.* Her silence is actively experienced as an other desire which momentarily collapses the ever-forward momentum towards death of dominant desire; she serves other forms of movement and potential as she embodies and enacts the web of *differance*.

The Voice of Wealhtheow: Peace-Weaver in a Double Bind

Immediately following Hildeburh's silence we hear the voice of Wealhtheow, the only woman in the poem who actually speaks. It is initially tempting to set up a clear parallel between these two women: what one does with silence, the other does with words; both are hysterics who challenge the violent, death-centred, symbolic order that systematically negates them as women, queens, wives or mothers. The fact that Wealhtheow uses language, however, necessarily adds another dimension of ambiguity to the hysteric's already complex function. She, like Hildeburh, simultaneously enacts and embodies *differance,* but as a weaver who also uses words, she adds yet another layering to the play of difference. Moreover, in her attempt to use language against violence, Wealhtheow stands at one of the poem's most important crossroads, embodying the problematic dialectic of a major social transition.

As a non-signifying participant in both the masculine social order and the symbolic order of language, Wealhtheow's double negation engages not only the problematic of self, and of the feminine, but also that of language in the poem. Before looking at the queen's specific use of words, I want to examine briefly the context that engenders them and look at the poem's general relation to language. The world of *Beowulf* is poised between language and violence as systems of representation.

Following Paul Ricoeur, we can posit language initially and simplisti-
cally as the opposite of violence, as a means of both understanding and
controlling violence:

> It is for a being who speaks, who in speaking pursues meaning, who
> has already entered the discussion and who knows something about
> rationality that violence is or becomes a problem. Thus violence has
> its meaning in its other: language. And the same is true reciprocally.
> Speech, discussion, and rationality also draw their unity of meaning
> from the fact that they are an attempt to reduce violence.[54]

On this level, the poem continually examines the efficacy of language,
especially the making, breaking and keeping of oaths, which are the
means of developing cultural memory through words. Language provides a different means of remembrance, replacing the function of
violence, cruelty and spectacle, which, according to Nietzsche, forge
memory in a barbaric society: "there is perhaps nothing more terrible in
man's earliest history than his mnemotechnics . . . Whenever man has
thought it necessary to create a memory for himself, his effort has been
attended with torture, blood, sacrifice."[55]

While *Beowulf* does not contain some of the extremes that
Nietzsche cites as examples (castration, murder of first-born), there are
many reminders in the poem of the ongoing link between violence and
signification. We are never far from what Deleuze and Guattari, in their
development of Nietzsche's discussion, call the "inscription in the
flesh." Coexisting with the speech of the poem are literal signs: Grendel's claw wrenched from its socket and nailed to the gables of Heorot,
his head severed from his dead body by Beowulf and dragged by four
men back to Hrothgar's hall; Æschere's head displayed on the path to
Grendel's mere; everywhere a pile-up of bodies, nameless victims and
famous heroes; funeral pyres consuming the dead.

The poem embodies both literal and representational orders of
signification, a blending that has often been examined in terms of
religious transition, as the movement from paganism to Christianity;
that Hrothgar and the Danes may revert to heathen practices in troubled
times and also thank God for deliverance via Beowulf is just one
instance of such blending which has caused considerable critical debate
about where exactly the poem stands. But instead of getting caught up
in the telos of transition, I think that the poem requires us to maintain a
kind of double vision. Consider, for example, some well-known words
in the poem which blend the literal and representational within language. The conclusion of Hrothgar's famous "sermon" to Beowulf, one
of the most analyzed and sophisticated examples of speech in Old

English poetry as a whole, offers thanks to God for the gory sight of Grendel's head:

> Þæs sig Metode þanc,
> ecean Dryhtne, þæs ðe ic on aldre gebad,
> þæt ic on þone hafelan   heorodreorigne
> ofer eald gewin   eagum starige!   (1778–81)

Thanks be to God, eternal Lord, that I have lived to see, that after long-standing strife I might stare with my own eyes on that blood-stained head.

Within this most "civilized" of linguistic representations in the poem, we see that inscription in the flesh remains very much alive as a form of signification.

Deleuze and Guattari maintain that these literal signs do not betoken "some ill-defined or natural violence that might be commissioned to explain the history of mankind; cruelty is the movement of culture that is realized in bodies and inscribed on them"; and, moreover, reiterating Ricoeur's point, "it is this cruel system of inscribed signs that renders man capable of language, and gives him a memory of the spoken word."[56] This memory comes and goes in *Beowulf,* and makes for a fluid boundary between speech and act.

This fluidity, this co-existence of literal and representational sign-orders, of violence and language, forms part of the context of language use in general in the poem, and of female language use in particular. In the masculine, heroic mode, words must translate into actions; the hero's spoken boast achieves signification only in literal, or bodily inscription. Elsewhere, in the masculine economy of the poem, we see the tenuous hold of language, of oaths sworn, exploded by memory— perhaps in the visual shape of an ancestral sword—of past violence. To break or rearrange this chain of signification, words must entirely substitute for deeds, not merely translate them, and this is one of the ways in which Wealhtheow's words differ from others in the poem. The attempt to move from inscription in the flesh to inscription in language, from bodily to verbal representation, is best demonstrated by the words of this woman, which we hear in a dual context, from within and without the masculine economy. Wealhtheow's speeches are, at this initial level of my discussion of language, an exhortation to warriors to remember their words, a plea for language to prevail, to replace its opposite, violence.

"This formal opposition," Ricoeur goes on to state, "does not exhaust the problem, but only encircles with a thick line surrounding emptiness" (90). We can abstract the idea of discourse and oppose it to violence simply enough, but language in use, language as spoken, used

by speakers (and vice-versa), all present another version of the initial
problem of violence. That language itself may be a highly systemized
form of violence is now a familiar critical assumption. Foucault maintains that the movement from literal to representational inscription is
neither forward nor progressive:

> Humanity does not gradually progress from combat to combat until
> it arrives at universal reciprocity, where the rule of law finally replaces
> warfare; humanity installs each of its violences in a system of rules and
> thus proceeds from domination to domination.[57]

Locating the queen's words within this continuum, or syndrome, of
progressively generated, and institutionalized, rhetorical forms of violence is further complicated by gender. Whether language creates violence or violence creates language, de Lauretis argues that "both views of
the relation between rhetoric and violence contain and indeed depend
on the same representation of sexual difference" and that violence
becomes "engendered" in the process of its institutionalized representation.[58]

As we listen to Queen Wealhtheow assert the rule of language over
the rule of violence, we see her own double subjugation: she is manipu-
lated by the same rule of language that she seeks to assert, and as a
speaking woman she must use and be used by the language of the
masculine economy. Wealhtheow's speeches offer a demonstration of
the Lacanian assumption that language is our inscription into patriarchy; language embodies the Name-of-the-Father, or phallocentric Law,
and is the point at which we enter the Symbolic order. In Wealhtheow's
language we see violence speaking and spoken against.

The queen's language is particularly interesting because of the variety of ambiguities it causes to surface—all of which make her a formidable hysteric. As a spokeswoman for the power of language, she directs
desire away from literal death and speaks for desire as representation,
offering, affirming ambiguity by the rejection of resolution inherent in
language. As a female speaker, she is simultaneously anomalous and
assimilated by, subject to the masculine order of language. There is also
the possibility that she is creating a new possibility; as she scrambles the
circuits of language she may be speaking herself, "against the other and
against men's grammar." To take language and turn it on its head is the
only way, according to Cixous and Clément, that the woman speaker
may "blow up the Law" (95).

The complexity of Queen Wealhtheow's character and her function
in the poem—a complexity that begins with the ambiguous connotations of her name itself—have met with a variety of critical responses, all

of which have been well chronicled by Damico;[59] but, as I have pointed out earlier, these often result in a reductive either/or assessment. She is either a type of victim, whether tragic or ironic; an antitype of Grendel's monstrous mother and therefore understood through opposition; or more recently Damico casts her as an actively powerful valkyrie figure, who nonetheless has been bifurcated into two personalities. The queen represents the more acceptable, less overtly violent attributes of the valkyrie, while the poet "follows the customary portrayal of the valkyrie as a deadly battle-demon in his characterization of Grendel's mother" (46). The division of attributes is a means of dissipating the menace and ambivalence of these "sublime noblewomen" with whom Damico ranks Wealhtheow; a Christian poet, she points out, would have to handle the valkyrie figure with care (53). It may not be necessary, or even appropriate, however, to make a choice between these extremes, to define Wealhtheow by means of oppositions that she both encompasses and resists; instead, we can try to perceive how she might define herself, glimpsing the process through the mirror of her language.

Complementing the notion that language may be seen as an attempt to control, codify or even eliminate violence is the idea of a "speech community," a group of individuals who undertake a kind of social contract in their agreement that certain words will work in certain ways: or, in the words of J.L. Austin and John Searle, *their* saying makes it so. I am going to use the premise that language is performative to ask what actual overall relation language bears to the violent social reality of its speakers, and will borrow on occasion some terminology from speech act theory to ask what specific relation the words of the female speaker have to the reality of the speech community in *Beowulf.* I propose that there are roughly three levels on which words, or more properly speech acts, function in *Beowulf.* The first I call the "Beowulfian" mode, the grand, simple and often devastating equation of words with reality, where intention or boast is tantamount to deed or actuality: saying will indeed make it so. Beowulf forms a speech community of one, however; he is judge and jury. His heroism demands a degree of self-absorption that closes the social circuit of language; he creates his separate relation to reality.[60] The second level is more mundane, more attached to the world of personal and social interaction: words of greeting, explaining, expressing gratitude or emotion, words of daily communication. (Beowulf is quite capable of using words in these ways as well). Oaths and promises and marriage vows fall into this category also, although they represent more serious, public versions of commitment to an agreed-upon code of social interaction.

The third level on which speech acts function, which is my present concern, is a form of opposite of the first: a level of failure where language is subsumed, overtaken by action, where violence breaks the linguistic social contract, where the connection of language to reality is shown to be tenuous, fragile and fraught with complexity. This is also the level at which desire as representation provides the initiation into ambiguity, and forces an acknowledgment of the violent potential of language. There are few "speakers" at this level in the poem. Hildeburh belongs here, a mute witness to the failure of marriage vows and oaths of peace. At this level we might also place the wordless sorrowing noise, a garbled parody of language, produced by the female mourners of the poem—Grendel's less-than-human mother included. The primary speaker for this third level is Queen Wealhtheow, who makes two formal, public speeches at the banquet in honor of Beowulf's first victory. These speeches, it is important to remember, follow immediately upon the "entertainment" of the story of Finn and Hildeburh: one queen takes up in language what the other had left in silence.

The Queen's first speech is addressed to her husband, in the presence of her two sons, Hrethric and Hrothmund, the visiting hero who is sitting next to them, her nephew Hrothulf, and the entire Danish court. The second is an equally public address to Beowulf. Dividing the speeches is the story of the valuable neck-ring that she gives to Beowulf, an account of its past and a depressing glimpse into its future, when it will be worn by Hygelac on his death-raid. I quote both speeches in full in order to examine the succession of ideas and the success or otherwise of her words as speech acts:

> 'Onfoh þissum fulle, freodrihten min,
> sinces brytta! Þu on sælum wes,
> goldwine gumena, ond to Geatum spræc
> mildum wordum, swa sceal man don!
> Beo wið Geatas glæd, geofena gemyndig,
> nean ond feorran þu nu hafast.
> Me man sægde, þæt þu ðe for sunu wolde
> hererinc habban. Heorot is gefælsod,
> beahsele beorhta; bruc þenden þu mote
> manigra medo, ond þinum magum læf
> folc ond rice þonne ðu forð scyle,
> metodsceaft seon. Ic minne can
> glædne Hroþulf, þæt he þa geogoðe wile
> arum healdan, gyf þu ær þonne he,
> wine Scildinga, worold oflætest;
> wene ic þæt he mid gode gyldan wille
> uncran eaferan, gif he þæt eal gemon,

hwæt wit to willan   ond to worðmyndum
umborwesendum ær   arna gefremedon.'

(1169–87)

'Accept this cup, my dear lord, giver of treasure! Be happy now,
goldfriend of men, and to the Geats speak with kind words, as a man
should do! Be gracious to the Geats, mindful of gifts that you now
possess from near and far. I have heard that you would have this
warrior for a son. Heorot, bright ring-hall, is cleansed; make use of
many rewards while you can, and to your own sons leave folk and
kingdom, when you shall go forth to see death. I know my gracious
Hrothulf, that he will hold these youths in honor, if you, friend of the
Scyldings, forsake this world before he does; I expect that he will
repay our sons with goodness, if he remembers all the kindnesses we
performed for his pleasure and honor when he was growing up.'

'Bruc ðisses beages,   Beowulf leofa,
hyse, mid hæle,   ond þisses hrægles neot,
þeodgestreona,   ond geþeoh tela,
cen þec mid cræfte,   ond þyssum cnyhtum wes
lara liðe!   Ic þe þæs lean geman.
Hafast þu gefered,   þæt ðe feor ond neah
ealne wideferhþ   weras ehtigað,
efne swa side   swa sæ bebugeð,
windgeard, weallas,   Wes þenden þu lifige,
æþeling, eadig!   Ic þe an tela
sincgestreona.   Beo þu suna minum
dædum gedefe,   dreamhealdende!
Her is æghwylc eorl   oþrum getrywe,
modes milde,   mandrihtne hold,
þegnas syndon geþwære,   þeod ealgearo,
druncne dryhtguman   doð swa ic bidde.'

(1216–31)

'Enjoy this neck-ring with safety, Beowulf, beloved youth, and make
use of this corselet, of our people's treasure; prosper well, declare
yourself with strength, and be kind of counsel to these youths. I shall
remember to reward you for that. You have brought it about that
men shall praise you from far and near for a long time to come, even
as far as the sea, home of the winds, encompasses the walls of the
shore. Be blessed, prince, while you live. I wish you well of your
treasure. Be kind in deeds to my sons, happy man. Here every
nobleman is true to the other, mild of heart, loyal to his lord; the
thanes are united, the people willing; the wine-drinking warriors do
as I bid.'

Both speeches offer a dense array of contradictions. Carmen Cramer
argues that the queen's language is "more commanding and authoritar-

ian, even as she displays proper and gracious feminine courtesy, than Hrothgar's. When Wealhtheow addresses her lord (1169–1185), she uses five imperatives." The general tone and style of Wealhtheow's language are more reminiscent of Beowulf's: "Wealhtheow, like the active Beowulf and unlike the rather passive Hrothgar, speaks in the present and future tenses . . . only twice in her two first speeches does she talk about the past; she is a person oriented to the active present."[61] While all of these observations are accurate, the speech of the hero and the queen differ in at least one important respect. Despite the occasionally uncertain tone of Beowulf's last speeches, Charles McNally, in his detailed analysis of all the hero's speeches, concludes that "the speech acts the main character of the epic performs throughout are primarily those of commitment: promises, intentions, boasts, all of which he sincerely delivers and carries out" (191). With the possible exception of her promise to reward Beowulf (1220), Wealhtheow's language is noticeably devoid of commissives, "those illocutionary acts whose point is to commit the speaker (again in some varying degrees) to some future course of action."[62] It would overstep the poem's bounds of congruity and possibility for a female speaker to commit an essentially nonexistent self—one which is outside the chain of signification—to a course of action. For the most part, she tries to get others to do things, or represents the conditions of her world as she observes them, not as she creates them. In language, as elsewhere in the poem, she must be translated into the terms of the masculine economy; obliged to speak herself through others, she must choose different varieties of speech acts.

In his analysis of the illocutionary point of all speech acts,[63] Searle introduces the dimension of "direction of fit," whether the speaker is trying to match the world to words or words to world, and the notion that the sincerity condition of any speech act must be located along a spectrum of psychological states; both concepts are useful in mapping out the complexity and ambiguity of the queen's speeches. When Wealhtheow uses directives (speech acts which try to move others to do something),[64] which she does a great deal, we have the difficult task of assessing where to place her along a spectrum ranging from pleading to commanding, and just how assured or desperate is the desire to make the world match her words. She begins her first speech by telling the king, in imperative form, to accept the cup from her and rejoice in his present happiness, but then attempts to undo her husband's past words by a kind of public admonition or embarrassment. Her exhortation to the king to do what is proper calls attention to his previous impropriety: his excessively generous offer to adopt Beowulf as his son when he already has two of his own. The public, ceremonial context of her words is a reminder of the power of the linguistic social contract and the law it upholds, and by her measured words she seeks to negate her husband's rash promise.

In the first part of her speech to Beowulf, she also makes skilful use of the ceremonial context, and her own formal role as cup-bearer and treasure dispenser, to extract a promise from the hero, summoning ritual to the aid of language. In her address to both husband and hero, she subjugates objects—drinking cup and treasures—to the rule of language. She tries to translate and confine their function to the representative domain of language, arrogating their previous translatability into literal signification. Indeed this cup-bearing scene may be visualized as a wonderfully complex enactment and embodiment of the weaving of *différance*. As the peace-weaver who is herself the representation and embodiment of her function, Wealhtheow physically draws lines of connection, enacts the process of weaving, as she carries the cup from one warrior to another. This literal and representational weaving resonates in her language, where the play of her own absence and presence continues to present, to represent, the echo or trace of her presence. This woman speaker trespasses in language as she is also trespassing in the masculine warrior stronghold of the hall—the "natural" invades the "cultural," or the women's world of the hut intrudes into the masculine domain of the hall in Earl's Freudian terms[65]—but only to turn this opposition into paradox. Her presence, her actions, and her words betoken connection, but at the same time they diagram an ongoing dialectic of separation and connection. The weaver, the activity of weaving and the web itself move continually in and out of focus in the play of levels of representation and layers of inconclusive, unresolvable ambiguity.

But I am getting ahead of myself here in anticipating the total ambiguity of her words; let me return to specific levels of its operation. Her persistent use of the imperative in the first part of both speeches appears to assert the rule of language. The formal or ceremonial directive "accept this cup" is paralleled to her directive to her husband to do what a man should do, to use kind—and appropriate—words to the Geats, and then to do what perhaps should appear obvious: leave the kingdom to its rightful inheritors. When she rewards the hero with ceremonial propriety, she aligns and publicly identifies the gifts of treasure with a future commitment on Beowulf's part to her young sons. This identification is further cemented by the one commissive Wealhtheow uses; she tells Beowulf that she will reward him in the future, asserting her power to do, to act, in the only way appropriate or permitted to her. The queen uses all the kinds of ammunition, actual and representational, that she has. Her language parallels, assumes ritual. But is the queen pleading or commanding? At what point does she believe the world will match her words, or even that language itself will control the violence which continually threatens her world?

Her imperative directives to enjoy and be happy are accompanied in both speeches by a conditional "while you now possess" (1174), "while you can" (1177), or "while you live" (1224), generating a free-floating temporal precariousness easily applicable to both the queen and her audience. Whether Wealhtheow is rather assuredly and urbanely reminding both the old king and the young hero of their mortality, or whether she is "a very worried mother in a very fragile world"[66] is difficult to determine. What the queen may or may not believe is entirely a matter of opinion. Her observations of her world are expressed in representatives, speech acts which, in Searle's words, "commit the speaker (in varying degrees) to something's being the case, to the truth of the expressed proposition" (10) Representatives also necessarily involve difficult and subtle decisions about sincerity conditions and psychological state, as Searle makes clear:

> The direction of fit is words to the world; the psychological state expressed is Belief (that p). It is important to emphasize that words such as 'belief' and 'commit' are here intended to mark dimensions. . . . Thus there is a difference between *suggesting* that p or *Putting it forward as a hypothesis* that p on the one hand and *insisting* that p or *solemnly swearing* that p on the other. The degree of belief and commitment may approach or even reach zero. . . . The simplest test of a representative is this: can you literally characterize it (*inter alia*) as true or false (10–11).

When the queen says that she knows her nephew will treat her sons well if their father dies before him, is she representing what she believes to be the truth? What is her degree of commitment to her own words, to the effective power of the language she wields against the violence that always seems to be imminent?

Analyzing the truth value of representatives is to some degree another way of talking about irony. The audience already knows, because the poet has already told them, that bad faith between Hrothulf and Hrothgar will erupt in the future (1018–19); also, we know very early in the poem that Hrothgar's great hall is destined to be burned down as a result of the Danish-Heathobard feud that Hrothgar is trying to patch up by using his daughter as a peace-weaver (81–85). But the queen does not have this overview. One could claim that the plain reality of reasonable expectation would undercut considerably the truth value of her statement regarding her nephew: "anyone who does not hear anxiety in Wealhtheow's speech about how Hrothulf will act towards her offspring," Robinson insists, "must think that Mark Anthony genuinely believes Caesar's murderers to be honorable men."[67] The audience and the queen would be foolish and naive not to expect the worst. The story of Hildeburh is no mere parable. The tenuous hold of language is well attested in the world of the poem, and in the queen's context especially. As she represents her view of her nephew and his future actions, the direction of fit becomes problematic; the simply representative coexists in tension with its opposite; these words are also an attempt to organize the world to match *them*, and the sincerity condition of belief is necessarily attenuated.

A similar situation arises at the end of her second speech when Wealhtheow represents her view of the harmony of the Danish court. Is she insisting, hypothesizing, or using a representative to express a covert directive, i.e. lying? Damico asserts that "the queen states unambiguously that the warriors in the hall pay her homage and obedience," rejecting the possibility of dramatic or tragic irony in this speech.[68] Military power is consistent with an autonomous warrior-woman image, which Damico argues is an important facet of Wealhtheow's compound personality as a valkyrie figure. Damico interprets the queen's words as authoritative and literal.[69] Others read this part of the speech quite differently. Given the poetic tradition of women as passive, suffering victims, "one may surely be excused for detecting the hint of a pathetic ring in her attempt at clinching her request (to Beowulf) with the assertion that the warriors in the hall always do her bidding."[70]

It may be impossible to determine the truth value of these representations, or what the queen actually believes. Larry M. Sklute thinks that her words are important and influential but somehow out of her control, as "she herself may not realize fully the implications of her admonitions."[71] Bernice W. Kliman does not even identify the woman with the words; she characterizes both of the queen's speeches as a series of "disjointed statements unconnected to any request or demand of her own." Kliman also suggests that "the argument by juxtaposition leaves the connections to be made by her husband."[72] But instead of trying to figure the queen out, or to pin her down, perhaps it is more useful to evaluate her words as an affirmation of the rule of representation. She is claiming the attention and invoking the rules of her speech community, holding up for public inspection the linguistic promises that the community has made to itself.

The domain of representation, however, opens up, even necessitates, a multitude of possibilities; in affirming the rule of language, Wealhtheow also affirms ambiguity and escapes definition. The queen may be

a consummate politician, able to manipulate her husband and Beowulf
with her verbal skill, engaging language to do the work of coercion and
therefore co-opted by the masculine economy; she may be a desperate
woman afraid for herself and her children, naively using words to stave
off violence; she may be a dignified, self-confident noblewoman who
believes in the civilizing, ordering power of language, unaware of its
violent potential; she may be a polite, proper and ineffectual ornamental
addition to the poem, whose verbal power is merely ceremonial; she may
be a military force in her own right with the actual power to back up her
words, whose language is thinly veiled violence. She may have more in
common with Grendel's monstrous, unwomanly and overtly violent
mother than with the feminine ideal of peace-loving peace-weaver. She
may be seen as controlling or controlled by her words, a fly netted in the
amber of her own language. Or perhaps there is no connection between
the language she uses and who she is, and the multiple personalities
suggested by her language are a means of escaping and resisting definition, of deflecting binary categorization.

When she falls silent, we are stranded unceremoniously on the
complex, thoroughly ambiguous shores of language. We hear a kind of
formless babble, the antiphon to Hildeburh's silence. As Hildeburh
reveals the trace of self through silence and absence, Wealhtheow may be
glimpsed through the mirror of language. But her image, like Hildeburh's, never resolves into clear black and white; it can only be apprehended through paradox. Wealhtheow, despite her eloquent speech,
does not speak herself, neither does she "blow up the Law." Her role as
hysteric calls language into question, subjects it to examination: this
woman speaker, who is as absent from language as she is from the
masculine symbolic order, temporarily introduces herself as female subject into the order of language, and her words, like no others in the
poem, strip bare the paradoxical core of the whole linguistic project and
her relation to it.

Wealhtheow leaves us with the riddle of unresolved and unresolvable
ambiguity. Her speech, like Hildeburh's silence and, as we shall see,
Modthryth's unpredictability, is a powerful and inescapable index to
ambiguity. But this is far less life-threatening than its opposite and
counterpart: the death-centred mode of desire affirmed throughout the
poem and especially in the words of its hero, where the illusion, albeit a
conscious or chosen one in Beowulf's case, of the subject in language is
translated into egocentric certainty and into yet another illusion of
control. The queen offers an alternative to this death-centred, tragic
morality, which "prefers the blind and lucid Oedipus at Colonnus to
Oedipus the King, blind to his sins,"[73] which elevates resolution, despite

its inherently reductive and blinding aspects, over toleration of the other. Like the silent Hildeburh, Wealhtheow offers a verbal plea for permission for the other, and also a disquieting glimpse of the presence of the other in the task of interpretation demanded by her language: "Only the unsolved riddle, the process of riddle-work before its final completion, is a confrontation with otherness."[74]

MODTHRYTH AS SPECTACLE AND SPECTATOR

Modthryth, or Thryth, whose very name has proved problematic to critics, occupies a brief and much emended section of the poem.[75] Her story is "very abruptly introduced and is the most difficult of all for 'whole-hearted admirers' to justify."[76] Perhaps even more than Wealh-theow, this queen's brief appearance has given rise to a critical conster-nation that well illustrates a binary pressure coming from without the poem, a need to define and somehow account for her as one of the most unruly details of a variously described but nonetheless assumed whole. Critics have attempted to explain her in a wide variety of ways; some have explained her away completely, taking *modþryðo* as a noun mean-ing "mindstrength" or "arrogance," and not as a proper name.[77] Bloom-field comes close to dismissing her when he emphasizes the "interrupt-ing quality" of her appearance in the poem, and sees her story and other scattered digressions in the last part of the poem as products of heroic senility. Her story is one of the references to the past that increasingly take over in the poem, which "reduplicates as far as is possible by structural means the mode of aged thinking" and generates "an atmo-sphere suitable to the story of an old and worn-out hero."[78] Others suggest that she is included in the poem on account of her marriage to Offa, whose Mercian descendant, Offa II, might have been flattered by the reference.[79]

She is mentioned in connection with Hygd, Hygelac's young and gracious queen, and is most often interpreted as an instance of the *Beowulf*-poet's technique of presenting contrasts. In order to make clear the nature and duties of the good king, Hrothgar cites the example of Heremod, who did everything wrong (1709–22). Modthryth, then, serves a similar function, operating in contrast to Queen Hygd. Adrien Bonjour rationalizes the problematic appearance of Modthryth by ex-tending this opposition principle even further: Modthryth, who eventu-ally reforms her behavior, and Heremod, who starts out auspiciously and then deteriorates, serve as foils for each other, and both of them are "implicitly contrasted with Offa, whose whole career was a long and continuous success and who, therefore, in the poet's brief and condensed eulogy, may give us a prefiguration of Beowulf's own future successful leadership" (55). By such a circuitous route, a place is found for the unmannerly queen in the larger context of the poem, one which connects, and assimilates her through opposition.

The figure of Modthryth herself and the notion of a possible separate or individual identity for her which is not dependent on binary classification have not received much critical attention. In her analysis of contemporary film narrative, de Lauretis raises a question that also sheds some light on this shadowy, ill- and over-defined queen. With particular reference to Hitchcock's work, she asserts that the development of suspense in film narrative, and the progress of narrative in general, always casts the question of desire in terms of "what will he do when he finds out?"[80] What effects do Modthryth's actions have, what response does she elicit, and how does she serve or thwart dominant desire in the poem—in effect, what is to be done about her? These are the kinds of questions that have been asked of her. Instead of trying to resolve the "problem" of what is to be done with her, I want to look at what *she* does when *she* "finds out," and what she does to us as readers. Her power to disturb, her "hysterical" potential, is enormous, and perhaps the more striking by virtue of the brevity of her cameo appearance.

With the notable exception of Grendel's mother, Modthryth is the most unwomanly, unqueenly female in the poem. She is vain, mean, proud, apparently gratuitously violent, aggressive, power-hungry and initially almost casually contemptuous of men. She is "tamed" by her marriage to Offa, transformed by the love and guidance of a good husband into a model wife and queen. In her ambiguous role as hysteric, she begins by rocking the boat, by challenging, even inverting the values of the prevailing symbolic order (much as Beowulf does when he hypothesizes the paralysis of indecision); she is then "cured" (as is Beowulf who finally chooses the "active" course of resolution, the closure of heroic binarism), a textbook example of the one-time hysteric assimilated by the familial symbolic order: "The family reassimilates her otherness, and like an amoeba, finds its single cell revitalized, stronger than before."[81] Modthryth causes a temporary shudder of discomfort, followed by a generalized sigh of relief that the disorder she threatens has been contained and things are once more under the control of the masculine economy.

Her assimilation, however, requires oversimplified binary rationalization: aggressive, "masculine" behavior is not a "lady/queen-like custom" (*cwenlic þeaw*, 1940), and is thus construed as a force for evil. Hansen makes this point clear: "Just as Beowulf, at the height of his career, can still control the malevolent elements in his world, so of course the wicked queen here can be subdued by the wisdom and love of her husband Offa" (115). Moreover, Modthryth's exceptional husband, according to Sklute, "was possessed of those rare qualities that can control women with confused libidinal drives" (536).[82] Although categorizing Modthryth as simply evil as a result of her sexually anomalous behavior is an efficient means of superficially restoring the poem's apparent moral status quo, it cannot address the persistent ambiguity she introduces into the narrative, nor accurately account for her power and "shock value" as an hysteric. To understand this, we have only to look more carefully at *what* she does, at the specific nature of her "evil."

At the center of Modthryth's rebellion is her refusal to be looked at, to become an object, which necessarily results in her rejection of the female peace-weaver role:

> Modþryðo wæg,
> fremu folces cwen, firen' ondrysne;
> nænig þæt dorste deor geneþan
> swæsra gesiða, nefne sinfrea,
> þæt hire an dæges eagum starede;
> ac him wælbende weotode tealde
> handgewriþene; hraþe seoþðan wæs
> æfter mundgripe mece geþinged,
> þæt hit sceadenmæl scyran moste,
> cwealmbealu cyðan. Ne bið swylc cwenlic þeaw
> idese to efnanne, þeah ðe hio ænlicu sy,
> þætte freoðuwebbe feores onsæce
> æfter ligetorne leofne mannan.
> Huru þæt onhohsnode Hemminges mæg . . .
>   (1931–44)

Modthryth, excellent queen of the people, carried out a terrible crime; there was none of the beloved followers so brave, except a great lord, who dared venture to stare at her with his eyes in the light of day; but he would discover appointed to him handwoven deadly bonds; soon after the seizure it was decided by the sword, the patterned blade would settle it, proclaiming death. That is no queenly custom for a lady to perform, even though she be beautiful, that a peace-weaver should deprive a beloved man of life on account of a pretended insult. However, the Hemming's kinsman (Offa) put a stop to that . . .

Her rebellion constitutes a direct confrontation with the masculine symbolic order of the poem. Despite her beauty, Modthryth will not consent to be a feminine spectacle in a masculine arena, refusing to join the ranks of the gold-adorned queens who circulate among the warriors as visible treasure (as does Hygd, for example). She rejects objectification, refuses to be an "objet petit a," Lacan's term for the appropriated, domesticated other which the masculine economy substitutes for the genuine, unrealizable Other (Autre). By refusing to be held in the masculine "gaze," Modthryth underscores the connection between seeing and masculinity, between the eye and the phallus, insisted on by Lacan: "It is in as much as, at the heart of the experience of the unconscious, we are dealing with that organ (the phallus)—determined in the subject by the inadequacy of the castration complex—that we can grasp to what extent the eye is caught up in a similar dialectic."[83] Modthryth's rejection of the gaze briefly exposes its particular oculocentric tyranny: both the illusion of subjectivity and the privileging of the subject that attends the apprehension of the world characterized as "I see myself seeing myself." "The privilege of the subject," Lacan asserts, "seems to be established here from that bipolar reflexive relation by which, as soon as I perceive, my representations belong to me." Modthryth's initial refusal to be "seen" is also a refusal to participate in a self-aggrandizing mode of perception, in a *"belong to me* aspect of representations, so reminiscent of property."[84]

Despite her dramatic rejection of a fundamental premise of the symbolic order, Modthryth does not achieve a rupture, or make a change in that order. Indeed, the violent form of her rebellion confronts the system on its own death-centred terms. Her complicity—also a form of mimicry—in the masculine objectifying, destructive mode, however, also demonstrates her dual role as hysteric, as both heroine and victim, whose ambiguity is part of her power to disturb. Her retaliation repeats the inscription in the flesh, the poem's insistent connection between violence and signification, that Wealhtheow tries so hard to sever. Modthryth turns the masculine gaze back upon itself, briefly becoming a spectator, an overseer herself, but then is co-opted in a joint spectacle. Her violent response to being "seen" reveals the barely displaced violence of the act of staring; she calls attention to, even makes a spectacle of, that same connection between violence and signification in which she also participates. She succeeds in making a spectacle of herself and of the masculine economy; her dramatic rearrangement, via inversion and restoration, of the spectator/spectacle, or passive/active binary dynamic, resists complacent resolution and affirms ambiguity; in spite of her reformed wifely personality, she remains a discomfiting presence.

Modthryth causes further disturbance from the point of view of motivation. Unlike the other overtly violent female in the poem, Grendel's mother, Modthryth does not appear to have a familial motivation. Although Chance and Damico find the closest parallels for her behavior in the masculine aggression of Grendel's mother,[85] even such alien monstrous proclivities find their rationalization in the familiar and familial code of vengeance which pervades the poem. Modthryth is not out there engaging in confrontation, as Grendel's mother does with actions, as Wealhtheow does with words, on account of someone else; she is nobody's mother. Her display of violence and her use of power are self-generated. She spurns male attention as vehemently as those chaste, aggressive female saints and martyrs, but not in the name of Christ. Her rebellion comes from no recognizable source or place, just as her story surfaces in the poem with no immediately apparent connection to the main narrative. She utterly rejects an hypothetical "identity" as a peace-weaver: instead she actively weaves the "deadly bonds" of death. Modthryth's behavior and motivation are not identifiable or explicable, unless we accept the poet's explanation that it is all in her head—an imaginary insult, pretended injury—or agree with Renoir that she is "so far gone on the unhappy path of paranoiac delusions" that she cannot function properly.[86] We might also entertain Sklute's suggestion that she suffers from "confused libidinal drives." Interestingly and appropriately, all these viewpoints fit the portrait of the "classical" hysteric.

As neither noblewoman nor monsterwoman, Modthryth escapes all definition offered by the poem; she is truly mysterious, perhaps eventually unthinkable,[87] qualities she shares with the silent, absent Hildeburh. Unlike Hildeburh, who leaves behind her profound silence and a glimpse of paradox through paralysis, we perceive the trace of Modthryth through the turmoil and upheaval she herself causes, and through the apparent narrative relief, in the form of good Queen Hygd's entrance, when she exits the poem. But my point is that she doesn't go away; even though she may appear to have been assimilated back into the family, the disturbance she brings to the poem does not subside with her quiescent marriage; nor is her disconcerting ghost laid to rest by her more comforting counterpart, Hygelac's young queen. She doesn't go away precisely because she remains a mystery, because she escapes, however briefly, the trap of binary definition.

Modthryth offers a variation on Hildeburh's silent declaration of paradox; she reveals the trace of something that we know cannot exist in the world of the poem: the trace of a woman signifying in her own right. Her initial gesture is strikingly alien, incomprehensible, until translated into the binary language of the masculine economy. Heremod and Beowulf as antitypes operate well within binary strictures; as good or evil as they are, they still speak the same language, as it were; one idea is comprehensible, indeed manageable, in terms of the other. But the Modthryth-Hygd opposition is slightly asymmetric; there is a part of Modthryth that will not translate or match up, and this, by the process of association so endemic to this poem, must reflect on Hygd, on the young Freawaru, on all the human females in the poem. I am not suggesting that Modthryth's response is one which substantially undermines or calls into overt question the prevailing symbolic order; what I am suggesting is that she intrudes herself briefly into the poem's chain of signification, introduces dis-ease, a thrill of disgust perhaps, a tremor of amazement at the unknown. The jolt in the narrative that she provides is just enough to make us think, as we watch the gracious temperate Hygd obediently performing her womanly duties, that one never knows . . .

POSTSCRIPT

I have paid most attention to the operation of desire within the poem, and some attention to critical desire and the demands it makes from without. In doing so I have been aware of both the arbitrariness and difficulty of separating the desires of text and reader, and the inevitable operation of my own desire as reader and critic—wherein I have also identified the kind of *Beowulf* I want.

Let us follow this line of reasoning for a moment. If this open-ended text, whose difference I claim mirrors the positivity of potential rather than the negativity of deferral of meaning, is produced by my own desire, where does that take us and what kinds of new questions are brought into language as a consequence? As continuity and irresolution have been critically identified with feminine forms of desire,[88] is one a condition for the other? When I read this poem, Beowulf's story of Hrethel with its agonizing ambivalence always exerts a tremendous pull; so, too, does the unsettled and unsettling Modthryth. Do these particularly ambiguous and unresolved parts of the poem match, or express, then, a feminine desire? If a feminist, psychoanalytic approach privileges parts and details over wholes, how might this reinscribe the detail in *Beowulf*? Modthryth and Scyld Scefing are details; the difference has been that Scyld is considered "central" to the theme of the poem, whereas Modthryth is peripheral at best, a muffled and incoherent voice from the margins of the poem's discourse. Suppose we move this hysterical, ambivalent queen closer to the "center," or privilege Hildeburh's absence over Beowulf's illusion of presence? Do these questions simply replace the imposition of masculine unitary desire with the imposition of feminine fragmentary desire upon a long-suffering, reader-produced text, or do they bring to language issues hitherto unexpressed? My answer to this last question is an unqualified and self-conscious "both." In posing either/or questions, I am setting up binary oppositions which I also hope to dismantle.

When I construct an argument for the women of *Beowulf* as deflecting or redirecting masculine desire, for example, I am aware that I am operating from within the same binary framework that I see as restrictive. Although I might also argue that such female hysterical characteristics may be shared by marginal monsters and mainline heroes, it could be said that I have simply set up another opposition, that of death-centred masculine desire versus female as life-giver, and ranked my pair according to ideological preference. This will obviously be the case to some extent, but I am also probing the possibilities of asymmetry and dialectic. One side of the opposition we know well, the other is relatively unexplored. Let me invoke the unsettling presence of Modthryth once more, and ask what might happen to the notion of a center if we bring her in from the margin and move her closer to it?

I have argued that this queen's power resides in paradox, in her ability to elude and foil binary categorization. She embodies an impossible dialectic, one which will continually generate new configurations of oppositional elements while at the same time introducing an asymmetrical potential. Such a view of Modthryth engages the question of desire from within and without the text, and suggests how new questions might be brought to language by the conscious examination of the interplay of our own desire with that of the text. Curiously but perhaps appropriately, this difficult queen has come to represent both the perils of over-definition and the unpredictable yet regenerative power of process. Perhaps it is fitting to conclude, then, with Modthryth, one of the least conclusive elements in the poem, as an affirmation of process in interpretation, and to look forward to the inscription of the reader's desire in that process.

NOTES

1. I wish to thank Southern Illinois University Press for permission to print this revision of material from my *Language, Sign, and Gender in "Beowulf."*

2. Line 197. This "refrain," which pinpoints the hero in time—"on *that* day of *this* life" (my emphasis)—is repeated again in line 790, and in line 806, where it refers to Grendel's doomed struggle against Beowulf. All references to *Beowulf* are from F. Klaeber, ed., *Beowulf and the Fight at Finnsburh,* 3rd ed. (Boston, 1950), and will be indicated by line number. The translations are my own, and I aim for literality and simplicity rather than elegance.

3. *Alice Doesn't: Feminism, Semiotics, Cinema* (Bloomington, 1984), 112.

4. "Economy" is used as a comprehensive term for the complex of cultural systems of change and exchange, wherein power is sought, claimed and distributed; "masculine economy" denotes the social and material conditions of patriarchy, in which women may be construed as commodities in the exchange system of power relations between men.

5. In *A General Selection from the Works of Sigmund Freud,* ed. J. Rickman (New York, 1957).

6. *The Subject of Semiotics* (Oxford, 1983), 57.

7. See for example the analysis of narrative technique in the Finnsburg episode in Thomas Shippey, *Old English Verse* (London, 1971), 19–30. Shippey emphasizes the ambiguity and problematic aspects of heroic choice, and shows how the poet is concerned with mental and emotional acts rather than physical ones, concentrating on the "inner maelstrom" (24) experienced by the characters.

8. See chapters one and two of *Language, Sign, and Gender,* cited above.

9. *The Newly Born Woman,* trans. Betsy Wing (Minneapolis, 1986), 71.

10. *Ibid.*

11. In Cixous and Clément, 168. When "Symbolic" is capitalized, it represents Lacan's specific use of the term. Betsy Wing, translator of Cixous and Clément, glosses the term (see 163–68); although there can be no pure instance of the Symbolic, Lacan sees language as the primary vehicle for the abstract order of discursive and symbolic action. Elsewhere I have followed Cixous and Clément's more general, uncapitalized use of the term; the symbolic order is that complex of symbolic systems that comprises and expresses a culture.

12. From *Moses and Monotheism,* quoted by Cixous and Clément in their discussion of "The Dawn of Phallocentrism," 100.

13. Jane Gallop, *The Daughter's Seduction: Feminism and Psychoanalysis* (Ithaca, 1982), 39.

14. Jacques Lacan, *Four Fundamental Concepts of Psychoanalysis,* trans. Alan Sheridan (New York, 1981), 34.

15. Gallop, *The Daughter's Seduction,* 47.

16. References to the non-existence/non-identity of woman are found throughout Lacan's *Télèvision* (Paris, 1973). See also Gallop, *The Daughter's Seduction,* for a discussion of Lacan's views on women, especially Chapter Three, "The Ladies' Man," 33–42.

17. These observations about masculine social organization find parallels in various contexts; for a discussion of bonds between men in a heroic, poetic context, see Joseph Harris, "Love and Death in the *Männerbund*: An Essay with Special Reference to the *Bjarkamál* and the *Battle of Maldon,*" in *Heroic Poetry in the Anglo-Saxon Period: Studies in Honor of Jess B. Bessinger, Jr.,* ed. Helen Damico and John Leyerle (forthcoming, Kalamazoo: Medieval Institutes Publications), or, with reference to the eighteenth- and nineteenth-century novel, Eve Kosofsky Sedgwick, *Between Men: English Literature and Male Homosocial Desire* (New York, 1985).

18. Norman E. Eliason, "Healfdene's Daughter," *Anglo-Saxon Poetry: Essays in Appreciation,* ed. L.E. Nicholson and D.W. Frese (Notre Dame, 1975), 10.

19. *Ibid.,* 9.

20. "Teaching the Backgrounds: History, Religion, Culture," in *Approaches to Teaching "Beowulf,"* ed. J.B. Bessinger and R.F. Yeager (New York, 1984), 118–19.

21. Gilles Deleuze and Felix Guattari, *Anti-Oedipus,* trans. R. Hurley *et al.* (New York, 1977), 165.

22. James W. Earl, "The Role of the Men's Hall in the Development of the Anglo-Saxon Superego," *Psychiatry* 46 (May, 1983): 143, 146.

23. Earl parallels the decline in the legal rights of women in the Anglo-Saxon period to the diminishment of the power and influence of the kinship system; this

process, he suggests, supports "Freud's view of woman's role as the antagonist of civilization: 'Women represent the interests of the family and of sexual life. The work of civilization has become increasingly the business of men, it confronts them with ever more difficult tasks and compels them to carry out instinctual sublimations of which women are little capable. . . . Thus the woman finds herself forced into the background by the claims of civilization and she adopts a hostile attitude towards it'" (146).

24. See Jacques Derrida's essay on "Differance" in *Speech and Phenomena*, trans. D.B. Allison (Evanston, 1973). He insists that "differance" is "neither a word nor a concept" (135), but rather a strategy, a process: "the kind of bringing together proposed here has the structure of an interlacing, a weaving, or a web, which would allow the different threads and different lines of sense or force to separate again, as well as being ready to bind others together" (132).

25. In Cixous and Clément, 7.

26. For a comprehensive overview of the connections between Anglo-Saxon critics and Anglo-Saxon studies, see Allen Frantzen's groundbreaking *Desire for Origins: New Language, Old English and Teaching the Tradition* (New Brunswick, 1990), and in particular see his study of the poem and its historical reception, "Writing the Unreadable *Beowulf*," 168–200.

27. This situation is gradually changing with the advent of some recent publications. For a comprehensive historical survey see Helen T. Bennett, "From Peace Weaver to Text Weaver: Feminist Approaches to Old English Literature," *Twenty Years of the Year's Work in Old English Studies,* ed. Katherine O'Brien O'Keeffe, Old English Newsletter Subsidia 15 (Binghamton, 1989), 23–42. For a brief overview see Helen T. Bennett, Clare A. Lees and Gillian R. Overing, "Gender and Power: Feminism and Old English Studies," *Medieval Feminist Newsletter* 10 (Fall 1990): 15–23. See also *New Readings on Women in Old English Literature,* ed. Helen Damico and Alexandra Hennessey Olsen (Bloomington, 1990). For further specific references see nn. 37 and 40.

28. "A Reading Context for *The Wife's Lament,*" in *Anglo-Saxon Poetry: Essays in Appreciation for John C. McGalliard,* ed. L.E. Nicholson and D.W. Frese (Notre Dame, 1975), 224, 235, 236.

29. I have selected Renoir's comments in "A Reading Context for *The Wife's Lament*" to characterize one view of the passivity of women in Old English poetry; I should add that Renoir has also argued for the assertive logic and intelligence of Eve in "Eve's IQ Rating: Two Sexist Views of *Genesis B,*" in *New Readings,* ed. Damico and Hennessey Olsen, 262–72.

30. "Female Characterization in Old English Poetry and the Growth of Psychological Realism: *Genesis B* and *Christ I,*" *Neophilologus* 63 (1979): 605, 606.

31. "Women in Old English Poetry Reconsidered," *The Michigan Academician* 9 (1976–77): 111, 113.

32. Hansen, 117.

33. "A Reading Context," 224.

34. *Woman as Hero in Old English Poetry* (Syracuse, N.Y., 1986), xv.

35. For a good selection of examples of Anglo-Saxon women in public, religious and political life, see Joan Nicholson, "*Feminae Gloriosae:* Women in the Age of Bede," 15–29, and Pauline Stafford's "Sons and Mothers: Family Politics in the Early Middle Ages," 79–100, both in *Medieval Women,* ed. D. Baker (Oxford,

1978).

36. Chance, xv, 53.

37. See Sheila C. Dietrich, "An Introduction to Women in Anglo-Saxon Society (c.600–1066)," in *The Women of England,* ed. B. Kanner (Hamden, Conn., 1979), 32–56. Dietrich sees a decline in the status of women within the Church later in the period (38); her essay also surveys differing views on women throughout the period. Christine Fell, in *Women in Anglo-Saxon England* (Oxford, 1986), discusses the issue of the critical division of views concerning the relationship of Christianity and women in her Introduction, and also offers another view of both male and female status: "the equality of the sexes which flourished in the eighth century in learning and in literacy, was replaced in the tenth century by equality in ignorance" (128).

38. Derrida, 156.

39. Derrida, 158.

40. For example, Barrie Ruth Strauss, "Women's Words as Weapons: Speech as Action in 'The Wife's Lament,'" *Texas Studies in Literature and Language* 23 (Summer 1981): 268–85; Bernice W. Kliman, "Women in Early English Literature, *Beowulf* to the *Ancrene Wisse*," *Nottingham Medieval Studies* 21 (1977): 32–49; Alexandra Hennessey Olsen, "Women in *Beowulf*," in *Approaches to Teaching "Beowulf"* (n. 20 above), 150–56; Pat Belanoff, "The Fall (?) of the Old English Female Poetic Image," *PMLA* 104 (1989): 822–31. See n. 27 above for further references.

41. *Beowulf's Wealhtheow and the Valkyrie Tradition* (Madison, 1984), 67.

42. "A Reading Context," 230.

43. Cixous and Clément, 70.

44. See n. 7 above.

45. Thorstein Veblen introduced the concept of "trained incapacity" in *Theory of the Leisure Class* (London, 1899), applying it primarily to businessmen whose very abilities and training worked against them, functioning in some cases as blindnesses and inadequacies. More recently sociolinguists Shirley and Edwin Ardener have applied the concept to the language of women as part of the "muted group" theory. As members of a "muted group," women must learn to speak the language of the dominant group, a language which is essentially an alien structure not of their own making. This situation makes for many kinds of distortions and incongruities: "For example, the dominant group may provide a style for them such that, if they are perceived as 'birds', when angry they may be required to 'roar like doves'" (Shirley Ardener, "The Nature of Women in Society," in *Perceiving Females,* ed. S. Ardener [New York, 1978], 20). For an extended discussion of the sociological "muted group" theory and its relation to female language use, see Cheris Kramerae, *Women and Men Speaking* (Massachussetts, 1981).

46. Chance, 74.

47. Chance, 79.

48. For a different view of Eve, wherein she is cast as a remarkably—if unfortunately—successful peaceweaver, see my "On Reading Eve: *Genesis B* and the Readers' Desire," in *Speaking Two Languages: Traditional Disciplines and Contemporary Theory in Medieval Studies,* ed. A.J. Frantzen (Albany, 1991), 35–63.

49. For an interesting and timely reassessment of the masculinity of both the hero and the poem, see Clare A. Lees, "Men and *Beowulf*," in *Medieval*

Masculinities: Regarding Men in the Middle Ages, ed. C.A. Lees, forthcoming, University of Minnesota Press.

50. This point was emphasized to me by Helen T. Bennett in a discussion of her paper "Revising the Germanic Tradition of Lament to Interpret the Female Mourner at Beowulf's Funeral" (presented at 23rd International Congress on Medieval Studies, Kalamazoo, 1988), where she affirms the female capacity to endure and survive in the poem, to persistently choose life over death. See also her essay, "The Female Mourner at Beowulf's Funeral: Filling the Blanks/Hearing the Spaces," *Exemplaria* 4 (1992): 35–50.

51. Deleuze and Guattari, 186.

52. See my semiotic analysis of the function of the objects in the poem and the ways in which the object-sign becomes an embodiment or reminder of past and future words and/or deeds in *Language, Sign, and Gender,* 33–67.

53. Although Freud credits women with the invention of the technique of weaving, he suggests in *New Introductory Lectures on Psychoanalysis,* ed. and trans. J. Strachey (New York, 1965) that the unconscious motivation for the achievement is shame: making "threads adhere to one another" (132) is an extension of braiding pubic hair to veil the shame of lack, to conceal the fact of castration. When one changes this premise of "lack" the activity of weaving might be more positively and interestingly revalued.

54. "Violence and Language," in *Political and Social Essays,* ed. D. Stewart and J. Bien (Athens, Ohio, 1974), 89.

55. Friedrich Nietzsche, *The Birth of Tragedy and The Genealogy of Morals,* trans. F. Golffing (New York, 1956), 192–93.

56. Deleuze and Guattari, 145.

57. Michel Foucault, "Nietzsche, Genealogy, History," in *The Foucault Reader,* ed. P. Rabinow (New York, 1984), 87.

58. *Technologies of Gender* (Bloomington, 1987), 32–33.

59. See especially Chapter Two, "Wealhtheow and the Heroic Tradition," 17–40. For a discussion of Wealhtheow's name, see 62–68.

60. The only full-length study of Beowulf's speeches from the point of view of speech act theory that I have come across is Charles E. McNally's dissertation "'Beowulf Maþelode . . .': Text Linguistics and Speech Acts," SUNY Binghamton, 1975. Elizabeth Closs Traugott makes interesting use of speech act theory in her discussion of Old English in *A History of English Syntax* (New York, 1972).

61. "The Voice of Beowulf," *Germanic Notes* 8 (1977): 43.

62. John R. Searle, "A Classification of Illocutionary Acts," *Language in Society* 5 (April, 1976): 11.

63. Austin and Searle divide the utterance, or speech act, into three stages or levels: the locutionary level, which is the content of the utterance itself; the intention of the speaker, the force or direction of the utterance, which is the illocutionary act (Searle calls this illocutionary point); and the perlocutionary act, which is the actual effect, intended or otherwise, of the utterance. Searle's method of classifying illocutionary acts is particularly useful for my purposes because he expands the criteria for examining the illocutionary act, and makes its complexity and ambiguity more accessible to analysis.

64. Searle defines directives as "attempts (of varying degrees, and hence, more precisely, they are determinates of the determinable which includes attempting) by

the speaker to get the hearer to do something. They may be very modest 'attempts' as when I invite you to do it or suggest that you do it, or they may be very fierce attempts as when I insist that you do it. Using the shriek mark for the illocutionary point indicating device for the members of this class generally, we have the following symbolism:

! ↑ W (H does A)

The direction of fit (indicated by the arrow) is world-to-words and the sincerity condition is want (or wish or desire). The propositional content is always that the hearer H does some future action A. Verbs denoting members of this class are ask, order, command, request, beg, plead, pray, entreat, and also invite, permit, and advise (11).

65. "The Role of the Men's Hall" (n. 22 above), 150.

66. Renoir, "A Reading Context," 229.

67. "Teaching the Backgrounds" (n. 20 above), 109.

68. P. 6. See also Damico's note on 185 in support of this interpretation.

69. See Damico, 123–32, for an extended discussion of both of Wealhtheow's speeches.

70. Renoir, "A Reading Context," 230.

71. "Freoðuwebbe in Old English Poetry," *Neuphilologische Mitteilungen* 71 (1970): 540.

72. "Women in Early English Literature" (n. 40 above), 34.

73. Cixous and Clément, 40.

74. Gallop, *The Daughter's Seduction*, 61.

75. See Klaeber, 195–99, for a discussion of this passage and an assessment of manuscript emendations. For an extended discussion of her problematic name, see also R.W. Chambers, *"Beowulf": An Introduction,* with supplement by C.L. Wrenn (Cambridge, 1963), 36–40, 238–43, 41–42.

76. Kevin Crossley-Holland, trans., *Beowulf* (New York, 1968), 139.

77. This is Norman Eliason's argument in "The 'Thryth-Offa Digression' in *Beowulf,*" in *Franciplegius: Medieval and Linguistic Studies in Honor of Francis Peabody Magoun, Jr,* ed. J.B. Bessinger and R.P. Creed (New York, 1965), 124–38; Eliason maintains that the entire 'digression' refers to Hygd.

78. Morton W. Bloomfield, "'Interlace' as a Medieval Narrative Technique with Special Reference to *Beowulf,*" in *Magister Regis: Studies in Honor of R.E. Kaske,* ed. A. Groos (New York, 1986), 58.

79. Kemp Malone, *"Beowulf,"* reprinted in *An Anthology of "Beowulf" Criticism,* ed. L.E. Nicholson (Notre Dame, 1963), 148–49. See also Adrian Bonjour, *The Digressions in "Beowulf"* (Oxford, 1950), 53–55.

80. *Alice Doesn't,* 155.

81. Gallop, *The Daughter's Seduction,* 133.

82. The phrase "confused libidinal drives" has drawn some critical attention. It was omitted from the version of Sklute's article reprinted in *New Readings,* 204–10 (see n. 27 above), which was previously unavailable to me. For a discussion of these problematic libidinal drives, included or excluded, and of the general critical disturbance Modthryth appears to cause, see my essay "Recent Writing on Old English: A Response," *Æstel* 1 (1993): 135–49.

83. *Four Fundamental Concepts* (n. 14 above), 101.

84. *Ibid.,* 81. Extending and often transforming the work of Freud and Lacan,

recent feminist critics have focused on the masculine tyranny of the gaze and the notion of woman as a mirror for male subjectivity as a fertile source for new theoretical metaphors and feminist insights. See chapter seven, "Patriarchal Reflections: Luce Irigaray's Looking-glass," in Toril Moi, *Sexual/Textual Politics* (London, 1985), 127–49, for a discussion of these. Moi pays specific attention to Irigaray's punning examination of female "specul(ariz)ation" and mimicry.

85. Chance suggests that the structural location of the passage "invites a comparison of this stubborn princess and the two other 'queens,' Hygd and the *wif* [Grendel's mother]" (105). She also points out that Modthryth and Grendel's mother are connected by the same irony: as Modthryth weaves "deadly bonds" for her suitors thereby severing the bonds of peace, "she resembles that other ironic peace-weaver, the *wif,* who tried to penetrate the braided breast-net of Beowulf with her knife" (106). Damico sees them as parts of a valkyrie-inspired whole: "Because they are parallel in function and nature, collectively Modthrytho and Grendel's mother may form one half of a valkyrie-diptych configuration" (51).

86. "A Reading Context," 230.

87. Although Modthryth's violence might seem anomalous in the human, female context of the poem, the Anglo-Saxon period offers plentiful examples of women who were less than temperate. Among others, Pauline Stafford (cited above in n. 35) recounts the story of Ælfthryth, mother of Æthelræd Unræd, who helped murder the son of her husband Edgar's first wife in order to secure the succession for her own son (79–80), and records the career of Eadburh, who murdered her husband's followers and finally her husband himself in her attempts to secure power (83). Coincidentally, Eadburh was the daughter of Offa of Mercia, supposedly the descendant of Offa of the Angles, Modthryth's husband.

88. Some analyses and reexaminations of the nature of feminine desire and its connection to process, fluidity, and linguistic forms that I have found of particular interest include: Jane Gallop, *Reading Lacan* (Ithaca, 1985); Luce Irigaray, "The Mechanics of Fluids" in *This Sex Which Is Not One,* trans. C. Porter (Ithaca, 1985); Jacqueline Rose's Introduction to *Feminine Sexuality Jacques Lacan and the Ecole Freudienne,* ed. J. Mitchell and J. Rose (London, 1982).

Kuhn's Laws, Old English Poetry, and the New Philology

by MARY BLOCKLEY and THOMAS CABLE

I. LAWS, DEFINITIONS, TAUTOLOGIES

FEW people who use the double set of statements known in Germanic philology as Kuhn's Laws think about the system from which they sprang. Hans Kuhn's long paper of 1933 sought to demonstrate the necessity of reformulating the categories of sentential stress upon which it crucially relies.[1] Stress is one of the ways that a linguistic system produces contrasts that differentiate syllables. Generally speaking, grammarians agree that some of the stress in a sentence belongs to the most prominent syllable in each individual word, and that some of these lexically stressed syllables get additional prominence from the word's position in a sentence. All the details of this generalization are currently disputed.

Kuhn's Laws are corrigible piecemeal, but the problem which that corrigibility indicates is essentially one of definitions. Kuhn's Laws define conjunctions as being essentially more like pronouns than like prepositions. They equate personal pronouns and finite verbs, although the former rarely figure in metrical stress and the latter often do. The most important bad effect they have is that they induce linguistic tunnel vision. There are certain grammatical categories that never appear in clause-initial position, but Kuhn's Laws do not predict their absence.

Kuhn's Laws have been far more respected by metrists than by syntacticians, although Hans Kuhn himself used *Beowulf* and other Germanic verse texts only as the necessary means to the otherwise unattainable end of recovering the syntax of the earliest recorded stage of the medieval Germanic languages.[2] Kuhn acknowledged the influence of Jacob Wackernagel's 1892 argument that the earliest texts in the Indo-European languages concur in their basic sentence structure: the lightest moveable elements of the clause, the *Partikeln,* immediately follow the first stressed element of the clause.[3] Wackernagel was building on Delbrück, who had observed that in the Avestas "Enklitische Wörter rücken möglichst nah an den Anfang des Satzes" ("enclitic words come as near as possible to the beginning of the sentence").[4]

Wackernagel takes his examples from Greek, Sanskrit, and Latin, though he makes passing reference to Celtic and Lithuanian. He mentions Germanic only at the end, and only with reference to the position of the finite verb. (See Kuhn's eagerness to "remedy" this, p. 5, n. 3). Kuhn is working with texts of a later state of the language that do not include some of the kinds of elements that Wackernagel's texts do. Nor does Kuhn use Wackernagel's terminology of *Partikeln* and *Enklitika*.

Kuhn's Laws in essence look to the poetry as an illustration of his syntactic theory. The meter therefore plays a crucial but unacknowledged role in the kinds of generalizations about syntax that Kuhn is able to make. Kuhn rejected the binary distinction between stressed words and unstressed words, by which a *Satzteil,* or sentence constituent, such as "the boy," can consist of an unstressed proclitic, or *Satzteilpartikel* ("the") and a stressed element ("boy"). He proposed that between these two possibilities for stress assignment lay a third categorically-defined group of words for which he had to coin the name of *Satzpartikel,* usually translated as "particle," although quite different from the present-day linguistic definition.[5] These are words whose stress, according to Kuhn, derives from their position in the clause. When they occur together early in the clause, either before the first stressed word or immediately after it, Kuhn notes that the meter shows that they are unstressed. But words that belong to the *Satzpartikel* group may occur later in the clause, and when they do, the meter shows that the word has stress. Kuhn proposed that the meter simply exploited the archaic syntax and revealed what the prose concealed about the tripartite division of words into categories eligible for sentential stress. In this we shall argue that he was wrong. Kuhn mistakenly credited syntax with the metrical dip that it allowed, but did not require. Kuhn's followers have used Kuhn's observations to correct meter, thus returning uncritically to the very system which Kuhn took as a given.

Calvin Kendall adeptly summarizes Kuhn's categories, providing a concise but complete statement of them:

> In 1933 Hans Kuhn formulated two highly important rules concerning word order and stress in the oldest poetry of the Germanic languages. To do so, he found it convenient to classify words (and some prefixes) into three categories on the basis of stress. . . . His three categories therefore are: (1) Stressed elements, which are principally nouns and qualitative adjectives, together with a few other forms. (2) Sentence particles, which include "substantive pronouns, many adverbs, and finite verbs, conjunctions, to some extent also adjectival pronouns, occasionally infinitives and predicate nouns, and possibly also vocatives." (3) Proclitics, which are the definite articles,

adjectival pronouns, some adverbs, prepositions, and unstressed pre-fixes.[6]

From these categories follow Kuhn's two laws about the structure of the clause. The first, already summarized, is the Law of Sentence Particles. All the members of category (2) must be in a dip of unstressed syllables that in any one clause appears in one of two places: immediately before or immediately after the first stressed syllable of the clause. Any sentence particles that occur later in the clause will receive positional stress, and the word will therefore have metrical stress. The Second Law is a further condition upon the place and contents of the clause's first run of unstressed syllables. This Law of Clause Openings states that if the dip comes before the first stress, then that dip cannot consist only of members of category (3). A member of category (2) must appear in it.

Our basic argument is that the levels of syntactic representation and of metrical representation must be kept distinct. The articulation of Kuhn's Laws, especially in their refinement by subsequent investigators, has taken the meter for granted. It has also taken the syntax for granted. Kuhn's attempt to trace a specific Germanic realization of the ancient classical languages' treatment of certain sentence elements fails because of the incompleteness and inconsistency of the method of defining the sentence elements. His correlation of grammatical category and stress works only sometimes and only epiphenomenally. The tripartite division directs attention to the influence of grammatical category on the contents of the metrical dip. But the method is sometimes too general—as in placing finite verbs, pronouns, and conjunctions together. It is also sometimes too specific: proclitics, as defined by Kuhn, are infrequent by themselves as clause openers, but, as we shall see, so are other parts of speech, including especially lone personal pronouns. Kuhn's Laws cannot address the infrequency of these pronouns without undoing the whole system.

As for meter, it is not that Kuhn's Laws and applications of Kuhn's Laws *ignore* it. To the contrary, they tacitly assume and appropriate a powerful metrical system and then claim the results of that system as their own. Whether stated as Sievers' Five Types[7] or as the alternative theory that we shall offer in the third part of this paper, Old English meter sets constraints which, when fully understood, cause much of the evidence for Kuhn's Laws to be neither compelling nor even very interesting. What seem to be surprising facts in need of an explanation (including facts about missing patterns) turn out to be the rather ordinary and expected results of other principles of meter, syntactic placement, and phrasal stress.

Consider, for example, verse 676b of *Beowulf*:[8]

> Gespræc þā se gōda   gylpworda sum,
> Bēowulf Gēata,   ǣr hē on bed stige   (675–76)

Then the good man, Beowulf of the Geats, spoke a certain boastful word before he went to bed.

In "ǣr hē on" we have a cluster of what Kuhn calls *Satzpartikeln* ("particles") and *Satzteilpartikeln* ("proclitics"): the subordinating conjunction *ǣr* (a particle), the personal pronoun *hē* (another particle), and the preposition *on* (a proclitic). These metrically unstressed words occur in the first dip of the clause and in so doing appear to follow Kuhn's Laws. Yet one should ask where else they might be *expected* to occur. Clausal conjunctions such as *ǣr* are simply going to come at the beginning of the clause. If they do not, then they cease to be clausal conjunctions. This is true for the scores of verses that begin with subordinating conjunctions (*þā, þǣr, þonne, swā,* etc.) as well as those that begin with coordinating conjunctions (*ond, ac,* etc.). If the conjunction appears, it must be the first syllable in the first dip of the subordinate clause. Such a beginning closes off certain syntactic and metrical options without necessarily requiring other things to happen. These things will happen for independent reasons.

The placement of personal pronouns closes off further options. There is nothing surprising about having the subject pronoun *hē* near the beginning of the clause. As in Modern English and Modern French, to name only two languages, subject pronouns tend to precede the verb. What is more interesting and what Kuhn's Laws have obscured is that Old English is like Modern French and unlike Middle English in the tendency for *object* pronouns to precede the verb:

> hī hyne þā ætbǣron (28a)
> Þā gȳt hīe him āsetton (47a)

Notice that there is no purely metrical necessity for the object pronouns to precede the verb. Both Sievers' metrics and Kuhn's Laws of Particles would allow the objects to follow the verb, as in our implausible rewrites of the Old English:

> x x x / x / x
> *hī þā ætbǣron hyne

> x x x x / x /
> *Þā gȳt hīe āsetton him

As "displaced particles," *hyne* and *him* would receive stress by a Kuhnian analysis. What then accounts for the rarity of the type? Ans van Kemenade is the most recent in a long line to posit syntactic rules that place Old English personal pronouns in preverbal position in prose and verse.[9] This placement has always been acknowledged, but recent investigations rightly emphasize the consequences of its restrictiveness. Bruce Mitchell's focus on variety of placement in the texts should not blind us to the fact that there are things that cannot happen. Mitchell himself notes the importance of nonoccurring patterns and points some out, as well as noting the difficulty of finding patterns that do not occur. Kuhn's Laws fail most signally in that they imply a modernist syntactic world where anything can happen.

In certain respects the traditional approach is compatible with the vast amount of work that has been done during the past fifteen years on clitic personal pronouns in many languages (especially Romance) within the theory of government and binding.[10] Whatever specific, technical analysis might turn out to be most appropriate among the various analyses possible within this framework, our argument is that the syntactic rules for personal pronouns and other grammatical categories must be considered in their own terms. Kuhn's Laws offer a spurious generality in lumping together personal pronouns and, say, finite verbs, along with conjunctions. In the next section we shall look more closely at some of the considerations that are relevant for individual grammatical categories.

II. Syntax

Conjunctions

What positive statements about Old English syntax do we derive from Kuhn's Laws? The much-praised accuracy of Kuhn's description of which elements are common in the beginning of a clause in Old English poetry might seem to rise miraculously out of this complex statement of prescriptions and constraints. Yet much of the First Law gets its descriptive power from categorial restrictions defining the parts of speech. Far from being peculiar to archaic Old English verse, these restrictions apply with equal truth to Old English prose and to all varieties of Modern English. For example, buried in the middle of category (2) are conjunctions. Despite the paratactic style of Old English poetry, conjunctions are still very numerous. *And* is the single most frequent token in the verse, occurring about every fourth line in *Beowulf.* Conjunctions, by descriptive definition, appear at the head of a clause or phrase in Old English just as surely as in Modern English. Old English homonyms like *ne* are adverbs or conjunctions depending on their position in the clause.

Moreover, the promulgators of Kuhn's Law have to patch the law concerning conjunctions and adverbs. Bliss writes in *An Introduction to Old English Metre*:

Words normally classed as particles may sometimes be used in such a
way that they are directly dependent on the following stress-word,
and in this case they are proclitics; grim *ond* grædig 121, *ne* leof *ne* lað
511, Þa wæs eft *swa* ær 642. (7)

That is to say, the italicized words do not get metrical stress. Rather than
taking them as evidence against Kuhn's Law, Bliss modifies the law to
accommodate them. But in so doing he undoes the very reason for
making a law out of what is otherwise a commonplace observation
about conjunctions: that they head the clause or phrase they connect to
its predecessor. When they connect clauses, they will be at the beginning
of a clause; when they connect phrases, they will be at the beginning of a
phrase.

If Kuhn's First Law were true in its original formulation about
conjunctions, it would make a very striking prediction about phrasal
conjunctions in Old English poetry: that conjoined phrases like *grim
ond grǣdig* occur only at the opening of clauses, where the particle *ond*
follows the first stress and is therefore not stressed. The usual pattern in
Old English poetry is just the other way around. Of the 313 instances of
the conjunction in *Beowulf,* 217 are phrasal. There are in fact no
instances in the poem of these conjoined phrases heading a clause.

With nouns, as in *grim ond grǣdig,* the particle *ond* can remain
unstressed only when the first noun is the first stress in the clause. If the
conjoined nouns appear later, the *ond* will not be in the first dip and
should therefore, as a particle, get stress. The 217 instances of conjoined
phrases appearing after the clause-initial dip (e.g., 1008b, 1063b, 1700b,
2431b, 2472a, 3157b) are contrary to the original formulation of Kuhn's
First Law; for example:

    Þǣr wæs gidd ond glēo (2105a)

With verbs, such a pattern of conjunctions will always satisfy the rule
for keeping particles unstressed, since the second verb will be the
beginning of its own clause:

    Manað swā ond myndgað (2057a)
    swefeð ond snēdeþ (600a)

These two examples show why Kuhn made *ond* a particle rather than a
proclitic. If *ond* were proclitic, then the clause beginning with *ond*
would begin with a proclitic immediately before a metrically stressed
verb, and so the clause beginning would lack a particle and be in
violation of the Second Law (of clause openings). The Second Law
would also have to declare ill-formed the fifteen instances of conjoined
clauses beginning with a conjunction and a prepositional phrase: *ond for
dolgilpe . . . nēþdon* in the following:

> ðær git for wlence   wada cunnedon
> ond for dolgilpe   on dēop wæter
> aldrum nēþdon   (508–10)

where the two of you, for your pride, made trial of the sea, and because of a foolish boast risked your lives in the deep water

Here, the clause would begin with two proclitics, *ond* and *for,* followed by a stress word without any intervening particles.

Conjunctions connecting phrases might be different from conjunctions connecting clauses. But Bliss's revision does not address this question. It dismisses the problem by definition: if a conjunction occurs at the beginning of a clause it is called a "particle"; if it occurs elsewhere it is called a "proclitic." The terms do not refer to differences in stress; indeed, Bliss makes the shift in terminology to account for the fact that in all instances the conjunctions are unstressed. The one place where meter may stress *ond*—when it introduces an A3 verse—is where a Kuhnian stress would usually require more, unmetrical stress in the rest of the verse. Thus, no empirical consequences flow from Bliss's taxonomy of conjunctions, and no evidence can be brought in support or refutation of it. By definition the two categories of conjunctions do not contradict either of Kuhn's Laws.

Prepositions

Kendall finds a "striking confirmation of Kuhn's second law" in the fact that of 253 verses beginning with a preposition (by his count), only six are clause-initial. Of these six he argues for repunctuating two and for assigning a "relative function" to the definite article in three, thus removing them as exceptions. The infrequency of prepositional phrases at the head of clauses in *Beowulf* may be an interesting fact. However, on closer inspection it may not be. Consider the parallel case of clause-initial personal pronouns.

Beowulf contains 284 instances of the subject pronoun *hē,* surely a better candidate for clause-openings than the prepositional phrase. And indeed, quite a few of these pronouns do begin clauses. But they rarely begin clauses all alone, though Kuhn's Laws predict that they can. There are 430 instances of the third-person personal pronouns in the nominative: *hē, hēo, hīo, hit, hyt, hī, hȳ, hīe,* and *hig.* Only seven have the nominative pronoun as the lone unstressed syllable at the beginning of a clause:

> Hē bēot ne ālēh (80a)
> ; hē fēara sum (1412a)
> ; hē fyrmest læg (2077b)

Hē frǣtwe gehēold (2620a)
Hī sīð drugon (1966b)
Hȳ bēnan synt (364b)
Hīe dȳgel lond (1357b)

More often, when the pronoun heads the clause, other unstressed words
fall into the dip. Sometimes the verb is in the dip together with the
pronoun, as in "*hē is* manna gehyld" (3056a), 1727b, 1837b. Quite often
object pronouns occur with the nominative pronoun.

The seven clause openings with the pronoun alone amount to about
one in every sixty-one occurrences of the nominative pronouns. This
frequency is even lower than that for the prepositions, where about one
in forty-seven stands alone (or with an adjectival pronoun) at the
beginning of a clause (by Kendall's count before his repunctuation and
reinterpretation). If anything is striking about these distributions, surely
it is that nominative personal pronouns occur so rarely by themselves, a
fact that Kuhn's Second Law in its focus on "proclitics" does not
address. One expects a high proportion of nominative personal pronouns at the beginning of clauses, although not necessarily many prepositions.

Indeed, a reason for the scarcity of prepositions as sole clause openers
can be seen in two exceptions to Kuhn's Second Law that Kendall fails
to include in his count, 1717b and 507a. Prepositional phrases without
other signals at the beginning of a clause can be ambiguous:

> ðēah þe hine mihtig God   mægenes wynnum,
> eafeþum stēpte,   ofer ealle men
> forð gefremede.   (1716–1718a)

although mighty God advanced him in the joys of strength, in might,
beyond all men(,) advanced him.

On what linguists call a garden-path reading, the clause in 1717b–18a
might be taken as a continuation of the *ðēah þe* clause that immediately
precedes it; the prepositional phrase *ofer ealle men* could easily be
construed with *stēpte* rather than with *gefremede*. A *hine* or *hē* before the
ofer would remove the ambiguity.

Similarly in 506–507:

> 'Eart þū sē Bēowulf,   sē þe wið Brecan wunne,
> on sīdne sǣ   ymb sund flite.

You are that Beowulf who contended with Breca(,) on the broad
sea(,) competed on the water.

The prepositional phrase *on sīdne sǣ* could as easily be construed with
wunne as with *flite*. It might be noted that either parsing produces a

violation of Kuhn's Second Law: by one reading, the clause-opening has only *on*; by the other, it has only *ymb*.

Because of the ambiguity of prepositional phrases and because of the deeper syntactic principles that require investigation, the infrequency of sole prepositions as clause openers is hardly remarkable. Other grammatical categories that might be more expected in that position also do not occur. One effect of the taxonomy of Kuhn's Laws is to obscure the need for further investigation that might reveal the more general principles regulating the opening of clauses.

Infinitives

Infinitives can be treated briefly because they show so clearly the contradictions and tautologies of Kuhn's Laws. They also show why assuming that the laws extract the relevant structures leads one into asking irrelevant questions. As part of his investigation that shows "a striking confirmation of Kuhn's second law," Kendall notes that there are thirty half-lines in *Beowulf* of the pattern infinitive with unstressed prefix + auxiliary (e.g., *onberan wolde* 990b). He observes that none begins a clause and credits this fact to the unstressed prefix, which would be in violation of Kuhn's Second Law. Kendall never considers the fortunes of infinitives *without* prefixes (e.g. *hȳran scolde* 10b), which are not prevented by Kuhn's Laws from being clause-initial. But of the 332 verses in *Beowulf* that begin with infinitives without a prefix, only one (449b) begins a clause. Kuhn's laws would easily have accommodated these infinitives at the beginning of a clause. Thus, the explanation for the gap in the data must be sought elsewhere.

Observations by Bliss and by Donoghue suggest a way toward the solution of this particular problem, although they stop short of the deeper principles that need to be articulated. Following up on Bliss's study of the order of the auxiliary and the verbal (a category that includes infinitives and participles), Donoghue draws the "reliable though not always infallible" generalization that in nineteen Old English poems, the "position of the auxiliary before the verbal characterizes principal clauses."[11] Thus, the order infinitive + auxiliary may indicate a dependent clause. To the extent that this generalization is true, the data on infinitives presented by Kendall are trivial and the operation of Kuhn's Second Law with respect to initial infinitives (with or without prefixes) is vacuous. If the clause is dependent, then obviously the infinitive cannot be placed at the beginning, because that position must be held by the subordinating conjunction or relative pronoun. The verbal prefix, to which Kuhn's Second Law assigns significance, does not explain the failure of infinitives to begin clauses, and it turns the inquiry in the wrong direction.

Finite Verbs

Perhaps more clearly than any other part of speech, finite verbs in Old English meter show why an inadequate generalization can be worse than no generalization at all. According to Bliss's interpretation of Kuhn's Laws, *song* in 323a "has been displaced from its normal position among the particles at the beginning of its clause" (10); it thus receives metrical stress, as the alliteration indicates:

/   x   /   x
song in searwum

However, in 217a *Gewāt* has not been "displaced"; therefore, according to Bliss's use of Kuhn's Laws (as with Kendall's use), the finite verb does not receive metrical stress and the alliteration is "non-functional" or "ornamental":

x x x xx   /   x
Gewāt þā ofer wægholm

Comparative statistics are difficult to state and analyze, because every metrist divides verbs into different kinds of categories. (Bliss finds nine patterns of finite verbs.) Roughly, however, one can say that Blissian interpretations of Kuhn's Laws are in accord with about sixty-nine verses of the *song in searwum* type; but those interpretations are problematic in that they classify as unmetrical or ignore (depending on whether verbal prefixes occur) far more verses than they accept—about 180 verses of the *Gewāt þā ofer wægholm* type if the verb is considered metrically stressed.

That the verb should indeed be considered metrically stressed is argued by metrists who reject Kuhn's Laws. For these metrists, two metrical stresses on alliterating syllables in *Gewāt þā ofer wægholm* are perfectly natural and in accord with other kinds of evidence. In fact, Kuhn himself scanned *Gewāt* with a stress. We find the criticisms on this point by Stockwell and Minkova, Russom, and Hutcheson convincing.

For these patterns of finite verbs Hutcheson actually gives a better interpretation of Kuhn's original intent than later followers of Kuhn do. If *Gewāt* is stressed, the verse seems to violate Kuhn's Second Law (according to which a proclitic like *Ge-* cannot occur by itself in the first dip of a clause). By distinguishing anacrusis (*Auftakt*) from upbeat (*Satzauftakt*) and by scanning *Ge-* as anacrusis, Hutcheson clarifies Kuhn's ambiguous terminology and confusing presentation. The verse in question is salvaged as metrical by a traditional Kuhn's Law reading and does not require the dubious scansions that Bliss and Kendall impose upon it. Having made sense of Kuhn's scansion of verses like this one, Hutcheson continues to make the devastating point that Kuhn's Laws, even when interpreted in the best possible way, really tell us very little: "Confining our discussion to verbs, recall that Kuhn asserts that if verbs are unstressed, they follow the law of sentence particles. But apparently the only verbs that Kuhn regards as unstressed are verbs that are in the positions that his first law allows: this is because these are the only verbs that Sievers regards as unstressed" (132). It is this circularity that those who dissent from Kuhn's Laws find maddening.

Kuhn's Laws seem to tell us why verbs in verse-initial position are sometimes stressed and sometimes unstressed (i.e. in the first part of a Type B or C verse). More specifically, they purport to explain that sixty-nine verbs like *song* in *song in searwum* are stressed because they are clause-medial and that about forty-six other verbs (other than the copula and finite verbs serving as auxiliaries) lacking alliteration and metrical stress and thus appearing in metrical Types B and C, such as *scōp him Heort naman* (78b), are unstressed because they are clause-initial.

Since most verse-initial verbs are stressed, and since most of the verbs that are stressed are clause-initial, it is hard to accept an explanation of the stress in *song in searwum* as coming about because the verb is clause-medial. Moreover, when we look at the second explanation, we must note that what Kuhn's Laws say cannot happen would not be expected to happen very often anyway. Given that more than eighty-four percent of the 374 verse-initial verbs are clause-initial, and that nearly eighty-eight percent of them are stressed, we would expect to find in all of *Beowulf* no more than eight verbs that are both clause-medial and unstressed.

Still, it seems impressive that except for 1109b, an instance of the copula *wæs*, we find no examples in Klaeber's text of verbs beginning verses of Types B and C that are not clause-initial as well. Kuhn's Laws seem to offer a nearly exceptionless description of metrically unstressed verbs in such verses as necessarily clause-initial. But are they? In at least four verses, an initial unstressed verb (other than an auxiliary) is preced-ed by a noun that can go just as well with an earlier verb—sometimes as the expressed subject or modifier of that subject, sometimes as an adverbial.[12] We can thank Klaeber's punctuation for directing us toward an interpretation of such verses that agrees with Kuhn. For example, at 607–10 we get not (a), but (b):

(a)   Đā wæs on sālum   sinces brytta
         gamolfeax ond gūðrōf; gēoce gelӯfde.
         Brego Beorht-Dena   gehȳrde on Bēowulfe,
         folces hyrde,   fæstrǣdne geþōht.

Then the giver of treasure, gray-haired and battle-brave, was glad; he
counted on help. The leader of the Bright Danes, the people's
guardian, heard a firmly-resolved intention from Beowulf.

(b)   Đā wæs on sālum   sinces brytta
         gamolfeax ond gūðrōf; gēoce gelӯfde
         Brego Beorht-Dena; gehȳrde on Bēowulfe
         folces hyrde   fæstrǣdne geþōht.

Then the giver of treasure, gray-haired and battle-brave, was glad; he,
the leader of the Bright Danes, counted on help. The people's
guardian learned of a firmly-resolved intention from Beowulf.

To say that Kuhn's Laws prove that only (b) is right assumes the
exceptionlessness that it sets out to prove. At least four examples of
unstressed verbs cannot count as evidence for either side. We would
therefore expect even fewer than eight examples of verse-initial but
clause-medial unstressed verbs. If Kuhn's Laws explain why we have
none, they offer no explanation for why most verse-initial finite verbs are
both clause-initial and metrically stressed.

We can illustrate this point with one final set of data. *Beowulf* has
thirty-five verse-initial verbs in the second half-line. Twenty-four of
these are clause-initial, and eleven are not. For the eleven verbs that are
not clause-initial, Bliss's interpretation of Kuhn's Laws seems to work
well, because the verbs receive stress (as though they were "displaced"
from the first dip). For the other twenty-four verses, however, Kuhn's
Laws (by any interpretation) are silent; stress is neither prescribed nor
proscribed. Those who invoke Kuhn's Laws assume that stress is assigned by metrical determinants. But if we need to specify the metrical
determinants for clause-initial verbs, then Kuhn's Laws are redundant,
because the same determinants must be specified for verbs that are not
clause-initial. Kuhn's Laws simply drive along compatibly with a small
set of the data and then shift into neutral for the rest, leaving the real
work of explanation to other metrical and grammatical rules.

III. METER

Our basic argument is that the syntax of Old English poetry is not as
simple, nor the meter as complex, as Kuhn's Laws would make them
appear. There are various independent but interacting syntactic con-

straints that can be understood only after the metrical constraints have been factored out.

The first step toward a more adequate theory of syntax than that described by Kuhn's two laws is a more adequate theory of meter than that described by Sievers' Five Types. Our theory of Old English meter is one that is basically built on a count of four positions and that can be stated as follows:

> The meter of Old English poetry is alliterative-syllabic, each verse containing four positions, which are realized as four syllables or resolved equivalents. There is one optional expansion of unstressed syllables in either of the first two positions of the verse.

Although this statement turns the constraints on Sievers' Five Types upside down, its effect is less radical than it might appear. Instead of the traditional conception of dips as variable in length except for restrictions to one syllable in the second dips of Types A, / x (x) (x) / x, and C, x (x) (x) / / x,[13] the idea is that dips are normally limited to one syllable except for suspension of the restriction in the first dips of Types A and C, which can be expanded. To these traditional categories for allowing expansion, we add the first dip of Type B (which, in our reverse way of doing things, limits the second dip of Type B to one syllable).[14]

Although stress is not mentioned directly in our paradigm of Old English meter, its relevance as a metrical feature is implied both by alliteration and by the allowance of "one optional expansion of un-stressed syllables in either of the first two positions of the verse." On the one hand, it is necessary to know which categories of words have enough stress to bear alliteration. (With a few exceptions these categories are limited to nouns, adjectives, participles, infinitives, finite lexical verbs, and adverbs.) On the other hand, it is necessary to know which categories of words are light enough to occur in what has traditionally been called the "gabble of weaker syllables," the optional expansion in one of the first two positions of Types A, B, and C. (These categories include articles, prepositions, auxiliaries, copulas, conjunctions, and pronouns, plus finite lexical verbs and adverbs from the first set.)

This taxonomy has a curious effect on the shape of Sievers' Five Types. For assigning alliteration, it is necessary to ask, "Which categories have enough stress?" For the optional gabble of weaker syllables in either of the first two positions of the verse, however, we must ask, "Which categories have enough *lack* of stress?" For the end of the long line, then, neither question is relevant: the gabble of weaker syllables can occur only in the first two positions of the verse, which in the b-verse is also the only place where alliteration can occur.

What, then, does one say about metrical stress, or metrical ictus, on *scealt* in 588?

x   x   x   /   x   ?

þæs þū in helle scealt

werhðo drēogan,   þēah þīn wit duge   (588–89)

for that you must suffer punishment in hell, though your wit is keen.

A Sieversian analysis assigns metrical stress to *scealt* to make it parallel to other Type B verses, such as 3069a:

x   x   x   /   x   /

Swā hit oð dōmes dæg

But in what sense is *scealt* metrically equivalent to *dæg*? The various forms of *sculan* never alliterate, and they rarely occur in what might be considered a stressed position (even by Sievers' Five Types) in the a-verse.

A better scansion might look like one of Bliss's "light verse" patterns (although Bliss never scanned Type B verses as light):

x   x x   / x   x

þæs þū in helle scealt

Indeed, if we had taken the sentence as prose rather than as poetry, our assumptions about the normal stress-timed patterns of Old English would have produced such a reading:

x   x x / x   x   / x   / x

þæs þū in helle scealt werhðo drēogan.

Since we know that the sentence is poetry and not prose, one might object to the lack of stress in *scealt* and insist that the patterns of poetry should prevail. But what *are* the patterns of poetry? Let us assume not Sievers' Five Types or an inevitable two-stress half-line but a four-position half-line realized as four syllables with one optional expansion. Then there is no imperative for stressing *scealt*. It simply counts as a full syllable, and thus as a position by itself—and not as part of a stretch of metrically unstressed syllables (like *þæs þū in* at the beginning of the verse). By this way of looking at things, the relevant question to ask (except when assigning alliteration) is not, "Which categories are stressed?" but "Which categories are light enough to be assigned to the optional expansion? or, as it is known, to the 'strong dip'?"

If this metrical analysis is right, then much of the point of Kuhn's Laws is lost, because the laws have it just backwards. Instead of assigning stress to particles that are "displaced" to the right, the idea is to determine which syllables can run together at the beginning. If Old English meter is basically a syllable-count meter and not a stress meter, the point is to determine when a syllable is *not* counted—or at least not counted as a position by itself.

As radical as this view of Old English meter may seem, it is part of a convergence of various approaches that has developed in recent years. For example, it is compatible with major aspects of Geoffrey Russom's word-foot theory of Old English meter.[15] Russom points to the rarity of Type B verses composed of monosyllables. By our view, sequences of monosyllables are especially associated with the optional stretch of unstressed syllables at the beginning of the verse, whereas a polysyllabic word gives a shape to the verse and narrows the possibilities for assigning ambiguous categories. Without the shaping effect of longer words, the Old English verse would be too flexible and too ambiguous to be clearly perceived. Thus, the effect of word shape, such as Russom builds into his system, is more significant than it would be in other theories of organizing the half-line.

IV. IMPLICATIONS

Although the syntactic and metrical structures dealt with in this analysis are fairly technical and specific, we believe that they call into question certain scholarly and popular conceptions of rhythm in English and the other Germanic languages. Our analysis also addresses current ideas about syntax, in both the older and the modern languages, but because scholarly and popular conceptions of syntax are less clear, the implications are rather different.

The Germanic languages are sometimes classified as "stress-timed," a description that means equal temporal intervals between stressed syllables, irrespective of the intervening number of unstressed syllables. In contrast are "syllable-timed" languages, such as French, in which equal temporal intervals occur between the syllables themselves. It is usually assumed that the patterns of Old English phonology and meter were at least as stress-timed as those of Modern English. Paul Fussell speaks of "our own Anglo-Saxon instinct to hear stress"[16] and makes the kind of statement that appears regularly in the handbooks:

> The powerful Germanic accents of the Old English language provide a natural basis for a very heavily accentual prosody in which sense rhythm rather than any abstract metrical imperative tends to supply the meter. The standard poetic line in Old English consists of four strongly stressed syllables arranged, together with any number of unstressed syllables, in two hemistichs (or half-lines) of two stresses each. (63)

In a classic essay that distinguished between strong-stress meter and syllabic-stress meter, W.K. Wimsatt, Jr., and Monroe C. Beardsley presented the view that appears in the standard handbooks: ". . . the clutter of weaker syllables in a strong-stress meter is against an accurate syllable-stress reading, most often prevents it entirely. A few lines of *Piers Plowman* or of *Everyman* ought to suffice to show what is what."[17] The authors contrast the meter of *Piers Plowman* with the syllable-stress meter of the English iambic pentameter (Chaucer, Shakespeare, Milton, Pope, Wordsworth) and suggest that Langland's meter is "older in English poetry and may be more natural to the English tongue, though again it may not be. Here only the major stresses of the major words count in the scanning. The gabble of weaker syllables, now more, now fewer, between the major stresses obscures all the minor stresses and relieves them of any structural duty. . . . Thus we have *Beowulf, Piers Plowman, Everyman,* Spenser's *February Eclogue,* Coleridge's *Christabel,* the poetry of G.M. Hopkins (who talks about 'sprung rhythm' and 'outrides'), . . . the poetry of T.S. Eliot, and many another in our day" (592).

The issues, then, concern not simply technicalities of this or that subtype of Old English verse but the rhythmical structure of the major forms of English poetry from its beginnings to the present. Both Sievers' metrical system and Kuhn's Laws are indeed technical in themselves; in combination they are dauntingly so. Yet the familiar generalizations about rhythm in English poetry rest upon these complexities. Kuhn's Laws seem to make Sievers' Five Types work—at least when one goes beyond the introductory presentation. The Laws seem to make the Five Types work because they claim to account for the *absence* of patterns that would otherwise be unexplained and that would form a deficit against the theory. Kuhn's Laws are like a governor on a motor, adjusting the distribution of metrically unstressed syllables that feed into the Five Types.

The problem is that the interaction of the two systems requires more machinery than is necessary. If we begin with either system, the other is needed as a complement. However, if we begin with the grammatical hierarchy and a metrical system that directly specifies the count of syllables (with one optional expansion), then the stressed syllables, particles, and proclitics fall into place. To the extent that there is what Wimsatt and Beardsley call a "gabble of weaker syllables," its placing and boundaries are precisely defined. But this precise definition also means that "strong-stress meter" does not have the essential character that their essay aimed to establish. It is not a thread that links *Beowulf, Piers Plowman,* and Eliot's *Four Quartets.*

The syntactic implications of the non-existence of Kuhn's Laws are that each grammatical category has its own story, its own environments where it is most likely to be eligible for metrical stress. The stress on nouns has always been clear, but the stress on finite verbs must be analysed anew. And so for each of the traditional parts of speech. About pronouns much remains to be said.[18] Future investigation will have to consider the implications of the choice possible in Old English between expressed and unexpressed subjects. The goal of all this particular activity is an understanding of how Old English syntax is no more primitive or simple than that of its direct descendant, which it may resemble more closely than the early nineteenth century imagined.

A recent issue of *Speculum* devotes its six essays to the New Philology. Because we consider Kuhn's Laws a prime example of the Old Philology, we would expect the authors of this set of essays to share our concerns. In principle, indeed, they do. Linguistics has always been central to philology even when philology has not kept up with linguistics. On the first page of the "Introduction" to the special issue, linguistics is the first of the "cognitive methodologies" named: ". . . a rethinking of philology should seek to minimize the isolation between medieval studies and other contemporary movements in cognitive methodologies, such as linguistics, anthropology, modern history, cultural studies, and so on, by reminding us that philology was once among the most theoretically avant-garde disciplines . . ."[19] Yet the isolation remains. The essay devoted specifically to linguistics skips completely the area that has been truly revolutionary in the twentieth century—generative grammar—and goes directly to issues of orality, pragmatics, and discourse analysis.[20] Elsewhere, reference to linguistics typically begins and ends with Saussure.[21] Our own position is that the individual grammar of the speaker and the structure of the sentence must not be neglected in investigations of discourse and culture.

It is not that we would advocate a particular theory of Chomsky's in order to understand the sounds and syntax of Old English poetry. Rather we would argue more generally that knowledge of current mainstream linguistics is a proven way of gaining new insights into the structure of a dead language—as it has been for the past two centuries. This is true whether the mainstream linguistics was the literal "Buchstabenlehre" of Rask, Grimm, and Bopp, the phonetics of the Neogrammarians, the phonemics of twentieth-century structuralists, or the higher abstractions of generative grammarians. Knowledge of mainstream linguistics enhances the philological effort even if linguistic constructs are not used. Although there is little that is "linguistic" in our analyses above, ideas of linguistic structure and description, including the goals of linguistic theory, underlie those analyses.

What is disconcerting in essays such as Suzanne Fleishman's in the issue of *Speculum* on the New Philology is the lack of interest in such concepts of structure itself, "stable system," "sentence," "forms of grammar," and certainly formalized "rules." What is favored instead is "a postmodern view of grammar as 'emergent', that is, not as a synchronically stable bedrock of form-meaning or form-function correlations, but as a set of linguistic transactions that are continually being negotiated in individual contexts of communication" (28). We can find nothing in this prescription or in its elaboration that helps us in understanding the sounds and syntax of Old English poetry, which we consider to be major elements of Anglo-Saxon culture. The alternatives that various philological theories offer, as we have tried to indicate above, are not trivial. A choice of one over another changes our perception of the text in fundamental ways. These alternatives are usually stated as *rules,* as we think they should be. Our rules may still not be the most adequate ones, but neither our theory nor any of the theories that we discuss deal with "emergent" phenomena. There is a certain bedrock stability to the interaction of sound and syntax in Old English poetry, a stability which generations of readers have intuited. The task of the philologist is to find the descriptions that make those intuitions explicit.

NOTES

1. Hans Kuhn, "Zur Wortstellung und -betonung im Altgermanischen," *Beiträge zur Geschichte der deutschen Sprache und Literatur* 57 (1933): 1–109.

2. Among studies of the past two decades that have made use of Kuhn's Laws, see Alan Bliss, *An Introduction to Old English Metre* (Oxford, 1962), *The Metre of "Beowulf,"* rev. ed. (Oxford, 1967), and especially "Auxiliary and Verbal in *Beowulf,*" *Anglo-Saxon England* 9 (1981): 157–82; Alistair Campbell, "Verse Influences in Old English Prose," *Philological Essays: Studies in Old and Middle English in Honour of Herbert Dean Meritt,* ed. J.L. Rosier (The Hague, 1970), 93–98; E.G. Stanley, "Verbal Stress in Old English Verse," *Anglia* 20 (1975): 307–34; Spencer Cosmos, "Kuhn's Law and the Unstressed Verbs in *Beowulf,*" *Texas Studies in Literature and Language* 18 (1976): 306–28; Calvin B. Kendall, "The Metrical Grammar of *Beowulf*: Displacement," *Speculum* 58 (1983): 1–30; Bruce Mitchell, *Old English Syntax* (Oxford, 1985); Daniel Donoghue, *Style in Old English Poetry: The Test of the Auxiliary* (New Haven, 1987); Peter J. Lucas, "Some Aspects of the Interaction between Verse Grammar and Metre in Old English Poetry," *Studia Neophilologica* 59 (1987): 145–75; Kari Ellen Gade, "Hans Kuhn's *Das Dróttkvætt*: Some Critical Observations," *Journal of English and Germanic Philology* 88 (1989): 34–53; Robert P. Stockwell and Donka Minkova, "On Kendall's Theory of Syntactic Displacement in *Beowulf,*" paper presented at a conference on Early Germanic

Syntax and Semantics, Berkeley, 3 March 1990; and B.R. Hutcheson, "Kuhn's Laws, Finite Verb Stress, and the Critics," *Studia Neophilologica* 64 (1992): 129–39.

3. Jacob Wackernagel, "Über ein Gesetz der indogermanischen Wortstellung," *Indogermanische Forschungen* 1 (1892): 333–436.

4. Berthold Delbrück, *Syntaktische Forschungen 3* (Waisenhaus, 1878), 47; cited in Wackernagel, 402.

5. See, for example, David Crystal, *A Dictionary of Linguistics and Phonetics*, 2nd ed. (Oxford, 1985).

6. "Metrical Grammar," 2.

7. Eduard Sievers, *Altgermanische Metrik* (Halle, 1893).

8. Unless otherwise noted, all quotations of poetry are from F. Klaeber, ed., *Beowulf and the Fight at Finnsburg*, 3rd ed. (Boston, 1950).

9. *Syntactic Case and Morphological Case in the History of English* (Dordrecht, 1987).

10. See, for example, Richard S. Kayne, *French Syntax: The Transformational Cycle* (Cambridge, Mass., 1975), and van Kemenade.

11. *Style in Old English Poetry*, 91.

12. The verbs are in lines 609b, 2431a, 2604b, and 2939a; additional examples of possibly clause-medial copula or auxiliary verbs like 1109b include 135b, 1338, 1903a, 2442b, and 3171a.

13. Sievers only stated what was usual, but see later developments such as Bright's presentation in Frederic G. Cassidy and Richard N. Ringler, *Bright's Old English Grammar and Reader*, 3rd ed. (New York, 1971) and the catalogue of Type B in John C. Pope, *The Rhythm of "Beowulf,"* 2nd ed. (New Haven, 1966).

14. A fuller explanation would exempt verbal prefixes from the count in a way parallel to their exemption in Type A with anacrusis.

15. *Old English Meter and Linguistic Theory* (Cambridge, 1987).

16. *Poetic Meter and Poetic Form*, rev. ed. (New York, 1979), 7.

17. "The Concept of Meter: An Exercise in Abstraction," *PMLA* 74 (1959): 585–98, at 592.

18. See, for example, Cynthia Allen, review of Ans van Kemenade, *Syntactic Case* (note 9 above), *Language* 66 (1990): 146–52.

19. Stephen G. Nichols, "Introduction: Philology in a Manuscript Culture," *Speculum* 65 (1990): 1–10.

20. Suzanne Fleischman, "Philology, Linguistics, and the Discourse of the Medieval Text," *Speculum* 65 (1990): 19–37.

21. As in Lee Patterson, "On the Margin: Postmodernism, Ironic History, and Medieval Studies," *Speculum* 65 (1990): 87–108.

On the Dating of *Beowulf*

by Roy Michael Liuzza

> I accept without argument . . . the attribution of *Beowulf* to the "age
> of Bede"—one of the firmer conclusions of a department of research
> most clearly serviceable to criticism: inquiry into the probable date of
> the effective composition of the poem as we have it.[1]

TIMES have changed since J.R.R. Tolkien made these remarks
in 1936. Not only has the traditional dating of the poem to the
somewhat elastic "Age of Bede" come under increasing suspicion, but few would nowadays consider the branch of *Beowulf* studies
concerned with dating to be "most clearly serviceable to criticism."
Around 1980 the question of "the probable date of the effective composition" of *Beowulf* was reopened in a dramatic way by the publication of
three works: Ashley Amos's *Linguistic Means of Determining the Dates of
Old English Literary Texts,* Kevin Kiernan's *"Beowulf" and the "Beowulf"
Manuscript,* and a collection of essays entitled *The Dating of "Beowulf."*[2]
The combined effect of these works was not only to raise the level of
discussion and quality of evidence to new heights of linguistic, palaeo-
graphical, and historical sophistication and subtlety, but to shift the
debate on dating from relative consensus to relative chaos, and many
critics since then have chosen to go about the business of reading and
teaching the poem without any firm public conviction about its precise
place in Anglo-Saxon history.

An emblem of this erosion of certainty may be drawn from the works
of Stanley B. Greenfield. In his 1965 *Critical History of Old English
Literature* he wrote, "a written text in the Anglian or Mercian dialect
probably existed by the middle of the eighth century";[3] in the revised
New Critical History of Old English Literature written with Daniel G.
Calder in 1986, this was changed: "the early consensus on dating . . . has
crumbled. Various linguistic, historical, and aesthetic arguments suggest
dates of composition from the late eighth through the early eleventh
century."[4] A sample of some works on *Beowulf* published since 1980
suggests that many scholars avoid the problem of assigning a date to the
poem, or present their opinions as a matter of faith rather than evidence.
In *"Beowulf" and the Appositive Style* Fred C. Robinson advises that
"when such learned and formidable challenges to an early date [i.e., as

those in Amos, Kiernan, and Chase] have been posed, minds must remain open.["5] This is quoted with approval by Alain Renoir in his 1988 *A Key to Old Poems.*[6] Helen Damico, in *Beowulf's Wealhtheow and the Valkyrie Tradition* defers to the essays in *The Dating of "Beowulf"* and provides the date of the manuscript (s. x–xi).[7] Nicholas Howe, in *Migration and Mythmaking in Anglo-Saxon England,* states that "nothing about the poem indicates that it was composed during a moment of crisis" and immediately adds in a footnote, "this statement should not be taken as evidence for the date of *Beowulf.*"[8] Edward B. Irving's *Rereading "Beowulf"* hesitates: "If the older scholarly assumption of an eighth-century date has been shown to be rather insecurely based (there was always a good deal of wishful thinking in that assumption), the late date has as yet been no more firmly established."[9] He declares his allegiance to the earlier date, but qualifies it by saying "the evidence for it is the merest gossamer" (7). Ruth P.M. Lehmann, in *"Beowulf": an Imitative Translation,* almost apologizes: "Since in my own mind I must try to settle the question, I feel that the eighth or ninth century consorts well with the language, the interest in Danish affairs, and the mixture of Christian and Germanic virtues."[10]

Others have continued to advocate an earlier date, often without reference to the uncertainty engendered by the works of Amos, Kiernan, and the contributors to *The Dating of "Beowulf."* David Williams, in *Cain and "Beowulf,"* accepts the traditional eighth-century date proposed in 1970 by Margaret Goldsmith in *The Mode and Meaning of "Beowulf."*[11] Mary Parker's *"Beowulf" and Christianity,* while acknowledging the work of Kiernan and the essays in *The Dating of "Beowulf,"* still proposes an early date.[12] George Clark's 1990 *Beowulf* provides a chronology with the following entry: "700–800. The poem, in something like its present form, first committed to writing, probably after a long circulation in oral tradition."[13] Elsewhere in this book he states that "*Beowulf* was already on parchment and somewhat resistant to recreation and updating by the time the Viking age began in earnest" (46). In a recent article, Robert P. Creed accepts what may be the earliest possible date for the poem: "I think the evidence—the prosody, geography, and subject of the poem—indicates that the poem was composed while being taken down in writing early in the Anglo-Saxon period, perhaps as early as the second quarter of the seventh century."[14]

A number of studies in the past decade have addressed but not settled the question of dating *Beowulf.* Important reviews of Kiernan and *The Dating of "Beowulf"* include those of Ashley Crandell Amos, R.D. Fulk, and Claus-Dieter Wetzel.[15] David Dumville has offered a methodological critique of textual and historiographical approaches to dating the poem; an important recent study of linguistic methodology has been made by Janet Bately.[16] Recent proponents of an early date include Michael Lapidge and M.J. Swanton; proponents of a later date include W.G. Busse and R. Holtei, Patricia Poussa, John D. Niles, Alexandra Hennessey Olsen, Rowland L. Collins, and Audrey L. Meaney.[17] Despite the learned and often passionate arguments of this prestigious array of scholars, the question remains open, though few critics are as candid as Alain Renoir: "I readily confess that I should be at a loss to tell when, where, by whom, and under what circumstances, this greatest of all early-Germanic epics was composed."[18]

   This critical confusion is perhaps the most trenchant of many ironies offered to the Anglo-Saxonist in an English department: the most historically-minded branch of English literary studies cannot place its most important poetic text more securely than in a range of three centuries. Without a doubt, the date of *Beowulf* matters; imagine the confusion that would result if some critics placed *Paradise Lost* in the late seventeenth century, others in the early sixteenth, still others in the middle of the nineteenth, and viewed Milton variously as a contemporary of Wyatt, Pope, or Tennyson. With only the most general notions of the poem's context, its backgrounds, its influences and its reception, it would be difficult, perhaps impossible, to perform any worthwhile critical activity upon it. Yet this is precisely the situation of the reader of *Beowulf.* It may well be the English literary text most in need of an interpretive context, but we have a pitifully vague notion of that context. This frustrating situation is itself of considerable interest, and rather than add to the already overburdened shelf of conflicting opinions I would like to examine in a general way the practice of dating the poem, not so much to sift truth from falsehood as to consider the implications of these methods for the discipline of Anglo-Saxon studies as a whole. I believe that the assumptions made in dating the poem, a branch of the study of Old English often regarded as ancillary, technical and perhaps a bit antique, tell us a great deal about our sometimes unspoken and unformulated critical attitudes towards Old English literary texts; each effort to date the poem contains an implicit *ars poetica.*

   One of the first problems raised by an effort to date the poem, for example, is that of definition—what we mean when we speak of *Beowulf.* To fix the moment of origin is to have some conception of the nature of the thing brought into being: is it the text contained in MS Cotton Vitellius A. xv? some earlier archetype of this manuscript, free from errors but without substantive variation from the surviving text? or some previously existing tale, or collection of tales, transmitted orally and finally written down some centuries after its original composition? Each of these alternative definitions has important consequences not only for how we date *Beowulf* but for how we read it; dating the poem forces us to make explicit our understanding of its form and content. The question of dating *Beowulf* foregrounds the most important questions of Old English poetry—creation and tradition, transmission and reception, context and the limits of interpretation.

Of the many methods which have been used to determine the poem's date, two call for special attention. One might call them "the beauty of inflections" and "the beauty of innuendoes": the first regards the internal evidence of meter and language, the second the external evidence of historical context both in explicit references to historical events and implicit attitudes towards man and society. The faith of the historicist method was simply expressed by Ritchie Girvan in 1935: "since the poem is English it ought not to be impossible to bring it into relation with some particular stage of Anglo-Saxon development, for it must have a background in time and place, and this will betray itself."[19] The stumbling-block in this faith is the assumption that *Beowulf* is an ordinary representative of an ordinary Englishman's attitude at a given moment in history; most of us would prefer to believe that the poem is of unusually high quality, and its author's beliefs may have been as uncommon as his poetic skill. The complexity of the poem's attitude towards the men and tribes it depicts suggests that its author did not "play the flat historic scale" and hold a monocular view of the world.[20] In fact wherever *Beowulf* is placed in Anglo-Saxon history it works rather like Wallace Stevens's jar in Tennessee—it makes the slovenly wilderness surround it; it takes dominion everywhere, and it becomes its own profound commentary on the political, moral and aesthetic conditions of the age, whether that age is Bede's, Offa's, Alfred's, Athelstan's, or Cnut's.

In its most basic form the historical method relies on a poem which is already interpreted, whose opinions and attitudes are beyond dispute; one of the most important goals of placing *Beowulf* historically, however, is to discover the context in which its ambiguities can themselves be interpreted. An example of the problem of simultaneously interpreting text and context is seen in the erosion of consensus regarding the *terminus ante quem* of the Viking Age for the poem's composition. Dorothy Whitelock, for example, believed that the poem must predate the onset of the Viking raids because of its praise of the Danes:

> I would doubt whether [the poet] would have spoken in these terms
> during the Viking Age, or whether his audience would have given
> him a patient hearing if he had. It is not how men like to hear the
> people described who are burning their homes, pillaging their
> churches, ravaging their cattle and crops, killing their countrymen or
> carrying them off into slavery.[21]

Assumptions about the nature of the poet and his audience—like all
assumptions about human cultural history—rely as much on prejudice
and desire as on research; Whitelock spoke, perhaps, from experience of
the English attitude toward German culture in the second World War,
when the appreciation of Beethoven and Goethe became guilty secret
pleasures, and could not imagine a Viking-Age collaborationist composing *Beowulf.* To ascribe the same nationalistic attitudes to the Anglo-
Saxons, however, may be unjust; other scholars have pointed out that
Anglo-Danish relations were neither simple nor unidimensional,[22] and
in fact *Beowulf* can be read as evidence that the Anglo-Saxons could
distinguish between the Danes who were pillaging their churches and
their Heroic Age ancestors. The Viking-Age limit was widely accepted
for other reasons as well; for most critics, the value of *Beowulf* increased
as its date of origin receded—the earlier the poem, the more "authentic"
its descriptions and values, the better and more accurate it was as an
historical document.[23] Perhaps the Viking-Age barrier fell, just as it was
erected, for reasons of prejudice and desire as well as research and
evidence: a late *Beowulf* is a text in some ways more interesting to the
contemporary reader than a pre-Viking Age poem, because it is more
involved in irony, politics, and the self-conscious ambiguities of literary
perspective.

In either case our preconceptions about the nature of the text, even
our sense of how it must serve our present needs, prescribes, to an
extent, the sort of context in which we will try to place it; the context
does not control the interpretation. Apart from this general hermeneutic
dilemma, however, placing *Beowulf* against a background is rendered
problematic by the facts that the background often refuses to stay put
and that *Beowulf* is itself a large piece of that background. Literary and
cultural historians in increasing numbers have come to realize that there
is often, sometimes inevitably, a circularity in historical argument when
it comes to literary subjects. Texts and the cultures in which they are
created exist in a dialectical relation[24] of mutual interpretability; rarely is
there an uninterpreted given, a fixed standpoint, a context which is not
also a text in need of decipherment, or a material object which is not also
the bearer of an immaterial meaning whose precise tenor can be only
approximated by the modern critic, and then often by reference to

literary works—one thinks, for example, of the relation of mutual interpretive dependence connecting *Beowulf* and the artifacts unearthed at Sutton Hoo.[25] The emphasis placed on this entanglement of text and context by contemporary historicism may encourage more efforts to situate *Beowulf* in some social or political environment through a complex mirror game of mutual interpretation,[26] but the difficulty of reaching firm conclusions about historical evidence which might then be turned on the murkier evidence of the poem, coupled with the sheer blankness of the historical record for much of Anglo-Saxon England, will probably continue to render these efforts suggestive rather than definitive.

The linguistic method, on the other hand, strives to avoid the problem of context by relying on purely internal evidence, most commonly metrical evidence, to reconstruct and date the putative original forms of the poem; systematic applications of linguistic tests followed quickly on the heels of Sievers' exposition of his discoveries on Old English meter.[27] The methods and results of these tests were discussed in some detail by Ashley Crandell Amos and need not be rehearsed here; her review of tests such as syncope, contraction, and parasiting of syllabic consonants concluded that no test based on language or meter is reliable in more than a vague way for establishing a chronology of the Old English poetic corpus.[28] For the most part Amos limited her inquiry into the validity and accuracy of the individual tests,[29] but much can be said about the plausibility of the metrical approach to dating and its assumptions in general.

The connection between metrics and dating relies on the belief that Old English verses "wild with motion, full of din" contain patterns of variation which are, however subject to individual style or ability, ultimately controlled by historical developments in the language—that is, there are metrical laws parallel to and dependent upon sound laws. Their analysis draws on two bodies of information, neither of which is certain: the reconstructed rules governing Old English meter and the chronology of Old English sound changes.[30] With regard to the first, at least, there is ongoing debate. The Anglo-Saxons left no text comparable to the Old Norse *Skaldskaparmal* to help us understand their poetry; all metrical rules for Old English are "a glass man, without external reference," induced from the evidence of the surviving manuscripts.[31] Alan Bliss suggests that this induction is a fortunate necessity: "in so far as they are based on the texts themselves the results are certain, whereas metrical treatises might prove to be misleading."[32] Others have criticized Bliss for precisely this faith in the textual evidence. Bliss's rage for order led him to construct 130 categories of half-line (though perhaps this ought to be seen as a conservative gesture in light of Pope's 286 categories in *The Rhythm of "Beowulf"*);[33] Thomas Cable suggests that in shifting Sievers's Five Types from a prescriptive to a descriptive system, Bliss creates "a long list of types and subtypes that in principle is open-ended";[34] Hoyt Duggan has pointed out that "systems that account for all the data, when that set of data axiomatically incorporates into itself an undetermined amount of scribal error and sophistication, are themselves defective to the extent that they authenticate the unauthorial material."[35] But Bliss set out to describe, not to interpret, the meter of the surviving Old English texts.[36] Such a complex metaphysical map of a physical corpus is an indispensable tool for textual analysis, and the power of its descriptive subtlety is seen in such recent works as Daniel Donoghue's study of auxiliary verbs and Old English poetic style.[37]

There are several problems, however, in using a purely inductive descriptive system, which makes no claims about the process of poetic composition, for the purpose of dating the poetry, which does implicitly make such claims. The first of these Donoghue neatly formulates as "distinguishing the tradition from the individual talent" (2)—separating the imitation of inherited patterns from the innovation of an author. All readers of Old English recognize that the poetry is formulaic; even translations from Latin like the *Paris Psalter* and the *Meters of Boethius* are full of conventional expressions and verses, the recapitulation of received tradition.[38] If poems were composed lexically rather than metrically—by improvising on the common stock of traditional collocations, remembered expressions, and accepted formulae with only secondary attention to the rules discerned by modern descriptive meter—then any notion of dating based on these patterns must be questionable; the swarming activities of the formulae would skew the percentages of a metrical analysis towards an earlier date of composition. Metrical evidence, even if it could separate "the poet's gibberish" from "the gibberish of the vulgate," might roughly date the formulaic phrases, but not their later incorporation into a given poem.

Nor is the process of poetic composition in Old English so well understood that we can rule out the wholesale borrowing of verses, lines, and episodes from one poem to another. The piecemeal process of accretion, conjuncture, and interpolation described by nineteenth-century critics under the influence of Lachmann's analysis of the *Nibelungenlied,* if even partly correct, would defeat any attempt at dating a poem by analysis of its meter;[39] though such grand-scale vivisections are no longer in fashion, the evidence of the manuscripts does not rule out a more modest version of such activity. Donoghue's theory of Cynewulf's compositional technique, for example, in which he proposes that the poet revised and added his runic signature to pre-existing poems in what is, to a contemporary reader, an act of plagiarism, would work against any metrical evidence for dating the poem.[40] If sections of *Beowulf*— from a few lines of description to an entire digression—were incorporated from the work of another, earlier poet, then statistical evidence for the behavior of the meter would be unreliable to the extent of the borrowing of another's words and verses. Poems such as *Genesis*, containing a vast portion of a transmogrified Old Saxon poem, and *Daniel*, containing a poem found elsewhere as *Azarias*, might be the norm rather than the exception in Old English poetic practice; there are not enough surviving texts to be certain. If such borrowing was common, then metrical evidence for dating is useless.

On the other hand, metrical tests for dating tend to subsume all variation under historical causation, thereby ignoring or severely restricting the extent of individual control in a poet's work. As Thomas Cable has said,

> the individual metrical style of a poet can override the presumed style of his age and turn our chronological typology into a wishful ideal. This is especially true as we focus on the subtleties of style, as we must, in the strongly uniform metrical tradition before the Conquest; a poet can diverge from the prevailing style through excellence or ineptness.[41]

Cable's own article in *The Dating of "Beowulf"* is an interesting case in point. He contends that verses with three levels of ictus (i.e., Sievers' types C, D, and E) are, in datable poems, less frequent in later verse; he considers poems with more than 30% combined C, D, and E lines to be pre-950. The problem, which he acknowledges, is that the datable Old English poems—*Cædmon's Hymn*, the poems of the *Anglo-Saxon Chronicle*, *Durham*, etc.—are all relatively short, and a few lines one way or the other would radically alter their percentages, calling into question the relation of the relative hierarchy to an absolute chronology. Moreover, he recognizes that the use of C, D, and E verses is a question of style, not language change, and that the chronology is based on his assumptions about Old English poetic taste: "I equate a higher proportion of types C, D, and E *over the long stretch* with a higher degree of technical competence and craftsmanship" (81).[42] Cable's criterion creates an interesting hierarchy in the Old English poetic corpus, but it is not *a priori* a chronological hierarchy.[43]

An example of the difficulty of distinguishing style and tradition from chronology is the use of contracted and uncontracted forms of words which were disyllabic in early Old English and became monosyllables later, words such as *þeon, hean, gan* and *don*.[44] This has been regarded as a particularly valuable test because it often does not involve much metrical subtlety; some verses, like *Beowulf* 25b *man geþeon*, contain only three syllables unless the contracted form is scanned as a disyllable. Apart from the uncertainty regarding the date at which uncontracted forms disappeared from the various dialects of Old English,[45] which calls the usefulness of the test into question in a general way, the problem with contraction as evidence of date is, simply, this: while *Beowulf* contains many forms which must be uncontracted to scan properly, it contains many others which must be scanned as monosyllables, such as 910b *geþeon scolde*.[46] Assuming that both lines are authorial—that the poet had both contracted and uncontracted forms in his poetic repertoire—then the use of one or the other is a stylistic rather than a linguistic phenomenon. Amos makes an analogy to Shakespearean pronunciation: just as Shakespeare used both monosyllabic and disyllabic pronunciations of the suffixes in words like *marriage, patience, division,* the *Beowulf* poet could have used both mono- and disyllabic pronunciations of *doð, gað, hean,* as the meter required.[47] Only if it can be demonstrated that a poet could not have used uncontracted forms after a certain date can this mixed proportion be taken as dating evidence, and it is certainly possible that a combination of traditional formulae, dialect variation, individual habit, imitation, and metrical exigency could have kept the uncontracted forms alive, perhaps for centuries. The fact that *Genesis A* has mostly disyllabic forms, the Cynewulf corpus has mostly contracted forms, and *Beowulf* and *Daniel* have both forms certainly creates a hierarchy within the Old English literary corpus, but again this is not necessarily a chronological order.[48]

It is disturbing that most models of Old English poetic composition describe activities that would, if practiced on any appreciable scale, frustrate all efforts to date the poetry by means of language or meter. In fact whenever the process of composition, performance, or transmission is taken into account, the methods of the metrical dating studies begin to look suspicious. In a recent paper John Niles suggests, by analogy to later ballad meters, that poems delivered orally are marked by a greater latitude of metrical variation than poems composed and delivered in writing;[49] it is also probable that different levels of style (popular, courtly, monastic) had different boundaries of acceptability in metrical practice. If the practice of oral recitation or the stylistic expectations of a poet or audience led to variety in metrical rules, then efforts to organize a limited corpus of poems by their adherence to or violation of the metrical norms of *Beowulf* would end up measuring style and tradition rather than date.

Given all these objections, the strict application of metrical evidence to the question of date begins to look, in Kenneth Sisam's phrase, like "guess-work hampered by statistics."[50] But apart from theoretical problems from the standpoints of the tradition, individual style, and social context of Old English poetry, a more serious objection to the metrical tests for dating *Beowulf* arises from the manuscript evidence for Old English poetic transmission. This may be introduced by considering the relation of metrical study to textual emendation. Metrical analysis, like emendation, works in part by removing layers of scribal corruption to reveal an author's original phrase; in some cases editors correct their manuscripts based on their conception of Old English meter. Emendation *metri causa* is a necessarily circular process, as Bliss notes early in his *Metre of "Beowulf"*: "the necessity for emendation may seem at first sight to discredit the rule on which the emendation is based" (4).[51] Bliss's capacious classification leaves only twenty-one verses as "remainders" or "defective", one-third of one percent of 6342 normal verses in the poem (not including twenty-two hypermetrical verses); he elsewhere records patterns whose legitimacy he himself is moved to doubt.[52] His implication is that some of the lines he accepts and classifies are scribal corruptions of the author's words. Moreover, emendation is normative rather than empirical, smoothing out irregularities in the meter by substituting similarity for difference. Among the nearly 400 emendations which Klaeber accepts in his edition of *Beowulf* are some based purely on metrical considerations, such as *mundgripe* for *handgripe* 965a and *lindplegan* for *hildplegan* 1073b, both made to provide necessary alliteration.[53] Tactfully applied, such editorial ministrations are not usually a bad thing; they raise a question, however, whose implications are fatal to the use of metrical evidence for dating: if scribes altered their texts through carelessness and inattention, were they always constrained to create nonsense and bad meter? In both of the cases just mentioned, the emendation assumes that a scribe has substituted a non-alliterating synonym for the original author's words—thus he was understanding and altering his text, not mechanically transcribing it, and while he may have been a bad poet in these cases he was at least a good reader. Editors generally limit their activity to the correction of obvious errors, large gaps in sense or outrageous breaches of metrical habit, but there is in fact little evidence that scribal activity was limited to the careless creation of these errors. An alternative model of manuscript transmission proposes that scribes were active participants in the process, mediating between the text and its readers, reconstituting the text in a performance on the manuscript page with sometimes scant regard for the precise reproduction of an authorial text; some of them, perhaps, even had a sense of the sound of a line of Old English poetry. The scribes may have altered the metrical form of a line in such a way that their words are, in the absence of a second copy of the text, not distinguishable from those of an author.[54]

In prose texts which survive in more than one copy, it is usually evident that scribes did not practice their craft with the honest simplicity and good intentions that metrical dating studies require. Most manuscripts contain, of course, a number of recognizable and uncontroversial errors which can plausibly be corrected by emendation, but beyond the garbling of sense into nonsense, there are few external grounds for determining the nature and extent of scribal "corruption." Scribes not only made mistakes; they also changed spellings and readings, rewrote passages they either did not understand or thought their readers might not understand, made connections between previously separate texts, omitted and recombined phrases, and generally participated openly and actively in the recomposition of the vernacular texts they copied. When a text survives in only one manuscript the amount of such interaction is unknowable. There are, however, a number of Old English poems found in more than one manuscript which can serve as evidence. The most attested poem in Old English, *Bede's Death Song,* which survives in twelve continental manuscripts and thirty-three insular ones, is not, however, one of them; the continental manuscripts were in all probability copied by non-native speakers, and the English ones date from the twelfth century and later, when familiarity with the language of the poem cannot be assumed.[55] In these cases the careful, often mechanical, copying of the scribes is a testimony to their distance from the language of the poem, and is not representative of the Old English scribal tradition.

A better, though still problematic, example is the West Saxon version of *Caedmon's Hymn*: in eighteen halflines, there are five significant metrical variants.[56] One must also note the freedom with which scribes ignored the original Northumbrian forms of the poem in their transmission of the text. As Kenneth Sisam notes,

> Bodleian MS. Tanner 10 of Cædmon's *Hymn* and the early-eighth-century Moore MS. are identical only in a few invariable words. Ample evidence from other sources confirms that copyists of Old

English texts were not expected to reproduce their originals letter for letter, as they were when copying Latin and especially Biblical texts. Modernization of forms in the course of transmission was allowed and even required by the use for which Old English works were intended, and the practice was obviously dangerous for the wording.[57]

Katherine O'Keeffe has recently discussed the variants in the version of *Cædmon's Hymn* contained in the West-Saxon translation of Bede's *Ecclesiastical History*. After noting the number of variants, she says, "we see a reading activity reflected in these scribal variants which is formula-dependent, in that the variants observe metrical and alliterative constraints, and which is context-defined, in that the variants produced arise within a field of possibilities generated within a context of expectations."[58] In other words, the scribes were collaborators in the construction of the text, and their activity was not limited to the garbling of authorial sense into scribal nonsense.

Other poems found in two manuscripts offer more evidence for the habits of Old English scribes with regard to meter and authorial wording; significant differences, from the addition or omission of an unaccented syllable to the substitution of one verse for another, are surprisingly frequent.[59] The two versions of *Soul and Body* in the Vercelli and Exeter books have 236 half-lines in common; these contain sixty-nine variants, of which fifty-two differ in a metrically significant way,[60] or 22% of all verses, not counting six half-lines in the Exeter *Soul and Body* which are not in the Vercelli Book text (94ab, 101ab, 107ab), and sixteen in the Vercelli Book text which are not in the Exeter Book text (14a, 23a–25b, 59a–60b, 85ab, 93ab, 111a). *Daniel* (Junius Manuscript) and *Azarias* (Exeter Book) have 150 half-lines that are sufficiently alike to be meaningfully compared (*Daniel* 279–364 corresponding to *Azarias* 1–75); these contain sixty-seven variants, of which fifty-two (35% of all lines) are metrically significant,[61] not counting thirty-one half-lines in *Daniel* not in *Azarias* (288a, 305a–312b, 319ab, 329ab, 343a–344b, 349ab, 353a–356b) and six in *Azarias* not in *Daniel* (36ab, 57a–58b) The two texts of *Solomon and Saturn* found in Corpus Christi College, Cambridge, 41 and 422 have 126 half-lines in common (lines 30–93); these contain thirty variants, of which twenty-two (or 17%) are metrically significant.[62] This does not include the two half-lines found in Corpus 41 (67ab) which do not occur in Corpus 422. The two texts of the *Gloria I* show comparatively little variation: in 114 half-lines, only sixteen are significantly different, and of these only twelve, or 10.5%, are metrically different.[63] Set against these other comparisons this is remarkable; it may be due to the quasi-scriptural nature of the liturgical text or the relatively close connection between the two surviving manuscripts.

Shorter texts show a degree of variation similar to the longer poems: the Exeter Book *Riddle 35* and the *Leiden Riddle* share twenty-four lines of which four are metrically different (17%),[64] not counting the four half-lines at the end which are different in the two texts. The two versions of the Exeter Book *Riddle 30* contain eighteen half-lines and four metrical differences, or 22% of all lines.[65] The poems of the *Anglo-Saxon Chronicle* are more difficult to compare; all are found in more than two copies, and some variants must be ignored as nonsense. *The Battle of Brunanburh*, edited from four manuscripts in Dobbie's edition for *The Anglo-Saxon Poetic Records*, contains 146 half-lines and twenty-six variants, twenty of which are metrically significant[66] (14% of all lines). *The Capture of the Five Boroughs*, edited from the same four manuscripts, contains twenty-eight verses and five metrically significant variants, or 18%.[67] *The Coronation of Edgar*, edited from three manuscripts, contains forty verses and six metrical variants, or 15%.[68] *The Death of Edgar*, edited from the same three manuscripts, contains seventy-four halflines and five metrical variants, or 7%.[69]

Excluding the poems in the *Chronicle*, the average percentage of variation in multiple-copy poems in Old English is 21.6%. It should be stressed that this is not the same sort of scribal interference with meter condoned by traditional metrical-dating studies, such as the writing of contracted monosyllabic forms where the meter requires a disyllabic form; these are alterations of the metrical shape of the half-line which do not, for the most part, result in nonmetrical or nonsensical lines, but in alternative acceptable versions. Assuming that the two surviving copies of these poems do not represent different authorial drafts, one must conclude that at least one of the surviving copies falsifies the author's metrical practice; from the figures it is tempting to extrapolate that, in a hypothetically average copy of an average Old English poem, approximately one half-line in five will vary from the author's original words. If one assumes, as most critics do, that most Old English poems went through several generations of manuscript copies before the one in which they are now preserved, then the figure rises still higher. Such scribal intervention is hardly conducive to the accurate transmission of the metrical details of an early poet; the extent of variation in Old English poetic manuscripts supports the theory that Anglo-Saxon scribes functioned rather like modern editors—unlike editors, however, they did not have as their goal the restoration of an original authoritative text.[70]

Manuscript transmission is characterized by what has recently been called *variance,* a radical instability or plurality of detail.[71] The manuscript existence of the Old English literary work means that textuality—in the modern sense of a fixed work separate from the circumstances of its transmission or reception—does not exist. It is therefore implausible to suppose that a poem might preserve for several centuries of written transmission the metrical shape of its first composition. The skepticism with which most critics greeted the reading *wundini golde* in line 1382, proposed with such enthusiasm by C.L. Wrenn as linguistic evidence for an eighth-century written text of *Beowulf,*[72] ought to be extended to any argument which supposes that the linguistic and metrical details of a poem remained substantially unaltered during the course of its transmission. Those who rely on minuscule characteristics of meter, and on the percentages of occurrences or non-occurrences of a given metrical type, to suggest that the *Beowulf* found in Cotton Vitellius A. xv existed in the same form (apart from scribal errors correctable by the same metrical evidence) for several centuries, are ignoring the realities of medieval textuality and literary transmission.

The lines of verse on the Ruthwell Cross and the preservation of a ninth-century text of the *Leiden Riddle,* poems which reappear in some form in the major manuscripts of Old English poetry, confirm the belief that the date of composition of an Old English poem may be centuries before its date of compilation. But as the texts of these poems themselves indicate, the process of manuscript transmission, like that of oral transmission, was not at all likely or even able to preserve the fixed form of a text or the sort of details on which metrical dating arguments must be based. Metrical dating studies must assume that there is a difference between the scribe's work and the author's; establishing a chronology by metrical means necessarily assumes that there is on the one hand a group of original texts, the full expression of their authors' intention, and on the other a series of divergent and derivative versions contained in the surviving manuscripts. The facts suggest otherwise: *texts* of Old English poems do not exist, only *manuscripts,* and these manuscripts are inherently the product of collaboration between the original composers and the transmitters of the verse. Our understanding of Anglo-Saxon manuscript culture and mixed oral/textual literary communities strongly suggests that their concepts of authorship and textuality differ sharply from those assumed by current metrical dating studies. Finally, if we accept that the manuscript text is a unique occasion, only one manifestation of a changing complex of variant versions, then we must accept that the only meaningful date for the "effective composition" of *Beowulf* is that of the manuscript, since any version previously existing would be different to an unknowable degree from the surviving text.

The implications of our ignorance and disagreement concerning the date of *Beowulf* are far-reaching. To begin with, it discourages any close interpretation of the poem that depends on a specific period of Anglo-Saxon history; conversely, the poem is of little use, except in a general way, in the interpretation of that history. The undated text forces Anglo-Saxonists, mostly historicists by inclination, to be formalists despite themselves; any approach to *Beowulf* is of necessity not documentary but monumental.[73] Logically the establishment of a date and historical milieu for a poem ought to precede and assist its interpretation, but in the case of *Beowulf* the dating is itself an act of interpretation, in some respects one of the hermeneutic activities most productive of knowledge of the poem and its meanings; reading this undated text reminds us of the fragility of our knowledge of Old English literary culture and the pervasiveness of interpretive activity in even the simplest matters of dating and context. By the same token it reminds us that the renewed interest in historicist criticism in the past decade is nothing new; Anglo-Saxonists have much to say to our colleagues about the interdependent relation between text and context, because trying to draw a conclusion on this matter is one of the most ancient and important questions of our field. Perhaps most important, it reminds us that our simplest actions as readers of Old English are not so simple, that our work, whether we like it or not, is constantly and intimately and profoundly involved in theoretical issues of language, literature, and textuality. When we talk about the dating of *Beowulf* we are talking about nothing less than the philosophical foundations of our discipline.

NOTES

1. J.R.R. Tolkien, "*Beowulf*: The Monsters and the Critics," *Proceedings of the British Academy* 22 (1936): 245–295; reprinted in Lewis E. Nicholson, ed., *An Anthology of "Beowulf" Criticism* (Notre Dame, 1963), 69.

2. Ashley Crandell Amos, *Linguistic Means of Determining the Dates of Old English Literary Texts* (Cambridge, MA, 1980); Kevin S. Kiernan, "*Beowulf*" *and the* "*Beowulf*" *Manuscript* (New Brunswick, NJ, 1981); Colin Chase, ed., *The Dating of* "*Beowulf*" (Toronto, 1981).

3. Stanley B. Greenfield, *A Critical History of Old English Literature* (New York, 1965), 82.

4. Stanley B. Greenfield and Daniel G. Calder, *A New Critical History of Old English Literature* (New York, 1986), 136.

5. Fred C. Robinson, "*Beowulf*" *and the Appositive Style* (Knoxville, 1985), 7.

6. Alain Renoir, *A Key to Old Poems: The Oral-Formulaic Approach to the*

Interpretation of West Germanic Verse (University Park, PA, 1988), 40.

7. Helen Damico, *Beowulf's Wealhtheow and the Valkyrie Tradition* (Madison, WI, 1984).

8. Nicholas Howe, *Migration and Mythmaking in Anglo-Saxon England* (New Haven, 1989), 177.

9. Edward B. Irving, *Rereading "Beowulf"* (Philadelphia, 1989), 31.

10. Ruth P.M. Lehmann, *"Beowulf": An Imitative Translation* (Austin, 1988), 1.

11. David Williams, *Cain and "Beowulf": A Study in Secular Allegory* (Toronto, 1982); Margaret Goldsmith, *The Mode and Meaning of "Beowulf"* (London, 1970).

12. Mary Parker, *"Beowulf" and Christianity* (New York, 1987), 2.

13. George Clark, *Beowulf* (Boston, 1990), xvi.

14. Robert P. Creed, "*Beowulf* and the Language of Hoarding," in Charles L. Redman, ed., *Medieval Archaeology*, Medieval and Renaissance Texts and Studies 60 (Binghamton, NY, 1989), 157.

15. Ashley Crandell Amos, "An Eleventh-Century *Beowulf?*" *Review* (Charlottesville, VA) 4 (1982): 335–45; R.D. Fulk, "Review Article: Dating *Beowulf* to the Viking Age," *Philological Quarterly* 61 (1982): 341–59; Claus-Dieter Wetzel, "Die Datierung des *Beowulf*: Bemerkungen zur jüngsten Forschungsentwicklung," *Anglia* 103 (1985): 371–400.

16. David N. Dumville, "*Beowulf* and the Celtic World: The Uses of Evidence," *Traditio* 37 (1981): 109–60; Janet Bately, "Linguistic Evidence as a Guide to the Authorship of Old English Verse: A Reappraisal, with Special Reference to *Beowulf*," in Michael Lapidge and Helmut Gneuss, eds., *Learning and Literature in Anglo-Saxon England* (Cambridge, 1985), 409–431.

17. Michael Lapidge, "*Beowulf*, Aldhelm, the *Liber Monstrorum* and Wessex," *Studi Medievali* 3rd ser. 23 (1982): 151–92; M.J. Swanton, *Crisis and Development in Germanic Society 700–800:* Beowulf *and the Burden of Kingship*, Göppinger Arbeiten zur Germanistik 333 (Göppingen, 1982); W.G. Busse and R. Holtei, "*Beowulf* and the Tenth Century," *Bulletin of the John Rylands University Library of Manchester* 63 (1981): 285–329; Patricia Poussa, "The Date of *Beowulf* Reconsidered: The Tenth Century?" *Neuphilologische Mitteilungen* 82 (1981): 276–88; John D. Niles, "*Beowulf*": *The Poem and its Tradition* (Cambridge, MA, 1983), 115–117; Alexandra Hennessey Olsen, "'Þurs' and 'Þyrs': Giants and the Date of *Beowulf*," *In Geardagum* 6 (1984): 35–42; Rowland L. Collins, "Blickling Homily XVI and the Dating of *Beowulf*," in Wolf-Dietrich Bald and Horst Weinstock, eds., *Medieval Studies Conference, Aachen, 1983: Language and Literature*, Bamberger Beiträge zur Englischen Sprachwissenschaft 15 (Frankfurt am Main, 1984), 61–69; Audrey L. Meaney, "Scyld Scefing and the Dating of *Beowulf*—Again," *Bulletin of the John Rylands University Library of Manchester* 71 (1989): 7–40.

18. Alain Renoir, "Old English Formulas and Themes as Tools for Contextual Interpretation," in Phyllis Rugg Brown et al., eds., *Modes of Interpretation in Old English Literature: Essays in Honour of Stanley B. Greenfield* (Toronto, 1986), 68.

19. Ritchie Girvan, *"Beowulf" and the Seventh Century* (London, 1935), 26.

20. The poem's attitudes towards the past are discussed by Robert W. Hanning, "*Beowulf* as Heroic History," *Medievalia and Humanistica* 5 (1974): 77–102;

Roberta Frank, "The *Beowulf* Poet's Sense of History," in Larry D. Benson and Siegfried Wenzel, eds., *The Wisdom of Poetry: Essays in Early English Literature in Honor of Morton W. Bloomfield* (Kalamazoo, 1982), 53–65; Fred C. Robinson, *"Beowulf" and the Appositive Style*; and Nicholas Howe, *Migration and Mythmaking*, 143–180.

21. Dorothy Whitelock, *The Audience of "Beowulf"* (Oxford, 1951), 24–5.

22. Among them Nicolas Jacobs, "Anglo-Danish Relations, Poetic Archaism, and the Date of *Beowulf*: A Reconsideration of the Evidence," *Poetica* (Toyko) 8 (1977): 23–43; R.I. Page, "The Audience of *Beowulf* and the Vikings," in Colin Chase, ed., *The Dating of "Beowulf,"* 113–122; and Alexander Callander Murray, *"Beowulf,* the Danish Invasions, and Royal Genealogy," in Chase, *The Dating of "Beowulf,"* 101–111.

23. This is the confession of Alexander Callander Murray: "It is as well to admit that to most of us the value of *Beowulf,* as either a literary or a historical monument, would increase in proportion to the earliness of its date" (101). For the history of this attitude, see Eric G. Stanley, *The Search for Anglo-Saxon Paganism* (Cambridge, 1975); Hugh A. MacDougall, *Racial Myth in English History: Trojans, Teutons, and Anglo-Saxons* (Montreal, 1982); and, more recently, Allen J. Frantzen and Charles L. Venegoni, "The Desire for Origins: An Archaeology of Anglo-Saxon Studies," *Style* 20 (1986): 142–156.

24. This phrase is taken from Stephen Greenblatt, ed., *Representing the English Renaissance* (Berkeley, 1988), viii.

25. For critical recognition and discussion of these problems see, e.g., Clifford Geertz, *The Interpretation of Cultures* (New York, 1973) and Hayden White, *Tropics of Discourse* (Baltimore, 1978). The problems of interpreting *Beowulf* and Sutton Hoo are hinted at in Allen J. Frantzen, "Documents and Monuments: Difference and Interdisciplinarity in the Study of Medieval Culture," in Allen J. Frantzen, ed., *Speaking Two Languages: Traditional Disciplines and Contemporary Theory in Medieval Studies* (Albany, 1991), 1–33.

26. Notable among these is Patrick Wormald, "Bede, *Beowulf,* and the Conversion of the Anglo-Saxon Aristocracy," in Robert T. Farrell, ed., *Bede and Anglo-Saxon England: Papers in Honour of the 1300th Anniversary of the Birth of Bede, Given at Cornell University in 1973 and 1974*, British Archaeological Reports no. 46 (London, 1978), 32–95. Wormald sets the poem against the background of Bede's time (and later), but a similarly rich interpretive conjunction is made for *Beowulf* and the age of *The Battle of Maldon* by James W. Earl, "*Beowulf* and the Origins of Civilization," in Frantzen, *Speaking Two Languages*, 65–89.

27. Eduard Sievers, "Zur Rhythmik des germanischen Alliterationsverses," *Beiträge aur Geschichte der deutschen Sprache und Literatur* 10 (1885): 209–314, 451–545, and *Altgermanische Metrik* (Halle, 1893); see also the translation by Gawaina D. Luster, "Old Germanic Metrics and Old English Metrics," in Jess B. Bessinger and Stanley J. Kahrl, eds., *Essential Articles for the Study of Old English Poetry* (Hamden, CT, 1968), 267–88. The major works proposing these tests are noted by Amos, *Linguistic Means*, 6–7 and 13–14.

28. Amos's conclusions, though widely accepted, have been recently questioned in a series of articles by R.D. Fulk: "West Germanic Parasiting, Sievers' Law, and the Dating of Old English Verse," *Studies in Philology* 86 (1989): 117–138,

"Redating *Beowulf*: The Evidence of Kaluza's Law," read at the Modern Language Association in Washington, D.C., December 1989, and "Contraction as a Criterion for Dating Old English Verse," *JEGP* 89 (1990): 1–16.

29. She declined to consider claims which might render all such tests invalid (see 9–12).

30. Amos cautions us on the limits of metrical evidence for dating: "The data the tests provide are no more secure than our understanding of Old English meter and no more precise than our ability to pinpoint Old English sound changes" (16).

31. Major theories of OE prosody include Sievers, Alan Bliss, *The Metre of "Beowulf"* (Oxford, 1963); John C. Pope, *The Rhythm of "Beowulf,"* revised ed. (New Haven, 1966); Robert P. Creed, "A New Approach to the Rhythm of *Beowulf,"* *PMLA* 81 (1966): 23–33; Thomas Cable, *The Meter and Melody of "Beowulf"* (Urbana, IL, 1974); and Geoffrey Russom, *Old English Meter and Linguistic Theory* (Cambridge, 1987).

32. Alan Bliss, *An Introduction to Old English Metre* (Oxford, 1962), 2.

33. Pope's categories are on 247–386 of that work.

34. Thomas Cable, "Old English Prosody," in Jess B. Bessinger, Jr. and Robert F. Yeager, eds., *Approaches to Teaching "Beowulf"* (New York, 1984), 176.

35. Hoyt N. Duggan, "The Evidential Basis for Old English Metrics," *Studies in Philology* 85 (1988), 162–3.

36. Compare the following comments in *The Metre of "Beowulf"*: "the study of any metre involves two distinct processes: firstly, the description and classification of the metrical forms which actually occur; secondly, the discussion and interpretation of the resulting classification" (1); "the purpose of this study is to provide an adequate statistical basis for an interpretation, not a detailed interpretation itself" (106).

37. Daniel Donoghue, *Style in OE Poetry: The Test of the Auxiliary* (New Haven, 1987), 13.

38. The oral-formulaic theory has ebbed and flowed through Old English studies since Francis P. Magoun's 1953 essay "The Oral-Formulaic Character of Anglo-Saxon Narrative Poetry," *Speculum* 28 (1953): 446–467; important contributions to the debate include Robert P. Creed, "The Making of an Anglo-Saxon Poem," *English Literary History* 26 (1959): 445–454; Robert E. Diamond, "The Diction of the Signed Poems of Cynewulf," *Philological Quarterly* 38 (1959): 228–241; Larry D. Benson, "The Literary Character of Anglo-Saxon Formulaic Poetry," *PMLA* 81 (1966): 334–341; Stanley B. Greenfield, "The Canons of Old English Literary Criticism," *English Literary History* 34 (1967): 141–155; Donald K. Fry, Jr., "Old English Formulas and Systems," *English Studies* 48 (1967): 193–204; and Jeff Opland, *Anglo-Saxon Oral Poetry: A Study of the Traditions* (New Haven, 1980). Further history and fuller bibliography can be found in John Miles Foley, *The Theory of Oral Composition: History and Methodology* (Bloomington, IN, 1988), 65–74.

39. For Lachmann's analytic method see Karl Lachmann, *Betrachtungen über Homers Ilias* (Berlin, 1847) and Peter F. Ganz, "Lachmann as an Editor of Middle High German Texts," in Peter Ganz and Werner Schröder, eds., *Probleme Mittelalterlicher Überlieferung und Textkritik* (Berlin, 1968), 12–30. Applications of his method to *Beowulf* include Karl Müllenhoff, "Die innere Geschichte des *Beovulfs*,"

Zeitschrift für deutsches Altertum 14 (1869): 193–244; Bernhard ten Brink, *Beowulf: Untersuchungen,* Quellen und Forschungen zur Sprach- und Kulturgeschichte 62 (Strassburg, 1888); R.C. Boer, *Die altenglische Heldendichtung,* I. *Beowulf* (Halle, 1912); Walter A. Berendsohn, *Zur Vorgeschichte des "Beowulf"* (Copenhagen, 1935); and Francis P. Magoun, *"Beowulf A':* A Folk-Variant," *Arv: Journal of Scandinavian Folklore* 14 (1958): 95–101 and *"Beowulf B:* A Folk-Poem on Beowulf's Death," in Arthur Brown and Peter Foote, eds., *Early English and Norse Studies Presented to Hugh Smith in Honour of His Sixtieth Birthday* (London, 1963), 127–40 (these and others are mentioned in Colin Chase, "Opinions on the Date of *Beowulf,* 1815–1980," in *The Dating of "Beowulf,"* 3–8). Several recent critics have revived the notion that *Beowulf* consists of separate poems joined at a subsequent time, among them Kiernan, *"Beowulf" and the "Beowulf" Manuscript,* 12, but other studies, including Bately, "Linguistic Evidence," see no evidence that the poem was not composed by one author throughout.

40. Donoghue, 115. See also R.M. Liuzza, "The Old English *Christ* and *Guthlac:* Texts, Manuscripts, and Critics," *Review of English Studies* n.s. 41 (1990), 9–11 for a vague suggestion to the same effect.

41. Thomas Cable, "Metrical Style as Evidence for the Date of *Beowulf,*" in Chase, *The Dating of "Beowulf,"* 77.

42. Emphasis in the original. He goes on to say, "I would judge *Exodus* at least as highly crafted metrically as *Beowulf,* and it is the only poem that I would so judge. Since the authors of these two poems rose above the ground of their tradition, they conceivably could have written at any period during the four centuries of classical Old English metre. Yet it is intuitively more plausible that they rose from the metrical highlands than from the plain that slopes to the sea. I would not expect such metrical skill in the second half of the tenth century."

43. See also the remarks of Klaus R. Grinda, who suggests that "there seems to be no method available as yet to translate statistics of language, style or metre into a chronological sequence, or, for that matter, to interpret stylistic features at all except as signs of greater or lesser mastery." "Pigeonholing Old English Poetry: Some Criteria of Metrical Style," *Anglia* 102 (1984), 306.

44. Contraction is described by Alistair Campbell, *Old English Grammar* (Oxford, 1959), §§ 234–239; the expansion of contracted MS forms was assumed by Sievers, "Zur Rhythmik des germanischen Alliterationsverses" 451–452. The use of contraction as a dating test was described by Moritz Trautmann, *Kynewulf, der Bischof und Dichter,* Bonner Beiträge zur Anglistik 1 (Bonn, 1898), 23–42 and 120–121, and Lorenz Morsbach, "Zur Datierung des Beowulfepos," *Nachrichten der königlichen Gesellschaft der Wissenschaften zu Göttingen, Philologisch-historische Klasse* (Göttingen, 1906), 262–63. It has recently been resurrected by Fulk, "Contraction as a Criterion." The test of contraction is discussed by Amos, *Linguistic Means,* 40–63.

45. See Amos, *Linguistic Means,* 40–43, and Randolph Quirk, "On the Problem of Morphological Suture in Old English," *Modern Language Review* 45 (1950): 1–5.

46. In this instance, if *gepeon* is scanned as a disyllable, the half-line must be read as a variant of Sievers's Type A with anacrusis; for the impossibility of this type see Bliss, *The Metre of "Beowulf,"* 40–43, and Cable, *The Meter and Melody of "Beowulf,"* 32–44. Cable goes so far as to say that "the avoidance of that pattern is a

basic part of the poet's craft" (32).

47. Amos, *Linguistic Means,*45.

48. The relevant numbers are found in Amos, *Linguistic Means,* and in Fulk, "Contraction as a Criterion," 5–12. Fulk, currently the most ardent proponent of metrical dating methods, proceeds with rigorous circularity: he begins with a chronology of the OE corpus largely derived from linguistic/metrical tests, a fact which he disguises by borrowing the chronology from Cable's article in *The Dating of "Beowulf"*; he then proposes that the tests he is examining, carefully applied, provide independent proof of the chronology they themselves have created. In all cases the datable poems (whether early, e.g., *Cædmon's Hymn, Bede's Death Song,* and the *Leiden Riddle,* or middle period, e.g., the metrical poems in the Alfredian corpus, or late, e.g., *Maldon, Brunanburh,* and the *Anglo-Saxon Chronicle* poems) provide no usable evidence; significant patterns of occurrence are inevitably drawn from major and undated poems: *Genesis, Daniel, Exodus, Beowulf, Judith,* and the works of Cynewulf. Fulk's disingenuous surprise at his inevitable results ("It is surprising just how well the list supports the presumed chronology", "WGmc Parasiting," 131; "It is surprising how well these results agree with earlier scholarship on dating," "Contraction," 9) belies the fact that his lists are simply restatements of a traditional ordering of poems. The fact that different OE poems show different metrical treatments of such features as contraction and parasiting is not in question; what is in question is the meaning of this variation—whether there is any reason to suppose that the relative hierarchy created by the tests in fact reflects an absolute chronology.

49. John D. Niles, "On Editing *Beowulf*: The Uses of a Comparative Perspective," forthcoming, *Oral Tradition.*

50. Kenneth Sisam, *Studies in the History of Old English Literature* (Oxford, 1953), 6.

51. Bliss is careful to limit the process to cases in which the meter is corrupt in more ways than one, the grammar is corrupt as well as the meter, and the same sort of emendation, made to several lines at once, may fix several different corruptions. Paul B. Taylor and R. Evan Davis support the manuscript's authority against that of the critic or editor in "Some Alliterative Misfits in the *Beowulf* MS," *Neophilologus* 66 (1982): 614–21.

52. E.g., "light" verses with final stress like *wæs min fæder* 262a, of which Bliss says, "it must be considered doubtful whether this type has any genuine existence" (61).

53. A fascinating tabulation of emendations proposed and accepted in editions of *Beowulf* is provided by Birte Kelly, "The Formative Stages of *Beowulf* Textual Scholarship," Part One *ASE* 11 (1983): 247–274; Part Two *ASE* 12 (1984): 239–275.

54. See Katherine O'Brien O'Keeffe, *Visible Song: Transitional Literacy in Old English Verse* (Cambridge, 1990) for a thorough and fascinating discussion of this problem.

55. E.V.K. Dobbie, *The Manuscripts of Cædmon's Hymn and Bede's Death Song* (New York, 1937), 115.

56. These are: 1a *nu/nu we,* 3a *weorc/weoroda/wera,* 3b *wundra gehwæs/wundra fela,* 5a *sceop/gesceop,* 7a *þa middangeard/ middangeard.* A variant in 4a, *or/ord,* is

without metrical significance.

57. Sisam, *Studies in the History of Old English Literature*, 36.

58. Katherine O'Brien O'Keeffe, "Orality and the Developing Text of *Cædmon's Hymn*," *Speculum* 62 (1987), 15–16. Reprinted in *Visible Song*, 23–46.

59. Comparisons are based on the edited texts in G.P. Krapp and E.V.K. Dobbie, eds., *The Anglo-Saxon Poetic Records* (New York, 1931–53).

60. These are (lines are cited once where the lineation in Krapp-Dobbie agrees, and in the order *Soul and Body I/Soul and Body II* where it does not): 2b, 4b, 12b/13a, 14b/13a, 16b, 21a, 26b/23b, 27a/24a, 30a/27a, 31a/28a, 33b/30b, 36a/33a, 37b/34b, 38b/35b, 42a/39a, 47a/44a, 48a/45a, 49a/46a, 50b/47b, 51a/48a, 52a/49a, 52b/49b, 54a/51a, 64a/59a, 65a/60a, 65b/60b, 69a/64a, 72a/67a, 73a/68a, 74b/69b, 79a/74a, 80a/75a, 82a/77a, 84a/79a, 89b/83b, 96a/89a, 98a/91a, 98b/91b, 100a/93a, 101a/95a, 102b/96b, 103a/97a, 106b/100b, 113a/108a, 114a/109a, 115a/110a, 117b/112b, 119a/114a, 119b/114b, 122b/117b, 123a/118a, 126b/121b. Variation which does not alter the meter occurs in lines 18b, 19b, 20a, 27a/24a, 43a/40a, 45a/42a, 51b/48b, 66a/61a, 70b/65b, 83a/78a, 88a/82a, 97a/90a, 107a/102a, 114b/109b, 116b/111b, 117b/112b, 124b/119b. See the outstanding edition by Douglas Moffat, *The Old English Soul and Body* (Woodbridge, 1990).

61. These are (cited *Daniel/Azarias*): 279a/1a, 282a/4a, 283a/5a, 287a/9a, 289a/10a, 290a/10a, 291a/12a, 294a/15a, 294b/15b, 297a/18a, 298a/19a, 303b/24b, 304a/25a, 305b/26b, 306b/27b, 314a/31a, 315a/32a, 317b/34b, 318a/35a, 320a/37a, 321a/38a, 321b/38b, 322a/39a, 322b/39b, 323a/40a, 323b/40b, 324a/41a, 325a/42a, 325b/42b, 326b/43b, 328a/45a, 330a/46a, 331a/46a, 331b/46b, 332a/47a, 332b/47b, 334b/50b, 336a/52a, 338a/54a, 338b/54b, 341a/59a, 341b/59b, 342b/60b, 345b/61b, 347a/63a, 350a/65a, 350b/65b, 358b/69b, 359a/70a, 362a/73a, 362b/73b, 363a/74a. Variants not affecting the meter occur in lines 286b/8b, 293a/14a, 297b/18b, 300a/21a, 302a/23a, 304b/25b, 306a/27a, 327b/44b, 328b/45b, 335b/51b, 339a/55a, 345a/61a, 346b/62b, 347b/64b, 357a/68a.

62. These are in lines 35a, 37a, 37b, 38b, 40a, 43a, 47a, 52a, 53a, 56a, 59a, 60a, 65b, 76a, 78b, 82a, 83a, 85b, 86a, 88a, 91b, 92b. Variants which do not alter the meter are found in lines 44a, 46a, 57a, 60b, 62b, 73a, 75b, 85a.

63. These are 1b, 5a, 7a, 15a, 23b, 30a, 31a, 34a, 41a, 48a, 49a, 55b; non-metrical variation occurs in lines 26a, 29a, 43a, 43b.

64. These are 6a, 7a, 8b, 11a; non-metrical variants are found in lines 7b and 12a and orthographic variants in every line.

65. These are 2a, 6b, 7b, 8a; non-metrical variants are found in 6a and 8b. See R.M. Liuzza, "The Texts of the Old English *Riddle 30*," *JEGP* 87 (1988): 1–15.

66. 1a, 20b, 24a, 26a, 28a, 29b, 30a, 31b, 35b, 41b, 51b, 54b, 55a, 56a, 57a, 58a, 60b, 62b, 66a, 71a; variants without metrical significance occur in lines 16b, 18a, 39a, 40b, 42a, 67a.

67. 1a, 7a, 8a, 8b, 13b.

68. 2a, 2b, 12a, 13b, 14b, 19a.

69. 2a, 8a, 10b, 24a, 29a.

70. It is this instability against which Ælfric complains in his Preface to the OE *Genesis*: "Ic bidde nu on Godes naman, gyf hwa ðas boc awritan wille, ðæt he hi gerihte wel be ðære bysne, for ðan ðe ic nah geweald, ðeah ðe hi hwa to woge gebringe ðurh lease writeras, and hit bið ðonne his pleoh na min: micel yfel deð se unwritere, gyf he nele his gewrit gerihtan" [I pray now in God's name, if anyone

wishes to copy this book, that he correct it well according to the exemplar, because I do not have the power, even though someone might bring it to error through false scribes; and then it will be his danger, not mine. The false scribe does much harm if he will not correct his errors.] S.J. Crawford, ed., *The Old English Version of the Heptateuch.* EETS o.s. 160 (Oxford, 1922), 80 (translation mine). The moral consequences of scribal activity were perhaps less dire in the production of vernacular poetic texts.

71. Bernard Cerquiglini, *Eloge de la variante: Histoire critique de la philologie* (Paris, 1989), 111. The term characterizes the contingency of the material text parallel to the *mouvance* of oral literature described by Paul Zumthor in *Essai de poétique médiévale* (Paris, 1972), 65–75 and "The Impossible Closure of the Oral Text," *Yale French Studies* 67 (1984): 25–42. See also Suzanne Fleischman, "Philology, Linguistics, and the Discourse of the Medieval Text," *Speculum* 65 (1990): 19–37, and Fred C. Robinson, "Print Culture and the Birth of the Text," *Sewanee Review* 89 (1981): 423–430.

72. C.L. Wrenn, ed., *"Beowulf" with the Finnesburg Fragment* (London, 1953), 35–6. The MS reading is also accepted by Johannes Hoops, *Kommentar zum "Beowulf,"* (Heidelberg, 1932), 166. For an argument against *wundini,* see Sisam, *Studies in the History of OE Literature,* 36; Kiernan reports that the MS reads *wundmi* (*"Beowulf" and the "Beowulf" Manuscript,* 30–37).

73. The distinction is discussed by Paul Zumthor, *Langue et techniques poétiques à l'époque romane* (Paris, 1963), 33–37.

Indexes

A. Passages cited

B. Words and phrases

WITHDRAWN